A SHARED WORLD

A SHARED WORLD

CHRISTIANS AND MUSLIMS IN THE
EARLY MODERN MEDITERRANEAN

Molly Greene

PRINCETON UNIVERSITY PRESS   PRINCETON, NEW JERSEY

Library of Congress Cataloging-in-Publication Data

Greene, Molly, 1959–
A shared world : Christians and Muslims in the early modern
Mediterranean / Molly Greene.
p.   cm.
Includes bibliographical references and index.
ISBN 0-691-00898-1 (hardcover : alk. paper)
1. Crete (Greece)—History—Venetian rule, 1204–1669—Influence.
2. Crete (Greece)—History—Turkish rule, 1669–1898.   3. Middle
East—Civilization—Religious aspects.   4. Mediterranean Region—
Civilization—Historiography.   I. Title.
DF901.C83G74   2000
949.5′905—dc21   99-41888

Seven of the nine illustrations appear courtesy of Marquand Library of
Art and Archaeology. Department of Rare Books and Special
Collections. Princeton University Library.

Publication of this book has been aided by Hellenic Studies Center,
Princeton University.

This book has been composed in Galliard

The paper used in this publication meets the minimum requirements
of ANSI/NISO Z39.48-1992 (R 1997) (*Permanence of Paper*)

www.pup.princeton.edu

Printed in the United States of America

10 9 8 7 6 5 4 3 2 1

To my parents, Sally and Charles ————————————

FOR THEIR LOVE AND SUPPORT. THANK YOU.

Contents

Illustrations

Acknowledgments

THIS BOOK has been many years in the making and I have incurred many debts, both intellectual and personal. Two people were absolutely central to my graduate education and I would like to thank them first. Professor Cemal Kafadar, formerly of Princeton, now at Harvard University, was the person who opened my eyes to the possibilities of Ottoman history. Under his guidance I began my journey away from the twentieth century, all the way back to the early modern period. Dimitri Gondicas, executive director of the Program in Hellenic Studies at Princeton University, was, and continues to be, unflagging in his support of my work. I would also like to thank Professor Emeritus L. Carl Brown and Professor Michael Cook, both of the Department of Near Eastern Studies at Princeton University. Professor Halil Inalcík passed through the Department of Near Eastern Studies from time to time and was always very generous in sharing his unrivaled knowledge of Ottoman history.

For the past six years I have found a home in the History Department at Princeton University. I would like to thank all my colleagues for the wonderful intellectual atmosphere that I have been able to benefit from during my years here. I would like to thank Professors Mark Mazower, Tia Kolbaba, and Peter Brown in particular for sharing with me their wisdom and insight on the Greek world and the world of the eastern Mediterranean. When she was here, Professor Judith Herrin was a wonderful colleague. A very special thanks goes to Professors William Chester Jordan and Suzanne Marchand, who have provided not only intellectual guidance but also given me the gift of their friendship. I would also like to thank the Program in Hellenic Studies here at Princeton; they have helped me every step of the way and have done so much to make a place for the study of the Greek world here at Princeton.

Most of the research for this book was undertaken at the Vikelaia Municipal Library in Herakleion, Crete, and I would like to thank the staff at the library for their support. Andreas Savvakes in particular gave me every possible assistance and became a very good friend. In Greece I would also like to thank Professor Elizabeth Zachariadou of the University of Rethymnon in Crete. Professor Zachariadou first suggested to me that I write about Crete and she helped me throughout my stay on the island.

In Turkey I would like to thank the staff at the Prime Ministry's Archives in Istanbul as well as the staff at the Cadastral Directorate in Ankara. I would also like to thank the American Research Institute in Turkey and Tony Greenwood for providing a very pleasant place to stay with a wonderful view of the Bosphorus. In Italy, the staff at the Venetian State Archives was extremely helpful. Professor Sally McKee provided invaluable assistance as I navigated my way through the Venetian archives, and she also shared with me her deep knowledge of Venetian Crete. The Greek Institute in Venice hosted me during my stay in Venice and I would like to thank them for their hospitality.

A number of foundations supported this research, both at the dissertation stage and as I turned it into a book. A grant from the Fulbright Hays foundation allowed me to spend a year in the archives in Greece and Turkey. I would also like to thank the Whiting Fellowship, the American Research Institute in Turkey, the Gladys Krieble Delmas Foundation, the American Philosophical Society, and the University Committee on Research in the Humanities here at Princeton for their support of my archival research. The History Department granted me a semester of leave and a Stanley Seeger Preceptorship from the Program in Hellenic Studies allowed me to extend that leave into a full year. During that time I was able to finish writing this book. The Program in Hellenic Studies also supported the publication of this book.

At Princeton University Press, I would like to thank my editor, Brigitta van Rheinberg, for her enthusiasm and her help in turning my manuscript into a book.

I would like to thank my sisters, Lydia and Alice Greene, for their love and support over many years. A very special thanks goes to my ex-husband, Jonathan Clements. This book could not have been written without him. He looked after our children during my long trips abroad, which were difficult and trying times for all of us. Although they certainly did not help me complete this book, I must mention, finally, my two wonderful children, Hannah, age 11 and Henry, age 7. They have brought me more joy than they can ever know.

Note on Transliteration

THIS BOOK draws heavily on sources in Ottoman Turkish and in Greek. I have followed the transliteration system of the *International Journal of Middle East Studies* for the Turkish material. When quoting directly from an Ottoman document I have given the Ottoman orthography but otherwise have preferred to use modern Turkish spelling (e.g., Mehmet rather than Mehmed). For the transliteration of Greek words I have followed the Library of Congress guidelines. For place names on Crete I have used the current Greek form, for example, Rethymnon rather than Resmo (Turkish) or Rethimo (Italian). The only exception is the capital city of Crete, today's Herakleion, which was known as Candia in the seventeenth century. Inconsistencies in transliterations from titles and citations are due to the variety of systems used at different times and in different places around the world.

A SHARED WORLD

Introduction ─────────────────────────────

IN THIS CENTURY two eminent historians, Henri Pirenne and Fernand Braudel, have produced compelling but very divergent portraits of the Mediterranean world, the former during the transition from antiquity to the Middle Ages, the latter in the reign of Philip II in early modern Europe.

Pirenne and Braudel differed not only in the periods which they studied, but also on the fundamental issue of Mediterranean unity or disunity. For Henri Pirenne, the Arab conquests of the seventh century and beyond crushed the common world of the Roman *mare nostrum* and replaced it instead with two hostile civilizations facing each other across the sea.

Rather than updating and reproducing this essential divide in a study of the sixteenth-century Mediterranean world, with the Spanish Hapsburgs representing Christendom and the Ottoman sultans the Dar ül-Islam, Braudel chose instead to write a history of the Mediterranean "from the bottom up," beyond the conventional boundaries of state, religion, and culture. By arguing for a common experience based on shared environmental constraints, Braudel deemphasized the very conflict that was at the heart of Pirenne's thesis.

Ottoman historians, by and large, have not confronted Braudel's thesis of a pan-Mediterranean world in the early modern era directly but have tended, however implicitly, to support the older idea of the Mediterranean as a zone of cultural contest and confrontation.

Andrew Hess is one Ottoman historian who has chosen to respond directly to, and sharply disagree with, Braudel's argument for the essential unity of the Mediterranean world. Braudel, he writes, rested his account "largely on examples drawn from the experience of Latin Christendom."[1] This was a natural course of action because "a sophisticated history from the bottom up could be written only for regions of the Mediterranean where sources and methodologies were well developed: the lands of Latin Christendom."[2] As a result of this unavoidable concentration on a geographical area that was "culturally neutral," Hess argues, Braudel's

---

[1] Andrew Hess, *The Forgotten Frontier: A History of the Sixteenth Century Ibero-African Frontier* (Chicago: University of Chicago Press, 1978), 2.

[2] Hess acknowledges Braudel's efforts to include the Ottoman Empire in his account but points out that this was an impossible task. "Braudel knew that he could not assume that what happened within the Hapsburg Empire also took place within the boundaries of the Ottoman state. And so he made a valiant attempt to include the preliminary results of research among the mountains of documents within the Ottoman archives. But modern Turkish historians were in no position to accomplish overnight what their European colleagues had taken centuries to do." Ibid.

Mediterranean world does possess an essential unity but this was not at all representative of the sea as a whole. Hess then turns to that part of the Mediterranean that is the focus of his book, the Ibero-African frontier as he calls the dividing line between the Spanish and the Ottomans in North Africa, to argue that "the separation of the Mediterranean world into different, well-defined cultural spheres" is the main theme not only of its sixteenth-century history, but of the centuries to follow when the chasm between Christianity and Islam only grew wider.[3]

In placing Hess's and Braudel's books side by side, two different early modern Mediterranean worlds emerge. In this book I suggest a third, the world of the eastern Mediterranean. This world, I argue, had a dynamic all of its own, one that is not adequately conveyed by a focus on the struggle—or absence of one—between Christianity and Islam. From the time of the Fourth Crusade in 1204 onward, the eastern Mediterranean was the point of intersection for not two, but three, enduring civilizations— namely, Latin Christianity, Eastern Orthodoxy, and Islam.

The early phases of this three-way struggle have, of course, received a good deal of attention. The seventh-century Arab conquests of Byzantine territory, the Crusades, and the Ottoman conquest of Constantinople are all well-established topics in the historiography of the eastern Mediterranean. In this book I want to consider instead the final stage in the history of this ancient triangle. It unfolded in seventeenth-century Venetian Crete when the long war (1645–69) between Venice and the Ottoman Empire resulted in an Ottoman victory and the beginning of the end of the Latin presence in the East. Although the Venetians would hang on until 1715, the loss of Crete, "the most beautiful crown to adorn the head of the Most Serene Republic," was a blow from which they never recovered.[4]

Crete was not only the last stop in the long contest between the Ottomans and the Venetians. It was also the site of the most enduring, and profound, interaction among Latins, Eastern Christians, and Muslims in the eastern Mediterranean. By the time the Ottoman navy appeared off the island's northwestern coast in the spring of 1645, Catholic and Orthodox Cretans had lived together for almost five hundred years in a relationship whose complexity had no rival in the Greek East. The Ottoman conquest added another layer to this already complicated past by setting off a process of conversion to Islam that eventually resulted in one of the largest Muslim communities in the Greek world.

This singular history makes the transition from Venetian to Ottoman rule in Crete well worth considering, not just for its own sake, but for the

---

[3] Ibid., 3.

[4] The words belong to Isepo Civran, provveditore generale in Candia in the mid-seventeenth century. Stergios Spanakēs, "Relazione de Sr. Isepo Civran tornato di Prov r Gen.l di Candia 1639," *Krētika Chronika* 21 (1969): 429.

larger themes of early modern Mediterranean history that Braudel and Hess have raised. A focus on Crete reveals the following dynamics at work in the eastern Mediterranean.

First, the transition from Venetian to Ottoman rule in Crete was a long process that included two major wars (1645–69 and 1684–99). In other words, it was the site of precisely that kind of civilizational clash which, Hess claims, wrung the ambiguity out of the Mediterranean world. But in Crete this extended period of upheaval—which continued until 1715— was characterized not by the crystallization of religiously defined communities but rather by an instability in religious identity. At the elite and popular level, the society created by the Ottoman conquest was full of individuals who were connected to both the Christian and the Muslim community on the island. Contemporary documents reflect this society, to the point of expressing, at times, an uncertainty as to the religious identity of the persons being written about.

Second, despite the high drama of the war, the Ottoman-dominated Mediterranean that emerged after the war did not look so different from the Venetian order that preceded it. This supports Braudel's view that religion and culture were not the critical dividing lines in the Mediterranean. Another dividing line, however, has not received sufficient attention. The essential continuity—with some important changes to be discussed here—between Venetian and Ottoman Crete stems from the fact that both powers represented, in the context of the Mediterranean, the ancien regime. By the seventeenth century these ancient adversaries were both powers whose world view was bounded by enduring geographical markers: the Italian peninsula, Istanbul, Aleppo, Alexandria, and possibly Algiers. An overemphasis on the Christian-Muslim divide obscures the fact that, in the early modern eastern Mediterranean, the real battle would prove to be between this ancien regime and the "northern intruders"—France, England, Holland, and, later on, Russia. They upset the balance in the Mediterranean not because they were Christian but because they were new. Their newness derived from the fact that their world, unlike the Venetian and Ottoman worlds, was larger than the Mediterranean.

Finally, the Ottoman conquest of Crete did bring about an important readjustment in the delineation of cultural spheres but it was not only, or even primarily, the extension of Islam at the expense of Christendom. The sultan's success also allowed for the completion of the Orthodox reconquest of the eastern Mediterranean, a process with its roots in 1453 when the Ottoman capture of Constantinople turned the balance of power in the eastern Mediterranean against the Italians and in favor of the eastern Christians. By conquering Crete, and reinstating an Orthodox hierarchy on the island, the Ottomans finally extinguished the last important state in the eastern Mediterranean that owed its origins to the Crusades.

Although the Crusades had begun as a Christian attack on the Muslim world, the Latin capture of Constantinople in 1204 left a legacy of bitterness between eastern and western Christendom that was, at times, even stronger than the antipathy felt by Muslims and Christian toward each other. Now, at last, the Ottomans were driving the hated Latins out of the Greek world.

This aspect of the Ottoman conquest brings us back to the value of Crete as a place where Orthodoxy, Latin Christianity, and Islam all intersected. I would like to point out two other other advantages to writing the history of the eastern Mediterranean from the vantage point of an island rather than at the imperial level.

The whiff of the interloper continues to cling to Muslims in the Mediterranean world. This is so for several reasons. Ottoman history is too often still treated as imperial history, as the history of the sultan and his army and their combined successes or failures. Since the sultan's navy was largely absent from the Mediterranean after the sixteenth century, it is as if the Ottoman Empire stopped at the shoreline. Individual Muslims whose lives were not bound up with imperial projects are simply invisible. This has manifested itself most clearly and consistently in the commercial historiography of the Ottoman Empire where, despite some recent stirrings, the Muslims are relegated to the overland routes while the Christians monopolize the sea.

The vantage point of an island is valuable for another, often overlooked reason. In the territorial division of labor that indelibly marks the nationalist historiography of the Balkan successor states, the Greeks have claimed the eastern Mediterranean as their own. Greek historiography, by and large, asserts the boundaries of religion and culture that Braudel seeks to minimize, and it tends to do this in two ways by excluding the Ottomans from the Mediterranean. The impression of a "Greek lake" has been bolstered by a scholarly concentration on the small Aegean islands, where there was virtually no Muslim settlement, to the relative exclusion of the larger islands, especially Crete, where there was a large and important Muslim community.[5] Where Muslims did appear in force, as in Crete, their arrival is treated as a cataclysmic event signaling a break with all that went before.

A focus on Crete in the seventeenth century renders visible the common world that Latins, Eastern Christians, and Muslims shared for many centuries, despite wars and considerable cultural hostility.

The book comprises six chapters and a conclusion. In chapter 1 I outline the peculiar features of this "last conquest" as Crete turned out to be for

---

[5] Cyprus has received a good deal more attention than Crete due to the ongoing political crisis on that island. The "Turks" of Cyprus have been studied intensively precisely because

the Ottomans. After this final addition to the sultan's domains, no more enduring victories were to be forthcoming; indeed, just a few decades later the Ottoman retreat from central Europe would begin. The incorporation of Crete was peculiar for several reasons. It came a century after the age of Ottoman expansion had come to an end and at a time when the classical institutions of conquest had fallen into disuse.

Profound transformations in Ottoman society during the course of the seventeenth century meant that the empire that conquered Crete was a different creature from that which had pursued conquest in the classical age between 1300 and 1600. The incorporation of the island reflected these changes. The oligarchy that conquered Crete—headed up by the famous Köprülü family—was careful to reserve the riches of the island for itself, rather than to parcel out the land to the sultan's soldiers. This policy was in line with empirewide trends in the second half of the seventeenth century, which saw the increasing commercialization of land and more entrepreneurial activity on the part of a wide variety of imperial and local elites. It was also not dissimilar to the situation that had prevailed in late Venetian Crete, where a weakened metropolitan center was unable to impose its will on the accumulated privileges of the local elite.

Although continued instability in the eastern Mediterranean up until 1715 prevented a thorough exploitation of the island's wealth, the strength of commercial interests from the very beginning meant that Crete was well placed to take advantage of the expansion in trade that characterized the eastern Mediterranean in the eighteenth century.

The Venetian threat was not extinguished in 1669; in fact, war between the Ottoman Empire and Venice broke out twice more, once in 1683–99 and again in 1714–15, before the Venetian withdrawal from the region in 1715 finally brought to an end almost three centuries of Ottoman-Venetian rivalry. Chapter 2 relates the difficulties that the Ottomans experienced in maintaining their hold on the island during these tumultuous years at the end of the seventeenth and beginning of the eighteenth centuries and shows that the Ottoman predicament was similar in important ways to Venice's predicament during its last century of sovereignty in Crete. The similarity issues directly from the fact that—unlike in previous Ottoman conquests—Crete did not pass from a crumbling system of rule to a strong and centralizing empire (as was the case with the Balkans) but rather from one struggling state to another. Here the similarity ends, however, because the Ottomans conquered Crete at a time when new conditions were beginning to emerge in the eastern Mediterranean, conditions that allowed the Ottomans to consolidate their sovereignty on Crete. One was the

---

they are still there, whereas the last of the Cretan Muslims were sent to Turkey in the population exchange in the 1920s.

dwindling of galley warfare, which allowed the Ottomans to treat the Cretan peasantry more liberally than had their Venetian predecessors. Even more important was the critical role that the French began to play in the eastern Mediterranean after 1670. France was a strong naval power, intent on erasing the last vestiges of Venetian domination in the eastern Mediterranean. This meant, among other things, that it was willing to help the Ottomans draw Crete firmly into Istanbul's domains.

Chapter 3 turns to the character of Crete's capital city, Candia, under the Ottomans.[6] This chapter, together with chapters 5 and 6, traces the fortunes of local, urban society. The last two centuries of Venetian rule have justifiably been presented as a time when, with ever quickening momentum, an urban society with local roots took shape. The famous "Cretan Renaissance" is, of course, the best-known product of the extraordinarily fertile mingling of Orthodox and Catholic elites in the urban centers.

The Ottoman conquest of the island did not level the cities. For some this will seem like an astonishing, even a heretical statement. The Greek historian Theodore Detorakēs' views on the matter are, I believe, representative albeit somewhat dramatic. "Urban life, which is the fundamental prerequisite of cultural production, was destroyed as the large cities turned into deserts in which mostly Turks lived." The Turkish conquest, he notes in the same paragraph, "abruptly and definitively cut down the rich and bright flower of the Cretan Renaissance."[7]

From the narrow viewpoint of elite intellectual production, Detorakēs is certainly right; the Cretan Renaissance sailed away with the last remnants of the Venetian fleet. But it should be obvious that only a very small number of people were ever caught up in artistic and literary life, and the history of Candia under the Venetians is not synonymous with the history of the Cretan Renaissance.[8] Deeper forces were at work in supporting an indigenous urban life, and these forces, somewhat altered admittedly, carried over into the Ottoman period. Chief among these during the Venetian period was the growing strength of local society vis-à-vis Catholic elites, a strength predicated in part on the declining ability of Venice to exclude the local population from the commercial life of the Mediterranean and even points beyond.

---

[6] This is the modern Greek city of Herakleion. I have chosen to use the better known Venetian spelling, Candia, rather than the Ottoman form of the word which is Kandiye. In the interests of consistency, I have used Candia even when quoting from Ottoman documents.

[7] Theocharis Detorakēs, *Istoria tēs Krētēs* (History of Crete) (Athens, 1986), 271.

[8] Anastasia Papadia-Lala, *To Monte di Pietà tou Chandaka, 1613–mesa 17 aiona: Symvolē stēn koinōnikē kai eikonomikē istoria tēs venetokratoumenēs Krētēs* (The Monte di Pietà of Candia, 1613–mid-17th century: A contribution to the social and economic history of Venetian Crete) (Athens, 1987), 26. Her book is published as a special edition of the journal *Parousia*, which is published by the University of Athens.

Although the long war undeniably exacted a very heavy toll on the capital city (including its total evacuation at the end of the war), it was not subsequently turned into an Ottoman garrison town. Nor was Crete the recipient of large-scale immigration from other parts of the empire. By the end of the seventeenth century conquest simply no longer called forth the mass of Turkish settlers that was so characteristic of Ottoman conquest in the Balkans. Very quickly, then, a population of local origin reasserted itself in Candia, supplemented by immigration from around the Aegean. Although recognizably Cretan, the new residents of the city were different from city dwellers during the Venetian period in two ways. First, many of them were Muslim and, second, many were of recent peasant origin. These two characteristics, along with the end of the Cretan Renaissance, have led historians, I believe, to equate the Ottoman conquest with the death of the cities.

In the next two chapters I turn to the important topic of commercial history. The commercial history of the eastern Mediterranean in this period is important not just in its own right but because it has traditionally supported the larger cultural arguments that I discussed earlier. In chapter 4 I outline the place of the island in the larger world of Mediterranean commerce between 1571 and 1720. To the extent that the question has been posed at all, historians have emphasized the flourishing wine economy of the sixteenth century, ignored the seventeenth century, and viewed the early Ottoman period (up until 1821), particularly in Candia, as one of decline.[9] I argue instead that in the course of 150 years the island moved through a cycle, such that the economy that emerged in the eighteenth century (after 1720) was not unlike that of the sixteenth century, although it was Chania, in the northwestern part of the island, and not Candia, that became the city of international trade under the Ottomans. At both ends of the cycle a profitable export economy with substantial involvement on the part of metropolitan elites was the rule. In between came a long period of localism in which the island lived off a dense, regional trade rather than the export of a single commodity—wine under the Venetians, olive oil under the Ottomans. This economic localism spanned the transition from Venetian to Ottoman rule in the second half of the seventeenth century.

If the movement in chapter 4 is cyclical, chapter 5 traces instead the linear development of a local group of merchants. Although Venice was initially able to exclude the Cretans from the world of trade, its grip on the commerce of the eastern Mediterranean eventually began to loosen.

---

[9] C. J. Heywood's comments are typical: "The Ottomans had entertained high hopes for the riches to be garnered from Crete after the conquest of Candia: a 'second Egypt' as Evliya Çelebi called it, but these hopes, particularly for Candia itself, were not to be realised." *Encyclopedia of Islam*, new ed., vol. 4, s.v. "Candia."

Beginning in the sixteenth century a community of local merchants is discernible in Candia. The same is true of the (already Ottoman) Cycladic islands in the early seventeenth century, a fact that strongly suggests that the rise of local merchants was intimately related to Venetian decline.

Again contrary to what historians have asserted, the Ottoman conquest of Crete did not arrest this process, nor is there any reason to expect that it should have. It was never the Ottomans' policy (unlike the Venetians') to reserve commercial pursuits for its own elites, and the Ottomans presided lightly over the Mediterranean world in the sense that their rule did not arrest the growing strength and vitality of local society, not just in Crete but throughout the Aegean basin.

Greeks, more than any other community of scholars, have explored the local and regional trade of this time. Yet as they survey the rocks and inlets that lie scattered across sea, the Aegean islands loom large while points further south simply fade from view. There are several reasons for this, I believe.

First, the relatively intense focus in the historiography on the second half of the eighteenth century has allowed the commercial activity in the eastern Mediterranean to be understood as part of the Greek commercial and literary revival that led up to the revolution in 1821; in short, it has been pressed into the service of the nation-state. If we include Crete, it becomes clear that the local resurgence in commerce, usually dated to the middle of the eighteenth century, started much earlier and grew out of the vacuum created by the end of Latin domination, rather than the temporary absence of the French from the eastern Mediterranean due to the Seven Years' War, as is commonly asserted. French domination of the eastern Mediterranean before 1750, although frequently asserted, was never as total as has been claimed.

The second reason is also closely related to the requirements of nationalist historiography and is part of the general exclusion of the Muslims from the sea that I mentioned earlier. Historians of modern Greece have chosen to ignore the Cretan maritime tradition because it is ethnically complex and does not fit into a recognizably Greek sea.[10]

Finally, chapter 6 takes up the question of cultural boundaries in the Mediterranean in the wake of the Ottoman victory in Crete. The Muslim-Christian divide is, of course, a natural point of emphasis. Crete was the last significant Venetian possession in the eastern Mediterranean. The loss of the island can be viewed as the final chapter in a process that began in the fifteenth century, when the rise of Spanish and Ottoman power at

---

[10] The Aegean is also favored because its naval forces—particularly from the famous trio of Hydra, Spetses, and Psara—played a vital and heroic role in the early days of the Greek independence struggle (1821–30).

opposite ends of the Mediterranean led to a division of the sea between Christian West and Muslim East. With the departure of the Venetians, the eastern Mediterranean finally became a Muslim lake.

Such an interpretation is not without value, particularly with regard to Crete itself, where the creation of a large Muslim community had enormous significance for the nineteenth century. In this chapter I argue that an Ottoman Mediterranean redrew the boundaries of Christendom as well and that this was equally significant for the future. The Ottoman victory in Crete meant that, after 500 years of Latin rule, the Greek Orthodox Cretans were rejoined to the Patriarchate in the old Byzantine capital. The reunion was not without its difficulties and the first half century of Ottoman rule on the island was marked by intense conflict between the Patriarchate and the local Christian community. The more peaceful relations that ensued after 1720 signaled the successful incorporation of Crete into the Orthodox world, under the aegis of Ottoman rule.

I also argue that the extended period of turbulence was the result, in part, of active Venetian support for opponents of closer control from Istanbul. Venice's continued aspirations in the eastern Mediterranean, combined with Istanbul's preoccupation with the Balkans, meant that the ancien regime was slow to die in Crete. One of the characteristics of this period of transition was an instability in religious identities, which was symptomatic of the uncertain nature of Ottoman sovereignty in these early years.

The ancien regime did finally die, and by 1720 the Ottoman Empire no longer had to concern itself with Venetian threats to its rule in the eastern Mediterranean. In the conclusion I look forward to argue that the Pax Ottomanica that emerged in the eighteenth century would prove to be short-lived in comparison with its Latin predecessor. The Ottoman Mediterranean was part of an expanding world in which new cultural choices were opening up. For the Orthodox Christians of the empire, the old boundaries of the Mediterranean world that they had shared with the Muslims and the Latins were giving way to new ventures into northern Europe. The creation of a Greek identity that resulted from this contact with the west is well known, but the place of Crete in this story has been less explored. Three points are worth emphasizing.

First, the successful incorporation of Crete into the Orthodox fold meant that the island's fortunes would now be closely tied to the fortunes of Greek nationalism. Second, the mixed world of the cities, where Christians and Muslims mingled, would fade from view as the exclusive narratives of nationalism took center stage. Third, the previously unstable line between the Muslim and Christian communities in Crete would give way to a society polarized along religious lines.

In that perennial balance in history between continuity and change, this book is a story more of the former than the latter. No sharp divide separates the Venetian era from the Ottoman one in Crete, and many of the forces that were already in motion in late Venetian Crete continued into the Ottoman period. The significant breaks that were occasioned by the conquest—the end of the Italian Levant, the creation of a Muslim community, and the reattachment of Crete to the Orthodox world—would only have consequences in the far-distant future. From today's vantage point it was almost as if the Venetian withdrawal from the eastern Mediterranean was the necessary precondition for the murderous struggles between Orthodox Christians and Muslim Turks that would begin at the end of the eighteenth century and which have continued into our own era.

Continuity is not, perhaps, a dramatic claim to make. Its value in this case lies in the fact that it allows a forgotten world to emerge, the common space, the Old World of the eastern Mediterranean, that Muslims, Latins, and Orthodox Christians inhabited and which had been evolving ever since the Ottomans reached the shores of the Mediterranean in the fourteenth century.[11]

The term "Old World" is chosen deliberately, to convey the durable geographical limits, known adversaries, incremental change, and established ways of doing business that characterized it. The Ottoman conquest of Crete is best seen not as an Iron Curtain of Islam thrown up around the eastern Mediterranean. Rather it marked the final extension of Ottoman political control over a world in which Muslims were already active participants, as well as the last gasp of the Venetian *oltremare*. Americans are used to thinking of Europe as the Old World, but from the point of view of Europe in the early modern era it was the Mediterranean that was old.

---

[11] Palmira Brummett has explored the idea of a common space in her work *Ottoman Seapower and Levantine Diplomacy in the Age of Discovery* (Albany: State University of New York Press, 1994). Brummett's work, however, is concerned with the Ottoman state and elite participation in trade, whereas society is the focus of my study.

One

The Last Conquest

*What can a Man say of a Country inhabited by
Turks?*
  *M. Pitton de Tournefort, a French botanist
who visited Crete in 1699*

The War for Crete

In a report sent to the Senate of the Venetian Republic in 1639, the
provveditore generale[1] of Crete, Isepo Civran, worried that pirate assaults
on Ottoman shipping by the Maltese or the Florentines would provide
the Ottoman Sultan with the excuse that he had been looking for to attack
the island.[2] He noted that the Venetian Republic was doing its best to
prevent such pirate attacks on Muslim shipping—mentioning an incident
in which Venice captured a pirate ship outside Leghorn and freed all the
Muslim slaves on board in order to show its goodwill toward the Ottomans—but clearly not every incident could be prevented.[3] In fact, Isepo
Civran's worst fears came true just five years after he wrote his report.

---

[1] This office was a new one for Crete, created in the second half of the sixteenth century.
Its creation was an attempt to wrest the control of Crete away from the locals who, it was
felt, had penetrated the lower levels of the administration and were bending it to suit their
own desires. Thus Venice took control away from traditionally powerful offices such as the
duca di Candia and created a new supervisory office, the provveditore generale, that had no
connection to the island. All the reform efforts during the last one hundred years of Venetian
rule attempted to ameliorate the position of the peasantry and thus gain its loyalty, but these
plans came to nothing due to the opposition of local landlords and the hesitancy of Venice.
See Anastasia Papadia-Lala, *To Monte di Pietà tou Chandaka, 1613–mesa 17 aiona: Symvolē
stēn koinōnikē kai eikonomikē istoria tēs venetokratoumenēs Krētēs* (The Monte di Pietà of
Candia, 1613–mid-17th century: A contribution to the social and economic history of
Venetian Crete) (Athens, 1987).

[2] Stergios Spanakēs, "Relazione de Sr. Isepo Civran tornato di Prov r Gen.l di Candia
1639," *Krētika Chronika* 21 (1969): 446.

[3] Ten years earlier General Moresini dwelt at length in his report to the Venetian Senate
on an incident involving the bey of Andros. Apparently as the bey was approaching the
harbor of Cerigo he was attacked by Venetian galleys, which mistook him for a pirate. As
soon as they realized their mistake, they did everything to make amends, including not
liberating the Christian slaves who were on board. The scribe of the Turkish ship was taken
to Crete to retrieve some of his belongings, and everything was returned, including the bey's
knife. The scribe and the Turkish girl who was with him (who was treated in Crete for a
wound) stayed at Moresini's house. But then going from Monemvasia to Andros the scribe
and the girl again met up with mishap, this time from Maltese pirates, who had—apparently—

In the autumn of 1644, a ship set sail from Istanbul with a number of notables on board, among them the chief of the harem Sünbüllü Agha and Bursali Mehmet Efendi, who had just been appointed to the judgeship of Mecca.[4] The ship stopped at Rhodes, where sailors warned them about a pirate boat lying in wait. Mehmet Efendi, however, insisted that they must reach Egypt in time for the haj, so the boat departed. Somewhere in the vicinity of Crete it was set upon by Maltese pirates. Sixty people were taken hostage (among them Mehmet Efendi) and the rest were killed, including Sünbüllü Agha, whose enormous treasure was shared out among the pirates. When he heard the news, Sultan Ibrahim accused the Venetians of having given safe harbor and aid to the Maltese in Crete. Thus, in Kenneth Setton's words, the impact of the Maltese attack on the Ottomans "fell with a deadly weight upon Venice."[5] From Istanbul, the Venetian bailo reported that a fleet of seventy-eight galleys and assorted smaller ships had set sail from Istanbul on 30 April, 1645. The Venetians continued to hope that the ships were headed for Malta, as the Ottomans said they were. In fact, the ships went as far as Navarino on the western coast of the Morea in order to disguise their intent. But when the armada was sighted off the northwest coast of Crete on 23 June, the Venetians knew that another war with the Ottomans had begun.[6]

---

gotten word of them from a French ship. The Venetians intervened again, secured their release and took them back to Andros. Stergios Spanakēs, "Relazione Francesco Moresini Provveditore Generale nel Regno di Candia 1629," *Mnēmeia tēs krētikēs istorias* (Monuments of Cretan history), vol. 2 (Herakleion, 1950), 86–87.

[4] See K. M. Setton, *Venice, Austria and the Turks in the Seventeenth Century* (Philadelphia: American Philosophical Society, 1991), 104–37, for an account of the beginning of the war.

[5] In some accounts the Venetians not only admitted the boat but also accepted Sünbüllü Agha's horses as a present. R. C. Anderson, however, says that the Maltese were refused admittance to any fortified port but did make use of various unfrequented and undefended harbors. See his *Naval Wars in the Levant* (Princeton: Princeton University Press, 1952), 121. Setton, who gives the most detailed account and makes extensive use of Venetian sources, writes that the Maltese put in on the unguarded southern shore of Crete to take on water and supplies. The Venetians were able to prevent them from landing at Castel Selino, also on the southern coast. Civran had worried in particular about the southern coast precisely because it was unprotected. "There are many places along the southern shore where, not only corsair boats can land, but also large armatas, without facing any obstacle at all." (Molti sono i sitti, e posti, quali dalla parte del mar d'Ostro possono far sbarco i Corsair non solo, ma ogni più grossa armata senza ostacolo, o contradittione alcuna.) Spanakēs, "Relazione de Sr. Isepo Civran," 429.

[6] See Setton, *Venice, Austria and the Turks*, 126, for the size of the Ottoman fleet sent out to Crete. The relatively modest number of ships assembled for the attack on Crete— unlike a century earlier, when 240 galleys had led the assault on Tunis—is indicative of the empire's declining naval power. The effort was significant, nevertheless, since the fleet represented approximately 80 percent of the empire's total capacity. Traian Stoianovich, "L'espace maritime segmentaire de l'Empire ottoman," in *Material Culture and Mentalities: Land and Sea*, vol. 4 of *Between East and West: The Balkan and Mediterranean Worlds* (New Rochelle, N.Y.: Aristide D. Caratzas, 1995), 51, 53. Manpower for the galleys was a chronic problem throughout the long years of the war. At the end of a successful season of naval campaigning in 1654, for instance, the sultan was presented with only 800 men, a number

Despite the seriousness of the Maltese attack, the decision to launch a war with the Venetian Republic must be explained. The Ottomans had had many opportunities in the past to launch an attack on Crete and had chosen not to do so.[7] Just a year before Civran wrote his report, the Venetians and the Ottomans had come to the brink of war, again over an incident of piracy. When North African pirates raided villages along the coast of Calabria, the Venetians had set out in pursuit. By the time they caught up with them, the pirates had taken refuge in the Adriatic port of Valona (today's Vlora in southern Albania). The Venetian commander decided to pursue them and entered the port, sinking fifteen of the sixteen ships he found there. Although agreements between the Venetians and the Ottomans allowed for the pursuit of corsairs, the sultan viewed the entry into an Ottoman port as a hostile invasion. Murat IV immediately had all trade with the Venetian Republic stopped and, according to the English ambassador in Istanbul at the time, it was only Venice's payment of large sums to various Ottoman officials, including the sultan, that prevented the outbreak of war.[8]

Evidence suggests that shifts both in the international situation and internal politics within the sultan's court explain the decision to invade Crete as a response to the Maltese assault. The earl of Castlemaine, Roger Palmer, who toured with the Venetian squadron in the Levant in the summer of 1664, was of the opinion that the Turks feared nothing more than a united Christian front against them. That was why they only dared to attack the West when the Christian powers were squabbling among

---

sufficient for just four galleys. Rhodes Murphey, "The Ottoman Resurgence in the Seventeenth Century Mediterranean: The Gamble and Its Results," *Mediterranean Historical Review* 8, no. 2 (December 1993): 191.

[7] The Ottoman intent to conquer Crete stretched back well over a century. Upon the conquest of Rhodes in 1522, the sultan's representatives tried to convince Rhodian merchants to return to the island by pointing out that Rhodes would soon be part of a larger, eastern Mediterranean market controlled by the Ottomans. Ahmet Pasha said to a Rhodian merchant: "Tu vois la belle situation de cette terre, qui est en liaison avec la Syrie, Chypre, Constantinople, e Candie et bien d'autres lieux. Sache que l'intention du Seigneur est de s'en prendre bientôt à Candie et à Chypre, car il ne veut pas que d'autres se mêlent des affaires de cette mer. Par conséquent ceux qui habiteront à Rhodes se trouveront dans un lieu très convenable et commode pour le commerce." Nicolas Vatin, *L'Order de Saint-Jean-de-Jérusalem, l'Empire ottoman et al Méditerranée orientale entre les deux sièges de Rhodes 1480–1522*, vol. 7 of *Collection Turcica* (Paris: C.N.R.S., 1994) 365. Again, in 1583 the valide sultan Nurbanu, who was of Venetian origin, was able to thwart the Ottoman admiral's plan to invade Crete in the next campaign season. Leslie P. Pierce, *The Imperial Harem: Women and Sovereignty in the Ottoman Empire* (Oxford: Oxford University Press, 1993), 223.

[8] Setton, *Venice, Austria and the Turks*, 109–10. On 6 September 1638 Sir Peter Wyche wrote to Charles I's secretary of state: "I have bin eaven now advertised in greate secresie that the Venice bailo (Alvise Contarini) for the accomodation of this business hath made proffers of 100 m. [thousand] dollers to the Grand signor, of tenn thousand dollers to the Captine Bassa, and of tenn thousand dollers to the Caymacam . . . and whereas the Caymacham would not formerlie suffer to departe two Venetian ships, which were in port, since those liberall offers hee hath given order for their departure."

themselves. When the Christian world was united, he continued, the sultan's armies occupied themselves on the Persian front. Ibrahim, he says, "unexpectedly" fell upon the Venetians when the "whole Christian world was at odds."[9] One may doubt just how much the Ottomans did fear a united Christian front since it so often failed to materialize. This may have been more of a plea on Castlemaine's part. Nevertheless, he was surely correct in pointing to the international situation as a determinate of Ottoman foreign policy. On the continent, the Thirty Years' War continued to distract Europe from its formidable neighbor. Venice was drawn into these wars and had been actively involved in the fighting for over two decades by the time the Ottomans chose to strike.

Even so, the Thirty Years' War was a situation of long standing. The more important shift for the Ottomans was the end of the long (1624–39) war with Persia. As long as the Ottomans battled the Safavids, any conflict in Europe would have meant the formidable task of sustaining a war on two fronts. Informed observers of the time saw this as an important consideration in Ottoman foreign policy. When Castlemaine was in the Lazaretto at Venice in the fall of 1664, the city received the news of the "dishonorable peace" concluded between the Ottoman grand vezir and the Holy Roman Empire. The reponse in Venice was one of fear and consternation precisely because now, with the Hapsburgs out of the way, the Ottomans could turn their forces on the Venetians and renew their seige of Candia.[10]

Changes at the imperial court may have been even more decisive in determining the response to the Maltese attack. When Ibrahim ascended the throne in 1640, the queen mother (valide sultan) Kösem and the grand vezir Kemankeş Mustafa Pasha took over the affairs of state, in response to the sultan's obvious emotional disturbance.[11] Both of them were seasoned and experienced politicians. Kemankeş Mustafa Pasha was known to be opposed to military adventurism because of the strain it put on the

[9] Earl of Castlemaine, *An Account of the Present War between Venetians and Turks with the State of Candie (in a Letter to the King from Venice)* (London: Printed by J.M. for H. Herringman, at the Anchor on the Lower Walk of the New Exchange, 1666), 2.

[10] In a "Postscript to the Reader" Castlemaine wrote that while he was confined at the Lazaretto in Venice he learned of the "dishonorable peace" made by Vienna with the grand vezir. This caused great consternation at Venice, he continued, because now the Ottomans could pursue the Venetians single-mindedly. Castlemaine, *An Account of the Present War.* The Treaty of Vasvar (1664) provided for a twenty-year peace between the Holy Roman Empire and the Ottoman Empire. Setton, *Venice, Austria and the Turks,* 102. The Venetian general Antonio Priuli, who served in Candia from 1664 to 1669, said it was an Ottoman principle of statecraft not to fight on more than one front at time. The conclusion of the war in Hungary, he writes, gave Köprülü Fazil Ahmet Pasha the opportunity to bring the long seige of Candia to an end. Stergios Spanakēs, "Relatione Del. Prov(r) genal dell'Armi in Candia E. Antonio Priuli 1667, 30 Marzo," *Mnēmeia tēs krētikēs istorias* (Monuments of Cretan history), vol. 6 (Herakleion, 1969), 3.

[11] Pierce, *The Imperial Harem,* 250. Ibrahim was brought to the throne because of Murat's death and the lack of any other heir.

treasury.[12] The situation changed dramatically, however, in 1643 when Ibrahim exiled Kösem and executed his grand vezir. A period of great chaos ensued during which the world of the court was turned upside down. Among other things, the sultan shocked the court by subordinating his sisters to his concubines, taking away their lands and jewels and forcing them to serve Hümaşah, the concubine he had married.[13] Ibrahim came to rely heavily on the notorious Jinji Hoja, a minor religious official who had been promoted to the second highest office in the religious hierarchy.[14] It was the Hoja himself, in fact, who interrogated the western ambassadors in an irregular manner about the Maltese attack. According to ambassadors' reports, he was a fervent advocate of war with the Venetian Republic, claiming that Crete, as part of the former Byzantine Empire, now rightfully belonged to the Ottoman Empire.[15] His ally in the war camp was the Kapudan Pasha Yusuf Pasha, who went on to conquer Chania in western Crete in just fifty-four days. He was a Dalmatian renegade, a convert to Islam whose original name was Josef Masković.[16] He and the Hoja were able to prevail on the sultan, over the objections of the grand vezir Sultanzade Mehmet Pasha, whom the Venetians considered a friend.[17]

Other factors also played a role. The Ottomans believed that Crete would fall easily to them, considering the dilapitated state into which most of the fortresses on the island had fallen.[18] It was certainly seen as an easier, and more tempting target than Malta, which was just barren rock. Finally, popular belief had it that soil trodden by Muslim horses was destined to belong to the faith. Rumors circulated in Istanbul that some of the horses captured by the Maltese had been unloaded in Crete.[19]

[12] J. von Hammer, *Histoire de l'Empire ottoman*, vol. 10 (Paris: Bellizard, Barthes, DuFour et Lowell, 1838), 43.

[13] Pierce, *The Imperial Harem*, 246. The sisters were forced to serve by "standing at attention like servants while she ate and by fetching and holding the soap, basin, and pitcher of water with which she washed her hands."

[14] Because of his reputation for occult powers, Jinji Hoja had been brought in to remedy the sultan's lack of heirs. Ibid.

[15] Setton, *Venice, Austria and the Turks*, 115.

[16] Setton, who claims that Masković hated the Venetians, seems to accept the Venetian point of view that there was a "Bosnian" clique in the palace and that they were implacably opposed to Venice. Setton, *Venice, Austria and the Turks*, 249. Bosnians were prominent at the highest levels of the bureaucracy in the second half of the seventeenth century. The Köprülü vezirs were themselves of Albanian origin, a group that was often paired with the Bosnians. Whether Bosnian-Albanian necessarily meant anti-Venetian is less certain. Köprülü Fazil Ahmet Pasha, for instance, had very cordial relations with the Venetians after the fall of Candia.

[17] Ibid., 124.

[18] Paul Rycaut, *The Present State of the Ottoman Empire* (London, 1669), 93, where he writes "Candy, the whole possession of which was imagined at the beginning of the war would upon a bare demand be quietly presented as the price and purchase of the peace."

[19] Hammer, *Histoire de l'Empire*, 10:81. In fact, reports from Crete at the time do not support this. Setton, *Venice, Austria and the Turks*, 116. For their part, Venetian administrators in Crete considered an attack on the island inevitable. Writing in 1639, Isepo Civran

At first it seemed that the Ottomans were justified in their belief that Crete would be an easy conquest. Chania was theirs by the end of the first summer of campaigning (1645), and Rethymnon fell before the end of the following year. In between the two assaults, and after the capture of Rethymnon, they went on to capture the rest of the smaller fortresses located throughout the island. Thus, less than two years after the beginning of hostilities, two of the three major Cretan cities had been captured as well as most of the countryside. In 1647 the invading army under the command of Serdar Deli Hüseyin Pasha turned its attention to Candia, the capital city of the island. But this fortress, with its ravelins, battlements, and various other outworks designed to withstand the ever increasing firepower of seventeenth-century warfare, would prove much more difficult to win. More than two decades had to pass before the Ottoman grand vezir Köprülü Fazil Ahmet Pasha finally received the keys to the city from the departing commander in September of 1669. Even as Candia stood in ruins, the Venetian attachment to this city that they called "the most beautiful crown to adorn the head of the most Serene Republic" was evident. The negotiators who rowed over to the Ottoman camp to surrender the city said, "We have come to surrender a fortress whose equal does not exist in the entire world. It is a priceless pearl the likes of which no sultan possesses."[20] As for the Ottomans, they were faced with the prospect of organizing an entirely new province, a task they had not faced for over a century.

The Last Conquest

Students of Ottoman expansion have neglected the incorporation of Crete into the empire at the end of the seventeenth century. This neglect is unfortunate because the circumstances of this last conquest are unique. Crete was the only territory won for the Ottoman Empire long after the golden age of expansion had come to a halt.[21] It was organized as an Ottoman province well after the classic institutions of Ottoman incorporation—the benefices known as timars and the provincial registers known

---

said that the Turks had suffered so much damage and so many *oltraggi* (outrages) that someday, surely, the kapudan pasha would decide to take his revenge.

[20] Silahdar Fındıklılı Mehmet Aga, *Silahdar Tarihi* (Istanbul: Devlet Matbaasi, 1928), 517–18. Writing in 1639, Isepo Civran referred to Crete as "the most beautiful crown." Spanakēs, "Relazione de Sr. Isepo Civran," 429. The Venetian attachment to Candia, however, did not prevent at least one Venetian official from considering blowing the entire city up before it was turned over to the Ottomans. Paul Rycaut, *A History of the Ottoman Empire from the Year 1623 to the Year 1677* (London, 1680), 272.

[21] The Ottomans did conquer some new territory in the Ukraine in the 1670s, but it was relinquished in 1699 as part of the Treaty of Karlowitz. Crete remained Ottoman until 1898.

as tapu tahrirs—had been transformed or even fallen into disuse. The Ottomans managed to acquire and to hold onto this major island—one of the "miniature continents" of the Mediterranean Sea—at a time when, according to conventional historiography, it was sinking into an irreversible decline.[22] What did a conquest look like in these unusual circumstances?

The two classical instruments of Ottoman incorporation—the timar, "the basic building block of Ottoman provincial administration," and the tapu tahrir[23]—were both intimately related to the military structure at the heart of the empire as well as the system of provincial administration. After a province was conquered, its revenues—both agricultural and urban—and its population were surveyed and entered into the tapu tahrir. On the basis of this record, the revenues of the newly conquered area were divided up into a certain number of timars and awarded to members of the military class.[24] Members of the Ottoman cavalry, the sipahis, were expected to settle in the village or town where their timar was located and to live off the tax revenue that had been assigned to them. In exchange they were required to help administer their area—in cooperation with the judiciary—and, most important, to be prepared to go to battle when called. The tapu tahrirs had another function: "survey books not only constituted a record and a reference to identify the resources to be assigned to the military, but also were a status book for the land and population which determined, until the next survey, the social position and tax liabilities of lands, persons and groups."[25] Thus through the system of timar and tapu tahrir the Ottomans managed both to provide for provincial administration and to assure themselves of an effective army.

The New Provincial Order

This system lasted from the fourteenth through the sixteenth century. By the beginning of the seventeenth century, however, shifts in the old institutional order meant that a long and painful period of transformation had begun. Changes in military and fiscal organization also meant that old methods of provincial administration were no longer workable. The shift from a land-based army to an eclectic mix of janissaries, volunteers,

---

[22] The expression "miniature continent" is Fernand Braudel's.

[23] The words are Halil Inalcık's. "Introduction: Empire and Population," in *An Economic and Social History of the Ottoman Empire*, ed. Halil Inalcık with Donald Quataert (Cambridge: Cambridge University Press, 1994), 14.

[24] The Ottoman timar has been the subject of an extensive literature. For a skillful overview of this debate, see Inalcık, "State, Land and Peasant," in Inalcík, *The Economic and Social History of the Ottoman Empire*, 103–78.

[25] Halil Inalcık, "Suleiman the Lawgiver and Ottoman Law," *Archivum Ottomanicum* 1 (1969): 135.

and the private armies of high-ranking Ottoman officials meant, among other things, that the timar holders were no longer available to run the provinces for the sultan.[26] State revenues that had formerly gone to the timar holders were reclaimed for the central treasury and then farmed out to tax collectors, whose importance grew enormously in the course of the seventeenth and eighteenth centuries. These tax farmers, rather than the soldiers of the old land-based army, became the key figures in provincial administration.

Happily for scholarship, and for this book, it is no longer necessary to stuff these facts through the famous meat-grinder known as the "Ottoman decline thesis." The decline paradigm, under sustained attack since the early 1980s, has begun to give way to a new picture of the seventeenth and eighteenth centuries.[27] An older generation of scholars understood Ottoman history after the sixteenth century as the story of a weak sultanate unable to impose his will on local potentates, armed with lucrative tax-farming contracts, who were intent on asserting their independence. This dynamic, viewed in strongly negative terms, was only reversed in the nineteenth century when modernizing reforms based on a European model returned the sultan to his rightful place at the center of Ottoman society. It follows that provincial history was understood primarily as a struggle between center and periphery.

The new scholarship on the seventeenth and eighteenth centuries, instead of falling into the old groove of center versus periphery, moves laterally away from the palace to emphasize how, beginning in the seventeenth century, "imperial power was diluted by an increasingly dense network of interest groups at the center."[28] These Istanbul-based elite households were interested, first and foremost, in more direct and longer-term rights over the empire's most lucrative revenue resources, and some of the most vicious battles of the seventeenth and early eighteenth centuries were fought precisely over this issue.[29] The switch to tax farming, and the sultan's

[26] In the middle of the seventeenth century the irrelevance of the timariot army was acknowledged by attempting to level a bedel-i timar, a tax in lieu of military service. Metin Kunt, *The Sultan's Servants: The Transformation of Ottoman Provincial Government, 1550–1650* (New York: Columbia University Press, 1983), 88.

[27] For examples of the new scholarship, see Ariel Salzmann, "An Ancien Régime Revisited: 'Privatization' and Political Economy in the Eighteenth-Century Ottoman Empire," *Politics and Society* 21, no. 4 (December 1993): 393–423; Suraiya Faroqhi, "The Ruling Elite between Politics and the Economy," in Inalcík, *The Economic and Social History of the Ottoman Empire*, 545–75; Pierce, *The Imperial Harem*; Linda T. Darling, *Revenue-Raising and Legitimacy: Tax Collection and Finance Administration in the Ottoman Empire, 1550–1660* (Leiden: E. J. Brill, 1996); and Jane Hathaway, *The Politics of Households in Ottoman Egypt: The Rise of the Qazdaglis* (Cambridge: Cambridge University Press, 1997).

[28] Jane Hathaway, "Problems of Periodization in Ottoman History: The Fifteenth through the Eighteenth Centuries," *Turkish Studies Association Bulletin* 20, no. 2 (Fall 1996): 27.

[29] Mehmet Köprülü, the reforming vezir, founded the first of these households in the 1650s. For the period 1683–1703 at least forty other households have been documented.

increasing reliance on the pashas' households for both staffing the state bureaucracy and military support, facilitated them in their quest. They gained one of their greatest victories at the very end of the seventeenth century (significantly, in the middle of another war) when the sultan conceded the important right of life-term tax-farming contracts (malikāne) on certain key revenue sources. This concession quickly became hereditary.[30]

The new elites were not necessarily at odds with provincial leaders. The two groups were often joined together in wide-ranging households that cemented the ties between center and periphery. These ties were less formal, and thus less understood, than the institutions of an earlier age but the distribution of tax farms among clients in a massive patronage network, extending from Istanbul to the provinces, seems to have been central.[31] Each side performed a valuable service for its partner. Under the new system the geographical link between one's assignment and the source of one's revenue, whereby the governor of Syria, for example, would draw most of his income from that province, was broken.[32] The fiscal map of the empire was increasingly a crazy quilt of particularist claims. Gone were the uniform blocks of timars, carefully graded in a hierarchy of military obligation, with the governor (and chief military commander) of the

See Rifa'at Ali Abou-El-Haj, *The 1703 Rebellion and the Structure of Ottoman Politics* (Leiden: E. J. Brill, 1984).

[30] See Salzmann, "An Ancien Régime Revisited," for an original and forcefully argued account of these changes. Her work on the provinces shows just how important the tax-farming contract of malikāne came to be. By the end of the eighteenth century, for instance, 47 percent of the tax revenue in the province of Aleppo was collected through malikāne, 41 percent was reserved for religious endowments (often to the exclusive benefit of a particular family), and only 12 percent was collected through timar. Ariel Salzmann, "Centripetal Decentralization: Life-Term Taxfarming in the 18th Century in the Ottoman Empire," in *Political Economies of the Ottoman, Safavid and Mogul Empires*, vol. 1, ed. Tosum Aracanli, Ashraf Ghani, and David Ludden (forthcoming).

[31] Recent work on Ottoman Egypt has shown how the households "served as a meeting ground for imperial and local interests by providing an opportunity for imperial functionaries to exercise local influence and to co-opt local luminaries." Jane Hathaway, "The Military Household in Ottoman Egypt," *International Journal of Middle East Studies* 27, no. 1 (February 1995): 41. Salzmann argues that in the course of the seventeenth century a division of the spoils emerged whereby central-state elites aquired the most lucrative tax-farming contracts at auctions held in the major urban centers of Istanbul and Edirne, while auctions held in provincial cities tended to dispose of less renumerative sources of income for the benefit of the provincial gentry. Even at the provincial auctions, however, high-ranking officials were often in attendance, and in practice the line between a central and a local notable is very hard to draw. The new elites did not rely solely on tax farming for their newfound wealth. They also engaged in urban real-estate investment, commerce, and money-lending and were behind the proliferation of private religious endowments. By the early nineteenth century as much as two-thirds of Ottoman land may have been endowed. Bruce McGowan, "The Elites and Their Retinues," in Inalcık, *The Economic and Social History of the Ottoman Empire*, 660. Thus Salzmann speaks of elites who held a "portfolio of assets." Salzmann, "An Ancien Régime Revisited," 403.

[32] Kunt, *The Sultan's Servants*, 83.

province at the top distinguished only by the fact that he received the largest timar. Thus the local notables—known in Ottoman historiography as the ayan—collected taxes and undertook military recruitment for their patrons who held assets spread out all over the empire. The ayan, in turn, were pleased to be included in the business of government.[33]

These shifts, as momentous as they were, nevertheless came about incrementally and over a long period of time. In addition, they were cast as illegitimate deviation from earlier, idealized norms by an important (and vocal) section of the Ottoman elite. Despite the importance of the provincial gentry from the seventeenth century on, for instance, it received no official recognition until the famous alliance (senet-i ittifak) of 1808.[34] These are just some of the reasons why, in the words of one scholar, the most important changes in Ottoman society after the sixteenth century were "gradual, unintended, usually unrecorded and therefore poorly understood."[35]

There is nothing gradual or unintended about a conquest, however, and in that sense Crete stands out from the pattern of incremental change that typified the seventeenth and eighteenth centuries. Conquests were typically an opportunity for the Ottomans to make manifest their vision of the proper imperial order. The conquest of the island, then, is a rare glimpse of Istanbul's intentions during this uncertain century. The record suggests a complex picture: the Ottomans were reluctant to abandon the outward form of earlier conquests, while at the same time they showed considerable realism in tailoring the new regime in Crete to the realities of the late seventeenth century as described here.

A New Province

Crete was important enough to the Ottomans for them to designate it an eyalet or province in its own right, the only island in the empire to enjoy such a status.[36] Unlike the smaller islands in the archipelago to the north,

---

[33] Salzmann, "An Ancien Régime Revisited," 402–3. Salzmann estimates that over the course of the eighteenth century some 1,000 to 2,000 Istanbul-based individuals, together with some 5,000 to 10,000 individuals based in the provinces, controlled an important share of state assets.

[34] Ibid., 408.

[35] McGowan, "The Elites and Their Retinues," 658.

[36] The sancaks (districts) of the eyalet of the Mediterranean islands (*Gezā'ir-i Bahr-i Sefīd*) in the first half of the seventeenth century were Gelibolu, Eğriboz, Inebahti, Mizistre, Rodos, Midilli, Biga, Sigala, Karli-eli, Kocaeli (Izmit), Sakiz, Naksos, and Mahdiyye on the Tunisian coast. Cyprus was part of this eyalet from 1670 to 1703, and then again from 1785 onward. In the interim the island's revenues were assigned to the grand vezir. See I. Yiannopoulou, *E dioikētikē organosis tēs stereas Ellados kata tēn Tourkokratian 1393–1821* (The administrative

Crete was the recipient of a significant influx of Ottoman officialdom. A pasha was assigned to each of the three cities on the northern coast, with the pasha of Candia enjoying precedence over the other two, and the city of Candia received not only a fortress commander (dizdar) but a janissary agha as well.[37] In addition, surviving documents indicate that the Ottomans paid a considerable amount of attention to their newest possession, both in terms of surveying it and dividing up its resources. Neither the survey, however, nor the division of the spoils followed the pattern of earlier conquests of Christian areas.

The Survey of the Island

Köprülü toured the island before departing Crete in the spring of 1670, and a general survey was carried out, probably under his supervision.[38] This survey, which is extant in the Istanbul archives, cannot be considered a tapu tahrir as it is generally understood in the literature, although the Ottomans used the terminology of the classical era, no doubt out of a desire to preserve the appearance of continuity with the past. It is not a general record of the land and population of the island with a view to establishing the social position and tax liabilities of the islanders. The customary taxes associated with the timar system—the çift-resmi and the ispence—are conspicious by their absence.[39] In other words this survey

organization of mainland Greece during the period of Turkish Rule, 1393–1821) (Athens: Athens University, 1971).

[37] A janissary agha was appointed only in certain important citadels. Ismail Hakki Uzun-çarşılı, *Osmanlı devleti teşkilâtından kapukulu ocakları* (The institutions of the Ottoman state: The military corps) (Ankara: Türk Tarih Kurumu Basimevi, 1943), 1:327, 330.

[38] Başbakanlık Arşivi (Prime Ministry's Archive), Istanbul, Tapu Tahrir Defterleri series, no. 825. It is undated but must have been compiled some time between 1080/1669–70 (the year of the final conquest) and 1084/1673–74 because on p. 819 there is an entry in the margins dated 1084/1673–74. This register covers the two eastern districts (*liva*) of Candia and Sēteia. Another marginal note, this one on the first pages of the register, adjusts the tithe from one fifth to one-seventh in 1086/1675–76, and the wording of this adjustment makes it clear that this document is, in fact, the general survey carried out soon after the conquest. The text reads: "bundan akdam Girit ceziresi muceddedan tahrir olundukta hasil [   ] olunup lakin cezire-i mezburenin arazi munbit olmamağla re'ayet zira'et ve hiraset eyledikleri hububatlari hasil ihat etmeyup senede hububatlarinin hamsindan olan hasillari eda(ya) öşret hukemler-ile zira'et ve hiraset-ten eraghet idup aksar-i arazi zira'et ve hiraset olunmamağla mu'attel olduğu mukarrer olmağin zira'et ve hiraset ragbet etmeleri içün hasil min as-sab' tayin olunmak üzere *defter-i mufassal getirup kaleminin tashih eylese diyu bu hakire varid olan emr-i şerif kayd ve [   ] olundu fil avasat 1086.*" The italicized text clearly refers to this document as the defter-i mufassal. Two other mufassal defterleri are also extant, both housed in Ankara at the Tapu ve Radastro Genel Mürdürlügü. Both are dated 1117/1705–6 or thirty-seven years after the conquest. One, number four, covers the livas of Sèteia and Candia. The others cover the two western livas of Chania and Rethymnon.

[39] Both of these taxes were paid to the timariot in compensation for the abolishment of certain services. Inalcık, "Suleiman the Lawgiver," 130.

did not have as its goal the implementation of the classical çift-hane system in the countryside.

For one thing, only those who possessed land were recorded in this detailed survey (mufassal defteri).[40] The arrangement of the register makes this clear. A village name is given, followed by a list of landholders and how much each possesses in terms of fields, orchards, and the like. At the bottom of each entry, the village's total holdings are given, followed by the tax in kind and money due from the village.[41] The taxes themselves are limited to a series of cash levies on agricultural produce, in keeping with seventeenth-century trends elsewhere in the empire. A ferman dated 1123/1711, which reviewed the tax system that had been in effect since the conquest, makes it clear that this system continued.[42]

The arrangement of the survey also bears the imprint of the reforms of the great Ottoman jurist of the sixteenth century, Ebu-su-ud, who abolished differential tithe rates for Muslim and Christian peasants. In Crete, despite complaints, Muslim peasants paid taxes at the same rate as their Christian neighbors and attempts by new converts to pay less were quashed (of course, the Christians had the added burden of the cizye).[43] This would

[40] Under the çift-hane system of the classical period peasants were recorded whether or not they owned an land: "He [the peasant] paid more or less according to his personal status—whether or not he controlled the labor of a wife and children, whether or not he possessed a piece of land and the requisite animal power." Halil Inalcık, "The çift-hane System: The Organization of Ottoman Rural Society," in Inalcík, The Economic and Social History of the Ottoman Empire, 153.

[41] For example, a village in the nahiye or subdistrict of Pediada lists 60 landholders. Between them these villagers possess 284 cerib of fields (tarla), vineyards (bağ), covering 71.2 ceribs, and 922 trees (escar). This village is recorded as producing 17,031 akçe of revenue. Tapu Tahrir, no. 825, p. 22. For a more extended discussion of the land regime put into place in Crete, see my article "An Islamic Experiment? Ottoman Land Policy on Crete," Mediterranean Historical Review 11, no. 1 (June 1996): 60–78.

[42] Turkish Archives of Herakleion (henceforth T.A.H.), 2:319. During the first survey (completed in the early 1670s) it was decided to collect 120 akçe from each dönüm (a measure of land, roughly one-quarter of an acre) planted with vineyards (bağ), or given over to gardens (bahçe) and vegetable plots (bostan). The rate was lowered in 1086/1675–76 and then at some point raised again. The reaya protested, pointing to the lower rate of 1086/1675–76, and this ferman appears to be the government's response to their complaint. It insisted upon a restoration of the higher rate.

[43] In classical Islamic law land was divided into two great categories: öşri land, which had remained in the hands of the Muslims at the time of the great Arab conquests and was subjected to a lower rate of tithe; and haraci land, which was conquered by war. Here the tenants had to pay a higher rate. Ebu-su-ud abolished this difference by ruling that all the land of the Ottoman Empire, having been gained through war, was haraci land and thus subject to the higher tithe. Halil Inalcık, "State-owned Lands (miri)," in Inalcık, The Economic and Social History of the Ottoman Empire, 113. This new standard represents an important shift in Ottoman society, which has been little examined, but see Halil Inalcık, "Islamization of Ottoman Laws on Land and Land Tax," in Festgabe an Josef Matuz, ed. Christa Fragner and Klaus Schwarz (Berlin: Klaus Schwarz Verlag, 1992), 101–19. See T.A.H. 1:28 for Muslims in Crete complaining about having to pay the tithe at the same rate as the Christians and T.A.H. 1:141, a ruling by the serasker (chief military officer) that Muslims pay taxes the same as Christians based on the extent of their property. If Ebu-su-ud's reforms leveled

explain why the surveyors in Crete recorded taxes due on the land, with due disregard for the status of whoever happened to be tilling it.

If the mufassal defters were originally an integral part of the timar regime in the Ottoman Empire, the Cretan mufassal defteri signals the demise of that regime. It must be viewed instead as a document that was called by its classical name but had nothing to do with either establishing a provincial cavalry in Crete or inscribing the status of each and every Cretan peasant. Rather its intent was to facilitate the collection of cash revenues from an unstable rural population.[44]

The Cretan Kanunnāme

As if to erase any room for doubt, the kanunnāme or law code that was issued for Crete very soon after the surrender of Candia explicitly states that the çift-resmi and ispence taxes, along with several others, were to be abolished entirely. The text of the kanunnāme brings us to another peculiarity of the conquest of the island.[45]

In the hybrid legal system of the empire, the Ottoman kanunnāmes covered all those areas of life regulated by the will of the Sultan, as opposed to Islamic law. The organization of the court and army, taxation, criminal law, the relationship of the individual to the state, and—most important for our purposes—land law were all areas that fell under kanun. Unlike any other kanunnāme that preceded it, the Cretan one insisted that the land and tax regime on the island be established in accordance with the şeriat or Islamic

---

the difference between Muslim and non-Muslim, other concerns in the seventeenth century worked to eradicate the difference between those belonging to the official class (askeri) and the ordinary taxpayer (reaya). In response to widespread peasant flight and dispossession as a result of uprisings across the empire, the Ottomans were faced with appropriation of peasant land by their own officials. The sultan's response was to shift tax status from the person to the soil rather than sustain the revenue loss. "One of the most frequent orders found in Ottoman judicial records is the demand by the central government that all individuals— regardless of their personal status—who lay claim to land formerly worked by the reaya (and still therefore miri) would have to pay the taxes incumbent upon the land." Bruce McGowan, *Economic Life in Ottoman Europe* (Cambridge: Cambridge University Press, 1981), 70.

[44] This shift in fiscal practice was a general one and dates to the very end of the sixteenth century. Salzmann, "An Ancien Régime Revisited," 398.

[45] Two copies of the kanunnāme for Crete are known to exist. One is in the Prime Ministry's archive in Istanbul and has been published by O. L. Barkan, *Osmanli Imparatorluğunda ziraat ekonominin hukuki esaslari* (The legal basis of the agricultural economy in the Ottoman Empire) (Istanbul: Burhaneddin Matbaasi, 1945), 350–53. The other is contained in the records of the Islamic court stored at the Vikelaia Public Libary in Herakleion, Crete. Neither one of the texts has a date, but the copy in Herakleion appears next to a kanunnāme-i gümrük (customs code) which is dated 18 Cemaziyel'evvel 1080/14 October 1669. Thus it seems safe to say that the general kanunnāme was drawn up on or around 14 October, ten days after Fazil Ahmet Pasha's formal entrance into the city. It appears in the third bound volume on p. 102 and will henceforth be referred to as T.A.H. 3:102.

law.[46] Thus a document that originated as the manifestation of the sultan's will is used to champion the supremacy of Islamic law, and the land regime is explicitly founded on Islamic principles, rather than on the will of the sultan.

Two different land taxes were established for Crete—the haraç-i muka-seme and the haraç-i mukata'a—and both were explicitly identified with the şeriat. Moreover, the ispence and the çift-resmi taxes, along with a wide variety of other taxes, were abolished precisely because they were not canonical.[47] Perhaps most radical of all, ownership of the land was granted unequivocally to the peasantry rather than to the sultan.[48] State ownership of arable land was the very bedrock of the Ottoman agricultural order with roots that reached back to the early Islamic period. Especially when one considers that these fiscal and military changes did not necessitate a change in the relationship between the cultivator and the land, it becomes clear how extraordinary was this departure in Crete.

Köprülü's motivations may have been ideological, influenced by the Islamic revivalist movement then raging in Istanbul. Köprülü was familiar with the kadizadelis, as the Muslim activists of the capital were known, and may have been sympathetic to some of their aims. The leader of the movement in the 1660s, a shaykh known as Vani Mehmet, was Köprülü's personal counselor.[49]

Although the view that the rejection of state ownership of the land was un-Islamic was a minority position in Islamic jurisprudence, it nevertheless did surface with some regularity throughout the centuries. In fact, such a

---

[46] T.A.H. 3:102. "cezîre-i mezbûreyi şi'âr-i şeri'at ve şevket-i Islāmiyye ile tenvir buyurub" (The island of Crete must be surveyed in accordance with the requirements of the *şeriat*). The peculiarities of the Cretan kanunnāme have long been known to scholars. Barkan was the first to note the special nature of the Cretan kanunnāme in his study of Ottoman kannunāmes. "Claiming that it was founding a land regime in accordance with pure Islamic tradition, [the kanunnāme] abolished the miri land regime—which had traditionally been applied in the Ottoman Empire and which had been confirmed by Ebussuut's *fetvas*—in its entirety." Barkan, *Osmanli Imparatorluğunda ziraat*, xli. For a further discussion of the peculiarities of the Ottoman land regime in Crete, see my article "An Islamic Experiment?"

[47] T.A.H. 3:102. "cezire-i mezbûrede ancak kütüb-i fikhiyeden istikhrac olunub bālāda mestûr olan rüsm-i şer'iye taleb olunub" (On this island only those canonical taxes which are written in the fiqh will be collected).

[48] T.A.H. 3:102. "ve arazi-i haraciye sahiblerinin mülk-i sarîhleri olub bey' ve şirāya ve sāyir tasarrufāta kadirlerdir. Ve fevt olduklarında emlāk-i sāyireleri gibi cümle vārisleri beyninde 'alel-farîza-i şer'iyye taksim olunur" ([The] land is clearly and unequivocally the freehold of its owners and as such they are able to buy it, sell it, and treat it as they wish. Upon their death it can be divided among their heirs, in accordance with the *şeriat*, just as all their other property). The conquerors of Crete abided by Ebu-su-ud's declaration that all the land of the empire was haraci—that is, acquired through military conquest—but they stood his definition on its head. Whereas Ebu-su-ud had declared all the land of the empire haraci in order to increase state control over the land, the Cretan kanunnāme explicitly denied the state's ownership of the land. See Greene, "An Islamic Experiment?"

[49] See Madeline Zilfi, *The Politics of Piety: The Ottoman Ulema in the Postclassical Age, 1600–1800* (Minneapolis: Bibliotheca Islamica, 1988), 146–49, for Köprülü's relationship to the kadizadelis.

position was being taken by a number of jurists in Egypt at the time of the conquest of Crete.[50] It is possible that the kadizadelis were aware of this dissenting school and, through their influence over Fazil Ahmet Pasha, affected policy in Crete. Against this line of speculation, however, we must counterpose the fact that the kadizadelis did not speak to the question of ultimate ownership of the empire's arable land. Their concerns centered around the relationship between individuals, rather than the relationship between the subject, the sultan, and the land.[51] The connection, then, between the land regime in Crete, the kadizadelis in Istanbul, and Fazil Ahmet Pasha is still to be established.

There is a more likely explanation. The seventeenth century was a time when elite households fought the sultan—more or less successfully, although with some temporary reversals—for more long-term control over revenue sources, particularly the right to pass on their wealth to their heirs. This was, after all, the attraction of both the malikāne contract, which swiftly became hereditary, and the establishment of religious foundations. Crete was the Köprülü family's triumph; it was Köprülü's mother who announced the victory to the Sultan, and it is not surprising that he would use this moment of triumph to make a radical move.[52] That move was to institute private control over the land in Crete. The kanun posited the peasantry, of course, as the beneficiaries of the new policy but, given the widespread disruption of the war, it was only natural that members of Köprülü's entourage, discharged soldiers and the like, would be able to gain access to the land. Abou-el-Haj has alerted us to the very different function of kanuns in the postclassical period. The grandee households, he argues, used the kanuns as a way of wrapping themselves in the aura of state authority while imposing regulations that were most beneficial to them in a particular situation. This was precisely the reason why no general empire-wide kanuns were issued after the end of the sixteenth century.[53] The Cretan

[50] These jurists argued that possession is a sign of ownership and rejected the majority view that land was state-owned unless proven otherwise. They also cited the importance of observable, everyday practices in establishing the legal status of the land. Jurists in Ottoman Syria and Egypt saw the peasants selling the land and passing it on in accordance with Islamic rules of inheritance, and this bolstered their argument that the land was privately owned. See Kenneth Cuno, *The Pasha's Peasants: Land, Society and Economy in Lower Egypt, 1740–1858* (Cambridge: Cambridge University Press, 1992), 76–81.

[51] For their program, see Katib Çelebi, *The Balance of Truth*, trans. G. L. Lewis (London: George Allen and Unwin, 1957).

[52] Silahdar, *Silahdar Tarihi*, 524.

[53] "We just noted that in early modern times the kanuns were issued as both general and specific regulations for conditions and under circumstances the central ruling elites thought they controlled. In circumstances when the situation was reversed, i.e., there was less unity within the ruling elite . . . no general, i.e., uniformally and universally appplicable central or provincial regulations were generated." Rifa'at Ali Abou-El-Haj, "The Ottoman Kanun as an Instrument of Domination," paper presented at CIEPO, International Committee of Pre-Ottoman and Ottoman Studies, Seventh Symposium, Pecs, 7–11 September, 1986, p. 5.

kanunnāme, then, represents not fundamentally the "resurgence of Islam" but rather an extraordinary victory on the part of the grandee households.

It is striking to notice how nicely a land policy based explicitly on the şeriat dovetails with the desire to wrest the control of Crete away from the Central Treasury. The rural order based on the timar was ending and thus the fiscal order that was instituted could pay little attention to those taxes which had supported such a cavalry. At the same time, such an arrangement could certainly be defended as more properly Islamic. The taxes so closely associated with the timar sytem were levies that the Ottomans had retained from an earlier, feudal era (this is particularly true for the Balkans) and clearly not part of an Islamic legal tradition that did not recognize such taxes.[54]

As for the provision in the kanunnāme for private ownership of arable land, extensive evidence from the religious court records of Candia indicates that this policy was adhered to. Unlike in other parts of the empire at this time, there was no attempt made to disguise the sale of arable land (tarla) around Candia, as well as its division through inheritance. Arable land appears with great frequency both in contracts of sale and in property distributions registered with the court.[55]

The principles of the kanunnāme were repeated in a court case from 1126/1714: "The land of this island being haraç land, vineyards, gardens, and vegetable gardens, and other land is mülk and must remain in the hands of the people. It is possessed like any other property and when someone dies it is to be divided among the heirs in accordance with the şeriat. It has been written and recorded thus in the Imperial Registers."[56]

It is interesting to note that this policy, formally based on Islamic principles, did not redound to the exclusive benefit of the Muslim community. During the long years of war and in the immediate aftermath, a good deal

---

[54] The çift-resmi tax was the cash equivalent of labor services due and, as Inalcık explains, derived from the slave or dependent subject status of the peasants. "As the Islamic Law does not recognize such a principle in terms of taxation, such taxes were categorized as 'customary' or more exactly 'sultanic' or 'state' (*urfi*) taxes, as distinguished from the Islamic taxes which are called 'rightful taxes' (*hukuk*)." Halil Inalcık, "Sources of Revenue," in Inalcık, *The Economic and Social History of the Ottoman Empire*, 70.

[55] This aspect of the land regime in Crete has been noted by scholars. Veinstein writes: "In the case of Crete the presence of *mülk tarlas,* as well as the inclusion of *tarlas* and *çiftliks* among the items registered by the kadis in probate inventories—a way of legitimating their character as freehold properties—is obviously related to the special land tenure system of this late Ottoman conquest, where the concept of *miri* land was categorically rejected, in order, so they argued, to return to the true Islamic conception." G. Veinstein, "On the Çiftlik Debate," in *Landholding and Commercial Agriculture in the Middle East,* ed. C. Keyder and F. Tabak (Albany: State University of New York Press, 1991) 40. For examples of sale and inheritance of tarla in Crete, see T.A.H. 7:96, 97; 2:31, 35.

[56] T.A.H. 2:235. "cezîre-i mezbûrenin arazisi, arzi-i hariciyeden olmağla ahlinin yedlerine ibka olunan bağ ve bağçe ve bostan ve sair arazi mülkleri olub emlak-i saire gibi tasarruf eyleyub fevt oldukda vereseleri beynlerinde vech-i şer'i üzere taksim oluna diyu defter-i hakaniye mestur ve mukayyed olmağla."

of land changed hands and the many land disputes that ended up in court shed some light on this process. Ottoman policy was to seize land that had been abandoned by those who fled to the Venetian side, and then to sell it off as private property (*mülk*) to bidders.[57] Whoever refused to accept the status of protected subject (*kabul-i zimmet*) by nonpayment of cizye and flight to Venetian controlled areas would lose their land. Not surprisingly, there are many cases where the new owner claims that the former owner was or is a Venetian sympathizer, an assertion that the dispossessed claimant vehemently denies.

A typical example involved a recent convert to Islam and a Christian. Soon after the conquest this convert appeared in court, trying to recover his family's vineyard from the new owner, whose name was Ioannes. The court denied his claim, pointing out that his family had fled to the Venetian side during the war. As a result of this flight, the state had taken over the property and auctioned it off. The vineyard now belonged to this Ioannes.[58]

This example (and there are others) shows that both Christians and Muslims were able to buy land from the public fisc. Christians could defend their property rights against Muslim challengers if the new owner could show that the challenger himself, or his family or village, had defected to the enemy during the war.

The New Entrepreneurs

Scattered references in the court records are a further indication of the enthusiasm with which the Istanbul elites threw themselves into Crete's agricultural economy. Some of the best land on the island, for instance, was granted to Köprülü, as a reward for his victorious seige of Candia. The sultan ceded to his grand vezir all the land surrounding the city of Candia that fell within the range of a cannonball shot from the walls of the city (*top altı*).[59] The land lying just outside the city walls had always been intensely cultivated due to the high quality of the soil, and archival evidence indicates that Köprülü spent considerable effort on his property, which endowed his foundation in Candia.

In 1084/1673 the departing administrator (*mütevelli*) of his foundation asked the court to value the improvements that had been made on

---

[57] Court records refer to a ferman ordering the seizure of land that had been abandoned. The ferman itself does not seem to have survived. T.A.H. 1:7. "hin-i feth cizye kabul olmayup Dar ul Harb'a ferar edenlerin emlak ve arzileri miriden zabr olunmak üzere hatt-i humayün [   ] varid olmağla" (It was decreed that the land of those who refused to submit and who fled at the time of the conquest be seized).

[58] T.A.H. 2:138. For other examples, see 1:7; 3:109; 2:421, 85.

[59] T.A.H. 4:255. In June 1673 the mütevelli of Köprülü's vakíf in Candia came to court to resolve some of the boundary issues resulting from the Sultan's grant to Köprülü and referred to the ferman the Sultan had issued.

Köprülü's farm (çiftlik). A new pipeline had been laid down to ensure the water supply. Using his own workers (*ergadlarim*), Köprülü had had twenty new rooms (*oda*) built, plus a large stable (*akhur*), a fountain (*çeşme*), several other structures, and finally a stonewall (*taş duvar*) that encircled the entire farm. Outside the çiftlik itself he had another two fountains built as well as several storehouses (*makhzen*). The mütevelli asked the judge to assign a value to the investment (including labor) which he did: 658,640 akçe. This was more than the tax farm for all the monasteries of Crete.[60]

In 1082/1672 the administrator for the endowment of the imperial defterdar (başdefterdar) came to court to record the sale of 190 sheep on behalf of the defterdar. These sheep were part of an enormous flock of 992 which the defterdar, through his mütevelli, had entrusted to two sheepherders from the coastal district of Mylopotamos, west of Candia.[61]

When the governor of Crete, Ahmet Pasha, was executed in 1096/ 1684, the kadi sent an inspector down to the harbor to take an inventory of the ex-governor's goods, which were loaded on a ship, ready to set sail, apparently, at the moment of the pasha's arrest. The list of his cargo was extensive and included 3,250 okka (over 4,000 kilograms) of grapes (*üzüm*) and 655 okka (over 800 kilograms) of honey, as well as numerous cloaks from Algeria, which were being sent on to Chios for dyeing. These and other items are a clear indication that the pasha was engaged in commercial endeavors.[62]

Entrepreneurial activity on the part of the conquering elites suggests that the hard-won victory on Crete represented not only the traditional opportunities associated with successful conquest but something more as well. Coming when it did, it presented the newly powerful Istanbul households with the chance to capitalize on their strength and make sure that the riches of this fertile island in the middle of the Mediterranean would belong to them and them alone.

Köprülü and Crete

The location of Köprülü's property is a striking example of just how strong this family had become by the last quarter of the seventeenth century.

---

[60] T.A.H. 4:249. Damage to the document makes it difficult to identify two of the structures in the declaration that was made to the court. The monetary assessment of the improvements was actually written as six "yük" and 58,640 akçe. The yük was the equivalent of 100,000 akçe. The tax farm for all the monasteries of Crete in 1083/1672–73 was 5 yük and 80,229 akçe. Elite claims on Candia's hinterland are clear from the court record. See, for instance, T.A.H. 4:161 for a Pasha's seray in a village in Temenos province, just to the south of the city.

[61] T.A.H. 3:171.

[62] T.A.H. 4:391. The incoming governor of Crete bought the entire cargo.

Sometime soon after the conquest of Rethymnon, the fertile lands lying just outside that city were granted to the imperial endowment of Sultan Ibrahim that had been established within the walls of the conquered city. As with Köprülü, the land was referred to as the sultan's top altı.[63] The similarity between the two land grants is hard to miss and seems to establish a sort of parity between the sultan and his grand vezir. In fact we can go further: Candia was the capital of the new eyalet and its pashas had precedence over the pashas of Rethymnon and Chania. The fact that it was precisely the capital city that was ringed round with Köprülü's estate suggests the enormous power that vezirial households had come to wield by the end of the seventeenth century.

When the disparate elements of the rural order in Crete—the disregard of personal status, the dearth of feudal taxes, the cash levies, the freedom to sell and divide land, the ability of both Muslims and Christians to acquire it, and the heavy commercial involvement of Ottoman elites—are considered as a whole, the fluidity of the new arrangements is striking. The typically Ottoman (and Byzantine and Roman) emphasis on the preservation of both state control and the individual production unit is relatively absent.

Many of these new conditions, of course, were emerging elsewhere in the seventeenth-century Ottoman Empire and it is not surprising to find them in Crete. What makes Crete different is that these new postclassical developments had to somehow be fit into the framework of a conquest. And it was conquest, after all, that had been the achievement par excellence of a different type of Ottoman society—one centered around the sultan and his timariot army—that the conquerors of Crete were determined not to return to.[64] Their solution was a hybrid one: to give the classical past its due by resurrecting the old terminology of conquest, while at the same using the potent language of Islam in a kanunnāme that allowed for unprecedented private control over the land. In the meantime, they pursued a path in Crete that made it a conquest unlike any other in Ottoman history. It is a testimony to their strength that they were able to do so.

The land regime in Crete is best understood as a reflection of conditions prevalent in the empire. Still, it is worth noting the continuity with certain features of late Venetian Crete. In the early centuries of Venice's rule, the

[63] T.A.H. 3:88.

[64] As several Ottoman historians have noted, the seventeenth-century chronicler Mustafa Naima was the apologist of this new class. Naima, drawing on the biological metaphors of the medieval historian Ibn Khaldun, spoke of the organic phases that a political entity must pass through. According to Naima, the age of the conquering soldier had come to an end and the well-being of the empire now depended on the civilian bureaucracy. Rifa'at Ali Abou-El-Haj, *Formation of the Modern State: The Ottoman Empire, Sixteenth to Eighteenth Centuries* (Albany: State University of New York Press, 1991), 45.

distribution of land was closely linked to the requirements, and particularly the military requirements, of the metropolitan power. Venice established a system of military colonization whereby fiefs were distributed to knights (*feudatarii* or *feudati*) who were obligated to serve the republic both as soldiers and as providers of grain to the Italian mainland.

By the sixteenth century this quasi-feudal system was in tatters; many of the estates had been divided up and passed into the possession of individuals, many of them Greek Orthodox, who were not bound by any sort of obligation to Venice.[65] Writing in 1575, Foscarini lamented that the vast majority of the knights neither owned horses nor even knew how to ride. When called upon to give an accounting of themselves, many would borrow a horse and stick a villager on it as the rider. The resulting demonstration was considered so hilarious that people would come from far and wide to watch and to throw rotten fruit and stones at the riders.[66] As we shall see in the next chapter, the Venetians also repeatedly failed in their attempts to force this new landowning class to put the interests of the state ahead of their own economic advantage. The creation of the office of the provveditore generale in the last quarter of the sixteenth century was an attempt to create a new level of administration, one that would not (it was hoped) be penetrated by local interests.[67]

The animosity that Venice felt toward this class saturates the reports of the administrators returning home to the lagoons from Crete. Again and again the island's elites were lambasted for their greediness, their ill-treatment of the peasantry, their lack of military preparedness, and their disloyalty. The duke Dolfin Venier, returning home in 1610, commented that the Cretans serving on the feudal council (who now outnumbered the Venetians) "seem peace-loving, but I don't know if this is how they truly are or if they are in fear of the many soldiers and fortresses they see on the island."[68]

The landed elites of the early Ottoman period shared a focus on economic gain, rather than military service, with their predecessors. The many differences between the two rural orders—such as the legal basis on which individuals controlled the land and the status of the landowners within the larger society—should not obscure the basic commercial thrust of agriculture in both the late Venetian and early Ottoman periods.

---

[65] In 1639 Civran lamented the fact that there were now more Greek feudatories than Venetian. Spanakēs, "Relazione de Sr. Isepo Civran," 380.

[66] Chr. Maltezou, "E Krētē ste diarkeia tēs periodou tēs venetokratias" (Crete during the period of Venetian rule), in *Krētē: Istoria kai politismos* (Crete: History and civilization), ed. N. Panayiotakēs (Herakleion, 1988), 143.

[67] See note 1.

[68] "se bene io giudico tutti coloro di animo assai quietto, non sò se per instinto proprio, o pure per il rimorso, che si vedono di Fortezze, et Militia." Stergios Spanakēs, "1610

The Janissaries' Island

In earlier conquests the Ottomans had relied on a landed army to rule the newly incorporated area, and had shown a willingness to concede certain feudal practices, albeit diluted, in order to provide for the provincial elite. No such class was envisioned or provided for in Crete. The Istanbul elites who held tax farms or religious endowments could hardly be expected to run their affairs directly. A local group of administrators would have to be found. By this time many other areas of the Greek peninsula enjoyed a high degree of autonomy and self-rule, but Crete did not follow this pattern. The Ottomans did create the office of the secretary to the divan (kapu yazıcısı), intended for a native who was expected to mediate between the local community and the Ottoman administration. In addition we hear of castel kethudas, provincial leaders whose responsibilities seem to have been confined to assistance in tax collecting. But the self-governing provincial bodies, with the right to appeal to the sultan over the head of the local governor, which were so characteristic of, for example, the Peloponnesos, were entirely absent in Crete.[69] Instead Crete became the island par excellence of the janissaries.

Timars: A False Start

After a survey, it was conventional practice for the Ottomans to draw up a summary register (defter-i icmal) indicating the distribution of tax revenue among the military. A summary register does exist for Crete, but, like the mufassal defteri, the continued reliance on classical terminology obscures more than it reveals.[70] The survey register of 1081 would have us believe that the timar system was implemented on the island, despite the fact that it had been largely abandoned elsewhere in the empire.[71] But close attention

a 9 Genaro, relation de s. Dolfin Venier ritornato di duca di Candia," *Krētika Chronika* 4 (1950): 317.

[69] For more on these positions, see chapter 6.

[70] Başbakanlık Arşivi (Prime Ministry's Archive), Istanbul, Tapu Tahrir Defterleri series, no. 801. The document was drawn up some time in 1081; a month isn't given. The Islamic year 1081 ran from 21 May 1670 through 9 May 1671. The list of timars distributed throughout the island is preceded by the following paragraph: "Icmal-i zeametha-i dizdar ve agayan ve gönüllüyan ve azaban ve agayan—ber muceb-i tahrir-i cedid el vaki' fi sene ihda ve tamanin ve elf" (Summary register of the zeamets [distributed to] the dizdar, the aghas, the gönül, the azabs, the aghas, in accordance with the survey conducted in 1081).

[71] See Halil Inalcık, "Military and Fiscal Transformation in the Ottoman Empire, 1600–1700," *Archivum Ottomanicum* 6 (1980): 283–337.

to the details shows that the survey register bore little resemblance to its classical namesake.

Although the governor (*muhafız*) of Candia did receive a very substantial revenue in the form of timar, the vast majority of grants were minuscule.[72] Four hundred eighty-two timars were carved out of the four districts of the island, most of them (340) in the two districts of Candia and Siteia.[73] The actual number of beneficiaries, however, was much greater—close to two thousand people—because of the practice that was followed. The village of Siyah in the subdistrict (nahiye) of Pediada is a typical example. This village had revenues worth 45,000 akçe, which were listed as one timar. However, the surveyor then went on to divide that timar into fourteen shares (*hisse*) each one worth only 3,000 or 4,000 akçe. Fourteen different soldiers ended up sharing the timar of Siyah.[74] The opposite situation also occurred: one solider might hold a small share of the revenue of two or three different villages.

The majority of the soldiers listed belonged not to the sipahi corps but to the volunteer irregular troops that had become so important to the Ottoman army in the seventeenth century. The small shares were distributed almost exclusively to members of the gönüllüyan, azaban, and farisan regiments.[75] Clearly the soldiers who received these revenue assignments would not be able to support themselves on such modest amounts, nor could they expect to have a serious role in governing the new province. Rather the motivation must have been to try to reward—however inadequately—the many volunteers who had fought in the long war. The Ottomans knew from bitter experience that demobilizing volunteers after a war was a risky business. At least this time, unlike earlier in the century, they had something to give them.[76]

In any event, the system did not last (and perhaps was not expected to). By the beginning of the eighteenth century the vast majority of eastern Crete's tax revenue had been redirected to the Central Treasury, in keeping with empirewide trends. This becomes clear by comparing the first cadastral survey with one carried out thirty-seven years later. Most of the timars, it

---

[72] Vezir Ahmet Pasha, the first governor of Candia, received a hass grant worth around 2 million akçe, all of it drawn from the eastern part of the island. Tapu Tahrir, no. 801, pp. 10–13.

[73] When Venice organized the system of fiefs in the early thirteenth century, it envisioned roughly 200 fiefs for the entire island. Maltezou, "E Krētē," 111.

[74] Inalcık points out that as early as the mid-fifteenth century a timar could be shared by several sipahis. Inalcık, "State-Owned Lands (*miri*)," 114. The system followed in Crete, however, stands out as an extreme—and no doubt unworkable—case. One village in the nahiye of Pyriotissa on the southern coast was divided up among an agha and twenty-four ordinary soldiers.

[75] Infantry, musketeers, and cavalry respectively.

[76] Demobilized peasant-mercenaries were behind the repeated insurrections of the first half of the seventeenth century.

will be recalled, were carved out of eastern Crete. It is not surprising then that in the district of Pediada, the largest district on the eastern half of the island, there was initially only one village whose revenues were assigned to the central fisc (*hass-i hümayun*). By the time of the second survey the revenues of 90 out of the district's 105 villages had been assigned to Istanbul; 81 of these villages were explicitly identified as new assignments to the fisc.[77] In the fertile district of Temenos, which formed Candia's immediate hinterland, 29 out of 36 villages were reserved for Istanbul. The situation was the same in the nine other districts of eastern Crete.[78] A note in the margins of the timar register discussed earlier suggests that timars were a very short-lived phenomenon on Crete. Just five years after the conquest a large timar (zeamet) worth 123,654 akçe was reassigned to the central treasury. The bereft timariot was given a new grant in Ohrid (Macedonia) in compensation.[79]

The Victory of Tax Farming

Crete represented a much greater opportunity for tax farmers than it did for individual soldiers hoping for a timar. The island was no exception to the general rule that, in the eighteenth century, the tax farmers effectively ruled the Ottoman provinces through their control of provincial resources. Tax farms (*mukataat*) covering all the major crops of the island were immediately put in place throughout Crete. Urban taxes and taxes on the island's monasteries were also farmed out.[80]

[77] The village is described as "hass-i hümayun-i cedid." Tapu ve Kadastro Genel Müdürlüğü, Ankara, register no. 4. Register no. 4, which covers the eastern livas of Siteia and Candia, is the second of the cadastral surveys (mufassal defterleri) that I discussed in note 38. A third register, which covers the two western livas of Chania and Rethymnon, is also housed in Ankara and does not form a part of this study. Both are dated 1117/1705–06, that is, thirty-six or thirty-seven years after the conquest.

[78] The revenues of Pyrgiotissa, Monofatsia, Ierapetra, Temenos, and Lasithi had been assigned to the Imperial Treasury from the very beginning. Their status had not changed by the time of the second cadastral survey. The revenue of the districts of Rizou, Kainourios, Malevizia, and Sēteia had not initially been assigned to Istanbul but was by the beginning of the eighteenth century.

[79] Tapu Tahrir, no. 801, p. 9. The date on the note is 1085 (or 1674/75). "zeamet-i mezkur hass-i humayun-a ilhaq . . . böylesinde mezkur Ahmad-a Ohrid sancakinda . . . haiyasinde . . . name qariye ve gayruhu." A Venetian report written sometime between 1703 and 1715 noted that, whereas previously the sipahis had been assigned villages, now they were drawing a salary: "*se ben horo non hano villagi come prima solo esigono paghe.*" Archivio di Stato, Venice, Senato, Provveditori da Terra e da mar, Lettere del. Provv. straordinario a Suda, Busta 891bis.

[80] Başbakanlık Arşivi (Prime Ministry's Archive), Istanbul, Baş Muhasebe Mukata'a Defterleri series, register nos. 10138–62. These documents, generated by the central administration, do not begin until 1101, or twenty-one years after the conquest. Local court records, however, make it clear that the tax-farming system was in place from the very beginning. For example, T.A.H. 4:5, Hajj Ahmet Agha, mütevelli of the vakıf of Defterdar Ahmet Pasha, asks for

Even before Köprülü had left the island, tax farms for the six districts that formed Candia's hinterland had been auctioned off.[81] The janissaries dominated the contracts awarded, which dwarfed the paltry amounts handed out to the volunteer soldiers in the form of timars.[82] Süleyman Agha, chief armorer of the military corps, bought the tax farm of four villages in two different districts for 69,543 akçe. Another individual, identified only as the head of the janissary corps, laid out 94,470 akçe for the revenues of eleven villages in Candia's immediate hinterland. Ali Agha, a janissary captain, bought the revenues of seven villages on the southern coast for 171,330 akçe. The tax farmer for monastic properties (worth 480,899 akçe) is not listed, but court records show that two years later a janissary named Hajji Ahmet Agha farmed this extremely rich revenue source.[83]

The janissaries were also important in the administration of the island's religious endowments.[84] The mütevelli who came to court to record the sale of the defterdar's sheep was a janissary, as was the mütevelli who came to court to arrange for the water supply of his patron, Abdurrahman Pasha, the janissary agha in Istanbul, who endowed a considerable amount of urban property in Candia.[85] The kethuda (chief lieutenant) of the imperial janissaries in Candia also administered his endowment through a janissary.[86]

Explaining a New Elite

There were several reasons for janissary domination of Candia and its hinterland. Soldiers were more numerous than any other social group.

---

and is granted the mukataa for the monasteries of Crete in 1083/1672–73. Urban taxes—which included customs and taxes on silk, cotton, coffee roasting, various market activities, candlemaking, dyeing, and the property of the deceased—are discussed in chapter 3.

[81] Başbakanlık Arşivi (Prime Ministry's Archive), Istanbul, Maliyeden Müdevver, register no. 2636. The opening page of this register states: "furukht-i mukata'a defteri 1080. defter-i furukht sudagan mukata'at-i eyalet-i cezire-i Girit der zaman hazret vezir-i mukarrem Ahmet Pasha ve Ebu Bekr Efendi Defterdar eyalet-i mezbure fi sene 1080" (Register of the sale of tax farms, 1080. Register of the tax farms sold in the province of the island of Crete in the time of the honored vezir Ahmet Pasha and Ebu Bekr Efendi Defterdar, in the previously mentioned province, 1080).

[82] In the six districts that formed Candia's immediate hinterland, janissaries farmed 40 percent of the revenues at the very least. The percentage was probably a good deal higher because in some cases the tax farmer is not listed and in others it is impossible to identify the individual with any certainty. For instance, someone identified only as Küçük Mehmet (little Mehmet) farmed revenues worth 265,336 akçe.

[83] T.A.H. 4:5. Hajj Ahmet Agha, mütevelli of the vakıf of Defterdar Ahmet Pasha was granted the mukataa for the monasteries of Crete in 1083/1672–73. By this time the amount of the tax farm had risen to 580,229 akçe. For a discussion of janissary control over urban tax farms, see chapter 3.

[84] Endowment administrators had many occasions to come to court and thus we can learn the identity of at least some of them. A comprehensive study of endowment administrators in Crete, however, would have to include the registers of the religious endowments themselves.

[85] T.A.H. 3:169.

[86] T.A.H. 3:226.

Most of the urban population was affiliated with some military regiment and the janissaries were the largest regiment by far. Contemporary estimates put the number of regiments in the city around nine or ten, with the janissaries accounting for as much as half of the military population.[87] In a city of slightly more than 10,000 people, the janissary troops alone (excluding dependents) numbered somewhere between 2,500 and 3,000 people.[88]

Military control over both the city and the countryside was also facilitated by an absence of competing indigenous elites. The countryside around Candia had been in Ottoman hands since the 1640s, and the end of the war witnessed the total departure of the Venetians from the capital as well. Köprülü Fazil Ahmet Pasha entered a deserted city. The prominent Greek families of the island—known as the archontopoula—that had spearheaded the resistence to the Venetians in previous centuries had long since made their peace with Venice. They chose to leave with the departing army.[89]

The absence of indigenous elites, however, does not mean that an alien military class was imposed on Candia and its hinterland. It would be a mistake to assume that Muslim meant foreign in the same way that Christian meant local. This was demonstrably not the case in early Ottoman Crete. Statistics are not available, of course, but it is certain that many—

[87] The sources are eight Venetian spy reports—all located in the Provveditori da Terra e da mar, Lettere del. Provv. straordinario a Suda series—dating from the 1680s, 1690s, and the first decade of the eighteenth century; the estimate was made by the traveler Tournefort, who received these numbers from the French vice-consul, who was, in turn, given them by the paymaster for the troops and, finally, an Ottoman salary register dating from 1080/ 1669–70. Başbakanlık Arşivi (Prime Ministry's Archive), Istanbul, Maliyeden Müdevver, register no. 658 entitled *Candia Kalesi Tahrir Defteri* (Survey of the citadel of Candia). The opening paragraph in this defter reads as follows: "Candia [   ] fethinden sonra kala'- i mezbure ve cezire-i Giritte vaki' kila' içün muceddidan tahrir olunan kul taifesinin defteridir" (This is a register of the kuls at the time of the new survey after the conquest of Candia on the island of Crete). For more on the Venetian reports, see the bibliography. Military orders proliferated in the urban centers of the Ottoman Empire in the seventeenth and eighteenth centuries, and it is sometimes difficult to know where to place a particular group. For instance, I have not included the group described by both Tournefort and the Venetians as "yamaks" as part of the janissaries, although some sort of affiliation was almost certainly the case. If included, the predominance of the janissaries would be even greater. See chapter 3 for a discussion of the phenomenon of the yamaks.

[88] See chapter 3 for a discussion of the city's population, including travelers' comments on the number of soldiers in the city.

[89] The history of the Chortatsē family is typical. They fled Crete with the Venetians and, when Venice reconquered the Peloponnesos, were given lands there to settle on. The Ottoman reconquest of the Peloponnesos (1715) forced them to flee again. Some members of the family then ended up as Venetian consuls in Smyrna, where they intermarried with the English and the French. One descendant of the Chortatsē family, Sir James William Whittall, published a family document from the late eighteenth century in which it was noted that "Most of the *archontopoula*, and among them the Chortatse family, not being willing to submit to the Ottoman yoke, abandoned all their land and fled to Venice, which—in recognition of the Chortatse family's many devoted years of service to her—granted them extensive holdings in the Peloponnesos." M. I. Manousakas, "Symvolē eis tēn istorian tēs Krētikēs oikogeneias Chortatsē" (A contribution to the history of the Chortatse family from Crete), *Epetēris Hetaireias Vyzantinōn Spoudōn* 26 (1956): 270.

if not most—of the soldiers in Crete were local converts to Islam. This situation is quite remarkable when one considers the fact that in places like North Africa, Egypt and Aleppo, where the local population was Muslim, entry into the military corps was denied to the ordinary subject, while in Crete the Christians managed to join in droves.[90]

The evidence for this comes from many sources. Court cases in Candia prove the Christian origin of many soldiers. In 1083/1672, for instance, Hassan Bey b. Abdullah from the gönüllü regiment went to court to claim his share of his cousin's inheritance, which had been taken over by the public treasury on the assumption that there were no heirs. His deceased cousin, Ahmet beşe b. Abdullah, had been an imperial janissary. Hassan Bey testified that his father, Georgi, was Ahmet beşe's father's brother, which would make Ahmet and Hassan cousins. Ahmet's father's name was Manolēs. Hassan Bey brought in Musli Bey b. Abdullah and Süleyman Bey b. Abdullah—the latter also from the gönüllü regiment and both no doubt converts as well—in support of his claim and won his case.[91] This court case provides another valuable piece of information. In Candia, as in other provincial cities at the time, the janissary regiments were traditionally divided into imperial (*dergāh-i āli*) and local (*yerli*) troops. Whereas in a city like Damascus, for instance, the two terms accurately reflected a real division between Turkish-speaking troops sent periodically from the capital and locally raised, Arabic-speaking soldiers, this was not obviously the case in Candia. The deceased in the case just cited, Ahmet beşe b. Abdullah, was certainly a local yet he was enrolled in the imperial regiment.[92] Similarly, yerli janissaries were not necessarily from Crete. Ahmet beşe, an immigrant from the Morea, was described as a yerli janissary at the time of his death in 1103/1691.

Travelers at the time remarked on the phenomenon. Tournefort, the French botanist in Crete in 1699, wrote, "The Turks throughout the island are mostly renegadoes or sons of such."[93] Later on, he included

---

[90] The Syrian historian Abd ul-Karim Rafeq was struck by the local takeover of the janissaries, in Damascus and points out that locals were forbidden from joining the corps in both Aleppo and Egypt. Abd ul-Karim Rafeq, "The Local Forces in Syria in the Seventeenth and Eighteenth Centuries," in *War, Technology and Society in the Middle East*, ed. V. J. Parry and M. E. Yapp (London: Oxford University Press, 1975), 280.

[91] T.A.H. 4:11. There are numerous such court cases in the early years. See T.A.H. 2:97, which records two convert soldiers fighting over their father's estate. The father's name was Frantzas veled-i Miseli, and the dispute was whether one of the brothers had converted to Islam before or after the father's death. In the former case, the brother in question would not be entitled to inherit from his father. See also T.A.H. 1:7, the case of a Christian taken to Istanbul as a slave. Eventually he was manumitted, whereupon he returned to Crete as an imperial janissary. Finally T.A.H. 2:420: In 1689 the bishop for the eastern districts quit in disgust over the conversion of so many Christians under his jurisdiction. The Christians on this island, he complained, were "devious, greedy apostates" (bu cezirede sakin olan kafire [   ] zerarik mürtedin olmağla).

[92] And see T.A.H. 8:29 involving another Dergah-i Ali janissary who is obviously local. His patronymic is Abdullah and he is referred to as a butcher.

[93] M. Pitton de Tournefort, *A Voyage into the Levant* (Paris, 1717), 32.

both "Greeks" and "Turks" in his comments on the Cretan physique and athletic prowess: "The inhabitants of Candia, both Turks and Greeks, are naturally tall proper Men, vigorous, robust; they love shooting with the Bow, an Exercise they have been distinguished for in all Ages."[94] Traveling in Crete in the early nineteenth century, the Austrian physician Sieber made similar remarks in a comment on Muslim attitudes toward the dead: "The Turks, particularly the Candiots, who are all descended from renegadoes, with the exception of a few, who have come to fill the public offices, and like proselytes in general, are the most zealous and enthusiastic adherents of their new doctrine, murder in cold blood a fellow-creature, who appears sacred to them as a corpse."[95]

The local origin of most of Crete's Muslims must explain why, despite a large Muslim community, the islanders remained Grecophone, as many travelers attested. Robert Pashley, traveling in Crete in the 1830s, referred to Greek as "the common language of the island." An official proclamation was read out to the villagers "in Greek, the common language of the island, and was therefore intelligible to his audience."[96] A demographic study of the island, undertaken in 1890 by a (Greek) member of the local administration, had this to say on the linguistic situation of the Cretans: "All of the inhabitants of the island without exception speak the Greek language. Both Ottomans and Christians speak Greek at home as their mother tongue. Very few—some city dwellers only—know Turkish at all."[97]

Finally, the reports sent to Venice by local spies regularly listed the troop strength in the capital city, regiment by regiment. They also carefully noted the origin of many of the troops, many of which were described as partially or completely composed of renegades. Next to the azab and dizdar numbers, for instance, they often wrote phrases like "la piu parte rinegati" and "anco d'costoro assai rinegati."[98]

Conversion and Conquest

Explaining conversion is a difficult task. Even when the reasons for an individual conversion are quite explicit—and there are such cases in Crete—that still does not help to explain why conversion to Islam was greater in

[94] Ibid., 89.

[95] F. W. Sieber, *Travels in the Island of Crete in the Year 1817* (London: 1823), 25–26. Robert Pashley, who was in Crete for most of 1834, wrote that the janissaries "consisted solely of Cretan Mohammedans." Robert Pashley, *Travels in Crete* (1837; reprint, Athens: Dion N. Karavias, 1989), 1:xxi.

[96] Pashley, *Travels,* 1:xxxiv.

[97] Nikolaou Stavrakē, *Statistikē tou plēthysmou tēs Krētēs* (A statistical survey of the population of Crete) (Athens: N. Kouravia 1890), 201.

[98] Archivio di Stato, Venice, Senato, Provveditori da Terra e da mar, Lettere del. Provv. straordinario a Suda, Busta 890, 891bis.

Crete than anywhere else in the Greek world.[99] The conversion rate is a particular puzzle when we consider the fact that the Ottomans did not offer as many financial inducements to convert as they had in earlier centuries.[100]

It seems to me that it is the war itself, more than any other factor, that explains the attractiveness of conversion to Islam in Crete. The very length of the war, nearly twenty-five years, must have brought considerable social dislocation in its wake, including the weakening of religious institutions. Within the Greco-Turkish world we have the (admittedly much more dramatic) precedent of Anatolia between the eleventh and the fifteenth centuries. Spyros Vryonis, in his classic work on medieval Anatolia, demonstrated the connection between extended social upheaval and conversion to Islam.[101] This connection must explain why, for example, so few Cypriots became Muslim in comparison to their compatriots in Crete. Although the similarity between the two islands is great—a Greek Orthodox population under Latin rule for many centuries, which is then conquered by the Ottomans—the war for Cyprus lasted only one year (1570–71).

As Vryonis has argued, one effect of extended upheaval in Anatolia was the weakening of Christian institutions. The successive Turkish conquests of Anatolia had the effect of cutting off contact between Anatolian Christians and the patriarch in Constantinople. This isolation was compounded by the political strategy of the Turks, who viewed the church as the ally of their enemy, the Byzantine emperor, and thus a force to be destroyed. This strategy stands in marked contrast to that followed by the Ottomans in the Balkans. The final incorporation of the Balkans into the Ottoman Empire took place *after* the conquest of Constantinople (1453). By this time the Ottomans viewed the patriarch as an ally, someone who could help them rule the very numerous Orthodox Christians who were now under the protection of the sultan. This was a key difference between Anatolia and the Balkans, and helps explain why in the latter the population remained largely Christian.

[99] For two examples of conversion in which the reason is explicit, see T.A.H. 2:56, T.A.H.10:11. In 1670 a Christian mother converted so that she could be the guardian for her underage daughter, Saliha. Saliha had received a certain amount of property from her father Mehmet beşe and there was a need for an adult to administer it. The second concerns a Christian who stood accused of associating with the Venetians (on Spinalonga, just off the coast) during the war (1684–69). He converted to Islam in order to avoid punishment.

[100] In fifteenth- and sixteenth-century Limnos it was common practice to exempt converts to Islam from the main land tax, the çift-resmi. Therefore Muslim converts escaped *both* the land tax as well as the head tax. Heath Lowry, "The Island of Limnos: A Case Study on the Continuity of Byzantine Forms under Ottoman Rule," in *Continuity and Change in Late Byzantine and Early Ottoman Society*, ed. Anthony Bryer and Heath Lowry (Washington, D.C.: Dumbarton Oaks, 1986), 235–59. As we have already seen from the Cretan mufassal defteri, the tax rate on Cretan villagers was the same (except, of course, for the head tax).

[101] Spyros Vryonis, *The Decline of Medieval Hellenism in Asia Minor and the Process of Islamization from the Eleventh through the Fifteenth Century* (Berkeley: University of California Press, 1971).

In Crete the Ottomans actually restored an Orthodox Archbishopric to the island. By so doing they defended and supported Orthodoxy, much as they did in the Balkans. Unlike the Balkans, however, Crete had been under Latin rule for nearly 500 years previous to the Ottoman conquest. As we shall see in chapter 6, the reunification of the island with the Orthodox world did not proceed smoothly. Serious internal dissension within the Christian community was very much in evidence during the early years of Ottoman rule and must have contributed to the attractiveness of Islam. Unlike in Anatolia, however, the sources of Christian weakness in Crete must be sought not in the policy of the conquerors, but rather in the legacy of Latin rule.

The close relationship between religious conversion and a military career in Candia, a peculiar consequence of the island having been conquered in the seventeenth century, must also have contributed to the high conversion rate in Crete. The link also suggests the more informal, although no less important, ways that Crete was incorporated into the Ottoman Empire.

The prevailing model for Ottoman conquests of Christian areas has been that of the Balkans in the fourteenth and fifteenth centuries. Students of this time and place have shown how, over time, the opportuntities for social mobility that had been extended to the local Christians closed down. By the sixteenth century it was no longer possible for a member of the defeated aristocracy to join the provincial cavalry as a Christian.

The conquest of Crete, however, provided significant opportunities as well, albeit of a different kind. By the time the island was conquered, changes in both the military and the ruling elite made it easier for members of the tax-paying class—the reaya—to join the political class, as long as they were willing to convert to Islam.[102] The Cretans clearly took advantage of this in great numbers and in several ways.

From the end of the sixteenth century onward, the Ottomans relied heavily on volunteers in their military campaigns. Crete was no exception to the rule, and it seems that the Ottoman army—faced with manpower shortages—used the islanders in the prosecution of the long war against the Venetians.[103] The Cretans, for their part, proved themselves willing to join. The gönüllü soldier from the previously cited court case almost certainly volunteered to fight on the Ottoman side, no doubt in hopes of

---

[102] The invasion of the military class by the reaya was an important target of the bureaucrats who produced the decine literature, beginning at the end of the sixteenth century: "In their diagnosis of the ills they found that the Muslim *re'aya*, the tax-paying subjects of the sultan, had invaded 'the military institution,' which, as an instrument of the sultan's power, had until then been reserved strictly for his *kuls*, slaves trained to this end." Halil Inalcık, "Military and Fiscal Transformation in the Ottoman Empire, 1600–1700," *Archivum Ottomanicum* 6 (1980): 283.

[103] See Setton, *Venice, Austria and the Turks*, 158, for a discussion of manpower shortages in the period between 1646 and 1653.

a reward at the end (which he would have gotten in the form of a timar, although a short-lived one). In testimony to the imperial divan after the war, according to Tournefort, the imperial treasurer said that 700,000 crowns had been spent on rewards to deserters who "turned Turk," to soldiers who had distinguished themselves and to those who had brought in the heads of Christians.[104] The correspondence of Greek spies in the service of Venice during the war years also makes it clear that some of the local population fought on the Ottoman side.[105]

The tremendous expansion in the janissary corps during the seventeenth and eighteenth centuries—as well as increasingly lax procedures for entering, was also a golden opportunity for Cretans who were willing to convert. The extension of military status and privileges to the Muslim population in general, so characteristic of the European provinces of the empire, also occurred in Crete, although the island was distinctive in that most of the soldiers were recent converts. It seems accurate to say that newly converted Cretans flooded the military orders to such an extent that the terms "Muslim" and "soldier" became virtually synonomous. Pococke, writing in the middle of the eighteenth century, said, "All the Turks belong to some military body."[106] The Venetian reports also emphasize the very widespread claim to some sort of military wage.[107]

No doubt the vast majority of converted Cretans who joined one of the military regiments remained at the humble level of a yamak or a beşe. Some, however, were clearly able to rise very high very quickly. A villager from southern Crete whose name was now Ali Bey b. Abdullah became the kethuda of Vezir Kapudan Mustafa Pasha, the commander of the Ottoman fleet during the final year of the seige. We learn about Ali Bey's Christian origins because he came to court to complain that Ioannes, a Christian from his former village, was illegally occupying a vineyard that Ali Bey should have inherited from his father Modatsos. He was careful to tell the court that he converted to Islam after his father's death because

[104] Tournefort, A Voyage, 41.

[105] Ath. Karathanasēs' work in the Venetian archives has unearthed a record of correspondence between Franceso Morosini, the commander of the Venetian forces, and Greek spies inside Ottoman territory. This correspondence reveals the deep involvement of the local population in the war, as well as the incredible confusion of the war years as Christians became Muslim and Muslims became Christian. Ath. Karathanasēs, "Anekdotē allēlografia tou Fr. Morosini kai allōn Venetōn me Krētikous stat chronia tou polemou (1659–1660)" (Unpublished correspondence of Fr. Morosini and other Venetians with Cretans during the years of the war [1659–1660]), Krētika Chronika 25 (1973): 21–124.

[106] R. Pococke, A Description of the East (London: 1739), 2:267.

[107] A report from 1688 said there was no "turco che no tiri paga o vilaggio e che no sia notato alli sopradetti generi." By "Turk" we should probably understand a native-born Muslim because the report considers converts in a separate category: "in tutto il Regno non si sono che 900 in circa rinegati che non tiri paga, e che no siano notati." Archivio di Stato, Venice, Senato, Provveditori da Terra e da mar, Lettere del. Provv. straordinario a Suda, Busta 889.

otherwise he would have no inheritance rights.[108] The head of the armorer's corps (*cebeci başı*) was identified by the Venetians as a native of Crete.[109] In a letter from the year 1688, a Venetian spy spoke of "Mehmet Aga, nominate commandante di Milapotamo rinegata bei da questo Regno."[110]

The mechanisms by which so many Cretans joined the military orders so quickly are still obscure. Nonetheless, several conversion documents describing how Christians came to court with Muslims of high standing, some of whom were obviously their employers, suggest that there was a process of sponsorship in place.[111] Sponsorship and conversion may well have been a key part of joining a household in Crete, for which there must have been many opportunities. A steady stream of officers and administrators came out of Istanbul, especially during the early years of Ottoman rule when the Venetian threat was still very serious.[112] They were undoubtedly anxious to develop clients on the island, for both military and economic reasons, and what better pool to draw upon than the newly converted soldiery?[113]

Finally, it was not only the state of the Ottoman Empire that encouraged the Cretans to enroll in the military orders. The legacy of the late Venetian period also paved the way. As we shall see in the next chapter, the local population made repeated attempts throughout the seventeenth century to join the paid militias that Venice maintained on the island. Venice, for its part, was equally resolved to exclude the Greeks, whom it didn't trust. Although Venetian administrators on Crete were anxious to paper over

---

[108] T.A.H. 2:138. Unfortunately for Ali Bey, his father had fled to the Venetian side and the court threw out the case, citing the order given during the war, that the property of all those who went over to the enemy side be seized and sold.

[109] "Meemet Aga ? nato in Regno zebezibasi de Gerli Zebezini tuti greci rinegati." Lettere del. Provv. straordinario a Suda, Busta 889.

[110] Ibid.

[111] See T.A.H. 16:171 for the case of a ten-year-old who lived in Candia and whose father, Nikola, had died. He was taken to court by Mehmet Agha and Mehmet Bey where he became a Muslim. Also T.A.H. 20:169 for a Christian adolescent from the countryside who converted to Islam in Candia. At the time of his conversion he was in the employ of a military officer, Cebecizade Hussein Agha. On the same day a Christian named George who was the partner of a janissary named Ali Usta, also became a Muslim. T.A.H. 42:43: At midcentury a villager named Nicholas, the son of George, converted and thereupon entered into the service of the governor of Candia. At the same time another Christian villager converted and became the standard-bearer (*bayraktar*) for Hassan Agha.

[112] T.A.H. 5:254: For instance, when Süleyman II ascended to the throne in 1099/1687, bonuses were distributed to the imperial janissaries throughout the empire and 2,728 soldiers received the bonus in Candia. Uzunçarşılı, who has studied the comparative strength of the janissary corps across the empire, notes the high number of soldiers stationed in Candia in the tumultuous years at the end of the seventeenth and beginning of the eighteenth century. Ismail Hakki Uzunçarşılı, *Acemi Ocaği ve Yeniçeri Ocaği*, vol. 1 of *Osmanli devleti teşkilātin-dan: kapukulu ocaklari* (The institutions of the Ottoman state: The military corps) (Ankara: Türk Tarih Kurumu Basimevi, 1943), 329.

[113] For one example of this, see T.A.H. 3:233 where a local janissary is the representative of the janissary agha in Istanbul, who has an endowment in Candia.

differences between Greeks and Latins, some of the Venetian attitude toward the islanders—and particularly their use in military service—is conveyed by Fra Paolo Sarpi's consul in 1615:

> For your Greek subjects of the island of Candia, and the other islands of the Levant, there is no doubt but there is some greater regard to be had of them, first, because that the Greek faith is never to be trusted; and perhaps they would not much stick at submitting to the Turk, having the example of all the rest of their nation before their eyes: these therefore must be watch'd with more attention, lest, like wild beasts, as they are, they should find an occasion to use their teeth and claws. The surest way is to keep good garrisons to awe them, and not use them to arms or musters, in hopes of being assisted by them in an extremity: for they will always shew ill inclinations proportionably to the strength they shall be masters of, they being of the nature of galley-slaves, who, if they were well us'd, would return the kindness, by seizing the gally, and carry it and its commander to Algiers: wine and bastinadoes ought to be their share, and keep good nature for a better occasion.[114]

The advent of Ottoman rule represented a real break with the past in this regard and the Cretans took advantage of the change in great numbers. Conditions prevailing in the empire at the time allowed the emergence of a local class of opportunists—closely linked to the military—who helped the Ottomans establish control over their last great conquest.

[114] Pashley, *Travels in Crete*, 2:297. In a "Historical Appendix" that Pashley inserted at the end of his two-volume work, he excerpted sections of various manuscripts. This is an excerpt from an English translation of Padre Paolo's address to the Venetian State Inquisitors in 1615. See Paolo Sarpi, *The Opinion of Padre Paolo of the Order of the Servites, consultor of State, given to the Lords the Inquisitors of State. In what manner the Republick of Venice ought to govern themselves both at home and abroad to have perpetual dominion. Deliver'd by publick order in the year 1615,* trans. W. Aglionby, (London: R. Bentley, 1689). Fra Paolo, who died in 1623, was both a priest and one of the most eminent scientists of his day. He was also a fervent Venetian patriot, and in the conflict between Venice and Pope Paul V, he sided with Venice. Jack F. Bernard, *Italy: An Historical Survey* (Newton Abbot: David and Charles, 1971), 311–12.

Two

A Difficult Island

I believe, and I think others will concur, that
to have fortresses and territories and coastlines
in places thousands of miles away, in front of
the open mouth of the enemy, without the
ability to supply the population and the militia
there with food, it is as if one doesn't, in fact,
possess that place at all to say the least. Your
Highness, your islands and fortresses in the
East—and particularly the island of Crete—
are in such a situation.
  Zuanne Sagredo, duca di Candia, 1604[1]

Postwar Conditions

Köprülü's army bombarded the city of Candia for over two years before
the Venetians finally surrendered. The capital city and the countryside
around it were devastated by this brutal war. The few Europeans who took
any notice of Crete once the Venetian army had departed fixed their sights
on the capital city and thus emphasized the extreme destructiveness of the
war. Historians have echoed them in this judgment. Paul Rycaut, who
was the English consul in Smyrna at the time with close connections to
Ottoman officials, observed that "there never could be a more sad spectacle
of desolation, nor a more clear mirror of the miseries of war."[2] Bernard
Randolph visited the city ten years after the surrender and noted that "all
the plain for above two miles without the Walls is like a new plow'd field,
where you cannot walk but must see pieces of dead mens bones. Not

---

[1] "ch'io stimo si come credo che faci ogn'altro, che l'haver fortezze e stati, et marine in
paesi lontanissimi migliara di miglia, situati nelle fauci dell'inimici, senza certo modo di poter
dar da viver, alli loro Populi, et militie, sij un non haverle, per on dir peggio, in tal stato.
Ser.mo Prencipe si ritrovano le sue Isole di Levante, et le sue fortezze, et in particolar l'Isola
di Candia." Stergios Spanakēs, "E ekthesē tou douka tēs Krētēs" (The report of the duke
of Crete), *Krētika Chronika* 3 (1949): 521–22.
[2] Paul Rycaut, *A History of the Ottoman Empire from the Year 1623 to the Year 1677*
(London, 1680), 277.

above one eighth part of the houses, that formerly were, are now inhabited, very few being left entire, nor do the Turks repair any but those where they dwell."[3] At the very end of the century the French naturalist de Tournefort described the city of Candia as "Little better than a desert, all but the marketplace and thereabouts where the principal Inhabitants dwell; the rest is hardly anything but rubbish, ever since the last seige."[4] In his history of the Ottoman Empire Hammer wrote "Jamais place-forte, non seulement dans l'empire ottoman mais dans aucun autre pays n'avait été disputée comme celle de Candie et n'avait coute tant de sang et tant d'argent."[5] Given this consensus, it is perhaps not surprising that the few modern historians who have written on early Ottoman Crete are unreservedly gloomy.

The Ottomans, of course, were interested in the nature of their acquisition as well. Rycaut mentions that, before leaving Crete in the spring of 1670, the grand vezir toured the island, "taking his progress through the whole circumference of it."[6] In the years following the conquest, administrators generated a number of documents that provide a more informed and systematic look at both rural and urban conditions on the island in the aftermath of the war. The city of Candia itself will be discussed in the next chapter. Here we will examine rural conditions in the eastern half of the island, an area that formed the capital city's hinterland. The evidence indicates that postwar conditions in the countryside were uneven and not uniformly bleak. More importantly, patterns of rural prosperity or poverty closely followed the outlines of the last century of Venetian rule.

The Countryside

Within five years of the conquest, the Ottomans commissioned a cadastral survey of the eastern half of the island, which consisted of the two districts (liva) of Sēteia and Candia.[7] This survey, although possessed of many peculiarities, provides valuable information on the rural areas of eastern

[3] Bernard Randolph, *Travels in Crete* (London, 1700), 82.
[4] M. Pitton de Tournefort, *A Voyage into the Levant* (Paris, 1717), 30.
[5] J. von Hammer, *Histoire de l'Empire Ottoman* (Paris, 1838), 11:330.
[6] Rycaut, *A History of the Ottoman Empire*, 281.
[7] Başbakanlık Arşivi (Prime Ministry's Archive), Istanbul, Tapu Tahrir no. 825. They may well have commissioned another survey for the western half of the island but this has either not survived or not yet been located. Under the Venetians the island had been divided into four "territorio" named after the four major cities on the northern coast. The Ottomans maintained this division. Moving from the east to the west they were the liva-i Istine (Sēteia), the liva-i Candia, the liva-i Resmo (Rethymnon), and the liva-i Chania. For the date of this survey, see note 38 in chapter 1.

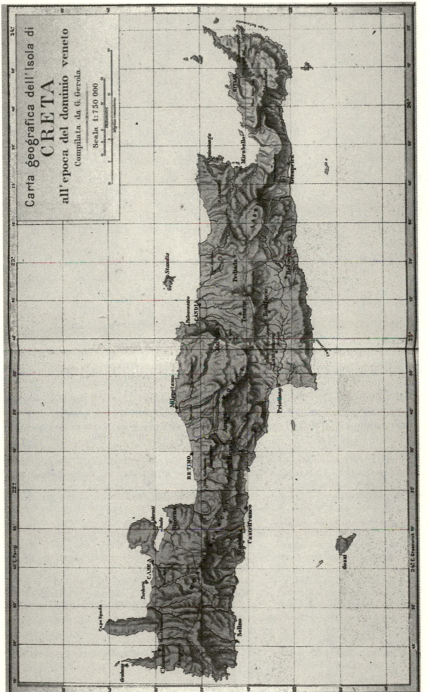

The Ottomans maintained the four-part division of the island which they had inherited from the Venetians.
Credit: Princeton University Library

Crete, areas that included the hinterland of the capital city at this time.[8]
As they toured the countryside, the surveyors carefully noted the extent
of abandoned land in each village.[9] If one uses this as a benchmark, it
becomes clear that the devastation in the countryside was neither widespread nor uniform. Moreover, regional differences were little different
than they had been in the Venetian period. Districts in the north and
center of eastern Crete, that is to say areas near the capital city, were well
cultivated, while the more arid southern regions of Rizou, Ierapetra, and
Sēteia had large stretches of abandoned land.

   Pediada was the largest district in the province of Candia, under both
the Venetians and the Ottomans. Starting just east of Candia, it was a
wide district that ran along the northern coast to the Bay of Malion. To
the south, it extended deep into the island, almost reaching the southern
coast. Most of this area is relatively low-lying, a broad plain eminently
suitable for cultivation.[10] In this first survey, 93 percent of the land in
Pediada was recorded as under cultivation. The immediate hinterland of
Candia, a district known as Temenos, also enjoyed a rate of cultivation of
over 90 percent.[11] To the south and west of Pediada lay the large district
of Monofatsìa, also well cultivated.[12] Although this lies toward the more
arid southern half of the island, this district is home to the Messara plain,
the most fertile land on the island.[13] Eight out of the eleven districts in
eastern Crete enjoyed rates of cultivation of at least 85 percent. But in the
districts along the arid southern coast—Rizou, Ierapetra and Sēteia—the

---

[8] The peculiarities will be discussed shortly. The form of the survey is as follows: a village
name is given, followed by a list of landholders and how much each possesses in terms of
fields, orchards, etc. At the bottom of the entry, the village's total holdings are given, followed
by the tax in kind and money due from the village. For example, the village of Chersonisos
in the district of Pediada, to the east of Candia, listed 46 landowners. These villagers cultivated
658.5 ceribs of fields and tended to 10 olive trees. Another 475 ceribs of land was deserted.
The village produced 22,245 akçe of revenue. Cerib (djarib) was the basic measure of surface
area in the early Islamic period. The fact that the surveyors in Crete used this term rather
than the more common dönüm may have been due to the emphasis on Islamic discourse
discussed in chapter 1.

[9] Abandoned land was designated as *arz-i hālī* or *arz-i hālī bila sahibi*.

[10] Pediada's preeminence continues today. It is the largest district in the province of
Herakleion, and the one with the greatest agricultural population. Stergios Spanakēs, *Poleis
kai choria tēs Krētēs sto perasma tōn aionōn* (Cities and villages of Crete throughout the ages)
(Herakleion: G. Detorakes, 1991), 2:618.

[11] Time constraints in Turkey allowed me to copy down complete information for only
two districts, Temenos and Pediada. The figures for the other districts are based on a
sample of villages from each district. No photocopying or microfilming or any other type
of reproduction of this register, which exceeds 900 pages, was allowed. Let us hope that
scholars based in Turkey publish this survey sometime in the near future.

[12] With a rate of 96 percent.

[13] "The large and fertile Mesara Plain, watered by the Ieropotamos stream, is the only
cultivable area of any size in the south." P. Cameron, *Blue Guide to Crete*, 4th ed. (London:
Ernest Benn, 1986), 686.

unclaimed land could reach almost one out of two dönüms (about a quarter of an acre).

Undercultivation of the land was a constant Venetian complaint in the century preceeding the Ottoman conquest. Reporting back to the Senate in 1589, the provveditore generale Mocenigo wrote, "It is known that there are only two types of well-cultivated land in the Kingdom of Candia today; that is land held by the nobility, by feudatories and persons of wealth, and land which the peasants hold by livello."[14]

This same report suggests that conditions might have actually been worse in the late Venetian period because even areas on the fertile northern coast remained uncultivated.[15] The districts of Sēteia and Lasithi were singled out in a Venetian report dated 1629 that warned about the dangers of relying on wheat imported from neighboring Ottoman territory.[16] The undercultivation of Lasithi is particularly striking, given that it was one of the most fertile areas on the island. It was one of the few areas that the Venetian state owned directly. Wheat from Lasithi was used to make biscuit for galley crews.[17] Although the Venetians do not actually give statistics, at the time of the Ottoman survey the district of Lasithi was comparatively well cultivated (85 percent).

If levels of cultivation emerged relatively unchanged after the long years of war, patterns of settlement also appear to have remained stable. Most of the villages in eastern Crete survived. Between 1575 and 1595 at least

---

[14] "si vede al presente, che due sorte di luoghi solamente sono nel Regno di Candia ben coltivati, cioè quelli che sono de nobili e feudati, e di persone commode, et quelli che posseggono li contadini a livello." Stergios Spanakēs, "Relazione del Nobil Huomo Zuanne Mocenigo ritornato provveditore generale del regno di Candia presentata nell'eccellentissimo consillio 17 Aprile 1589," *Mnēmeia tēs krētikēs istorias* (Monuments of Cretan history), vol. 1 (Herakleion, 1940), 188. *Livello* was the name of a feudal tax which the peasants paid to either the feudatory or the state, depending on who held the land. In exchange for this tax he had the right to cultivate the land in perpetuity and to pass it on to the next generation. Ibid., 457. In 1602 Benetto Moro wrote "ritrovandosi molte parte dell'Isola mal coltivate, le quali si potriano con la fatica ridurre a coltura" (There are many places on the island which are not well cultivated, which could be returned to cultivation with some work). Stergios Spanakēs, "Relatione dell Sr. Benetto Moro ritornato di proveditor general del regno di Candia, letta in pregadi a 25 giugno 1602," *Mnēmeia tēs krētikēs istorias* (Monuments of Cretan history), vol. 4 (Herakleion, 1958), 160.

[15] "Quasi tutti li terreni del Chissamo in quel Territorio della Canea vanno inculti, se ben ve ne sono atti a produrre." Spanakēs, "Relazione del Nobil Huomo Zuanne Mocenigo," 189. The territory of Kisamos lay to the west of Chania on the northern coast of the island.

[16] "si trova nel Regno un paese grandissimo non coltivato. Prima la campagnia del Vai a Settia longa 18 miglia et larga quattro et più, che questa sola basteria a nutrir mezo il Regno. Dopo il rimamnente della campagnia del Lassiti et luoghi vicini." Stergios Spanakēs, "Relazione Francesco Moresini provveditore generale nel regno di Candia 1629," *Mnēmeia tēs krētikēs istorias* (Monuments of Cretan history), vol. 2 (Herakleion, 1950), 89–90. The Venetian general then went on to name other areas in western Crete that were similarly left uncultivated.

[17] Spanakēs, "Relazione del Nobil Huomo Zuanne Mocenigo," 105, 186–87.

five different Venetian reports put the number of villages on the island somewhere between 1,000 and 1,100.[18] Almost half a century later, on the eve of the war, Isepo Civran reported that there were 1,020 villages on the island. Half of them—554 villages—were in the two eastern districts of Istinye and Candia. Thus little was changed from the late sixteenth century when Mocenigo reported that there were 569 villages in the two eastern provinces.[19] In 1644 Andrea Corner, the provveditore on Crete, ordered that a general survey be done of the island's settlements and population. This survey listed 496 villages in the district of Candia and 148 in Sēteia. This is certainly the highest number of settlements in eastern Crete that we encounter for the Venetian period, but still within the general range. What is more striking about Corner's survey is the shift in balance between the fertile and central province of Candia and the relatively remote and arid province of Sēteia. Previous to this almost 85 percent of the population in eastern Crete lived in the province of Candia. On the eve of the war this had shrunk noticeably to a little over three-quarters of the population. This trend obviously accelerated during the war.

When the Ottomans conducted their own cadastral survey in the early 1670s they found that the number of villages in eastern Crete had remained stable at 560. Now, however, one out of three villages was to be found in Sēteia, historically a very high number.[20] It is clear that, beginning with the very first years of the conflict, villagers chose to flee the main arena of war, which raged around the walled city of Candia, in search of greater security far from the battle. Overall, however, the density of settlement in the countryside was not greatly disturbed by the war.

Trends in population, both before and after the war, are much more difficult to establish. Toward the end of the sixteenth century, but before the great plague of 1592, Crete's population was around 200,000 souls.[21] The plague of 1592, the first in seventy years, hit the island very hard. Filippo Pasqualigo, a Venetian administrator who was present throughout that period, devoted fifty pages of his report to an account of the plague. By the summer of 1593, when the plague had yet to run its course, half

[18] Venetian estimates on the number of villages in Crete are numerous. The numbers are not wildly divergent but neither are they identical. This suggests that they are probably quite credible. I have not been able to find any information on how these surveys were carried out.

[19] In 1589 Mocenigo recorded 83 villages in Sēteia, 486 in Candia. Spanakēs, "Relazione del Nobil Huomo Zuanne Mocenigo," 6. Fifty years later there were 76 villages in Sēteia and 478 in Candia. Stergios Spanakēs, "Relazione de Sr. Isepo Civran tornato di Prov r Gen.l di Candia 1639," *Krētika Chronika* 21 (1969): 369.

[20] Başbakanlık Arşivi (Prime Ministry's Archive), Istanbul, Tapu Tahrir no. 825: a total of 560 villages, of which 379 were in Candia and 181 in Sēteia.

[21] In 1589 Mocenigo estimated the population at 208,000. Spanakēs, "Relazione del Nobil Huomo Zuanne Mocenigo," 12. Earlier estimates, all from the second half of the sixteenth century, were 219,00, 183,798, and 206,934. Spanakēs, "Relazione de Sr. Isepo Civran," 369.

the population of the capital city—almost 9,000 people—had died.[22] The effect of the epidemic in the countryside is harder to assess. Pasqualigo tells us that 13,908 people died by that summer, and it appears that he is referring only to the territory of Candia. If that is indeed the case, the mortality rate was lower—as expected—but still close to 20 percent of the population.[23] Pasqualigo was clearly shaken by what he had witnessed in Crete; he said the island he left was quite changed from the island he had found upon his arrival.[24]

With the plague of 1592 Crete was marching in step with the rest of the Mediterranean world, in which the 1590s were a disastrous decade.[25] Unlike the rest of the Mediterranean in the seventeenth century, however, official reports would have us believe that the island's population grew, and grew substantially, in the fifty years between the plague and the beginning of the war with the Ottomans. Provveditore Generale Civran told the Senate that there were 254,040 souls on the island in 1639.[26] Five years later Andrea Corner, the current provveditore, commissioned a population survey that gave the very high number of 287,165 Cretans.[27] A report on the number of Cretan men serving in the local militia, the ordinanze, in 1630, suggests a more modest rise in population, but a rise nonetheless.[28] It is difficult to reconcile these numbers with the general downward trend in population in the rest of the seventeenth-century Mediterranean (and European) world. Whatever the population trends on the island, they do

[22] The count was taken in July 1593, a little over a year after the onset of the plague. Stergios Spanakēs, "Relatione di Me Filippo Pasqualigo ritornato di cap.o di Candia et prov.r della Canea 1594," *Mnēmeia tēs krētikēs istorias* (Monuments of Cretan history), vol. 3 (Herakleion, 1953), 102. This was only somewhat worse, however, than the usual mortality rate from the plague in the Mediterranean at this time. Braudel estimates that throughout the sixteenth century "a quarter or a third of the inhabitants of a town could suddenly vanish." Fernand Braudel, *The Mediterranean and the Mediterranean World in the Age of Philip II* (New York: Harper and Row, 1973), 1:332.

[23] In 1589 there were 76,000 people in the territorio of Candia.

[24] "ma bene, perche informata dello stato in che al presente io l' ho lasciate; assai differente da quello, che la trovai." Spanakēs, "Relatione di Me Filippo Pasqualigo," 66.

[25] Suraiya Faroqhi, "Making a Living: Economic Crisis and Partial Recovery," in *The Economic and Social History of the Ottoman Empire*, ed. Halil Inalcık with Donald Quataert (Cambridge: Cambridge University Press, 1994), 441.

[26] Spanakēs, "Relazione de Sr. Isepo Civran," 369.

[27] M. I. Manousakas, "E para trivan Apografē tēs Krētēs (1644) kai o dithen katalogos tōn krētikōn oikōn Kerkyras" (The 1644 census of Crete [found in] Trivan and the supposed list of Cretan families in Corfu), *Krētika Chronika* 3 (1949): 37.

[28] Venetian administrators were in the habit of giving not only the total population of the island but also the number of men fit for some kind of service to the state (*anime da fattione*). Most commonly the villagers of Crete were expected to serve as rowers in the galleys, but they could also be recruited to serve in the ordinanze. Thus in 1589 700 men were enrolled in the ordinanze of Sēteia province, as opposed to 600 in 1630. A modest rise is evident for the province of Candia, from 2,060 to 2,400 while in Chania the numbers enrolled doubled from 2,361 to 4,479. Finally in Rethymnon province 2,700 men were enrolled in 1589 and 2,890 in 1630.

not necessarily indicate an improvement in other areas. Undercultivation of the land, for example, continued. Other chronic problems of the late Venetian period will be discussed shortly.

Reliable estimates of the population in the wake of the Ottoman conquest are difficult to come by. Bernard Randolph, the English writer who visited the island in 1680, gave the extremely low figure of 80,000 people (50,000 Christian and 30,000 Muslim) on the entire island. Randolph's unreliability is suggested by his wildly exaggerated notion of the Venetian period when, he says, there were more than a million souls.[29] He is also demonstrably wrong on the number of villages. He said there were only 300, whereas the Ottoman survey records 560 villages on the eastern half of Crete alone. His estimate is important less for what the population of Crete actually was in the wake of the war than for what it tells about the European conviction that Crete was decimated by the war.

Paul Rycaut is a much more valuable source because of the close ties he had to Ottoman officialdom. He very likely learned about the first cizye survey undertaken in Crete from his Ottoman sources and put the number of non-Muslims liable to pay the head tax at 22,000.[30] This number accords closely with the number in an Ottoman cizye survey dated 1080/1669–70 that recorded 26,674 potential taxpayers.[31] The total number of Christians indicated by this figure is much more difficult to ascertain, ranging anywhere from 71,000 to 111,000.[32] But this seemingly huge population decline is only a very partial picture, excluding the island's Muslim population, which was substantial due to local conversion.[33] Randolph estimated

[29] "Before the Turks conquered this Island, there were above a million of Souls, wereas now there are not 80,000, of which not above 30,000 Turks on the whole island." Randolph, *Travels,* 93–94.

[30] Rycaut, *A History of the Ottoman Empire,* 281.

[31] Başbakanlık Arşivi (Prime Ministry's Archive), Istanbul, Tapu Tahrir, no. 980. Although this is before the reform of the cizye system in 1691, when the Ottomans returned to counting individuals rather than heads of households, I believe the Ottomans *were* counting individuals, not *hanes* (households). This is because the total given for each village is followed by the word *nefaran* (individuals) and the cizye payers are divided up into low, middling, and high, which is the Islamic way.

[32] Venetian numbers provide a guide to the vexed question of which multiplier to use in calculating population. As explained in note 28, administrators were in the habit of providing not only total population figures, but also the number of men "fit for work." The rest of the population—explicitly identified as women, children, old men and the disabled—can be considered the dependents of these men. The numbers given in 1589 produce a multiplier of 4.16, whereas the 1639 numbers give a multiplier of 3.25. I am equating the Venetian category of *anime da fattione* with the Ottoman cizye payer (although obviously for Christians only) and assuming that roughly the same multiplier applies. The range of the numbers given is accounted for by the two different cizye estimates, as well as the two different multipliers.

[33] There is a tendency among nationalist historians to equate conversion with population decline. See, for instance, Detorakēs' discussion of population trends on the island in the advent of Ottoman rule: "The population had declined significantly with the long years of the war, with the mass expatriation from the urban centers *and the numerous conversions to*

that there was almost one Muslim for every Christian, and Richard Pococke, who visited the island in 1739, gave a Muslim-Christian ratio of 1:2.

Unfortunately, no documents from this period consider the island's Muslim population directly.[34] The peculiarities of the two cadastral surveys discussed in the first chapter—they represent a survey of landowners rather than the population as a whole—limit their utility in helping us to estimate the population of eastern Crete. Even so, a consideration of the first of these surveys, along with other anecdotal information, shows that any estimate of the island's population that excludes the Muslims is very misleading.

The cizye survey of 1080/1669–70 listed 14,206 non-Muslim taxpayers in the two eastern provinces of Candia and Sēteia. The first cadastral survey, which was carried out at the same time, put the total number of landowners in these two provinces at 43,349.[35] Even if every Christian taxpayer was also a landowner, there are still another 29,143 individuals who do not appear in the cizye survey. Basing ourselves on the cadastral survey, the population in the two eastern provinces alone might have been as high as 140,000 to 180,000 souls.[36]

If the cadastral survey provides a general overview, local court documents provide concrete evidence of Muslim population in specific villages. This can be profitably compared with cizye numbers on the same village. For instance, the village of Larani in the southern district of Monofatsi had seven Christian taxpayers in 1080/1669–70, thus probably a total Christian population of somewhere between twenty and thirty. Just a year later, the village of Larani appears in the court records of Candia. A village near Larani named Agios Tomas had been granted as freehold (temlik) to the conqueror of Crete, Köprülü Fazil Ahmet Pasha. A representative of the kadi court was sent to the area to ascertain the boundaries of the village

---

Islam" (emphasis added). Theocharis Detorakēs, Istoria tēs Krētēs (History of Crete) (Athens, 1986), 271–72.

[34] Ottoman administrators in the seventeenth century rarely produced counts of Muslim taxpayers. Suraiya Faroqhi, "On Population," in Inalcık, The Economic and Social History of the Ottoman Empire, 442.

[35] Three cadastral surveys of the island (and perhaps more that have not yet been discovered) survive in state archives in Istanbul and Ankara. None have been published so far. The first survey, which covers the two eastern provinces of Candia and Sēteia (this includes Candia's immediate hinterland) is the Tapu Tahrir no. 825 referred to previously. The other two surveys are both dated 1117/1706 and cover the entire island between them. They are stored in the Tapu ve Kadastro Genel Müdürlüğü in Ankara. Register no. 4 covers eastern Crete—the liva of Candia and Sēteia—and is the only register that will be discussed here. Information is organized by individual village. A list of landowners is given, along with the amount held by each, followed by a list of tax obligations both in money and in kind. For a detailed discussion of this source and its peculiarities, see my article "An Islamic Experiment? Ottoman Land Policy on Crete," Mediterranean Historical Review 11, no. 1 (1996): 60–78.

[36] Again, using the multipliers indicated by a consideration of ratios that held for the late Venetian period.

by asking villagers from the surrounding area. Among the people asked were Hussein b. Abdullah, Recep b. Abdullah, Mustafa b. Abdullah, Ali b. Abdullah, and other Muslims all from the village of Larani. Clearly, there were at least as many Muslims in Larani as Christians, and maybe even more. This very different demographic profile of the village would never be evident by considering the cizye survey alone.[37]

The war, however, almost certainly took a heavy toll on two of the island's main export crops, olive oil and wine. Rycaut says so directly, at least for olive oil: "and great numbers of Olive Trees being cut down and burned by the Soldiery in the time of the War, is the reason that the island yields not half the quantity of Oils as in former times."[38] Both vines and olive trees would need many years before they could start producing their fruits again.

The situation in the countryside, then, was uneven. In the more fertile areas of the island, Ottoman records indicate that the peasants were quick to move back onto the land, if indeed they had ever left it. While yearly crops could be quickly resumed, vines and olive trees would take much longer. Undercultivation of the land, where it existed, should not be explained by the difficulty of the war years because these same problems plagued the Venetian rulers of the island. The population of the island is extremely difficult to ascertain; however, the Muslim population cannot be ignored and, when it is included, the assumption of catastrophic population decline becomes untenable. This mixed picture, after so many years of war, is not as paradoxical as it seems. After the initial burst of fighting in the late 1640s, the war on Crete itself (as opposed to the battle at sea) proceeded rather fitfully. Contracts of sale from the archives show that, as early as the mid-1650s, conditions in the countryside were peaceful enough for individuals to be buying and selling property.[39] When the war did pick up again, in the late 1660s, it was the city of Candia that was pounded night and day by Köprülü's guns. As he toured the island, then, in the triumphant winter of 1669/70, the grand vezir must have felt satisfied that the Ottomans had indeed wrested a fertile paradise from the Venetians. The exploitation of the island's riches, however, would prove to be a difficult task for the Ottomans.

[37] T.A.H. 2:129. See also T.A.H. 2:127, which shows that we must adjust our population figures for the villages of Lango, Perama, Dalablo, and Orthe in the district of Mylopotamos to the west of Candia.

[38] Rycaut, *A History of the Ottoman Empire*, 281.

[39] Lord Castlemaine, who toured with the Venetians in the eastern Mediterranean in 1664, commented on how the war could drag on indefinitely. The sultan, he wrote, was prepared to wait it out since the war in Crete at least was costing him little: "the Island maintaining the Force he hath there; and for the present havock at Sea, it commonly belongs to Merchant-men." Lord Castlemaine, *An Account of the Present War between Venetians and Turks with the State of Candie (in a Letter to the King from Venice)* (London: printed by J.M. for H. Herringman, at the Anchor on the Lower Walk of the New Exchange, 1666), 61.

A Difficult Island

Köprülü Fazil Ahmet Pasha formally entered the city of Candia on 8 Cemaziy'ül-evvel 1080/4 October 1669. He went directly to the Hunkār Camisi—newly converted from the Church of Saint Francis—to pray.[40] Evliya Çelebi, the inveterate Ottoman traveler who was witness to Candia's surrender, describes the city on that first night of celebration: "That night there were so many thousands of torches and lanterns among the soldiers who lined all the walls of the city, so much pitch and naphtha, tar, oil and wax burning in the arsenals, so many candles that there was not a single spot on the walls where a light was not burning. Candia glowed like a torch in the night."[41]

This moment of victory after more than twenty years of war was no doubt very sweet: Randolph wrote that Köprülü was "overjoyed" when the city was surrendered to him, and Rycaut said that the sultan, who was found hunting in Negroponte, received the joyful news "like a Dream, being at first so surprised with such an unexpected happiness, that he could scarce believe it."[42] But, in fact, the Ottomans in Crete were going to be plagued by many of the same problems that had plagued the Venetians in their last century of rule. The similarity is not surprising. Although different in many ways, both the Ottoman Empire and the Serenissima Repubblica proved themselves unable to meet the military and technological challenges of the seventeenth century. States that were unable to do so had to content themselves with only a limited amount of control over their own territories, particularly the outlying areas. In passing from Venetian to Ottoman rule, Crete was, in fact, passing from one feeble state to another. This similarity is perhaps most dramatically evident in the question of piracy. Unlike the Aegean in the mid-sixteenth century, Ottoman victory in Crete did nothing to cleanse the seas of pirates.

In 1604 the duke of Crete vented his rage and frustration at the pirate ships that had infested the waters around Crete: "These damn bertons which sail in these waters to their heart's content, stealing from and plundering everyone, and not permitting even one caramousal, loaded with grain, to approach, as they used to."[43] Seventy years later the Ottomans

---

[40] Stergios Spanakēs, "Relatione dell Sr. Benetto Moro Ritornato," 87. This church was the most important and most opulent of all the Latin monasteries in Candia. It stood where the archaeological museum stands today.

[41] Evliya Çelebi, *Seyahatnamesi* (Travelogue), vol. 8 (Istanbul: Develet Matbassi, 1928), 467.

[42] Rycaut, *A History of the Ottoman Empire,* 278.

[43] "quelli maledeti Bertoni, che infestando fin che a loro paiono quei mari, robbando et depredando ogn'uno, non permettendo che comparino a quelle Isole come era solito, pur un Caramusal de formenti." Spanakēs, "E Ekthesē tou douka tēs Krētēs," 523–24. In 1639

found themselves similarly unable to control the waters around their newest possession and, to add insult to injury, the Venetians were able to join in the harassment because of their continued possession of the three islands of Gramvoussa, Souda, and Spinalonga. One of the more brazen attacks came in the year 1675 when a Monsieur Crevellier, a "famous Privateer" in Randolph's words, attacked the southern city of Ierapetra with 500 men: "Travelling in the night, he came next morning, just at the dawning of the day, and found the Turks at their Sabbah names morning prayer, so he made himself master of the Town, carryed away 200 slaves, nailing up the Guns which were in the Castle."[44] The pasha of Candia sent three galleys out to look for Crevellier, but they returned empty-handed. The local Venetian commanders were no doubt complicit in the attack because the pirates had docked in the bay of Spinalonga, which was held by the Venetians, and traveled to Ierapetra by foot, since that city had no secure port. The pasha complained to the provveditore on Spinalonga, threatening to alert Venice if any more privateers were allowed into that bay.[45]

The Burden of Defense

In its heyday in the fourteenth and fifteenth centuries, Venice's control of the seas meant that the defense of Crete was secured through the prowess of its navy, with little or no need to mobilize the population of the island. Questions of security, to the extent that they existed, had much more to do with quelling rebellion on the part of the local population so that Venice would be free to enjoy the advantages that the possession of Crete conferred, in terms of both the eastern trade and the luxury wine produced on the island for export. By the seventeenth century this situation had shifted dramatically.

The collapse of the Venetian navy and merchant marine at the beginning of the seventeenth century coincided with—and was partly caused by— an upsurge of piracy in the Mediterranean. If this had grave consequences for Venice itself, it had even graver consequences for continued control of Crete, its main colony.[46] The disintegration of Venice's naval and com-

---

Isepo Civran fumed that the pirates around Crete were "as bad as the Uskoks." Spanakēs, "Relazione de Sr. Isepo Civran," 445.

[44] Randolph, *Travels*, 75.

[45] Cases of piracy appear frequently in the Muslim court records, and even ranking Ottoman officials were not immune. A court entry from 1714 reveals that the kadi, or Muslim judge, for Santorini, was living in Candia, no doubt for the greater security it afforded. In that year he went with great reluctance to Santorini to attend to certain matters there. When he arrived, a pirate ship was in the harbor, and he was carted off to Malta for two years. T.A.H. 2:247.

[46] The consequences of piracy for Venice have been masterfully laid out by Alberto Tenenti, *Piracy and the Decline of Venice, 1580–1615* (Berkeley: University of California Press, 1967).

mercial power rendered the problem of provisioning the island even more acute, as the seas grew more dangerous, as Ottoman exports dried up, and as the military threat from the sultan grew. Zuanne Sagredo, whose assessment of the situation opened this chapter, went so far as to wonder whether Venice could still claim sovereignty on Crete.

Venetian administrators, then, could no longer be content with simply keeping the local population quiet. More and more they were forced to turn to the island's peasants to participate in the republic's defense, both by serving as lookouts along the coastline, and as rowers in the galleys that Venice maintained. These duties were vigorously resisted by the Cretans. They also had to worry about an adequate grain supply for the island, particularly in case of war, and this brought them into conflict as well with local elites, who were more interested in, first, viticulture and, later on, olive oil.

The Venetians in Crete desperately wanted the peasantry to view them in a benevolent light. Pleas to the Senate for more money, more soldiers, and more ships were always justified not only in terms of military preparedness, but also in terms of relieving the "poor people" of the island. The endless discussion of the grain problem was always presented as a mission of mercy to a countryside on the verge of starvation. The justice system was repeatedly criticized for failing to deliver justice to the people. Venier, discussing a case in which several murderers had been able to avoid any punishment, claimed that things had reached the point where the poor were not only oppressed but even murdered without any recourse. He recommended that inspectors be sent down because their very appearance in Crete would bring satisfaction and relief to the long-suffering people.[47] Civran, writing in 1639, obviously expected to move his audience when he related an anecdote from a recent tour he had taken of the Aegean, in search of grain for Crete. Apparently a bishop in the Morea (at that time under Ottoman rule) had given him a letter and, with tears in his eyes, said that they were all willing to fight if war should come, because their longing to return to Venetian rule was so great.[48]

This preoccupation with the peasantry did not stem from altruism. The point of view from Venice is given very succinctly in Civran's report in the context of discussing the possibility of an Ottoman assault:

[47] "che essi sindici, sono tanto desiderati da quei Popoli, che quando anco facessero molto poco con la sola presenza, apporterebbono in universale, infinita sottisfatione et sollevamento" Stergios Spanakēs, "1610 a 9 Genaro, relation de s. Dolfin Venier ritornato di duca di Candia," *Krētika Chronika* 4 (1950): 319.

[48] "conservo anco appresso di me la lettera stessa, scrittami da quel Vescovo, coll'intervento de tutti i principali; che son avvisato habbino, con le lacrime a gli occhi, inteso l'accomodamento, nelle speranze concepite di sottrarsi dalla Tiranide del Turco, et ridursi alla devotione di Vostra Serenità, tanto da loro bramata, et desiderata." Spanakēs, "Relazione de Sr. Isepo Civran," 444–45.

There is no doubt that the strongest defense will always be a strong navy. . . .
The defense of the inhabitants is just as important. They must always be treated
well so that they will remain faithful and devoted. Because when they are
oppressed and used too much in forced labor by the fief holders and sometimes
even by the representatives of the state, and subjected to extraordinary harshness,
they are driven to despair. Then they abandon the kingdom and go to the
Turkish territories and, enraged as they are, they devote themselves to evil doing.
They incite the enemy and open the way toward attacks, which perhaps he [the
enemy] would not otherwise have thought of.[49]

Despite his plea for harmony, the antagonism between the state and
the peasantry is alluded to in his own speech. Although he placed most
of the blame for exploitation of the peasantry on local elites, he had to
confess that sometimes *even the state* overdid it with forced labor. In fact,
Civran was very much understating the case. Ever since the time of the
last Ottoman-Venetian war (1570–71), the Venetians had put frightful
demands on the island's population, in effect squeezing the peasantry
between the demands of the state and obligations to local landlords.[50] This
dilemma resulted in peasant flight and the depopulation of the countryside,
which, of course, only exacerbated the problem of insufficient grain yields.

Although the Venetians initially relied on free labor to staff both their
merchant marine and their navy, the increasing use of galleys meant that
free labor would not suffice. They began recruiting oarsmen (*galeotti*)
from Dalmatia as early as the fourteenth century, and the burden only got
worse as time went by.[51] At the Battle of Lepanto in 1571 the Venetian
galleys were so understaffed that they accepted detachments of Spanish
soldiers on board.[52]

[49] "Non è dubbio, che la più vigorosa diffesa, sarà in ogni tempo, un conveniente nervo
d'armata . . . niente inferiore stimo la diffesa de sudditi, che devono esser sempre accarezzati,
ben trattati, mantenuti in fede, e devotione, perche oppressi, et angarizati soverchiamente
da. Cav.ri padroni de feudi, alcune volte da rappresentanti stessi, con essecutioni, e rigori
estraordinari, si riducono poi alla disperatione, abandonano il Regno, si portano in paese
Turchesco, et inviperiti procurano tutti i mali, fomentano i nemici, l'aprono, e facilitano la
stradda a quei tentativi, a quali forse non pensano." Ibid., 438.

[50] Moro complained that the peasants were being shielded from the state corvée by their
masters, in exchange for which they were expected to labor for the master's own account.
Spanakēs, "Relatione dell Sr. Benetto Moro," 101.

[51] Even as the use of sailing ships for war increased elsewhere, galley warfare continued
into the seventeenth century in the Mediterranean because any ship without oars was at the
mercy of the unreliable winds of that sea. Much of the Cretan war consisted of Venetian
galleys chasing Ottoman supply ships headed for Crete, trying to prevent them from provisioning their army. If they relied on sailing ships, they ran the risk of watching the Ottoman
fleet go by, unmolested, while the Venetians ships remained idle due to lack of wind. The
galleys demanded enormous numbers of men. The merchant galleys in use in the fifteenth
century required 200 men each and the numbers required for warfare kept rising as larger
states formed all around Venice.

[52] Frederic Lane, *Venice: A Maritime Republic* (Baltimore: Johns Hopkins University
Press, 1973), 362.

The strain of recruitment was acutely felt in Crete, a traditional center for galley labor.[53] In the 1570s the reforming provveditore Foscarini attempted to regularize the supply of galeotti from the island but problems continued throughout the seventeenth century. In 1610 Venier reported that the city of Candia, which was usually a sure thing, had not managed to outfit even two galleys with rowers. There were two reasons for this, he continued. First, the rolls had not been kept up to date and, second, recruitment started too late in the year, in May, when the peasants were already busy with the harvest. Recruitment should begin on the Day of the Virgin (February 2) because at that time of the year the peasant had very little to eat.[54]

In 1629 Francesco Moresini wrote "Praise be to God, galeotti can be found in this kingdom," about 40,000 strong and used to hardship. But he admitted that they ran away and that, in case of dire need, it would be very hard to actually get ahold of them, even though the records of the names—village by village—were very carefully kept. Although Foscarini had limited the amount of money that could be paid to substitutes, as well as the total number of substitutes permitted, these rules were not being observed.[55] A year later Capitan Generale Pietro Giustiniano spoke at length about the recruitment problem. Before the last war (1570–71), he said that finding rowers had been easy. But conditions during that war, and subsequent to it, had so horrified people that now it was impossible to get anyone to come of his own free will. Whole families would be destroyed as people frantically sold vineyards, fields, and cattle in an attempt to find the money to pay substitutes. This, he observed, only made the system even more hated.[56] The Venetians may have had 40,000 names entered in their records, but Giustiniano makes it clear just how difficult it was to find even the 400 men required for the ordinary galleys in peacetime.[57] One particularly harrowing account of a recruitment drive includes the information that in the village of Anapoli, a man hung himself rather than be taken away to the galleys.[58] In 1639 villagers were still running away and going broke paying a substitute so that they could avoid service.[59]

The loss of naval superiority in the wider arena of the eastern Mediterranean threw into question Venice's very ability to hold onto Crete.

---

[53] At the Battle of Lepanto the Venetians commanded 110 galleys. Of these, 30 were manned by Cretans. Ibid., 369.

[54] Spanakēs, "1610 a 9 Genaro, relation de s. Dolfin Venier," 339.

[55] Spanakēs, "Relazione Francesco Moresini," 66.

[56] Stergios Spanakēs, "Relazione Pietro Giustiniano capitan generale de Resmo 1630," *Mnēmeia tēs krētikēs istorias* (Monuments of Cretan history), vol. 5 (Herakleion: 1969), 230, 233.

[57] Ibid., 234.

[58] Spanakēs, "Relatione di Me Filippo Pasqualigo," 36.

[59] Spanakēs, "Relazione de Sr. Isepo Civran," 371.

Unfriendly ships, both pirate and Ottoman, could now approach the shores of the island with impunity. The extent of Venetian paranoia over this new development is made clear in a remark by Moresini. The fortress of Candia, he said, was wide open from Dermata gate to the bulwark of Saint Andrea. This area, which faced out onto the sea, had to be fixed because, as things stood now, anyone can go in and out at will and, most important, *could send out a signal.*[60]

Thus Cretans were also required to help defend the island itself as both piracy and the perceived threat from the Ottomans grew. These local militias were known as cernide and, though service in this was much to be preferred to service in the galleys, it was a hated burden nonetheless. In 1629 about 14,000 people were enrolled, charged with patrolling the coasts. Like so much else about Venetian defense at this time, their quality left much to be desired. Moresini complained that the commanding officers, who were from noble families, refused to train properly with these soldiers from humble backgrounds and chose to suffer punishment instead. Many of the ordinary soldiers neglected their posts.[61]

In addition to leaning heavily on the peasantry, the Venetians also poured soldiers onto the island after the loss of Cyprus to the Ottomans. It is doubtful that the presence of large numbers of soldiers in the cities and elsewhere contributed much to the island's defense. Instead, by stationing a large number of soldiers in Crete and yet not providing for them adequately, Venice simply exposed the local population to abuse by the military.

When Moresini wrote his report in 1629, 4,000 paid infantry were serving on the island. But they were in a "miserable situation" because their pay—seventeen riyals a month—was not nearly sufficient. As a result, it had become established practice to give permission to some soldiers to exercise a profession on the side, and some had become tailors, haircutters, shoemakers, and bakers. Some had even gone so far as to take up agriculture, tilling fields lying near the city and growing grapes and olives.[62] The cavalry, charged with patrolling the coasts, had to be prevented from wasting public monies and harassing the peasantry. The military was an extremely costly affair from every point of view. Moresini estimated that the state was owed 480,000 ducats in old debt, *all* of it owed by sea captains, galley commanders, and officers of the various militias. This was at a time when state revenues in Crete only amounted to 110,000 riyals.[63]

[60] Spanakēs, "Relazione Francesco Moresini," 26–27.

[61] Spanakēs, "Relazione de Sr. Isepo Civran," 436.

[62] Spanakēs, "Relazione Francesco Moresini," 50. Moresini estimated that this situation had been going on from "at least" the time of Foscarini.

[63] Spanakēs, "Relazione Francesco Moresini," 74, 81. The local cavalry, supposedly maintained by the feudatories, was also deeply in debt. At the time of Moresini's writing, the riyal—a Spanish silver coin that was "the most widely used coin of the world economy during

Ten years later Civran described an equally miserable situation: Captain Bobo, captain of one of the six cavalry regiments, had to be punished by Civran for misuse of public funds, while another captain had been in Crete two years, waiting for his regiment to show up. They were stuck on Zakynthos for lack of transport.[64]

Despite low pay in the military, the local population clearly wanted to enroll. The people's determination to avoid the galley service and watch duty that Venice sought from them was matched by equally persistant attempts to join the mercenary forces from which the ruling power, in turn, was resolved to exclude them. Moresini chastised the Senate for not sending the five replacement companies it was supposed to every year. "When the requisite five companies are not sent as they should be, the militias start to deteriorate as Greeks and some villagers enter them." The same thing happened with the cavalry. It was supposed to be entirely Albanian and Croat, yet the Greeks managed to join.[65] Civran wrote that the Greeks in the militia served "very badly" and stressed that only Croats and Albanians, not Greeks, should be recruited.[66]

Although Venetian administrators were fond of making a show of compassion for the *popoli* of the island, in fact their distrust of the Greek peasantry was profound and is evident throughout all of the reports. The extent of their paranoia is strikingly demonstrated by Giustiniano's suggestion on how to handle the island's population during a war with the Ottomans. He envisioned putting, essentially, the entire male population of the island out to sea on the galleys. Not only would the men perform a valuable military task but "The people [back on the island], each having their father, their son or their brother basically held hostage by the navy, would be very careful to remain faithful and to not engage in activities that could be harmful to themselves."[67]

More than the pay itself, the power they would gain prompted many Greeks to join the military. By donning a uniform, the Greeks might hope to establish themselves both in urban professions and on the choice land near the capital city that Moresini mentioned. The reports to the Senate are mostly concerned about the military shortcomings of the forces that the Serenissima maintained (or, more accurately, did not maintain) on the

---

the sixteenth and seventeenth centuries"—was worth twice as much as the ducat. See Şevket Pamuk, "Money in the Ottoman Empire, 1326–1914," in Inalcık, *The Economic and Social History of the Ottoman Empire*, 964–65.

[64] Spanakēs, "Relazione de Sr. Isepo Civran," 377–78.

[65] Spanakēs, "Relazione Francesco Moresini," 52, 58. "Il muttarli a suoi tempi e più che necessario perche de Albanesi o Crovati si fanno tutti greci et li cavalli diventano Ronzini" (Changing them in good time is more then necessary because from Albanians and Croats they all turn into Greeks, and the horses become wild and unruly).

[66] Spanakēs, "Relazione de Sr. Isepo Civran," 378.

[67] Spanakēs, "Relazione Pietro Giustiniano," 242.

island. Yet there are hints of a military tyranny over the civilian population. Moresini put it quite bluntly when he wrote: "The captains who serve in Crete and their officers are not saints. To speak frankly, they are not good at all."[68] When the state tried to collect on its debts, for instance, by selling off the property of soldiers in debt, few people cared to come forward out of a fear that their ownership rights would not be enforced.[69]

Provisioning and the Local Elite

In their battle to maintain control over the island, and to make sure that it was properly defended, the Venetians had to worry about local elites as well as the armed forces. Venice clashed with the feudatories on many issues, but none more dramatically than the struggle to ensure a proper grain supply for the island.

If Crete had become difficult to defend, it had also become difficult to feed. Like defense, this was a problem that the Venetians had not faced in earlier centuries. The island had actually once served as Venice's breadbasket, particularly in the fifteenth century when huge amounts of Cretan grain were sent to the Italian mainland to feed Venetian armies fighting in Lombardy. But that same century saw the beginnings of viticulture on the island and, by the sixteenth century, the export of the sweet luxury wine known as malvasia had come to dominate the island's commercial economy.[70]

The wine trade was extremely profitable and the local population threw itself into the export economy with enthusiasm. But by the end of the sixteenth century Venetian administrators had become concerned about the military implications of such a heavy concentration on viticulture. Because so much land was given over to vineyards—vines were planted in even the most fertile plains of Crete, plains that could have produced an abundant wheat crop—the island had developed the habit of importing grain from the surrounding Ottoman lands for three or four months out of every year. This could continue only as long as the Ottomans had grain to export and were willing to do so. In the sixteenth century both these provisos became uncertain. In 1555 the first Ottoman ban on the export of grain was imposed, and their wheat policy became ever more draconian as the century wore on and the empire's population grew.[71] At the same time, and particularly after the loss of Cyprus, Venice became convinced

---

[68] Spanakēs, "Relazione Francesco Moresini," 48. Moresini actually wrote these lines in defense of the militias in Crete. These militias, he said, had been much maligned but in fact they were no worse than any of the mercenary forces serving the republic elsewhere.

[69] Spanakēs, "Relazione de Sr. Isepo Civran," 83.

[70] For more on the island's wine economy, see chapter 4.

[71] Bruce McGowan, *Economic Life in Ottoman Europe* (Cambridge: Cambridge University Press, 1981), 35.

that a war with the Ottomans over Crete was inevitable. When such a war came, they had to make sure that the island would be able to feed itself. Finally, even if the Ottomans were willing to continue to supply Crete with grain, the proliferation of pirates toward the end of the sixteenth century came close to isolating the island.

Moved by such concerns, the authorities took severe measures. Predictably, it was Foscarini who initiated the policy of ripping out vines in an attempt to force landowners, both large and small, to plant grain instead.[72] But the attempt to restrict viticulture and encourage wheat cultivation in Crete enjoyed only limited success. It was vociferously resisted by the landowners, as the Venetians bitterly noted in their reports. In 1584, when another order was issued to rip out the vines in the vicinity of Candia, the landowners declared that they would make "no distinction between being subjects of Venice or of the Turks."[73] In 1602 the provveditore generale had to recommend again that vineyards be ripped out in order to make way for wheat, and in 1630 the capitan generale suggested the appointment of a special wheat supervisor whose duties would include a tour of the island, to make sure that the best fields were given over to wheat cultivation, not viticulture.[74]

The authorities had difficulty gaining access even to the wheat that was grown on the island, most of it on privately owned fields. Sagredo reported to the Senate that the previous year's harvest in Crete had been so bad that he sent out ships to all the Ottoman ports in a fruitless search for grain. When the ships returned empty, he was forced to beg for grain from the lords and nobles, speaking to them "with words of great love and concern."[75] This produced nothing as well, so he had to think of another strategy. He assured the Senate that he wanted to avoid what had been done in the past, namely breaking down the doors of the granaries. Apparently landowners were under obligation to sell a certain percentage of the annual wheat crop to the state, but they partially avoided this by underreporting the harvest. Sagredo decided to undertake a detailed survey of the taxes paid by the peasantry that year to deduce the real amount of the harvest.[76]

[72] Although Foscarini's report has not been published, Sagredo refers to the new policy in his report: "fece l'Ecc.mo. s.r Proc.r all'hora Prov.r Gn.a in quel Regno Foscarini di f.e m.; una infinita di opere Eroiche, ma fra le principalissime, e necessarie, fece far un stretissimo Editto, che alcuno non potesse sotto pene gravissime pinatar vigne in terreni atti a coltura, anzi ne fece sradiccar buona quantita, obligando li possessori alla coltivationi di essi" Spanakēs, "E ekthesē tou douka tēs Krētēs," 522–23.
[73] Manuscript 7299 (9 June 1584), Marciana, quoted in Braudel, *The Mediterranean*, 1: 157.
[74] Spanakēs, "Relazione Pietro Giustiniano," 220.
[75] "piu d'una volta gliene facessimo grandissima instanza, con parole di molto amore, et affetto." Spanakēs, 'E ekthesē tou douka tēs Krētēs," 527.
[76] According to Sagredo, the actual amount of the harvest was five times what had been declared. Ibid., 527–28.

Armed with the survey, he was able to buy the wheat he needed—although he complained about the high price he had to pay—for the military and the galley crews.

When Dolfin Venier arrived in Crete a few years later and found no wheat in the storage bins, he himself traveled to the plain of Messara on the south side of the island in order to find grain. He did find some but the primitive state of transportation made the trip back an excruciating one: the "small animals" (probably donkeys) that he had to use to bring the grain back to Candia could only carry modest loads on their back.[77] The next year saw a dramatic improvement, however, because Venice itself sent grain and the bailo in Istanbul secured permission from the Ottoman government to import wheat into Crete. Thirty years later, Isepo Civran was still sending ships throughout the archipelago, looking unsuccessfully for grain.[78]

More grain could have been grown, of course. Venetian administrators lamented the fact that, at a time when grain was desperately needed, large tracts of land on the island were going uncultivated. They blamed the landholding class for this as well. Writing in 1589, Mocenigo claimed that the entire province of Kisamos, in southwest Crete, was uncultivated not for lack of hands, but because the landlords were asking such high rents that the peasants preferred to remain idle. He recommended that, in order to encourage cultivation, fields should be rented out on a perpetual lease so that the cultivators could be assured of passing the land onto their heirs. He conceded, however, that a law recently passed by the republic, whereby anyone could claim uncultivated land as long as he was willing to work it, had failed miserably. Only a handful of villagers had come forward, convinced as they were that, once the land was in use again, it would be taken from them by the feudal lords. [79]

The comments of Moresini in 1629 are almost identical and show that the situation had changed little in forty years. He told the Senate that with the recent poor harvest one-third of the population had been faced with the choice of either starving to death or fleeing to Ottoman lands. In order to avoid such a situation in the future, all the lands lying fallow (he listed them) had to be brought into cultivation. Moreover, it had to be given to the peasants on a perpetual lease and with a grace period of two or three years from certain obligations.[80]

---

[77] A "staro" each. A staro was a wooden measure, in the shape of a barrel, used for measuring grain. It was equal to 83.3 liters or 4.5 mouzour. Spanakēs, "1610 a 9 Genaro, relation de s. Dolfin Venier," 330.

[78] Spanakēs, "Relazione de Sr. Isepo Civran," 418.

[79] Spanakēs, "Relazione del Nobil Huomo Zuanne Mocenigo," 188.

[80] Spanakēs, "Relazione Francesco Moresini," 89.

The republic was largely unsuccessful in getting local elites to reorient the economy and to put military above economic concerns. It also faced a struggle in its attempts to force the wealthy of the island to contribute toward the ever increasing cost of maintaining Venetian rule in Crete. Although the fountain that Moresini had built in Candia at the end of the 1620s was celebrated for its beauty—the base was supported by four marble lions and a marble statue of Poseidon graced the top of it—the wealthy residents of the city were in fact extremely reluctant to fund the entire project of ensuring a more reliable water supply for the city.[81] Moresini listed their objections to the project in his report to the Senate, which shows a skeptical elite, unwilling to fund the grandiose plans sent down from Venice.[82]

Official frustration with what was viewed as the ungratefulness of the local population is clear in Mocenigo's proposal for a new tax on wine. Explaining that he had saved the most important matter for last, he said it was well known that the revenue received from Crete was not nearly enough to cover the cost of maintaining it: "For all those who consider the matter, it is very strange that a Kingdom as rich and strong as this one does not manage to yield enough to cover its own expenses even in times of peace. The republic is forced to buy at a very high price the armed galleys that she will certainly need in times of war."[83]

While the state struggled to meet its commitments, he continued, the citizens of the island enjoyed the security provided by Venice without paying the taxes that even the citizens of Venice were obligated to bear. A new tax was needed, and he had determined that a tax on wine would be the most appropriate. Those involved in the wine trade would certainly grumble, but Mocenigo was confident that they would eventually accept it when they considered the amount that the state had to spend on maintaining the island's fortresses and the large number of soldiers who were stationed there, all to protect the security of its inhabitants. In fact, the wealthy classes had actually benefited from the militarization of the island:

[81] In years of drought the wealthy of the city simply sent their servants to a source of water lying five or six miles outside the city. Ibid., 27.

[82] The residents objected that the water was too far away to ever reach the city; that most of the water would be lost along the way; that mountains would have to be cut through and this was an impossible task; that the water would have to go through many valleys, and thus many bridges and walls would have to be built; that if such a thing were really possible it would have been built at some time during the past 400 years of Venetian rule; that the expense would be enormous, possibly as much as 100,000 scudi, and all that for a project whose success was uncertain; that the time remaining in the provveditore's term in Crete would not be sufficient to complete the project; that no provveditore ever wanted to complete the projects of his predecessor but rather preferred to start his own. Ibid., 31–32.

In the end, Moresini did manage to get the *fontana* built, but the fountain with the lions and Poseidon was destroyed within a decade by the Inquisition. See Spanakēs, "Relazione de Sr. Isepo Civran," 392.

[83] Spanakēs, "Relazione del Nobil Huomo Zuanne Mocenigo," 204.

They must bear in mind the fact that, due to the large number of soldiers stationed on the island, the price of wine, wheat, and all other provisions has doubled. They spend their money as they wish and also receive numerous obligatory "gifts" from the peasantry, gifts that they did not even bother to demand before the war [of 1570–71] since buyers could not be found. On account of all this they have accumulated huge amounts of money, which they then lend to the government, which uses it to pay the soldiery. Thus all the notables, and many of the citizens, have become rich, and some of them extremely rich. This is obvious from the luxurious dress they have adopted, from their celebrations, their banquets and their funerals. . . . Such things were not seen here until after the war. . . . This wealth came about as a result of state spending dedicated to the maintenance of the kingdom and thus they are obligated to pay cheerfully this one, very insignificant tax.[84]

Given this antagonism between the provveditore and the local elite, it is perhaps not too far-fetched to believe that some prominent local families invited the Ottomans to invade Crete in the wake of the pirate attack of 1644, as contemporary sources assert. The provveditore at the time, Andrea Corner, was widely hated for many reasons, not least of which was the fact that he had cornered the market in olive oil.[85]

The last Venetian rulers of Crete were caught in a vicious cycle. In their struggle to hold onto the island, the centerpiece of their empire in the Levant, they leaned ever more heavily on both the peasants and the nobility, trying to force them shoulder what Venice saw as their fair share of the burden of defense. In the case of the peasantry, this meant a willingness to serve as rowers in the galleys and as lookouts along the shores of the island. The elites were expected to give priority to military concerns when making decisions about which crops to plant, as well as to make contributions, both in money and in kind, toward costs of maintaining Venetian rule on Crete. In general Venice expected the elites to forgo

[84] Ibid., 207.

[85] In his discussion of the beginning of the Cretan war, Setton quotes at length from a manuscript in the Correr library entitled "Relazione dell'invasione fatta da Turchi del regno di Candia": "che veramente il pensiero del Turco fosse solo contro Malta, ma che poi il combattimento con le doglianze degli Affricani lo disponesse contro a Veneziani, e finalmente in tutto lo facesse risolvere il ricoro che fecero a lui delle prime famiglie di Cania che disgustate dal governo aspríssimo di Andrea Cornaro, non sapendo dove trovar giustizia, per esser in Venezia la famiglia Cornara troppo potente, implorarono il braccio del Gran Signore, rappresentandogli la facilità dell'impresa et il desiderio che haveva quel Regno di soggettarsi a lui." Quoted in K. M. Setton, *Venice, Austria and the Turks in the Seventeenth Century* (Philadelphia: American Philosophical Society, 1991), 119. Similar charges were made in another contemporary manuscript, no. 1625 in the Marciana, entitled "Aneddoti Politici," referred to in Amy Bernardy, *Venezia e Il Turco nella seconda metà del secolo XVII* (Florence: G. Civelli, 1902), 8.

economic gains in the interests of keeping the island Venetian. But the pressure that Venice applied served only to weaken its position. Caught between a harsh feudal nobility and a demanding state, Cretan peasants fled to Ottoman territories. The depopulation of the countryside exacerbated the problem of provisioning the island. As local interest increasingly diverged from that of the metropole, local elites decisively chose the former. In the end, dissatisfaction with Venetian rule may have led them to give an opening to the sultan's troops. Although Venice's policy was ultimately self-defeating, it would have been hard to behave differently. As the costs of war climbed, and its control of the seas slipped away, Venice had to rely more on the cooperation of the local population, and this cooperation proved not to be forthcoming.

Ottoman Crete

Unlike earlier Ottoman conquests in the Balkans, the conquest of Crete did not replace a weak and divided government with a strong, centralized regime. Precisely because Venetian weaknesses at this time were also Ottoman weaknesses, the new rulers came to be plagued by many of the same problems that had dominated the last century of Venetian rule on the island. Yet certain key differences made it easier for the Ottomans to hold onto Crete. Various aspects of Ottoman rule in Crete are discussed more extensively in the chapters that follow. The purpose here is to provide a general overview of the difficulties the Ottomans encountered in ruling Crete. Like the Venetians, the Ottomans found the defense of the coastline to be a challenging job, and their failure to do so adequately had an adverse impact on rural conditions. Provisioning the island, however, proved to be much easier since Crete was no longer a Christian outpost surrounded by enemy territory. The Ottomans also benefited enormously from their alliance with the French.

Rural Decline

If the rural areas of Crete survived the war quite well, conditions actually deteriorated with the coming of the peace. Thirty-seven years after the conquest the Ottomans conducted another cadastral survey of the island, which showed that the amount of land under cultivation had dropped, in some cases dramatically.[86] Nor was the countryside generating the revenue that it had been capable of almost forty years previous. Within this overall picture of decline, however, there were important regional differences. These regional disparities, moreover, followed the pattern of the late Venetian period.

In the province of Candia tax revenue dropped by 27 percent. The hardest hit areas, however, were in the south. In the remote district of Pyrgiotissa, southwest of Candia, revenues dropped by 41 percent. Areas lying close to the capital city fared much better. Temenos district, which forms the immediate hinterland of Candia to the south, actually showed an increase in revenue, and over 90 percent of the land was in cultivation.[87] The exception to this was the large district of Pediada directly east of Candia. There, cultivated land tumbled from 68,651 to 51,874 ceribs. Abandoned land shot up from 7 percent to 18 percent of the total. Tax revenue dropped a dramatic 35 percent, from 2,632,462 to 1,687,976 akçe.[88] The explanation here must be that Pediada had a long coastline and was thus prey to pirate and other attacks. By the same token, Temenos's relative prosperity must have derived, in part, from the fact that it was one of the few districts that was completely inland.

Conditions in the remote province of Sēteia, far from the island's capital city, were clearly much worse. Tax revenue declined by 43 percent on average and in one district by more than 50 percent.[89] The cadastral survey shows that, like the Venetians before them, the Ottomans established more or less effective control in the fertile areas lying near Candia and reaped the rewards in terms of tax revenue. Very soon after conquering the island, however, they resigned themselves to only a limited presence in the more remote parts of the island.

The reasons for this are not hard to understand. Given Ottoman weakness at sea, it would have taken considerable military effort to guard the southern coasts from pirate attacks. The Venetians, for instance, normally maintained twenty-five soldiers and one cavalry regiment in the fortress of Sēteia in the extreme eastern part of the island. When pirates attacked the area in the late 1630s, the provveditore felt obliged to send down another 200 men plus an additional cavalry regiment.[90] Such a commitment was extremely costly, especially when one considers the inferior agricultural possibilities in the south. The mountain ranges that run like a backbone through the center of the island all drop off abruptly on the southern side

---

[86] See note 35 for a description of this source.

[87] From 632,657 akçe to 656,095 akçe, a rise of 4 percent. To the southwest of the city, the district of Malevizi dropped a modest 5 percent.

[88] These numbers are based on a comparison of the earlier and later registers.

[89] The district of Rizou on the southern coast.

[90] Spanakēs, "Relazione de Sr. Isepo Civran," 398.

of the island, making cultivation difficult. The south also suffers from a lack of natural harbors. Throughout the year, but particularly in the summer months, the south of the island is blasted with the hot winds coming up from Africa. It was precisely because the southern shore was deserted and unguarded that the Maltese pirates chose to land there in 1644, rather than on the northern coast of the island.[91]

Rural population appears to have been in decline as well. The records of a cizye survey from 1195/1693—a quarter century after the first one—survive in the archives: the island's non-Muslim population had actually declined from 26,674 to 18,246 souls.[92] Widespread conversion to Islam makes it difficult to know if the cizye figures indicate an absolute decline in the island's population, or just a shrinking of the Christian and Jewish communities to the benefit of the Muslims. But the wealth of negative indicators in the second cadastral survey—declining revenues, declining cultivation—make it likely that rural population was, in fact, smaller than it had been twenty-five years previous.

The number of landowners in the two eastern provinces recorded in the cadastral survey was also way down, from 43,349 in the immediate postconquest period to 26,736 in 1117/1705–06. In this case of land-holding, however, it is difficult to know whether this is an indication of population decline or, equally likely, an appropriation of peasant holdings.[93]

The impression of rural underpopulation is supported by the comments of Tournefort from his visit in 1699. He visited the famous Arkadi Monastery southeast of Rethymnon and noted that the monks had gathered in 400 measures of oil "though one-half of their fruit was lost for want of hands to get it in."[94] On the island in general, he wrote: "Though there is not in the Island half enough people to cultivate it, yet it produces more grain than the inhabitants can consume. It not only abounds in wines, but it also supplies strangers with oils, wool, silk, honey, wax, cheese, ladanum. Though Candia is a rich country, yet the best land in it is cultivated but by halves."[95] Tournefort's comments on undercultivation could have been made by any Venetian adminstrator half a century earlier. Plentiful grain supplies, however, were certainly an anomaly and strongly suggest that the population was smaller than it had been during the late Venetian period.

---

[91] Setton, *Venice, Austria and the Turks,* 111.

[92] Başbakanlık Arşivi (Prime Ministry's Archive), Istanbul, Maliyeden Müdevver series, register no. 745.

[93] Appropriation of peasant holdings was certainly the trend. For examples of the new scholarship, see Ariel Salzmann, "An Ancien Régime Revisited: 'Privatization' and Political Economy in the Eighteenth-Century Ottoman Empire," *Politics and Society* 21, no. 4 (December 1993): 393–423.

[94] Tournefort, *A Voyage,* 55.

[95] Ibid., 69.

Defending the Island

Unfortunately, the Ottoman governors of Crete were not in the habit of presenting reports to the sultan upon their return from the island but the reasons for rural decline are not difficult to ascertain. In a general way rural population trends in Crete were in keeping with the situation in the Ottoman Empire (and the Mediterranean world) as a whole.[96]

As for the particular situation of Crete, local court records show that, like the Venetians before them, the Ottomans had great difficulty in preventing attacks along the coastline. These attacks certainly hurt agricultural yields and probably contributed to peasant flight, both because of the attacks themselves and because of the guard duties that the Ottomans demanded from the peasantry in response.

The Venetians had had to worry about pirates and the Ottomans. The Ottomans, in their turn, had to worry about pirates and, until 1715, the Venetians. By the terms of the peace treaty of 1669, the Venetians maintained sovereignity over three rocky islands just off the northern coast of Crete.[97] Venice was not at all reconciled to the loss of Crete and hoped to use these islands as a base to launch a reconquest. In the meantime, Venice used locals to launch raids against the mainland from the three islands, particularly during the long war of 1684–99, and these were clearly very damaging.

In 1106/1694, a delegation from Istanbul was sent to Crete to ask why the sums collected from villages whose revenues belonged to the imperial purse (hümayûn kariyeleri mukataat) had fallen so far short in the previous year. The answer was a litany of woes that were characteristic of Crete during the early years of Ottoman rule. The proper planting and harvesting of any fields near the coastline had not been possible, village representatives explained in court, because of the presence of enemy ships from Spinalonga in many of the harbors of Crete. In addition, many pirates and hains had conducted raids against Crete during this period.[98] Finally, the Venetian siege of Chania, although brief, had meant the loss of most of the agricultural produce of Chania province.[99]

---

[96] "While evidence concerning the fate of Ottoman towns in the seventeenth century is ambiguous, population decline in the countryside is fairly well documented." Faroqhi, "Making a Living," 442.

[97] Souda, Spinalonga, and Grambousa.

[98] The Ottomans used the Arabic term *hain* (traitor) to refer to men who conducted raids on the island, then fled to one of the Venetian strongholds for refuge.

[99] T.A.H. 8:110. Between 17 July and 29 August, the Venetian naval commander Domenico Mocenigo laid seige to Chania, using the island of Suda as a base. He abandoned the attempt when Turkish prisoners of war informed him that the Ottoman Kapudan Pasha was headed for Chania with a large naval force. Setton, *Venice, Austria and the Turks*, 386.

In 1107/1696, at which time the Ottoman Empire and Venice were at war once again, a ferman to the pasha of Crete noted that boats from Venetian-held Souda were constantly intercepting ships coming into Chania, Rethymnon, and Candia, thereby preventing grain and other goods from reaching the island. A certain Mustufa Kapudan from Monemvasia had apparently offered to repair three old frigates lying in the harbor of Candia, in order to chase the Venetians, and the sultan ordered that these boats be turned over to him.[100]

Like the Venetians before them, the Ottomans organized the villagers into bands in an attempt to protect the coasts. Several documents from the late 1680s indicate the system they followed, as well as the kind of attacks to which the countryside was subject. Provincial leaders from four coastal districts were called into court in Candia and told that henceforth they would be held personally responsible for any Muslims of their province who were taken hostage by the hains, as well as any damage to Muslim property that was inflicted during the course of these raids. In the northern coastal districts of Malevizia and Rethymnon (to the west of the capital city) the villagers were obliged to serve as sentries at established lookout points, and to send up a signal whenever a ship was spotted. Villagers in Pediada, as well as in the southern districts of Rizou and Ierapetra, were organized into martolos bands and charged with arresting any hains that appeared in their areas.[101] They were also ordered to report to the authorities any villager that they suspected of planning an escape to one of the Venetian islands. Finally, the provincial leaders were threatened with severe punishment if any aid or succor was extended to the hains or to pirates. The pasha of Candia suspected such an alliance in the case of the villagers from Malevizia and Rethymnon.[102]

The pasha probably had good reason to be suspicious. Although the hains and the pirates inflicted damage on the countryside, they also represented an opportunity for the villagers. Cooperative villagers could claim a share of the booty and, in case of trouble, run away themselves. The Cretans had long used their position between the Venetian and Ottoman empires to run to the other side in a bid to escape punishment. Now, with Venetian garrisons just off the northern coast, escape was easier than ever. This situation must have encouraged a certain amount of lawlessness in the rural areas. Tournefort remarked on the hain and their relationship to the Ottoman-Venetian wars: "In times of Peace tis pleasant living in this

---

[100] T.A.H. 11:41.

[101] *Martolos* was a term in wide use during the Ottoman period. It referred to Christian irregulars used by the Ottomans along the military frontier. See Catherine Wendy Bracewell, *The Uskoks of Senj: Piracy, Banditry and Holy War in the Sixteenth Century Adriatic* (Ithaca: Cornell University Press, 1992), 36–37.

[102] T.A.H. 5:299, 300, 301.

island, but when there's a War, the whole country is ravaged and laid waste by the Cains."[103] The career of one hain who was eventually caught and executed by the Ottomans conveys the atmosphere of the time. Hassan b. Abdullah, brought into court in 1109/1697, had already been caught associating with the enemy at Spinalonga once before. A Christian at the time, he had saved himself by converting to Islam. Apparently his newfound identity as a Muslim did not prevent him from continuing his activities, raiding Muslim villages and murdering Muslims. When he was caught a second time, his execution was ordered.[104]

Despite these difficulties, Ottoman rule in Crete did bring about one dramatic improvement in rural conditions: the end of recruitment for the galleys. Although the Ottomans continued to have acute labor shortages for their navy both during and after the war for Crete, they apparently never tapped the island's villagers for this service.[105] The orders that were sent out from Istanbul to the Aegean, Thessaloniki, and other coastal areas of the Greek world, ordering the recruitment of rowers (*kürekciler*), do not appear in the records of Candia. In subsequent discussions of the crews for the sultan's navy, Crete is conspicuous by its absence.[106] Although the last Venetian rulers of Crete were deeply worried that, by conquering even a part of the island, the Ottomans would gain a large new supply of manpower for their galleys, the Ottomans, in fact, chose not to use the Cretans in this way. The reason for this is difficult to know. One Venetian general did break with the prevailing wisdom when he predicted, accurately as it turned out, that the Ottomans would not use the islanders as galley slaves. Giustiniano wrote:

> I think the enemy will behave more prudently. In order to win the trust of the kingdom's population he will try not to frighten them, and will ask only that they remain in their village to attend to their fields and their vines for their own account. By enticing them in this way, and with this false pretense of liberty and munificence, the enemy will gain their devotion.[107]

This motivation, while quite possible during the war years, does not explain why the Cretans were not tapped for galley service after the war was over. The sultan also did not recruit them as sailors, later on, when

[103] Tournefort, *A Voyage*, 98.
[104] T.A.H. 10:11.
[105] The Ottoman historian Naima noted with disapproval how, in the 1650s during the Cretan war, children were pulled off the streets to serve in the galleys. Rhodes Murphey, "The Ottoman Resurgence in the Seventeenth Century Mediterranean: The Gamble and Its Results," *Mediterranean Historical Review* 8, no. 2 (December 1993): 189. In 1711 the Ottoman Kapudan Pasha broke down the doors of a monastery in Naxos to find people. Vassilis Sfyroeras, *Ta hellēnika plerōmata tou tourkikou stolou* (The Greek crews of the Turkish fleet) (Athens, 1968), 39.
[106] See Sfyroeras, *Ta hellēnika plerōmata*.
[107] Spanakēs, "Relazione Pietro Giustiniano," 241.

naval reforms in the empire replaced the galley with the sailing ship as the basis of the Ottoman navy.[108] The Aegean continued to be the main recruiting area. Quite unwittingly, Giustiniano's remarks suggest what the real reason might have been. Unlike the rocky Cycladic islands, Crete had the potential to become a great agricultural resource. To that end, people had to be encouraged to stay home and farm, rather than to head off to sea.[109] The tiny Venetian Republic had access to only very small amounts of manpower and thus had to recruit among the Cretans. The Ottoman lands were vast by comparison, and thus the sultans could turn to other areas for their rowers and sailors and reserve Crete for agriculture.[110] As a result, Crete and the Aegean islands played very different roles within the empire.

Although detailed studies are lacking, the island's population seems to have entered a period of growth after 1720.[111] The long eighteenth-century peace in the Mediterranean (1718–68) suggests that Crete's previous population woes were due first and foremost to the ongoing wars.

Provisioning

The Ottomans may have had difficulties ruling effectively in Crete, but they did manage to hold onto it. In addition to an accommodation with local elites—to be discussed in the next chapter—two factors were critical in allowing them to do so. The first was that, as part of the Ottoman Empire, Crete now had access to supplies of grain that had been denied the island when it was under Venetian control.

In a striking departure from the late Venetian era, Crete actually went through a brief period as a grain exporter. During the war, the Ottoman military commander had ordered the governor of Rethymnon province to forbid the loading of wheat and olive oil onto ships arriving from

[108] Sfyroeras, *Ta hellēnīka plerōmata*, 37. In 1683 the Kapudan Pasha decided to make the sailing ship known as the galion the basis of the fleet. When a new tax was levied on the Greek islanders in 1710 in order to pay for the upgrading of the arsenal in Istanbul, protests came from places like Patmos but not Crete. Ibid., 39. There is still some dispute in the literature as to how quickly galleys went out of service. Stoianovich, on the basis of French archival sources, points out that as late as 1730 the Kapudan Pasha was still using a galley with rowers for his sorties into the Aegean for the head tax, the tithe, and—when war did not prevent it—the wheat from Egypt. Traian Stoianovich, "L'espace maritime segmentaire de l'Empire Ottoman," in *Material Culture and Mentalities: Land and Sea*, vol. 4 of *Between East and West: The Balkan and Mediterranean Worlds* (New Rochelle, N.Y.: Aristide D. Caratzas, 1995), 57.

[109] I thank Viriginia Aksan for this insight.

[110] This is what Braudel calls the problem of city-states in an age of territorial empires.

[111] Yolanda Triandafyllidou Baladie, *To emborio kai e oikonomia tēs Krētēs 1669–1795* (The commerce and economy of Crete) (Herakleion: Municipality of Herkleion, 1988), 34.

elsewhere.[112] Just four years after the war, however, a ferman sent to the pasha of Candia complained that produce was going unsold and that, therefore, "no one [should] prevent the islanders from selling their produce to the merchants that come to the harbors of the island in their boats."[113] French archival records and local court records show that grain was regularly exported from the island up until 1715, with a particularly strong burst at the end of the seventeenth century.[114] The French traveler Jean Baptiste Tavernier, becalmed off the coast of Crete for two days in the early 1670s, wrote that "Out of the island of Candy strangers export great quantities of wheat and sallet-oyl, all sorts of pulse, cheese, yellow wax, cottons, silks, but more especially malmfey, wherein consists its chief trade."[115]

Braudel notes that a greater security in grain supplies was a "paradoxical" characteristic of "the poorer and more backward islands, which had fewer inhabitants and above all were not exploited by crops grown for export."[116] Crete would seem to fit this profile in the immediate aftermath of the war.

The records also show, however, that when grain shortages occurred, the islanders could count on Istanbul to send supplies. In the spring of 1083/1672 the imperial navy brought 14,875 kilograms of millet (*dari*) and 15,000 kilos of wheat (*hinta*) to Candia, all of which was received by the fortress commander Yusuf Agha and stored in the public granaries.[117] These two shipments alone were three times as great as the largest amount ever loaded onto French ships in a single year.[118] Later on, when Crete once again had to import grain, regular shipments arrived from other parts of the empire.[119] For those who had to worry about feeding the island's population, this was a vast improvement over the days when provveditori regularly pleaded with Venice to send grain, usually to no avail.

The French Connection

The international situation that that Ottomans faced from Crete was also quite different from that faced by the Venetians. At the end of the sixteenth century, Venice confronted the daunting prospect of trying to hold onto a faraway island even as its naval power went into sharp decline. This was particularly worrisome because the Ottoman threat loomed ever larger on

---

[112] T.A.H. 1:148. The order was given in 1659.
[113] T.A.H. 5:131.
[114] See chapter 4 for a discussion of the grain trade.
[115] Jean Baptiste Tavernier, *Six Voyages through Turkey into Asia* (London, 1698), 138.
[116] Braudel, *The Mediterranean*, 152.
[117] T.A.H. 3:190, 3:254.
[118] See chapter 4 for French exports of grain.
[119] In 1715 the city of Foca in Anatolia sent 10,000 kilograms of wheat. T.A.H. 14:113. In 1722 alone the Morea sent more than 22 shipments of wheat. Baladie, *To emborio*, 291.

the horizon. For the Ottomans in Crete, there was no comparable threat. When they defeated the Venetians, a Mediterranean rivalry with its roots in the late medieval period was finally extinguished. Furthermore, future challengers to Ottoman dominance in the eastern Mediterranean—the French, the English, the Russians, and, in a different way, the Greeks—were not yet ambitious. Although the Venetians continued to be a problem until 1715, in retrospect it is clear that the era of great galley clashes in the eastern Mediterranean—clashes that were such a drain on both the Ottoman and Venetian treasuries—came to an end in 1669.

More important than this, however, was a factor that can be called "the French connection." By the time the Ottomans conquered Crete, the special relationship that France had with the Ottoman Empire was already a century old. This relationship was vital in allowing the Ottomans to hold onto Crete with relative ease. The Venetians, by contrast, were friendless by the seventeenth century. Time and again the French showed themselves to be willing to put their ships at the service of the Ottoman sultan.

The sultan's navy was not absent from the Mediterranean after 1669. It would be more accurate to say that a division of labor with the French was established. The sultan's ships undertook tasks relating to imperial defense. Soon after the fall of Candia, weapons, wheat, and wood were sent down from Istanbul. The Ottoman navy was particularly active during the war years (1683–99), when ships were regularly sent to Crete to pick up old cannons and other armaments. These valuable bits of iron were then taken back to Istanbul to be melted down at the Imperial Foundry.[120] Yet even during the war years a feeble Ottoman naval presence is indicated by Mustafa Kapudan's offer to repair, at his own expense apparently, the three frigates in Candia's harbor.[121] After the Peace of Karlowitz (1699) the navy rarely came to Crete.

For local shipping along the island's coasts and more routine matters of communication, the islanders relied on the French and the Ottomans were seemingly content to have them do so. The court records and other contemporary documents provide glimpses of the myriad tasks that the French performed in Crete, all of which contributed to the strengthening of Ottoman sovereignty. Randolph, in Crete in 1680, noted that a French merchant had had the harbor of Candia cleaned in order "to ingratiate himself with the Pasha."[122] In 1694 a French merchant helped a local Muslim sea captain chase away a pirate from the coast of Sēteia.[123] As with the Ottoman navy, the French role was particularly evident during the war years. Shipments of wheat from Candia to the soldiers in Chania, which

---

[120] T.A.H. 4:312; 7:21, 22, 24, 114; 11:24, 93.
[121] T.A.H. 11:41.
[122] Randolph, *Travels*, 81.
[123] T.A.H. 8:30.

was particularly vulnerable to assault because of the Venetian presence on Souda, were regularly taken on French ships. The representative of the French consul in Candia appeared in the local court on numerous occasions during the 1680s and 1690s to guarantee these shipments against attacks by corsairs or the enemy.[124] Ottoman officials relied on French shipping as well for their own transportation. In 1686 the pasha of Crete and his retinue sailed for home on a French ship, which the consul had guaranteed against pirate attack.[125] A few years later the new pasha of Crete sent a shipment of butter plus some cash home to his family in Istanbul. Again, the safe arrival of the ship was guaranteed by the French.[126]

French support for the Ottomans must be understood not just as a function of the special relationship between the sultans and the French kings, but also as a direct result of French-Venetian rivalry in the eastern Mediterranean. The Venetians were well aware that, as their hold on the Levant loosened, the French were moving in to assume prerogatives that had traditionally belonged to the Italians, including protection of local Catholics.[127] During the long War of the Holy League (1683–99) Louis XIV's support of the Ottoman sultan became increasingly apparent. When the Venetians abandoned their seige of Chania in the summer of 1692, it was widely assumed that it was the result of the French having passed secret information on to the Ottomans, thereby allowing them to foil Venetian plans. The previous fall French troops serving on the Venetian flagship of Bartolo Contarini had mutinied, wounding Contarini in the process.[128] When the Venetian garrison on the island of Grambousa gave themselves up to the Ottomans in 1692, it was a French ship that took the fugitive soldiers to Istanbul, much to the outrage of Venice.[129] Once Venice was out of the way, French policy toward the sultan and Ottoman merchants would not always be so solicitous. By the end of the eighteenth century, far from helping local merchants chase pirates, concern about their competition had grown to the point where a French consul wrote that, without the fear of pirates, local shipping would decimate the French coastal trade.[130] But in that crucial half century between 1669 and 1720,

[124] See T.A.H. 4:385, 390, 474; 6:152; 7:81, 86. The unwillingness of the Ottoman navy to go beyond Candia is strikingly illustrated by the fact that, in 1694, a shipment of weapons from Istanbul was turned over in Candia to a Greek from Mytilene for transport to Chania. T.A.H. 8:70.

[125] T.A.H. 6:119.

[126] T.A.H. 7:12.

[127] See B. J. Slot, *Archipelagus Turbatus: Les Cyclades entre colonisation latine et occupation ottomane c. 1500–1718* (Istanbul: Nederlands Historisch-Archaeologisch Instituut te Istanbul, 1982), particularly chap. 8, for acute Venetian-French rivalry over patronage of the religious orders in the Cycladic islands at this time.

[128] See Setton, *Venice, Austria and the Turks*, 386–87. Thomas Coke, an English diplomat in Istanbul, wrote the following on 29 October 1692: "The Venetians have rais'd their seige at Canea with losse and disreputation, which is imputed to the French, who gave notice of their designe to the Turks."

[129] T.A.H. 8:7.

when the Venetian threat was still very real in the eastern Mediterranean, the French did everything in their power to strengthen the sultan's grip on the island and thus deny Crete to the Venetians.

The dominant role of the French in the coastal trade of the empire in the eighteenth century is, of course, well known. But the significance of French maritime strength—and France's willingness to put it at the disposal of the Ottomans—stretched far beyond the world of commerce in the case of Crete. The Ottomans may have conquered the island, but it was French ships that allowed them to hold onto it with relative ease. In France, the sultans found the friend that Venice had so sorely lacked.

---

[130] "Il est absolument necessaire pour le soutien de la caravane (français) que des corsaires paraissent de temps en temps sur le Gobas de Damiette et qu'ils y fassent même des prises; sans cela les bateaux du Pays feraient presque tout le commerce de la cote de Syrie." André Raymond, *Artisans et commercants au Caire au XVIII siècle* (Damascus: Institut Français, 1973), 1:170.

Three

Ottoman Candia

Ottoman Policy in Candia

The collapse of Venetian rule in the city of Candia was dramatic. It brought to an abrupt halt that cultural blend of Catholicism and Orthodoxy that had produced the Cretan Renaissance in the sixteenth and seventeenth centuries. Virtually all of the city's many churches and monasteries, both Catholic and Orthodox, were converted to other uses, as mosques, of course, but also as private homes and as housing for the military. The urban institutions associated with Italian cities—scuole, the Monte di Pietà—vanished.[1] All this was ushered out with the last refugees who clambered onto the boats going to Dia, the small island that lies just outside the harbor of Candia, for passage to the Ionian islands and beyond. Köprülü and his entourage entered a deserted city.

Under the Ottomans, the city became a center not only of Islam but also of a newly reconstituted Orthodoxy ill-disposed toward the West. It became a city of soldiers, a city of converts, and a city of immigrants, both from the countryside and other parts of the empire. To the Europeans, it was a forbidding place. Baume, the French vice-consul in Candia in 1723, wrote, "Quant à nos français, en général tant sédentaires que marins, ils se trouveraient dans une situation passablement bonne pour un pays de Turquie, si le chef du gouvernement qui réside à Candie était moins opposé et antipathique à tout qui s'appelle franc."[2] The Europeans preferred Chania, center of the olive oil trade, where the rulers seemed to be more tractable and the Capuchins had a small mission.[3] Only the Venetians persisted in trying to penetrate the exterior of this newly transformed city. In this they were remarkably successful and Venetian reports on the city in the early years of Ottoman rule provide a perspective that no other western source approaches.

---

[1] St. Alexiou, "To kastro tēs Krētēs kai ē zoē tou ston 16th kai 17th Aiōna" (The fortress of Crete and its life in the 16th and 17th centuries), *Krētika Chronika* 19 (1965): 146–78, for a description of the capital city in the sixteenth and seventeenth centuries.

[2] K. Konstantinides, "Ekthesis kai ypomnēmata apo tēn allēlografia tou gallikou prokseniou Krētēs" (Essays and notes from the French consulate in Crete), *Krētika Chronika* 8 (1954): 356.

[3] M. Pitton de Tournefort, *A Voyage into the Levant* (Paris, 1717), 20. There were two Capuchins in Chania.

The dramatic departure of the Venetians, however, should not be allowed to obscure the very real similarities between the new Ottoman city and Candia under the Venetians, at least during the later period of Venetian rule. In the early centuries the cities of Venetian Crete stood as Catholic fortresses on the edge of an Orthodox countryside, but over time, as the ranks of the nobility thinned and Venice's grip on trade loosened, the urban centers were infiltrated by the local population. By the sixteenth century, if not earlier, a majority of the population in Candia and elsewhere were Greek-speaking and many were Orthodox Christians.

This "localization" of the cities was not arrested by the Ottoman conquest. Candia was not claimed by either Ottoman officialdom or Turkish colonists from elsewhere in the empire, and the population of city continued to be overwhelmingly indigenous, even if many of these Cretans were now Muslim.

The relationship of religion to other cultural markers also shows interesting continuities with late Venetian Candia. Both Muslims and Christians shared a common language, Greek, just as the Latins and the Orthodox had previously. As in the Venetian period, a serious level of religious tension and animosity coexisted with very close and, from the point of view of the authorities, rather irregular relations between the two religious communities.

A Deserted City

The city that Köprülü wrested from the Venetians had been founded by Arab Muslims, adventurers from Spain, early in the ninth century. In antiquity the city had been known as Herakleion (hence today's name) and was the harbor for Knossos. The Arabs must have been attracted in part by the harbor created by the indentation of the coastline, but even more so by the rich hinterland that extends southward for more than twenty miles. Unlike Rethymnon and Chania, Herakleion is not cut off from the south by a steep mountain range. Instead the land rises only modestly all the way down to the Messara plain. This soil is the best on the island and even today the villages behind Herakleion are the richest on Crete. The gentleness (for Crete) of the terrain is also the reason why the easiest north-south crossing of the island—then and now—is made from Herakleion.

The Arabs called the city Kandak, after the great ditch they dug around it, a name that the Venetians corrupted to Candia and the Greeks retained quite faithfully, calling the city Χανδαχας (Chandakas). When the Byzantines reconquered the island in 961 they retained Candia as the capital city of Crete, rather than returning to their old capital, Gortyna, in the south.

The city of Candia (Herakleion) viewed from the sea in the opening years of the twentieth century. Credit: Princeton University Library

It was under the Venetians that Candia acquired its fame as one of the best-fortified cities of the eastern Mediterranean. Over the course of three centuries (fourteenth through the seventeenth) Venice steadily built walls, gates, and bastions in a bid to keep up with improving methods of seige warfare. By the seventeenth century this city of something less than 20,000 people was surrounded by seven large bulwarks in the shape of a heart. Its heavy fortifications led the Greeks to give it a second name, Το Κάστρο (To Kastro), the Castle, which they used alongside the older name of Chandakas. During this time, too, the city gradually expanded westward and southward, moving the city limits far beyond the original Byzantine walls. The core of the old city—now the northeastern quadrant of the city—emerged as the quarter of the elite, the place where the public buildings and the most opulent churches were located. This was true throughout the Venetian period, it remained true under the Ottomans (of course, the churches were now mosques) and it is still the case today.

By the time Köprülü's representative was given the keys to all the public buildings in the city (1 Cemaziy'ül-evvel/27 September 1669), this famous city had withstood over two years of daily bombardment, as well as a vicious underground mining war.[4] It was also a deserted city. In accordance with the terms of the peace treaty (6 Rebiülahir 1080/3 September 1669) the civilian inhabitants of the city were free to leave together with all their belongings, and most chose to do so. "Candia appeared as the skeleton

---

[4] Mines were exploded on a daily basis by both the Venetian and Ottoman armies. The two sides were constantly digging underground and would on occasion run into each other, at which point hand-to-hand combat underground would ensue. Nicholaos Stavrinidēs, *E teleutaia periodos tēs poliorkias tou M. Kastrou* (The final stage of the siege of Candia). (Herakleion, 1979), 23.

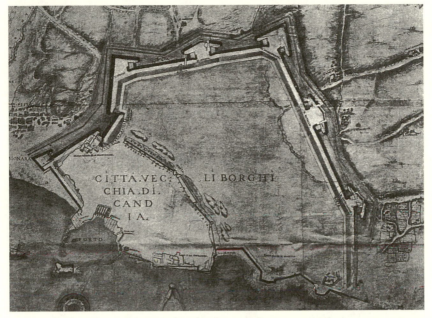

This map of the city, which dates from the late Venetian period, shows how the city expanded southward and westward over time. Under both the Ottomans and the Venetians the Old City remained the elite quarter. Credit: Princeton University Library

of a city," wrote Battista Nani, the procurator of San Marco, whose history of Venice discussed the war and its aftermath at length. Only two Greek priests and three Jews, along with a handful of soldiers who converted to Islam, remained in the city. The rest, roughly 4,000 in number, boarded the ships waiting in the harbor "con gran quiete e silentio."[5] A monk writing from Mount Athos at the time noted the fall of the city in the margins of a manuscript: "The Kastro of Crete has surrendered and the ill-fated souls have fled to foreign parts, and this because of our sins."[6] Ottoman policy in the city, as we shall see shortly, supports the contemporary observation of a deserted city.

[5] Battista Nani, *Historia Veneta di Nani* (Venice, 1687), 2:518–19. Nani's reference to the two Greek priests and the three Jews was repeated by Rycaut and, ten years later, Bernard Randolph.

[6] "Eparadothike to Kastron tēs Krētēs kai exeniteutēkamen oi kakarizēkē eis xenous kosmous kai etoutō ex amartiōn mas." From a manuscript from the Monastery of Stavronikita on Athos, dated 1669 August. Signed "Ego ireus Mathaos." Sp. Lambros, "Enthymiseon, etoi chronikōn semeiomatōn" (Enthymeseon, or notes in the margins of chronicles), *Neos Ellēnomnēmōn* 7, nos. 2–3 (1910): 196.

The emptying out of the city makes sense given that it had first been attacked in 1647 and was under continuous threat of attack for over twenty years subsequent to that. Anyone who was willing to consider abandoning the city and submitting to the Ottomans (and there were innumerable such cases) would probably have left long before 1669.

Although no systematic study has been done of the phenomenon, the arrival of the refugees—both Christian and Jewish—in the Ionian islands is well attested to. In 1699 a "Cretan" synagogue was inaugurated on the island of Zakynthos (Zante), and a poem written to commemerate the occasion mentions the city of Candia in the first line.[7] The Jewish population of Zante rose dramatically during the years of the war and in its aftermath, from 385 to about 1,000.[8] Registers compiled in Corfu and Zakynthos in 1683 listed 206 refugee Cretan families still in Corfu and 223 still in Zakynthos.[9] These registers were modifications of lists drawn up in the early 1670s and may or may not have included all the refugee families in the two islands. The chevalier d'Arvieux, future French consul in Aleppo, stopped at the island of Cephalonia in the 1670s and noted "Elle est habitée par des Grecs pauvres et miserables qui font la plupart des debris de Candie." The governor of the island had been a major in Crete who had received this post as a reward for the service he had rendered to Venice during the war.[10] A sharp increase in the number of marriages contracted by Cretans in Venice after 1669 points to the arrival of a number of refugees in the capital city as well.[11]

---

[7] Judith Humphrey drew my attention to this reference. See *Mosè: Antologia Israelitica* 2 (Corfu, 1879).

[8] Three hundred eighty-five in 1652; 700 in 1667 and about 1,000 in 1689.The numbers are given in Anthony Seymour, "Caveat Lector: Some Notes on the Population Figures of the Jewish Communities of the Ionian Islands: II," *Bulletin of Judaeo-Greek Studies* 15 (Winter 1994): 33–40.

[9] M. Mertzios, "Dyo katalogoi tōn en Kerkyra kai Zakyntho krētōn prosfygōn kata ta etē 1682 kai 1683" (Two lists of Cretan refugees in Corfu and Zakynthos in the years 1682 and 1683), *Krētika Chronika* 5 (1951): 8. These lists were compiled for the purpose of estimating the amount of help that would have to be extended to the refugees.

[10] Laurant d'Arvieux, *Memoires du Chevalier d'Arvieux, contenant ses voyages à Constantinople, dans l'Asie, la Syrie, la Palestine, l'Egypte et la Barbarie*, comp. by J. B. Labat (Paris, 1735), 5:474–75. For other information on Cretan refugees in the Ionian islands, see L. Ch. Zois, "Krētes prosfyges tou 1667" (Cretan refugees from 1667), *Krētika Chronika* 9 (1956): 346–52, and G. N. Moschopoulos, "Metoikēsē krētōn stēn Kefalonia stē diarkeia tou krētikou polemou (1645–1669) kai ystera apo tēn alosē tou Chandaka" (The emigration of Cretans to Kefalonia during the course of the Cretan war and after the fall of Chandaka), in Pepragmena tou D Diethnous Krētologikou Synedriou (Proceedings of the Fourth International Cretological Symposium) (Athens: 1981) 2:270–91.

[11] S. Antoniadēs, "Oikonomikē katastasē tōn poleōn tēs Krētēs 1645–1699" (The economic condition of Crete's cities, 1645–1699), *Thēsaurismata* 4 (1967): 48. The records are preserved in the Greek Scuola S. Nicolo in Venice. Antoniades' article also provides information on the measures taken in Venice to provide for the refugees there. According to Nani, many of the refugees were settled in Parenzo on the Istrian peninsula. Nani, *Historia Veneta*, 518.

The Repopulation of the City

Some aspects of Ottoman policy in Candia were reminiscent of Ottoman urban policy in formerly Christian cities in earlier centuries.[12] The landmarks of the city were quickly distributed among the elite. The magnificent Church of Saint Francis became the Friday mosque of Candia.[13] The other major Christian landmarks of the city, all of them within the original walls, went to high-ranking Ottomans as well. The basilica of the Dominican Monastery of San Pietro was converted into the Sultan Ibrahim mosque.[14] Köprülü claimed the Metropolitan Church of Saint Tito in the elite northeast quadrant of the city for his own complex, the Vezir Camisi.[15] The Church of Saint Mark in the very center of the city, opposite the Ducal Palace, became the Defterdar Camisi.

But after the parceling out of the most prestigious buildings, the Ottomans were still faced with the problem of how to dispose of all the abandoned property that had come into their possession. The city had been obtained through surrender and the usual practice in such cases was to leave urban property in the possession of its owners. This would not work in Candia precisely because the urban population had left with the Venetians.[16] As a result, the Ottomans implemented a two-pronged approach.

As in past centuries, the state relied heavily on religious endowments, founded by elite Ottomans, to repopulate and refurbish the city.[17] The scope of some of these endowments indicates the considerable investment that members of the elite were willing to make in the city. The former

[12] But note the interesting problems of converting Catholic, rather than Orthodox, churches to mosques. I. Bierman, "The Ottomanization of Crete," in *The Ottoman City and Its Parts,* ed. Irene A. Bierman, Rifa'at A. Abou-El-Haj, and Donald Preziosi, 68 (New Rochelle, N.Y.: Aristide D. Caratzas, 1991).

[13] This church was the most opulent and important of all the Latin monasteries in Candia. It stood where the Archaeological Museum stands today. Alexiou, "To kastro tēs Krētēs," 152.

[14] Zvi Ankori, "From Zudecha to Yahudi Mahallesi: The Jewish Quarter of Candia in the Seventeenth Century," in *Salo Wittmayer Baron Jubilee Volume,* ed. Saul Lieberman (Jerusalem: American Academy for Jewish Research, 1974), 1:91.

[15] Ibid., 104.

[16] For Ottoman policy on cities that surrendered, see H. Inalcık, "The Policy of Mehmed II towards the Greek Population of Istanbul and the Byzantine Buildings of the City," *Dumbarton Oaks Papers* 23–25 (1969–70): 231–49, and Traian Stoianovich, "Model and Mirror of the Premodern Balkan City," in *Economies and Societies: Traders, Towns and Households,* vol. 2 of *Between East and West: The Balkan and Mediterranean Worlds* (New Rochelle, N.Y.: Aristide D. Caratzas, 1995), 82. Article 12 of the peace treaty did specify that the property of all those who remained would not be harmed: "kala'da kalub sakin olanlara mani' olmayub, mal ve canlarina zarar olmaya." The peace treaty is given by the Ottoman chronicler Silahdar Fındıklılı Mehmet Aga, *Silahdar Tarihi* (Istanbul: Devlet Matbaasi, 1928), 520.

[17] Inalcık, "The Policy of Mehmed II."

Jewish neighborhood, or Zudecha, was endowed in its entirety to the valide sultan mosque in Candia.[18] Over 100 buildings in Candia were dedicated in support of Köprülü's pious endeavors. The Köprülü family also assigned the revenue from urban sources in Izmir to selected public buildings in Candia.[19] Unlike many other religious endowments in the Ottoman Empire, the mosques and other public buildings in Candia were supported primarily through urban revenue, rather than agricultural resources. Again, this indicates the eagerness of the Ottoman elite to rehabilitate the ruined city. Abd ur-Rahman Agha, the head of the imperial janissaries in Candia, dedicated the revenues of nearly forty buildings—shops, storehouses, and private homes—to the support of his mosque, as well as 1,000 guruş, the interest from which would also go to the support of the mosque and its staff. All of the various properties were bought from the public fisc and a title deed was issued to this effect.[20]

The second part of the strategy was to sell off all available urban property, whether part of a religious endowment or not, to anyone of any religion who was willing to put up the purchase price. The endowment deed for the mosque dedicated by Abd ur-Rahman Agha in the summer of 1081/ 1670, describes how properties became available: "after the divinely ordained conquest of the fortress of Candia which took place in the year 1080 and after the repair and restoration of all the houses and plots lying within that fortress, they [the houses and plots] were sold by the Public Fisc to those who desired them."[21]

Records of real-estate transactions in the early 1670s are extremely numerous in the court records, indicating that the authorities were success-

[18] Ankori, "From Zudecha to Yahudi Mahallesi," 96.

[19] I. M. Kunt, "The Waqf as an Instrument of Public Policy: Notes on the Köprülü Family Endowments," in *Studies in Ottoman History in Honour of Professor V. L. Ménage*, ed. Colin Heywood and Colin Imber (Istanbul: Isis Press, 1994), 197. This endowment was drawn up in 1679 and contained donations of both Fazil Ahmet and his brother Fazil Mustafa. Obviously it was drawn up after Fazil Ahmet's death. It is explained in the document that Ahmet Pasha built many public and charitable works but died (in 1676) before he had endowed them with sources of revenue. His brother then took it upon himself to endow them. The Köprülü brothers dedicated a very large amount of real estate in Candia: 142 shops, markets, and houses as opposed to 103 such establishments in Izmir. Izmir, of course, was a much larger city. This is an indication of how deserted the city was, and the willingness of the Köprülüs to buy up large amounts of real estate in an attempt to build up the city's economy.

[20] T.A.H. 2:111. "tarf-i miridan mülk-name-i hümayun ile temlik olundukdan sonra."

[21] Ibid. "bin seksen senesinde [   ] ek-akbar feth-i müyesser ve mukadder olan Candia kal'asi mesahasi ta'mir ve bi-l-cümle ihya olundukdan sonra derunda olan menazil ve arazisini mesaha tahdid ve malikāne tasarruf olunmak üzere [   ] taraf-i saltanat-i Aliyyeden talibine bey' ü temlik olundukda." The date of the document is 19 July 1670. Despite the claim that all necessary repairs had been made within the fortress, both travelers' accounts and archival evidence show that many buildings persisted in a state of ruin for decades after the war. Several of the buildings that the janissary agha bought are described as being in a state of ruin (*kharabe*).

ful in attracting people into the city. In the spring of 1081/1670, for instance, several Jews bought four plots of land that had been abandoned by their Christian former owners. In addition to the purchase price of 100 guruş they were also obliged to pay four akçe a day to the endowment of the valide sultan.[22]

Not all the abandoned houses and commercial buildings were included in the city's religious endowments. Some property taken over by the incoming Ottomans was sold through auctions as *mülk* (private property) much as it was in the countryside. Property transactions between the fisc (*miri*) and a private individual—or between two private individuals where it is mentioned that the seller originally acquired the property from the fisc— are also extremely numerous in the court records of early Ottoman Candia, and the documents indicate that the owner owned the shop or house in question free and clear. The scale of transactions varied widely, from the purchase of a small house by an ordinary resident to much more lavish purchases by the city's elite.

In the spring of 1081/1671, for instance, Ali beşe b. Ahmet sold a house he had bought from the fisc to Mustafa beşe b. Abdullah. The court noted that Ali beşe had bought the house from the fisc (*miriden*) and that it was his private property (*mülk menzil*). Now that Mustafa beşe had bought the house for thirty-five guruş, it belonged to him free and clear and he could do with it as he liked.[23]

Almost a year later Ahmet Agha, a janissary officer, bought the entire Church of Ayios Yiannis Chrysostomos, as well as an eleven-room house that had belonged to a Venetian. The house had three wells, two court-yards, storehouses, and a spring. He also bought five stores and converted the Venetian Monastery of Akrotirianis into a janissary barracks, where he built a small mosque and bathhouse.[24] Ibrahim Agha, another janissary officer, appeared in court five times during October and November of 1672 (1083) to register his purchase of houses, empty lots, and gardens throughout the city.[25]

The right to buy property in the city was not limited to Muslims but included Jews and Christians as well. The disposal of urban property in Candia, preserved in the court records, shows this open settlement process very clearly.

---

[22] T.A.H. 2:137.

[23] T.A.H. 2:33. "zikr olunan menzil merkum Mustafa beşe'nin mülk-ü menzilsidir keyfe-ma yeşa ve yektac mutasarrif olsun." The house consisted of two upstairs rooms in a state of ruin. Real-estate transactions concerning endowed property do not contain the same language that appears in deeds of sale for property that was owned outright. Endowed property could not be sold, although there were abuses.

[24] T.A.H. 2:88. See also T.A.H. 7:149 for the sale of a luxurious house, including a kiosk. The house was sold by one high-ranking officer, who was going back to Istanbul, to another.

[25] T.A.H. 4:112, 117, 120, 123–24.

A year after the conquest Mehmet b. Abdullah sold the house he had bought from the fisc to a Christian named Markos veled-i Cōnstantine. Mehmet owned another property adjoining the house he was selling to Markos, suggesting that speculators bought up as much property as they could in the days immediately following the conquest, only to sell it later on at a profit.[26] An Armenian resident of Candia bought a house from the fisc in the spring of 1080/1670.[27]

In a significant departure from the Venetian period, when they were confined to the Jewish quarter (Zudecha), the Jews were permitted to bid for property anywhere in the city. Within a year of the fall of the city Jews were already moving out of the Zudecha and buying houses that had been abandoned by departing Christians.[28] A document of 1105/1694 shows a Jewish shop on the main street (in Venetian times known as the Ruga Maistra) in a very fashionable part of the city.[29]

Observers at the time commented on the policy of allowing non-Muslim settlement. Randolph wrote, "Since taking the place, they have granted liberty to all who will come to inhabit there, but all their encouragement cannot bring the Candiots to dwell there."[30] An Orthodox Christian source is more specific.

> As soon as the Turks took Candia, all the Christians fled the confusion. And the vezir saw how the Romeioi all left, pulled up their roots, and fled to the islands. In order to induce them to come back, he called Panayiōtēs. And he asked him why everyone had left. And Panayiōtēs said they left because they don't have a church. That's why they left from here and stay away. Then the vezir said, find a church. Make sure it's small and inconspicuous.

The Panayiōtēs of the poem was Panayiōtēs Nikousios, the first Greek to hold the position of grand dragoman to the Sublime Porte. The writer of the poem, no doubt impressed by Nikousios's relationship with the powerful Ahmet Köprülü, attributed the presence of Christians in Candia to Nikousios's influence.[31] It is certainly true that Nikousios worked on behalf of the Christians of the island and that he was a well-known figure, not only on the island and in Istanbul, but in the West as well.[32] But the presence of Christians and Jews in Candia, as well as their ability to acquire

---

[26] T.A.H. 2:61. Real-estate documents are very informative because, in addition to the property being sold, all the surrounding property, as well as the owner, is listed. Both Mehmet and Constantine lived in the Kethuda Bey neighborhood.

[27] T.A.H. 2:71.

[28] Ankori, "From Zudecha to Yahudi Mahallesi," 93.

[29] Ibid., 101. The landmarks of that area were the Moresini Fountain (partially dismantled by the Inquisition), the Ducal Palace, and the San Marco Church.

[30] Bernard Randolph, *Travels in Crete* (London, 1700), 84.

[31] For a discussion of this poem and its author, see chapter 6.

[32] We return to the important topic of Panayiōtēs Nikousios in the final chapter.

property, was not due mainly to Nikousios, but rather to the urgent problem of populating a deserted city, especially in the absence of any serious influx of Turkish Muslims as in the Balkans in previous centuries.[33]

Although we lack court records for the city of Chania, travelers' comments suggest that the Christians of that city were confined to the suburb outside the city known as the varoş.[34] This was the policy followed by the Ottomans in Cyprus a century earlier, when an imperial command prescribed that the Christians of the fortress of Famagusta should be resettled in a varoş or unfortified place outside the city walls.[35] The fact that this policy was not followed in Candia only emphasizes how deserted the city was, and how eager Köprülü was to repopulate it. Even during the renewal of hostilities with the Venetians and other Christian powers (1684–99 and 1714–15), there was no attempt to remove the Christian population from Candia.[36]

A City of Soldiers?

A ferman, issued in 1082/1671, brings us to the question of the encouragement of Muslim settlement in the capital city. The ferman stated that, if the Yerli Yeniçeri, or locally recruited janissaries, so desired, they could choose a house from among those not yet sold and live in it without

[33] There is a debate over the extent of Turkish Muslim settlement in the Balkan cities between the fourteenth and sixteenth centuries. An earlier generation of Turkish scholarship by Ömer Lutfi Barkan, for example, argued for massive Turkish colonization, supported systematically by the state, that in effect created cities anew. According to Barkan, the most important cities of the empire were Turkish and Muslim in their population. Nikolai Todorov, the historian of the Balkans and particularly of Balkan cities, disputes this and sees much more continuity with pre-Ottoman times. "According to the latest information, the scope and dimension of Turkish colonization was far less than what might be suggested by the size of the Muslim population in the nineteenth century." Nikolai Todorov, *The Balkan City, 1400–1900* (Seattle: University of Washington Press, 1983), 45. Even if the scope of Turkish colonization in the Balkans proves to be much less than was previously thought, still it was more extensive in the Balkans than in Crete.

[34] Both Rethymnon and Chania had varoş. A head-tax register from 1105/1693–94 lists a varoş for Rethymnon and Chania but not Candia. Başbakanlık Arşivi (Prime Ministry's Archive), Istanbul, Maliyeden Müdevver, register no. 745. Randolph clearly referred to the varoş in his comments on Chania: "No Greeks live within the city. They have a new town built to the South, about half a mile off, where there are two long streets, very commodious, and here they enjoy all the liberty they desire." Randolph, *Travels*, 90. A Venetian dispatch from Chania, dated 3 May 1670, reported "In Canea the vizir has imposed great hardships upon those few Christians who have remained there, for he has confiscated all their houses and properties . . . allowing them to build themselves habitations only in the villages that existed on the fringes of the city before the war." K. Setton, *Venice, Austria and the Turks in the Seventeenth Century* (Philadelphia: American Philosophical Society, 1991), 245.

[35] Stoianovich, "Model and Mirror," 102.

[36] See T.A.H. 11:73 where the administrator of a vakıf rented a shop to a Christian during the Ottoman-Venetian wars.

payment. After their death the house could pass to their children. Their only obligation was a promise to fix up the property, as well as to refrain from selling the house at some future date.[37]

Köprülü was clearly willing to allow Christian and Jewish settlement within the city's walls. Despite this, there is no doubt that Candia very quickly became a city with a large Muslim majority. As with the Muslim population in the countryside, the Muslims living in the capital city were not Turkish immigrants to the island but rather local converts to Islam. No evidence suggests that the Ottomans brought in Muslims from elsewhere in the empire and settled them in Candia. There were certainly cases of individual Muslims settling in the city, but the population, by and large, remained local in origin.[38]

Candia was a typical Balkan town of the seventeenth century in this respect. The age of Muslim, Turkish colonization of southeastern Europe and the creation of new, Muslim-dominated, urban centers had come to a close by the end of the sixteenth century. Henceforth, the growth of the Muslim population of the Balkans was to be explained by reproduction and local conversion to Islam.[39] The late date of Candia's conquest must explain why Turkish settlement was so minimal, and why the presence of local converts was so striking in comparison to other Balkan towns.[40]

[37] T.A.H. 3:220. Damage to the document has obscured the date but the surrounding documents are from December 1671. A similar directive appears in a survey of the city conducted by the Ottomans within just a few weeks of the Venetian surrender. Forty-five houses were assigned to janissary soldiers as long as they promised to actually live in them. Başbakanlık Arşivi (Prime Ministry's Archive), Istanbul, Maliyeden Müdevver, Register no. 634.

[38] T.A.H. 5:160. When Recep b. Ali registered his purchase of a sword from Osman çavuş b. Ali in 1674, the court described him as an immigrant from Nauplion on the eastern coast of the Morea: "fil asl vilayet-i rumelinden Mora sancaginda Anablou kazasina tabi' zade nam kariyeden Receb b. Ali."

[39] Todorov, *The Balkan City*, 49–50. Conversion affected both the indigenous population as well as Vlachs who had been settled there by the Ottomans. As to the ratio of Muslims to Christians in Ottoman cities, evidence suggests that, as time went by, the urban Christian population grew relative to the Muslims. Stoianovich, for instance, notes that, in the seventeenth and eighteenth centuries, Muslim population decline was "momentarily thwarted" by conversion to Islam so that in the countryside it was "barely perceptible." The cities, however, were rapidly becoming more Christian. In 1669, the very year that Candia was finally won for the Ottomans, Sultan Mehmet IV issued a ferman sanctioning the settlement of Jews and Christians in Muslim quarters in Sofia in today's Bulgaria. Stoianovich, "Model and Mirror," 94. See also Suraiya Faroqhi, "Social Life in Cities," in *The Economic and Social History of the Ottoman Empire*, ed. Halil Inalcık with Donald Quataert (Cambridge: Cambridge University Press, 1994), 602. Todorov notes an overall gain in the Muslim population of the Balkans between the sixteenth and the nineteenth centuries, but he does not comment on the cities specifically (*The Balkan City*, 312). Candia may be considered atypical in that it retained a strong Muslim presence throughout the eighteenth century. In 1817 the Austrian naturalist and doctor F. W. Sieber reported that there were 15,000 residents, half "Greek" and half "Turk." F. W. Sieber, *Travels in the Island of Crete in the Year 1817* (London, 1823), 60.

[40] See the comments of European travelers in chapter 1.

If most Muslim residents of the city were converts, the evidence suggests that most were soldiers as well. These two characteristics are the key to understanding the nature of Muslim settlement in Candia.

By the late seventeenth century the janissary corps throughout the Ottoman Empire was deeply involved in the production and exchange of goods—that is to say, in economic life—to the detriment of military duties.[41] The janissaries and other soldiers in Candia were no exception to this rule. Indeed convert soldiers in Candia would have already been familiar with this aspect of military life from the late Venetian period. The Venetians, like the Ottomans, were faced with a city full of soldiers that they couldn't pay, and they tolerated military involvement in production and exchange as a result.[42]

Within a year of the conquest the court records tell us of a nonranking soldier, a beşe, who was a baker. Hassan beşe b. Abdullah of the twenty-first regiment had bought some wheat from a janissary officer and the imam of a religious endowment, and then died before he could pay for it.[43] A survey of the bakers in the city at the end of the century listed fourteen names, nine of which were Muslim. Of those nine, six had the epithet "beşe" after their name.[44] In 1081/1671 a Christian named Sefer veled-i Simaron sold his shop (*dukkan*) in the center of the city to Ali bey b. Abdullah. Most likely the shop had some connection to the textile trade since Sefer was identified as a member of the textile guild (*bezzaz taife*).[45] Mehmet beşe, the standard-bearer (*bayraktar*) for the local janissaries had a license (*gedik*) for a store at the time of his death.[46] Another beşe, Yazici Mehmet beşe, was appointed head of the market (*bazar başı*) in 1129/1717.[47] A ferman sent to Candia in the early 1690s implicated the janissaries as a whole in the illegal wine trade in the city. The sale and consumption of wine within the fortified city (*kala'*) was forbidden but the janissaries stood accused of leaving the city gates open at night, in order to allow wine to come in. They charged a bribe for this, of course, as well as collecting protection money from the winehouses (*mey-khane*) operating within the city.[48] Finally, soldiers were heavily involved in the buying and selling of real estate.

---

[41] The literature on this is immense. For an excellent discussion of the phenomenon, see Cemal Kafadar, "Yeniçeri-Esnaf Relations: Solidarity and Conflict" (Master's thesis, McGill University, 1981).

[42] See the discussion in chapter 2.

[43] T.A.H. 2:67, 76.

[44] T.A.H. 10:21.

[45] T.A.H. 2:92.

[46] T.A.H. 4:475.

[47] T.A.H. 15:87.

[48] T.A.H. 7:133.

If soldiers-turned-merchants became increasingly common in the seventeenth century, so too did merchants-turned-soldiers. In Candia, as elsewhere in the empire, urban merchants and craftsmen established relationships with the various military corps, either as a way of gaining privilege or out of duress.[49] Many poor urban residents simply enrolled themselves in the corps and this, too, contributed to the extremely rapid growth of the urban "military" population.[50]

Thus in seventeenth-century Ottoman cities we see the proliferation of a new group of individuals, "half civilian, half military" in André Raymond's words, whose names were on the military lists but who had no military background and were highly unlikely to serve in any case. As the line between the civilian and military population (at least for the Muslims) became increasingly blurred, new terms were created as a way of trying to establish and maintain difference. These individuals went by various names: *yamak* (literally, recruit) in the Balkans, *yoldaş* in Cairo, and *beşe* in Candia.[51] The term beşe is extremely common in the Cretan court documents

[49] Ottoman historians disagree on the effects of military control over merchants and craftsmen. Suraiya Faroqhi writes on Cairo in the second half of the seventeenth century: "By and large the corps provided effective protection against the exactions of Mamluk beys and Ottoman governors and the later years of the seventeenth century, when the power of the corps reached its apogee, were also a time of prosperity for merchants and artisans." Faroqhi, "Social Life in Cities," 595. Bruce McGowan takes a very different view of Cairo in the eighteenth century: "But Janissary control of the corporations seems to have gone farther here than at Istanbul since craftsmen also were placed under 'protection' by the Janissary *agha*. . . . Little wonder that the average income of Cairo's craftsmen, who comprised half the city's population, declined drastically during the course of the century." "Merchants and Craftsmen," in Inalcık, *The Economic and Social History of the Ottoman Empire*, 706.

[50] The lucrative trade in janissary pay stubs was, of course, vastly important in inflating the rolls. But this phenomenon is not directly related to the changing nature of Muslim urban populations in the seventeenth and eighteenth centuries.

[51] The term *beşe* was also used in Bulgaria. Rossitsa Gradeva, "War and Peace along the Danube: Vidin at the End of the Seventeenth Century" (paper presented at a conference on *The Ottomans and the Sea* at the Skilliter Centre for Ottoman Studies, Newnham College, Cambridge University, 29–30 March 1996). McGowan discusses yamaks: "By the late eighteenth century virtually all the Muslim guildsmen of Belgrade, Sarajevo and Salonica called themselves janissaries or at least recruits (*yamaks*)." McGowan, "Merchants and Craftsmen," 702. On the eve of the Serbian uprising (1804) during the Napoleonic Wars it was the yamaks who stayed behind while imperial troops went off to fight on the European front. We know more about this process in Cairo than we do in any other Ottoman city, thanks to the work of Andre Raymond. The term used in Cairo was *yoldaş*. Andre Raymond, *Artisans et commercants au Caire au XVIII siècle* (Damascus: Institut Français de Damas, 1973), 2:728. Daniel Crecelius and 'Abd al-Wahhab Bakr, who have edited a seventeenth century chronicle by a soldier stationed in Cairo, make the relationship even clearer: "As used by al-Damurdashi, the term *yoldash* refers to the common troops in the regiments. *Ojaqs* used to accept the tradesmen and craftsmen into the ranks in return for a sum of money. The tradesmen and craftsmen then fell under the protection (*himaya*) of the *ojaqs*. These civilians, who were recognized formally as members of the corps, were called *yodashat, aldashat,* or *yoldashat himaya*." Ahmad Damurdashi, *al-Damurdashi's Chronicle of Egypt, 1688–1755,* trans. and annotated by Daniel Crecelius and 'Abd al-Wahhab Bakr (Leiden: E. J. Brill, 1991), 128. In at least one case the court in Candia used both terms, yoldaş and beşe, to refer to a particular soldier. T.A.H. 2:67.

and I believe that it indicates precisely one of these individuals who stood midway between the civilian and military populations. The term was applied only to nonranking soldiers, never to officers such as aghas or çorbacis.[52]

The frequent use of the term beşe in the court records of Candia is a clear indication that many "soldiers" were, in fact, ordinary urban residents who had managed, somehow or other, to establish a relationship with one of the military corps in the city. In addition the extant comments of several observers indicate that this was so. Pococke, in Crete in the 1730s, wrote:

> There are in the garrisoned towns seven military bodies: First the janissaries, of which there are in each a certain number of different companies, or chambers called odas. But besides these there are a great number of janissaries called jamalukes who belong to chambers which are in other parts of the empire, and are settled here as merchants or tradesmen, and yet receive their pay as janissaries; and if any one of the companies are ordered away, those only go who please, and they make up their number as they can, and then the persons who refuse to go belong no more to that company, but they frequently go to Constantinople to be put into another company, and return to Candia with a patent to receive their pay.[53]

Even well into the nineteenth century, after the first violent incidents related to the Greek War of Independence had broken out on the island, a Greek priest referred to the relationships of protection and patronage established between artisans and merchants and local strongmen: "In order to avoid injury, many Christian artisans accepted Turks as partners and merchants chose as commercial partners the most notorious, fearless, and the strongest (among the Turks) in order to be protected."[54]

The ordinary soldiers of early Ottoman Candia were not so much soldiers—although there certainly were some—as they were Muslims (and some Christians) who belonged to various military corps as a way of pursuing their professional concerns. Ottoman military commanders were aware of this situation. On the eve of the war with the Hapsburgs in 1683, the governor of Candia worried to the janissary agha about the state of the troops in Crete:

---

[52] Damurdashi, *Chronicle of Egypt*, 21. A çorbaci was a captain in the janissary corps.

[53] Richard Pococke, *A Description of the East* (London, 1739), 2:267. There was no military regiment in Candia known as the jamalukes. It is probably a garbled version of the word *cema'at* or regiment, which was one of the organizational divisions of the janissary corps.

[54] This is from a chronicle of a monastery, written in Crete in the wake of the 1821 uprising. Nicholas V. Tomadakēs, "E Iera Monē Agias Triados tōn Tzangarolōn en Akrotirio Melecha Krētēs" (The Blessed Monastery of the Holy Trinity on Cape Melecha in Crete), *Hetaireia Byzantinōn Spoudōn* 9 (1932): 319. André Raymond discusses this type of arrangement in his article "Soldiers in Trade: The Case of Ottoman Cairo," *British Journal of Middle Eastern Studies*, 18 no. 1 (1991): 16–37.

"The Vezir says that the place [*piazza*] lacks troops. There are only a few janissaries. They can be trusted [*che si può fidare à questi*] but the Greek renegades have become Turks only to avoid the cizye [*ma questi renegati Villani Grechi, che per fuggir Carazzi si sono fatti Turchi*] and, by implication, cannot be trusted. They do not know how to handle the weapons and would only cause confusion [*che non sanno maneggiare Armi sorte alcuna, ne vagliono per altro, che per far confusion in tempo di bisogno*]."[55]

The nature of the janissary corps, then, in Candia (and probably in the other Cretan cities as well) was little different from elsewhere in the empire. What is striking about Candia is how fast the interpenetration of the military and the general urban population occurred. It took until the end of the eighteenth century for virtually all of the Muslims in Balkan towns like Belgrade, Sarajevo, and Salonica to claim some sort of membership in the janissary corps.[56] Andre Raymond also describes a gradual process for Cairo, where extensive ties between the local population and the militias took over a century to develop.[57] In Candia the Venetians wrote the following less than two decades after the fall of the city to the Ottomans: "On the island there are not any Turks who don't draw a salary or have a village and who are not enrolled in the above-mentioned corps. Similarly, there are not more than about 900 renegades on the island who don't draw a salary and who are not enrolled in the above-mentioned corps."[58]

In that same report the writer added that there were over 1,000 adolescents and children (*putelezzi et bambini*) between the ages of ten and twelve who were drawing a stipend but who were completely incompetent.[59] It is not surprising that, when the Venetians tried to retake Chania in the summer of 1692, the Ottomans were not able to round up more than 4,000 men in the entire island.[60] The military became synonymous with the (Muslim) urban population in Candia with uncommon speed. Thus Pococke wrote: "There are in Candia six thousand men belonging to the six bodies of the Turkish soldiery, but those include all the Turks who are fit to bear arms for they all belong to some military body."[61]

---

[55] Copia di Lettera scritta dal Confidenti di Candia all Ecc(mo) Sig. Pietro Querini Prov(v) Estr. alla Suda collas: sotto li 24 Agto 1683 S.V. Archivio di Stato, Venice, Senato, Provveditori da Terra e da mar, Lettere del. Provv. straordinario a Suda, Busta 888.

[56] McGowan, "Merchants and Craftsmen," 702.

[57] Raymond, *Artisans et Commercants,* 725.

[58] "Nelle Piazze non [   ] e [   ] turco, che non tiri paga o vilaggio e che non sia notato alli sopradetti generi. In tutto il Regno non si sono che 900 in circa rinegati che non tiri paga, e che non siano notati." Archivio di Stato, Venice, Senato, Provveditori da Terra e da mar, Lettere del. Provv. straordinario a Suda, Busta 889.

[59] "Dal numero delli sudetti passano mille in putelezzi, bambini, che Latano insino L'eta di dicci, in dodeci anni, che godono per buoni menti de Padri Li Loro stipendi ma inutili totalmente." Ibid.

[60] Tournefort, *A Voyage,* 41. In Chania itself at the time of the siege there were barely 200 men in the town fit to bear arms. Ibid., 20.

[61] Pococke, *A Description,* 257.

There is nothing in the sources to indicate why or how the Muslim population in Candia (and evidently in Crete as a whole) became so quickly affiliated with the military. Probably it cannot be disentangled from the phenemenon of massive conversion to Islam. In the much earlier Ottoman conquests of the Balkans it had been possible to join the ruling class, the askeri, as a Christian but by the late seventeenth century this possibility was no longer open. Membership in the military corps, however, had become easier. Admittedly the janissaries were no longer the well-paid force that they had once been, but some sort of a liaison with the military was clearly still attractive to many people. Cemal Kafadar has suggested that a military connection was particularly attractive to the newly urbanized elements who flocked to Ottoman cities everywhere in the seventeenth century, fleeing oppressive and chaotic conditions in the countryside.[62] This makes good sense for Candia, where everyone was a newcomer.

In other words, it is doubtful that there would have been so many converts to Islam if the avenue toward a military career had not been so wide open. Tournefort was frankly puzzled by the extent of conversion, given that, in his view at least, the head tax was not a serious burden: "It must be confessed that these wretches sell their souls a pennyworth: all they get in exchange for their religion is a vest, and the privilege of being exempt from the capitation tax, which is not above five crowns a year."[63] What the converts gained, however, was not simply relief from the burden of the cizye but rather the generalized benefits of askeri status.

Second, it is hard to avoid the impression of widespread chaos and abnormality after the war. This impression comes, admittedly, from bits and pieces of scattered evidence, but it all points in the direction of a temporary relaxing of social boundaries and hierarchies, which may have facilitated massive entry into the military corps. The fact that most of the city's residents were newcomers would have contributed to the sense of disorder and confusion. Venetian reports make it clear that some high-ranking officers were local Cretans who were no more than adolescents. There was, for instance, Atraman Agha, "putelezzo di 15 anni natto in regno figlivolo[64] di Ziaboli rinegati greci," or "Mustafa Sagiol Allai bei giovine natto in regno," and "Cusleri (?) Sacola Allaibei ancor questo putelezzo, natto in regno."[65]

The conversion of women to Islam also reflects an anomalous situation. Individual women were apparently free enough to approach the court on their own and convert. The personal liberty gained by such a conversion could be considerable. Since under Islamic law a Christian man cannot be

---

[62] Kafadar, *Yeniçeri-Esnaf Relations,* 81–82.

[63] Tournefort, *A Voyage,* 9.

[64] In modern Italian it is *figliolo,* son or boy.

[65] The word *putelezzo* is very common and refers to an adolescent.

married to a Muslim woman (the reverse is permitted), a Christian woman could dissolve her marriage by converting to Islam, and the court records in Candia contain such cases.[66] In the case of newly converted Ayşe hanım, no sooner had she dissolved her marriage with Michael, who refused to convert, than she turned around and married Ali b. Abdullah, no doubt a convert himself. It seems highly likely that a previous relationship had existed between Ayşe and Ali.[67] By converting and *not* remarrying, a woman could not only rid herself of a husband but also gain legal control over her children. In 1083/1673 a woman from the island of Santorini named Maria became a Muslim, as did her two minor sons, Konstantinos and Andones. One day later her husband Ioannes was asked three times in court to convert to Islam and three times he declined. The marriage was dissolved; the legal status of the relationship between the father and his two sons was not commented upon.[68] Some years later, in 1118/1707 a villager named Sofia came to the kadi court to convert. She brought her small daughter with her, who also became Muslim and was renamed Ayşe.[69] The father was not mentioned.

Even the seemingly basic dividing line of religious identity appears not to have been firmly established in the years following the conquest. There was clearly suspicion about who was, and who was not, a Muslim. In 1081/1670 a guardian for a young boy went to court for his Muslim charge because the janissary kethuda had illegally collected the head tax from his young charge, who was the son of a convert.[70] There is also the strange story of Ayşe b. Mehmet.[71] Ayşe had been living with her mother, a Christian, when Ahmet b. Ali arrived from Galata and claimed that the girl was his niece, the daughter of his brother Mehmet, also originally from Galata, now deceased. She was evidently living as a Christian because her purported uncle accused her of apostasy.[72] Ayşe insisted that her father was Georgi, not Mehmet, but Ahmet was able to produce three witnesses (all from Galata) who swore that she was, in fact, the daughter of Georgi. Although this case is difficult to interpret, it seems entirely possible that, except for her father, all of Ayşe's relatives were Christian and that upon the death of her father she had hoped to simply melt back into the Christian fold.

[66] T.A.H. 2:18, 4:288, 16:165. The proceedure followed was always the same. The Christian husband would be asked three times if he wished to convert. If he refused three times, the marriage was dissolved. This happened in two of the cases; in the other the husband converted as well.
[67] The case is T.A.H. 2:18.
[68] T.A.H. 4:223, 288.
[69] T.A.H. 13:100.
[70] T.A.H. 2:106.
[71] T.A.H. 4:344.
[72] "halla mürtedi olmuştur" (Now she has become an apostate).

Certainly the extended upheaval of such a long war created a complex religious situation, to say the least, and the effects of this must have spilled over into the postwar period. Christian conversion to Islam and the related issue of crypto-Christianity are well-known phenomena, not only in Crete but elsewhere in the Greek world. In 1068/1658, while the war was still going on, the head of the Ottoman army in Crete sent a note to the kadi of Rethymnon, telling him that he had been informed by the circumciser (*sünnetçi*) Şeyh Rustem that many Muslims were trying to avoid paying their taxes, while at the same time they only appeared to be Muslims since they remained uncircumcised. The kadi was instructed to let the sünnetci proceed with the circumcision of all converts.[73]

What is less well known is that during the war years there were also cases of Muslim conversion to Christianity, seemingly out of a fear of an ultimate Venetian victory. Spy correspondence directed to the Venetian forces in Candia in the years 1660 and 1661 refers repeatedly to the *rinegadi*, by which they mean not Christian converts to Islam (as the term is used by travelers to Ottoman Crete) but rather Muslims who have become Christian.[74]

Finally, as discussed in chapter 1, the Ottomans relied in part on the fighting capabilities of the islanders in their long struggle for Crete. Fifteenth- and sixteenth-century conquests had relied much more on the professional army—the timariots and the janissaries—but by the seventeenth century irregular troops formed the backbone of the Ottoman army. Local participation in the war no doubt facilitated widespread entry into the military corps.[75]

Population Levels and Origins

Population estimates in the aftermath of the war can be made with more confidence for Candia than they can for the rural areas. In addition to the cizye survey from 1693, already discussed in chapter 2, we also have a considerable amount of information on the city's Muslims. The reason for this is that most of the city's Muslims were soldiers, and both the Ottomans and the Venetians were interested in knowing how many soldiers there

[73] T.A.H. 1:33. And not all converts had Muslim names. Thus we come across a convert named Varnalake (T.A.H. 8:125) who fled to the Venetians in 1684. The owner of a börek (pastry) shop in Candia was named Georgi Mehmet beşe.

[74] Ath. Karathanasēs, "Anekdotē allēlografia tou Fr. Morosini kai allōn Venetōn me Kretikous sta chronia tou polemou (1659–1660)" (Unpublished correspondence of Fr. Morosini and other Venetians with Cretans during the years of the war [1659–60]). *Krētika Chronika* 25 (1973): 22, 29.

[75] It was during the war with the Hapsburgs at the end of the sixteenth century that the Ottomans turned to irregular troops on a much greater scale than in the past.

were. Finally, the infrequent travelers who passed through Crete at this time were in a better position to estimate the city's population than they were to estimate the population of the island as a whole.

The best source for the non-Muslim population of the city in these early years is the cizye register of 1195/1693, which includes both the rural and the urban population of the island. In that year the tax collectors counted 426 Greek Orthodox, 126 Jewish, and 40 Armenian individual taxpayers within the walls of Candia.[76] It is difficult to deduce from this the total size of the minority community but given that this survey was carried out just two years after a major reform of the cizye system, it is safe to assume that the scribes were counting individual taxpayers, not heads of households.[77] If we consider the cizye payer, as an adult male, to be the rough equivalent of the Venetian "man of action" (*anima da fattione*), then ratios from the late Venetian period can perhaps be applied. This suggests a total minority population of somewhere between 2,000 and 2,500 souls.[78] It might well have been larger than that, since the long years of war would have increased the ratio of women and children to men.

Tournefort, who visited the city six years after the cizye survey, said there were 800 Greeks subject to the capitation tax, 1,000 Jews, and 200 Armenians. These numbers are very high if they refer only to taxpayers; more likely Tournefort was indicating the total size of the non-Muslim population, around 2,000 souls.[79] The cizye survey indicates that the Or-

[76] Maliyeden Müdevver, register no. 745. The non-Muslim population of Candia is divided up into six different categories: "defter-i cizye-i gebran taife-i Yahudiyan sakin der derun kala'-i Candia," "defter -i perakende taife-i yahudiyan ma'a sibyan," "defter-i cizye-i gebran taife-i Rumiyan der sakin derun-i kala'-i Candia," "defter-i perakende taife-i Rumiyan ma'a sibyan ve ehl-i safa'in," "defter-i cizye-i gebran taife-i Ermeniyan der sakin kala'-i Candia," and "defter-i perakende taife-i Ermeniyan ve ma'a sibyan." The word *sibyan* (boys, youths) is misspelled *sabiyan* in entries four and six. Since this word makes no sense, it is safe to assume that the scribe actually meant *sibyan* as it is, in fact, correctly spelled in the second entry. Why the Ottomans would specifically be counting boys is not clear.

[77] For the reform of the cizye system, see Suraiya Faroqhi, "Finances," in Inalcık *An Economic and Social History*, 532. Until 1691 the tax was collected from households rather than from individuals. Women, children, and old and disabled individuals were exempt. The reform of 1691, when the Ottomans were in dire need of more revenue, was a return to the Islamic system. Every taxable individual was to pay separately.

[78] See chapter 2 for a discussion of the relationship of the *anima da fattione* to the larger population.

[79] Tournefort, *A Voyage*, 42. Venetian estimates, while they exist, are of limited utility because they seem to refer to specific groups within the population as a whole. For instance, a report from 1694, just one year after the cizye survey counted 426 Greek taxpayers in the city, refers to only 200 "Greci Artisti e Mercanti." A report compiled sometime between 1703 and 1715 is more useful. It says there are 200 "Christiani habitanti in questo citta." This number seems very low. It may indicate that Christians left the city during the difficult years of the war against Venice (1684–99). Archivio di Stato, Venice, Senato, Provveditori da Terra e da mar, Lettere del. Provv. straordinario a Suda, Busta 890, 891bis. The Venetian reports, however, consistently report more Greeks than Jews, just as the cizye survey does. It is difficult to reconcile this with Tournefort's 1,000 Jews to 800 Greeks. Possibly he included a number of Jewish merchants residing in the city temporarily.

thodox population lived mainly, although not exclusively, in the outlying areas of the city rather than in the prestigious neighborhoods within the old walls. The survey distinguished between non-Muslims living "within the fortress" and those "on the border." By this expression, the Ottomans no doubt meant to indicate the newer part of the city, since Candia did not have an actual suburb or *varoş*.[80] A total of 276 Greek taxpayers were recorded "on the border" as against 150 "within the fortress." This settlement pattern is not unlike the Venetian period when the old city was the preserve of the ruling elites.[81]

The Jewish and Armenian populations did not follow the Greek pattern. Twice the number of Jews lived within the fortress as lived in the outlying neighborhoods, and the Armenians were more numerous in the old city as well.[82] This difference can be interpreted in several ways. It is likely that the Jewish and Armenian communities were more concentrated in mercantile pursuits and thus tended to congregate down by the port. The Greek population, being larger and so more diverse, no doubt included people of modest means who would have been attracted to the less expensive housing available further out of the city center. It is unlikely that the Greeks were prevented from settling in the old city due to concerns about their loyalty. A large enough number (150 taxpayers and their dependents) did live there to preclude the idea of a policy of exclusion, and court documents hint at an important Christian role in the city from the earliest years of Ottoman rule. A Christian named Paschalēs bought the tax farm for wax in 1081/1671.[83] In 1095/1684 (the year that the war with the Holy League began) a Christian grocer named Dimētrē was elected bazar başı, or head of the bazaar, an indication of Christian prominence in the city.[84] In the earliest list (1723) of soap producers in the city (soap was to become the most important industry in eighteenth-century Candia), a Christian appears among the six individuals registered by the kadi court.[85]

Information on the city's Muslim population is more extensive but also more difficult to interpret. The blurred line between the military and civilian populations makes it difficult to know who is being included in the frequent surveys of the military population, and the inconsistency in

---

[80] The minority populations are divided depending on where they live. For the Jews, for example, the scribe divides them into "defter-i cizye-i gebran taife-i Yahudiyan sakin der derun kala'-i Candia," and "defter-i perakende taife-i yahudiyan ma'a sibyan." The literal meaning of *perakende* is "in the margin."

[81] Archaeological excavations have revealed that most of the cisterns of Candia were in the old city where the Venetian elite lived. Very few cisterns have been found in the more outlying neighborhoods populated by the native population. Stergios Spanakēs, "Relazione de Sr. Isepo Civran tornato di prov r gen.l di Candia 1639," *Krētika Chronika* 21 (1969), 393.

[82] For the Jews eighty-five to forty-one, and twenty-five to fifteen for the Armenians.

[83] T.A.H. 3:252.

[84] T.A.H. 4:483.

[85] T.A.H. 16:144.

the terms used also renders comparison over time difficult. Despite these reservations, it is clear that at all times the "military" population was always much larger than the janissaries sent down from Istanbul.

A record of all the soldiers serving in Crete in 1080/1669–70, drawn up for the purposes of salary disbursement, listed almost 3,000 soldiers serving in the citadel of Candia, over half of whom were identified as local.[86] Reinforcements from Istanbul did pour in during the long war with the Holy League, when the Ottomans maintained more troops in Candia than they did in Belgrade.[87] In 1099/1688 the imperial janissaries alone numbered almost 3,000, not including other regiments in the city.[88] Yet in that same year a Venetian report listed 1,500 "Gianizeri Gerli Culi La piu parte greca del Regno renegati."[89] In fact the local corps of armorers (gerli zebezini), of bombadiers (gerli topicibasi), the troops of the fortress commander (dizdar), and the troops of the fortress in the port (Castello del Porto) were all identified as renegades in the report. Tournefort, visiting in 1699, said there were 1,000 imperial janissaries (kapikulu yeniçeri) but also 2,500 Local (yerli) troops as well as 1,400 Azabs and 1,500 Yamaks.[90] Writing in 1739 Richard Pococke said, "There are in Candia 6,000 men belonging to the six bodies of the Turkish soldiers *but these include all Turks who are fit to bear arms* for they all belong to some military body."[91]

The various reports from this early period indicate a military population that fluctuated between 3,000 and 6,000 men. This was somewhat more than Venice mantained at the end of the sixteenth century, a time of tension but not actual war. Jerome Dandini, a Jesuit who passed through Candia in 1599, noted a garrison of about 2,000 men.[92]

[86] Başbakanlík Arşivi (Prime Ministry's Archive), Istanbul, Maliyeden Müdevver series, Mevacib Defteri (salary register), no. 658. In this register 1,560 individuals are described as "yeniçeriyan-i yerliyan der kala'-yi Candia ma'a zabatan" and another 215 are described as "cebeciyan-i yerliyan i kala' i Candia." The muhafız janissaries (in Candia called mustahfizan), or those sent out from Istanbul to guard the most important fortresses, were only 801. A ferman to the defterdar of Candia, dated March 1671, is in close accord with these numbers. It lists 2,888 individuals serving in Candia, divided into yerli, cebeci, mustahfizan, and aza-plar. This is T.A.H. 3:245.

[87] In the year 1685 there were 13,793 muhafiz Janissaries stationed in thirty-six citadels throughout the empire, with the largest number, 3,086, stationed in Candia. Belgrade, on the front line with the Hapsburgs, had 2,358. I. H. Uzunçarşılı, Osmanli devleti teşkilâtindan: kapukulu ocaklari (The institutions of the Ottoman state: The military corps) (Ankara: Türk Tarihi Kurumu Basimevi, 1943), 1:329.

[88] A ferman from 1687 reveals that 2,728 dergâh-i mu'allem yeniçeri in Candia received a bonus upon the ascension of Suleyman II to the throne. T.A.H. 5:254.

[89] In Turkish "Yeniçeri Yerli Kulu." Lettere del. Provv. straordinario a Suda, Busta 888.

[90] Azabs were also volunteer irregulars, most likely locally raised. A Venetian report from the 1690s describes the 400 "Asapi" as "La più parte rinegati." Lettere del. Provv. straordinario a Suda, Busta 890.

[91] Pococke, A Description of the East, 257 (emphasis added).

[92] Girolamo Dandini, "A voyage to Mount Libanus; wherein is an account of the customs and manners of the Turks. Also, a description of Candia, Nicosia, Tripoli, Alexandretta etc. Written originally in Italian by the Rev. Father Jerom Dandini," in A General Collection of

Sources of Population

Probably most Christians, and many Muslims, were recent arrivals from the Cretan countryside who had come to take advantage of new opportunities now that the war was over and the Ottomans wanted to encourage settlement. We have seen that members of the local janissary corps were allowed to move into the city's deserted houses as long as they promised not to sell them. There is some evidence in the court records to suggest the rural origin of some of Candia's residents. In 1081/1671 Giannakēs Frankias, a resident of Candia, sold his house back in the nahiye of Kainourios to another Christian.[93] In 1084/1674 a Christian woman from Candia settled a ransom debt contracted twenty-seven years previous between her father and a man from the eastern district of Mirambello.[94] According to a Venetian spy report, the Ottoman governor of Candia referred to the converts as "questi renegati Villani Grechi," suggesting a rural origin for many of the city's converts. It is also possible that, when Candia surrendered, people who had been living in Chania moved to the capital city.[95]

But not all immigrants were from Crete. The Greeks who petitioned the court for land for a burial ground in the summer of 1082/1671 were not native to the island since they were identified in the documents as being from "the Greek community that came from other countries and is now settled in Candia." An Armenian group that approached the court with the same request may well have been recent arrivals as well, but the document does not identify the Armenians as such.[96] A few years later a Christian named Yannaki veled-i Panyiot asked the public treasurer for the return of his deceased nephew's property, which had been taken over by the treasurer when it appeared there were no heirs. Yiannaki, a baker, had emigrated from the town of Monemvasia as had his nephew. He was able to produce two other Christians from the same town to swear to the familial link, at which point the property was turned over to him.[97] In 1084/1673 a Greek from Arta in western Greece, now settled in Candia, was in court to sell his garden (*bahçe*) in Arta to a Christian from his

---

the *Best and Most Interesting Voyages and Travels* (London, 1811), 10:11. The original Italian version was published in 1656.

[93] T.A.H. 2:97.

[94] T.A.H. 5:124.

[95] T.A.H. 2:145.

[96] T.A.H. 3:7, 16. Separate Greek and Armenian delegations requested and received land to be used as a burial ground for the community. The Greeks were described as "ahir diyardan gelüp medine-i Kandiyede mütemekkin olan Rum taife."

[97] T.A.H. 4:206. The religious court records always distinguish between natives and immigrants. The neighborhood of residence is always given for a native, while the place of origin is given for a recent arrival. In this case Yiannaki is described as "fi'l asl vilāyet-i Rumeli'den Benefşe kazasi ahalisinden olub" and the witnesses as "kaza-i mezbûre ahalisinden."

hometown who was temporarily in Candia. When Recep b. Ali registered his purchase of a sword from Osman Çavuş b. Ali in 1085/1674 the court described him as an immigrant from Nauplion, in the Peloponnesus.[98] Haci Abd-ur Rahman and Haci b. Abdullah emigrated to Crete from Rhodes and entered into the coffee trade.[99]

Finally, an all too brief remark in the report of a Jesuit secretary to Pope Innocent XI raises the distinct possibility that some of the Christian refugees from Venetian Candia returned soon after they had left. Urbano Cerri, writing in the 1670s, gave the following account:

> The Holy Congregation, received at the End of the Year 1676, a Letter from one Andrew Barozzi, a Native of Candia, importing, that upon the Surrender of the City of that Name, all the Catholicks went away with the Venetian General, having a Promise that they should be maintained elsewhere; and that when they came to Zante, they were deprived of all sorts of Provisions, and forced to return into Candia and to be Tributaries to the Turk.[100]

When Randolph visited the city in 1680, he put the population at 10,000 plus "2000 Janissaries besides the Pasha's guards."[101] Randolph's description, vague as it is, implies that he differentiated between the local population of 10,000 souls and those soldiers in Candia for a three-year term of office. When one considers that the non-Muslim population was around 2,000 or 2,500 people in 1693, and that the local Muslim community throughout the period was certainly no less than 4,000 and perhaps as much as 10,000 people, it is safe to assume that Randolph's estimate was reasonably accurate for the first half-century of Ottoman rule in the city. Although the soldiers from Istanbul cannot be considered in the same way as the more permanent residents of the city, it is true nonetheless that they too settled in while they were there and were an integral part of the urban fabric. They established religious endowments, bought real estate themselves, and entered into the life of the city in numerous other ways.

When we consider that the city's population stood at 14,451 on the eve of the war, it is clear that—unlike in the rural areas—the effort to repopulate the capital city was fairly successful.[102] Rural folk, as well as settlers from further afield, were no doubt attracted by new possibilities

---

[98] T.A.H. 4:257, 5:160. For other examples of immigration, see 8:90, a Muslim from Yenişehir, and 7:82, a Muslim woman from Mistra who fled after it fell to the Venetians in the early 1690s.

[99] T.A.H. 7:86. They came sometime before 1691.

[100] *An Account of the State of the Roman-Catholick Religion throughout the World. Written for the Use of Pope Innocent XI by Monsieur Cerri, Secretary of the Congregation de Propaganda Fide* (London, 1716), 57.

[101] Randolph, *Travels,* 84.

[102] M. I. Manousakas, "E para Trivan apografē tēs Krētēs (1644) Kai o dithen katalogos tōn Kretikōn oikōn Kerkyras" (The 1644 census of Crete [found in] Trivan and the supposed list of Cretan families in Corfu), *Krētika Chronika* 3 (1949): 39. In 1659, eight years before

in Candia, and Köprülü was eager to have them come.[103] The Ottoman conquest of the city may have represented the first time that the rural population was able to come freely to the city and in great numbers. Because of plague Balkan cities had long relied on in-migration from the countryside to maintain their population, but this seems not to have been the case in Venetian Crete. In the wake of the plague of 1592 the Venetian official Filippo Pasqualigo worried about how to resettle the city:

> We can no longer settle [the city] with foreigners brought from the islands of the archipelago as was done in the past, when great areas of the island were destroyed by the continuous wars or by the southern winds. At that time they [the islanders of the Archipelago] were under the rule of the Greek emperors of Constantinople. At the time such a thing wasn't so difficult but now the world has changed and it is no longer appropriate to do this, but rather to try and repopulate the city with people from the countryside.[104]

The extent of the divide between city and countryside is made clear when Pasqualigo considers one of the benefits of bringing Cretan peasants into the city: such a policy, he writes, might induce the peasants left behind to take a greater interest in the city's defense since their relatives now live there.

The Control of Urban Revenue

Janissary control of rural tax farming was matched by its domination of the capital city's tax farms as well. The all important customs tax farm,

---

the beginning of the daily bombardment of the city, the Latin archbishop of the city estimated the population at 500 Latins and 10,000 Greeks. Setton, *Venice, Austria and the Turks*, 135.

[103] So in a limited way the depopulation of the countryside was related to the more successful effort to repopulate the city. In this sense Candia's development was not unlike that experienced by other seventeenth-century cities in the Arab provinces, such as Aleppo where peasants were fleeing the countryside (especially Armenians coming from Van) helped to swell the city's size. As with the court records in Candia, the court records in Aleppo identify where a person is from and many Armenians from the Lake Van area appear in the seventeenth-century registers. Bruce Masters, telephone conversation with author (1991). Of course, the relatively small population of Candia could not account for the full extent of rural population decline.

[104] "ne potendosi provederle di gente forestiera, come si fece anticamente, che in tempo, che l'Isola fu in gran parte distrutta, per le continue guerre, et da venti dall'ostro, con il mezo degli habitatori delle Isole dell'Arcipelago, all'horo sottoposte all'Imperatori Greci di Constantinopoli. . . . Onde, si come all'hora, fu materia non molto difficile, cosi al presente, havendo il negotio del Mondo mutato forma, non è bene pensarvi, per molti rispetti; ma prender altra risolutione, et con il mezo delle proprie genti, et habitatori del paese provedere al bisogno." Stergios Spanakēs, "Relatione di Me Filippo Pasqualigo ritornato di cap.o di Candia et prov.r della Canea 1594," *Mnēmeia tēs krētikēs istorias* (Monuments of Cretan history), vol. 3 (Herakleion, 1953), 115–16. By "continous wars" he means the rebellions of the Cretans against the Venetians.

which usually included the other major urban taxes as well, was under janissary control. Eight contracts for the customs of Candia port (*gümrük mukataasi*) during the first half century of Ottoman rule appear in the records of the şeriat court. In the year 1082/1671 one Süleyman Agha bought the customs tax farm.[105] This is probably the same Süleyman Agha who was described as the head of the Local Armorers (Yerli Cebecibaşi) in a tax-farming document two years earlier.[106] It is highly likely that he was a convert.[107]

Two years later another janissary officer, Abdullah Agha, bought the customs tax farm, which this time included various other revenue sources besides the customs tax. He subcontracted out the monopoly on wax to a beşe.[108]

Fifteen years later the same tax farm was purchased jointly by Ibrahim beşe—previously employed as the public weighmaster (*kantarci*) for Candia—and Haci Ibrahim.[109] Ibrahim beşe was certainly a soldier of low rank. A year later the former customs chief (*gümrük emini*) Ibrahim Çelebi bid 547,740 akçe for the tax farm, but Ali Agha, the agha of the harbor fortress (Su Kale Ağasi) offered 50,000 akçe more.[110] Ali Agha's petition was eventually rejected because "he does not have good relations with the merchant community and with the market in general," but Ibrahim Çelebi had to come up with an extra 50,000 akçe in order to secure the tax farm.[111] To do so, he brought in a partner, Ibrahim beşe, probably the tax farmer who had purchased the customs revenue the year before.

In the last three customs tax farming contracts that are recorded for this early period—dated 1099/1688, 1118/1707, and 1132/1720—the tax farmers were all janissary officers and merchants identified as janissaries. Part of the 1099/1688 tax farm was subcontracted out, again to a beşe.[112]

---

[105] T.A.H. 3:250.

[106] See chapter 1.

[107] Two Ottoman documents refer to him as "b. Abdullah." T.A.H. 3:79 and Başbakanlık Arşivi (Prime Ministry's Archive), Istanbul, Maliyeden Müdevver, register no. 2636. The Venetian reports consistently describe the Local Armorers as renegades, including the information in 1688 that the current head of the corps, one "Meemet Aga," was "nato in Regno."

[108] T.A.H. 5:132. The customs tax farm (*gümrük mukataasi*) included a head tax on visiting merchants (yave cizye), a tax on coffee (tahmis) and wax (şemhane), market dues (ihtisab), a tax for weighing and measuring (resm-i qintar), the tax on fermented drinks (bozhane), the tax on dyeing (boyahane), the tax on tripe houses (işkembehane), revenues of the public treasurer (beyt ül-mal), and a slaughterhouse tax.

[109] T.A.H. 4:295. This tax farm was described as customs (*gümrük*) plus a head tax on visiting merchants (yave cizye) plus unspecified "attachments" (mülhakat). No doubt these attachments were the same as those bought by Abdullah Agha since the amount bid was roughly the same.

[110] T.A.H. 4:442.

[111] "mümaileyh ebna-i tüccar ve ehl-i suk ile hasen olmayub mezbur Ali Ağa mukata'a-i merkumdan ref' idub."

[112] T.A.H. 5:251, 13:99, 15:332. In the first case the Dergah-i Ali Cebeciler Başı, in the second to a janissary captain (çorbaci) and a merchant named Osman çelebi, in the third

The janissaries also moved swiftly to establish their control over the salt that was gathered near Spinalonga and sold in Candia. A note from 1082/ 1671 granted the janissaries the salt monopoly in the city.[113]

Alongside the tax-farming opportunities, a large chunk of the city's revenues were directed toward the many religious endowments (vakıf/ evkaf) that were established. In 1100/1689 eighteen endowments paid out over 1 million akçe annually in salaries of personnel employed by the various religious institutions.[114]

Soldiers were closely associated with the vakıf economy, both as founders of religious endowments and as administrators.[115] Abd ur-Rahman Agha, the head of the imperial janissaries whose foundation was discussed earlier, appointed a beşe as the mütevelli or administrator of his foundation.[116] Other high-ranking officers followed suit, establishing endowments and appointing both ranking and ordinary soldiers as administrators of the urban revenues dedicated to the foundations.[117] The defterdar had an agha, possibly a convert, as mütevelli of his vakıf, centered around the converted Church of San Marco, in the very heart of the city.[118] The kethuda of the imperial janissaries named a beşe as his mütevelli.[119]

Intercommunal Relations

If we step back now and consider early Ottoman Candia as a whole, it must be admitted that the emerging picture is a sobering one. Here was a city filled with recent converts to Islam, many of whom were also new arrivals from the countryside. Some of the highest military posts were filled by local young men, little more than boys, who evidently managed to capitalize on their willingness to convert. The arrogance of the young, the

---

and final case to Ali çelebi, a janissary merchant. For more on the janissary merchants, see chapter 5.

[113] T.A.H. 3:250.

[114] T.A.H. 5:257. For an idea of the numbers employed by the religious endowments, we may look at the endowment deed of Abd-ur Rahman Agha, which dates from 1670. T.A.H. 2:111. The proceeds of the vakıf went to support seventeen different positions including a preacher, Koran readers, an inspector and an overall administrator. Often one person would hold more than one position so the endowment employed something fewer than seventeen people and paid out 147 akçe a day in salaries and expenses.

[115] The largest endowments, however, were founded by officials associated with the palace such as the valide sultan (queen mother) and the grand vezir. See T.A.H. 5:257.

[116] See T.A.H. 3:169 where Mehmet beşe b. Mehmet appeared in court to arrange for water rights for the janissary agha's foundation.

[117] Several kethudas and aghas established endowments in the first two decades of Ottoman rule in Candia. T.A.H. 5:257.

[118] See T.A.H. 3:171 where his mütevelli, Ahmet Agha b. Abdullah, came to court on matters connected with the vakıf.

[119] T.A.H. 3:226.

zeal of the convert, and the peasant's resentment of the city could be expected to combine into a fearsome mix in Candia, particularly for the Christians.

This is exactly what some historians of Ottoman Crete have argued. Detorakēs calls the Islamicized Cretans "the terrible Turco-Cretans" and "the notorious Turco-Cretans who were often more savage and tougher than the true Muslims." Vasileiou Psilakēs, who early in this century wrote a history of Crete, said "The atrocities of this class surpassed even that of the most monstrous crimes."[120]

This view of Cretan history fits into a larger argument made by Ottoman historians, which sees military, and specifically janissary, rule in the seventeenth and eighteenth centuries as a disaster for the local population. The Muslim soldiers of local origin were particularly notorious in the Balkan provinces of the empire. The abuses of the dahi class, as the janissaries around Belgrade were known, led directly to the peasant uprising in Serbia in 1804, which launched the Serbians on the long road to independence.[121]

Historians of the empire, particularly those working on the Arab provinces, have recently begun to reconsider this view. For one thing, it fails to distinguish between urban and rural experience.[122] In the cities the janissaries could act as the defenders of local interest against Ottoman officials, as Suraiya Faroqhi has argued for Cairo. They also provided an avenue of social mobility as certain members of the subject population, by joining the military corps, secured a modest position in the ruling class. Thus the transformation of the military into a paramilitary actually

---

[120] Theocharis Detorakēs, *Istoria tēs Krētēs* (History of Crete) (Athens: 1986), 113, and "E Tourkokrateia stēn Krētē" (The Turkish period in Crete), in *Krētē: Istoria kai politismos*, (Crete: History and civilization) ed. N. Panagiotakēs (Herakleion: Synthesus Topikōn Enōseōn Deniōn kai Koinotētōn Krētēs, 1988), 353. Psilakēs is speaking specifically of Venetian converts to Islam who, he said, "combined the fanaticism of the newly converted with the traditional Venetian hatred for the Orthodox." Vasileiou Psilakēs, *Istoria tēs Krētēs* (History of Crete) (Chania, 1909; reprint, Athens: Akradi, 1970), 3:8–9. All the cases of Venetian conversion to Islam concern the western part of the island, around Chania. This phenomenon is noticeably absent in Candia. Robert Pashley, who was in Crete for a number of months in 1834, was equally negative about the local converts to Islam: "In one or other of their regiments almost every Cretan Mohammedan was enrolled; and it is easy to conceive what must have been the condition of the Christian population." Robert Pashley, *Travels in Crete* (1837; reprint, Athens: Dion N. Karavias, 1989), 1:xxi.

[121] Charles Jelavich and Barbara Jelavich, *The Establishment of the Balkan National States, 1804–1920* (Seattle: University of Washington Press, 1977), 26–29.

[122] Most of the work on the social relations of the seventeenth and eighteenth centuries has focused on the conflict between city and countryside. Much less is known about the urban experience, particularly with regard to intercommunal relations. Faroqhi writes, "But on the whole, little is known about social relations between Muslim and non-Muslim townsmen." Faroqhi, "Social Life in Cities," 603.

stabilized Ottoman rule in Cairo, rather than hastened its demise as in Belgrade.[123]

Adel Manna has suggested the same dynamic for eighteenth-century Jerusalem where "the localization of the janissaries made them potential rebels and protectors of the inhabitants rather than representatives of the Ottoman authority."[124]

Whether this model of urban life could also apply to the Christian-Balkan cities of the empire is a question for the future. What can be said at this point is that, in the city of Candia, the Muslim and Christian communities were bound by numerous ties.

Both the court documents and travelers' accounts show that mixed marriages were not uncommon, facilitated by the fact that Islamic law permits the marriage of a Muslim man with a Christian woman (but not the reverse).[125] These Muslim-Christian unions did not take place in isolation, outside of society, but in fact received the imprimatur of important institutions. From the court records we know that the Muslim courts had no objection to registering these marriages. Even on the Christian side there is evidence that the church—admittedly at the low level of the village priest—was willing to bless these marriages. An anonymous chronicle written by a monk, early in the nineteenth century, complained, "Sometimes the Turks interfered in religious matters. . . . They interfered in the marriages and baptisms of Christians by being *koumbari* and taking their children for baptism. They got the priest to crown the [wedding] couple, and he would often do this illegally and without the permission

[123] "In eighteenth century Istanbul, Cairo and many Rumelian cities, a large number of artisans were members of one or the other paramilitary corps. This was a comparatively new development. . . . The change largely occurred in the seventeenth century, and to date has been well studied only in the case of Cairo." In Cairo it was the wealthiest merchants that sought military protection most assiduously: "Since the corps farmed a considerable number of urban dues, which were collected from the same craftsmen and merchants, the chiefs of the corps possessed a means of pressuring the more recalcitrant Cairenes to comply. In exchange for this protection, merchants and artisans paid a fee to the corps. In addition, about 1/10th of the estate of every protected 'member' of the corps was turned over to the organization after his death. By and large the corps provided effective protection against the exactions of Mamluk beys and Ottoman governors and the later years of the seventeenth century, when the power of the corps reached its apogee, were also a time of prosperity for merchants and artisans. . . . the close connection between merchants and craftsmen on the one hand, and the corps on the other, provided an avenue for social mobility as certain members of the taxpaying subject population entered the ruling class. From this point of view, the transformation of the military into a paramilitary corps may well be regarded as one of the factors stabilizing Ottoman rule in the provinces." Ibid., 593.

[124] Adel Manna, "The Rebellion of Naqib Ul-Ashraf in Jerusalem, 1703–1705" (unpublished manuscript), 10. A Hebrew language version of this paper was published in *Cathedra* 53 (1989): 49–74.

[125] See T.A.H. 1:3; 2:11–14, 21, 117; 3:2, 11; 4:344; 8:45, 13:77, for examples of these mixed marriages.

of either the higher clergy or of the parents."[126] This account, incidentally, shows that ties of godparentage also linked the two communities, a phenomenon that Sieber encountered as well.[127]

Mixed marriages produced Muslim children (according to Islamic law, the father's religion determines the religion of the child) who had Christian mothers. Conversion, too, resulted in Muslim children with Christian parents. It is not surprising that the bond of parent and child cut across different religious affiliations. Such was the case of a Muslim daughter who came to court on behalf of her Christian mother to complain that her mother was still being harassed by Hassan Bey, who had divorced her three days previous. Two other Beys from the same village supported the daughter's suit and Hassan Bey was told to stay away from the woman.[128] A Muslim named Mustafa represented his Christian father in court in order to make sure that his father received all his (the father's) deceased daughter's property, against the claims of the daughter's Muslim husband.[129] In 1081/1671 Yusuf Çelebi came to court with his father, Nicholas, to register the sale of a vineyard.[130]

In court proceedings in Candia Christians and Muslims were willing to testify on each other's behalf. Although, according to Islamic law, a Christian litigant would have to rely on a Muslim witness only in a case that involved another Muslim, in Candia Christians used Muslims even in intra-Christian disputes. Muslims also had frequent recourse to Christian witnesses and the court apparently accepted this testimony as legally valid.[131]

In 1081/1670 Apostolos Liontarēs became embroiled in a dispute with Metsos Stathē over a shop that they had rented in the city from the vakıf of Kethuda Bey. Apostolos claimed that he had bought Metson out, yet his former partner continued to occupy the shop. When Metson denied the charges, Apostolos brought in Ali beşe b. Mehmet and Mustafa b.

[126] "Eniote de oi Tourkoi epemvainon eis ta thrēskeutika . . . epemvainon de kai eis tous gamous kai stefanōmata tōn Christianōn ōs koumbaroi, kai anedechonto paidas ek tou agiou vaptismatos. Outoi ediōrizon, os epi to pleiston, pote kai pou na stefanōsē o iereus to androgynon. Pollakis kai aneu archieratikēs adeias kai afeseōs . . . estefanōnan androgyna paranoma ē asymfōna ek merous tou enos ypokeimenou kai aneu synkatatheseōs tōn goneōn." Nicholas V. Tomadakēs, "Syndomon diagramma tēs istorias tēs ekkēlsias Krētēs epi Tourkokratias" (A short sketch of the history of the church of Crete during Turkish rule), *Deltio tēs Istorikēs kai Ethnologikēs Etaireias tēs Ellados* 14 (1960): 15.

[127] Sieber's guide on the island was a man named Georgi, who had a Muslim godson. Sieber, *Travels in the Island of Crete*, 56.

[128] T.A.H. 3:11.

[129] T.A.H. 2:115.

[130] T.A.H. 2:93. See also 3:4 for another property sale between a Christian father and a Muslim son.

[131] Only a few of the very numerous cases can be cited here. For other instances of Muslims and Christians testifying for each other, see also T.A.H. 1:120; 2:60, 94; 4:94; 5:46; 10:23; 11:73.

Ibrahim and was able to win his case.[132] When Panayiot veled-i Kosta's shop was robbed in 1083/1672 by one Ahmet Bey b. Abdullah, he was able to get two janissaries, both converts, to testify on his behalf against Ahmet Bey.[133]

Eight years before the final conquest, when Candia was still in Venetian hands, two women came to the court in Rethmynon to complain that Mehmet Sipahi b. Ahmet was occupying a mill and a field that they had stood to inherit from their father. Mehmet protested that the property in question had, in fact, belonged to a Venetian named Yiannitzan Vrele and that the women's father had only had a sharecropping arrangement on the island. To support his case, which he won, he relied on four of the women's Christian covillagers.[134] When Hassan Bey b. Abdullah, a convert, was trying to retrieve a deceased cousin's property from the public treasurer who had seized it, he called in numerous witnesses to prove the familial connection. Among those called were four Christian villagers from the family birthplace (*maskat ras*) who affirmed that Hassan Bey's father, Georgi, was indeed the deceased father's brother.[135]

The court was also willing to accept a Christian man, Georgis veled-i Nikolas from the district of Monofatsia, as the agent (*vekil*) for a Muslim woman, Razie bint Abdullah, who was most likely a convert.[136] Georgis was selling a vineyard for her.

Finally, Muslim and Christian merchants each enjoyed commercial relations with merchants from the other community. These business ties will be discussed separately in chapter 5.

It is clear that converts and steadfast Christians remained linked through innumerable ties. This is not to say that religiously based animosity played no role in society. It is to say, however, that conversion in Crete did not automatically create a fierce and brutal divide between the two communities. A possible explanation for this may be a history of religious ambiguity that predated the Ottoman period. It is instructive to compare Sieber's remarks on mixed marriages in the early nineteenth century with those of a Venetian writing in 1589. Sieber wrote:

> The custom of young Turks to choose handsome Greek women, or to carry them off by force to make them their wives, is a principal cause that Christianity

---

[132] T.A.H. 2:54.

[133] T.A.H. 4:87.

[134] T.A.H. 2:9.

[135] T.A.H. 4:13. This case and others like it show that conversion did not cut the convert off from his extended family.

[136] T.A.H. 2:41. The nature of the ties between the two communities shows endless variation. See T.A.H. 7:99, the property distribution of a wealthy Muslim who left numerous bequests, some of which went to non-Muslims; or T.A.H. 2:45, where a Muslim resident

has found its way into many Turkish families, not only in Candia but in other parts. . . . The Turk who has thus become connected with the relatives of his wife, and in constant intercourse with them, governed by the beauty and talents of his wife, is often inspired by her warm attachment to her religion, with increasing indifference to his own. The children, more attached to the mother, are prepared for the part they will have to act as Turks, and Islamism is easily undermined in the heart of the child by turning it into ridicule. Thus a foundation is laid for an approximation to Christianity.[137]

More than 200 years earlier a Venetian official described a remarkably similar situation:

> Although the nobili Cretensi are descendants of residents of the city of Venice— both noble and ordinary citizens—they lost their privileges due to various misfortunes and now live "alla Greca" as do all the residents of the cities and indeed many of the nobili Veneti. The reasons for this are the strong influence of local custom and manners and respect for their wives who speak Greek and are all of the Orthodox faith. If the nobili Veneti were not threatened with the loss of their privileges if they embrace Orthodoxy, I believe very few of them would follow the Latin rite.[138]

Nor would the Islamic principle that the religion of the child derives from the father be unfamiliar to the Cretans. Unlike anywhere else in western Europe, Venetian law in Crete allowed for the possibility that an offspring's juridical status could be determined by his father's. If a son could prove that his father was Latin, even though his mother was a slave, he was declared to be of free status because Latins could not be enslaved. Whatever the reason for this innovation, which was peculiar to Crete, it raises the possibility that the Cretans were already accustomed to thinking in terms of a "public" religion (Latin Christianity, Islam), traced through the male line, which brought certain concrete benefits, and a "private" religion

---

of Candia sold his house and a field in the village of Panayia to two villagers, a Christian and a Muslim convert.

[137] Sieber, *Travels in the Island of Crete*, 58. In some cases Muslim landowners built private churches on their farms for their wives to worship in. Tomadakēs, "Syndomon diagramma," 17.

[138] "Et benche li nobili Cretensi habbiano per lo più tratta l'origine da questa Cittá, dalle famiglie de Cittadini, et da nobili ancora, che per diversi accidenti sono caduti dalla nobiltà; viveno nondimeno la maggior parte alla Greca; come fanno tutti gli'altri, che habitano nelle Città, et come pur anche fanno alcuni dei nobili Veneti, per la forza dell'uso del paese, et per rispetto dell'educatione, e delle donne loro' le quali, come il parlare, così anche usano quasi in tutil resto il medisimo rito Greco; et se non fosse l'impedimento, che haveriano li nobili Veneti nella prova della nobiltà vivendo alla greca, pochi credo seguiriano il rito latino." Stergios Spanakēs, "Relazione del Nobil Huomo Zuanne Mocenigo ritornato provveditore generale del regno di Candia presentata nell'eccellentissimo consillio 17 Aprile 1589," in *Mnēmeia tēs krētikēs istorias* (Monuments of Cretan history) (Herakleion, 1940), 1:13.

(Orthodox Christianity), which was maintained by the women of the family.[139]

Given the relatively small number of outsiders who were stationed on the island—the pasha, top janissary officers, and some of the military regiments—it seems much more likely that the more salient divide was between local society and the Ottoman officials sent down to rule over it. Something of the Istanbul elite's scornful attitude toward the local converts is conveyed in several of the Venetian reports. A spy for the Venetians reported a conversation that took place in 1683 between the pasha and the janissary agha, as they worried about the possible outbreak of another war with Venice.[140] The pasha was concerned that the place (*piazza,* i.e., Crete) lacked troops. The janissaries "could be trusted" (*che si può fidare à questi*) but there were only a few of them. As for the Greek renegades, in the pasha's opinion they had become Muslims only to avoid the cizye, did not know how to handle the weapons, and would only cause confusion.[141] Several years later, another pasha of Candia worried that the sultan would call upon the janissaries stationed in Crete to go to the front in the Balkans. At that point the "Turchi veri" would leave and "solamente li Turchi novi" would be left to defend the island.[142]

[139] S. McKee, "Greek Women in Latin Households of Fourteenth Century Venetian Crete," *Journal of Medieval History* 19 (1993): 237. The categories of juridical status in Venetian and Ottoman society were, of course, completely different. The essential differences in Ottoman society were based on religion and the concept of civil status was unknown. Although slaves were extremely numerous, within the Muslim community itself the concept of a "free" Muslim versus an "unfree" one was nonexistent. Despite this difference, the nature of Cretan society under the Venetians—where the population was divided into Orthodox and Latins with important advantages accruing to the latter—meant that the Venetian law served to differentiate the population on the basis of religion. This would have been familiar to the Ottomans.

[140] Copia di Lettera scritta dal Confidenti di Candia all Ecc(mo) Sig. Pietro Querini Prov(v) Estr. alla Suda collas: sotto li 24 Agto 1683 S.V. Lettere del. Provv. straordinario a Suda, Busta 888.

[141] "ma questi renegati Villani Grechi, che per fuggir Carazzi si sono fatti Turchi . . . che non sanno maneggiare Armi sorte alcuna, ne vagliono per altro, per far confusion in tempo di bisogno." Ibid.

[142] In a letter dated 17 November 1687. Lettere del. Provv. straordinario a Suda, Busta 889. This conversation records the attitude of the Ottoman elite toward the converts. A letter written by the metropolitan of the island of Limnos in 1500 gives a sense of the attitude of local Christians toward their fellow islanders who chose to convert. A Muslim convert named Soulayimaneis Agalianos, from a prominent family, retained his position on the island's Council of Elders, despite his conversion. Thirteen Christians served on the council along with three local converts to Islam. In his letter to Mount Athos, the metropolitan referred to the Ottoman rulers of Limnos as "foreigners" and "barbarians," but he did not apply these epithets to the local converts. Heath Lowry, "The Island of Limnos: A Case Study on the Continuity of Byzantine Forms under Ottoman Rule," in *Continuity and Change in Late Byzantine and Early Ottoman Society,* ed. Anthony Bryer and Heath Lowry (Washington, D.C.: Dumbarton Oaks, 1986), 248–49.

Four

Between Wine and Olive Oil

The Island of Wine

The economic history of Crete in the early modern period, to the extent that it has been conceptualized at all, has been presented in discontinuous and linear terms. The flourishing wine economy of the sixteenth century is followed by the black hole of the seventeenth century. Once the Ottomans arrive, economic decline sets in.

In this chapter I argue instead that in the course of 150 years, roughly the period between 1570 and 1720, the island moved through a cycle: the economy that emerged in the eighteenth century (after 1720) was not unlike that of the sixteenth century, although it was not identical. This cyclical movement is to be explained by certain enduring environmental and social factors, above all the ability to focus on profitable exports as a function of the overall military situation and the proven eagerness of local elites to respond to market incentives.

The agricultural profile of Crete has shown remarkable consistency throughout the island's very long history. Wine and olive oil, followed by cheese, have always been the most important commercial crops.[1] The balance between the two, however, has shifted on more than one occasion. Crete has also swayed between the two poles of a monoculture agriculture oriented toward export and a more diversified economy. Between the late sixteenth century and the early eighteenth century the island moved through one of these periods of reorientation.

In the fifteenth and sixteenth centuries Crete enjoyed notoriety as a producer of celebrated sweet wines, of which the wine known as malvasia was the most famous.[2] Exports of malvasia went as far as England, where several literary references to the wine survive, and from the beginning of

---

[1] Chr. Maltezou, "E Krētē stē diarkeia tēs periodou tēs venetokratias," (Crete during the Period of Venetian rule), in *Krētē: Istoria kai politismos* (Crete: History and civilization), ed. N. Panayiotakēs (Herakelion: Synthemos Topikōn Enōseōn Demōn Kai Koinotētōn Krētēs, 1988), 139, gives these three products for the Venetian period. Writing in 1818, the author of a description of Crete gives the same list but adds raisins. Zachariou Praktikidou, *Chōro-grafia tēs Krētēs* (Description of the places of Crete) (1900; reprint, Herakleion: Technical Board of Greece, 1983).

[2] The term malvasia—a corruption of the name Monemvasia, a fortified town in the southeastern Peloponnese—referred to both the wine and the grape that produced it. The heart of the wine district was in Malevizia, a coastal area just to the west of Candia. The

the sixteenth century an English consul was resident in Candia for the sole purpose of assuring the wine supply to his country.[3] As early as 1455 a Venetian administrator observed that the export of wine ensured the prosperity of the Cretans.[4] A large part of the population in Candia in the sixteenth and seventeenth centuries made its living from constructing wine barrels.[5] Braudel includes Crete among those islands where a monoculture economy was imposed in the sixteenth century: "Here . . . we must imagine a countryside converted by man for the cultivation of the vine, producing raisins and the wine known as malmsey."[6] The extensive cultivation of vines periodically threatened the island with famine, particularly in the seventeenth century when wheat imports from the Ottoman Empire had become much less certain.

The conversion of the island into a vast vineyard geared toward high-priced exports was very much a phenomenon of the fifteenth and sixteenth centuries. Earlier and later phases of the island's economy looked quite different. When the Venetians initially took possession of the island in 1211—as part of the division of the Byzantine Empire in the wake of the Fourth Crusade—they had little interest in what the island itself might produce. Rather they were concerned to have a reliable way station in their phenomenally lucrative trade to the Levant.[7] The port of Candia was important as a center for redistribution, as well as the home port for Venetian military ships patrolling the eastern Mediterranean. This view of the place of the island in the Venetian maritime empire was no doubt reinforced by the fact that the rural areas of Crete were in almost constant revolt during the first two centuries of Venetian rule. Such instability effectively prevented the extension of Venice's power, as well as intensive agriculture, beyond the three fortified cities on the northern coast: Candia, Rethymnon, and Chania.[8]

English called this wine malmsey. Moscato, or muscadel, was the other famous wine of Crete, produced from the muscat grape.

[3] Maltezou, "E Krete," 139.

[4] Ibid.

[5] St. Alexiou, "To kastro tēs Krētēs kai ē zoē tou ston 16th kai 17th aiōna," (The castle of Crete and its life in the 16th and 17th centuries), *Krētika Chronika* 19 (1965): 155.

[6] Fernand Braudel, *The Mediterranean and the Mediterranean World in the Age of Philip II* (New York: Harper and Row, 1973), 1:156.

[7] F. Thiriet, "L'empire colonial source de prospérité pour la dominante," in *La romanie venitienne au Moyen Age* (Paris: De Boccard, 1959), 303–9. Maltezou, "E Krete," 140, in her discussion of the Cretan economy under the Venetians describes extensive warehousing facilities. Sometimes the warehouses were so full that Venice had to send boats to unload some of the goods.

[8] Candia's fortifications were already old by the time the Venetians conquered the island. Chania, by contrast, was very much a Venetian creation. Built on the site of the ancient city Kydonias, it was little more than a settlement until 1252, when the Venetians fortified it and gave it the name La Canea. Theocharis Detorakēs, *Istoria tēs Krētēs* (History of Crete) (Athens, 1986), 143, and Nikolaou Stavrakē, *Statistikē tou plēthysmou tēs Krētēs* (A Statistical survey of the population of Crete) (Athens: N. Karavia, 1890), 168.

By the beginning of the fifteenth century, change was underway. The co-optation of the leading Byzantine families did much to derail the revolts and increasing demand in Europe created an incentive to extend cultivation in the countryside.[9] Venetian wars on the Italian mainland, as well as defensive efforts against the Ottomans further to the east, required huge amounts of grain, and Venice came to rely on the fertile plain of Messara, near the southern coast of the island, to feed its troops.[10] At the same time, increasing prosperity both on the Italian mainland as well as further west created a market for the island's sweet wines as well as other luxury products.[11] The three essentials of the Cretan export economy—grain, wine, and cheeses—were all cultivated in the hinterland of the capital city and exported through its port. Grain came from Messara to the south of the city. Cheese production was concentrated in the district of Pediada, just to the east of the city, which had a large number of goats. Vines covered the rolling hills just behind the city. Already important as a military base and redistribution center, the port of Candia now became the main conduit for the export of Cretan agricultural goods, as well as a breadbasket for the rest of the island. Candia's pride of place is conveyed by Civran's description: "The kingdom is divided into four territories: Candia, the capital city, with a fertile hinterland and the largest population, rich in every sort of grain, which is often sent to the other [territories]."[12]

Less is known about the agricultural economy in other parts of the island at this time. The major cities and most of the island's population were concentrated on Crete's northern coast and it is safe to assume that agriculture in the south—aside from the plain of Messara—was limited to a subsistence economy.[13] Crete has four principal mountain ranges, which

---

[9] There is a large literature on these developments. See Thiriet, *La romanie venitienne*, pt 3, chap. 1; Maltezou, "E Krētē"; Detorakēs, *Istoria tēs Krētēs*, 206–50; and Alexiou, "To kastro tēs Krētēs." This literature organizes itself around the Greek/Venetian (or Orthodox/Latin) division. For a revisionist critique that argues for a more colonial picture, with local elites often in opposition to the metropolitan city, see Sally McKee, "Uncommon Dominion: The Latins and Greeks of Fourteenth Century Venetian Crete" (Ph.D. diss., University of Toronto, 1993).

[10] Messara is the largest and most fertile plain on the island. Measuring twenty-five miles in length and three to four miles across, it has the benefit of being watered by two of the four principal rivers in Crete. The description in Praktikidou's *Chōrografia* (1818) makes it clear that Messara continued to be important during the Ottoman period: "the fruits (of this plain) feed not only almost the entire island, but are also sometimes exported to Malta and other islands" (31).

[11] Such as sugarcane. In 1428 the Senate granted a ten-year concession to Marco Da Zanono for the cultivation of sugarcane around the area of Apokoronas (on the northern coast between Rethymnon and Chania). For a general discussion of Candia's trade at this time, see Thiriet, *La romanie venitienne*.

[12] Stergios Spanakēs, "Relazione de Sr. Isepo Civran tornato di Prov. r Gen.l di Candia 1639" *Krētika Chronika* 21 (1969): 368.

[13] This was not always true. Gortyn, in the south central part of the island, was the capital of Roman Crete. The Arab conquerors of the island (ninth century) founded the city of

run like a backbone across the length of the island, effectively dividing it into northern and southern halves.[14] The southern half suffers from a number of disadvantages: very high temperatures in the summer as a result of the hot winds coming up from Africa, stony soil, and a lack of natural harbors along the coast. In addition, all of the mountains drop off abruptly on the southern side of the island, creating "a virtual wall along the sea," while in the north they slope gently down toward the coast.[15] The aridity of the south is reflected in the comments of Venetian administrators writing in the fifteenth and sixteenth centuries. Civran described the southeastern province of Sēteia as "sparsely populated and extremely sterile; it cannot feed itself without constant outside help."[16]

Although it suffered from undercultivation, the hinterland of Chania was apparently already the center of olive oil production as early as the late sixteenth century.[17] Under the Ottomans, when olive oil became the leading export, it would become the preeminent commercial city of the island. It is unlikely that Rethymnon played a significant commercial role in the sixteenth and seventeenth centuries because the Venetians repeatedly complained that the harbor was completely silted up. Rethymnon may as well not even have a harbor, Mocenigo said dismissively, since it could accommodate no more than one galley at a time.[18]

Any area without good access to the sea was necessarily isolated on the island because overland transportation was limited to mule paths, and primitive ones at that. This was true not only in the Venetian period, but under the Ottomans as well and continuing on up until modern times.[19] Dolfin Venier had grain brought back from Messara at the beginning of the

---

Herakleion (on the basis of a small settlement that was already in existence) and from that time on settlement has been heavily concentrated in the north.

[14] The four ranges are the Levka or White Mountains behind Chania, the Psiloritis range in the center of the island behind Candia, the Dhikti Mountains between Candia and Ierapetra and, on the eastern promontory, the more modest mountains of Sētia.

[15] Leland Allbaugh, *Crete: Case Study of an Underdeveloped Area* (Princeton: Princeton University Press, 1953), 42.

[16] Spanakēs, "Relazione de Sr. Isepo Civran," 368.

[17] In the context of discussing Chania's inability to feed its inhabitants at the end of the sixteenth century, the provveditore generale Mocenigo wrote that Chania's hinterland produced more olive oil than any other part of the island: "onde rende maggior quantita di oglio d'ogni." Stergios Spanakēs, "Relazione del Nobil Huomo Zuanne Mocenigo ritornato provveditore generale del regno di Candia presentata nell'eccellentissimo consillio 17 Aprile 1589," *Mnēmeia tēs krētikēs istorias* (Monuments of Cretan history), vol. 1 (Herakleion, 1940), 189.

[18] Stergios Spanakēs, "Relazione del Nobil Huomo Zuanne Mocenigo," 6, 179. Also Stergios Spanakēs, "Relatione dell Sr. Benetto Moro ritornato di proveditor general del regno di Candia, letta in Pregadi a 25 giugno 1602," *Mnēmeia tēs Krētikēs istorias* (Monuments of Cretan history), vol. 4 (Herakleion, 1958), 43.

[19] As late as 1953 half the rural villages of Crete still had no other form of transportation than mule pack trails. Allbaugh, *Crete*, 311.

seventeenth century on the backs of "small animals," probably donkeys.[20] French consuls in Ottoman times complained that olive oil, too, had to be gathered into "petites parties qu'on porte sur des mulets, en manière de cueillete."[21] Coastal trade, in contrast, was heavy and constant. Writing in 1629 Franceso Morosini stressed that the harbor of Rethymnon must be kept from silting up, since the traffic between the harbors of the northern coast was constant and heavy—"perche essendo la navigatione continua e frequentissima."[22] Boats traveling from Candia to Chania, he continued, had nowhere to take refuge if caught in bad weather and thus many boats got lost in the course of this journey.

The Seventeenth-Century Economy

The wine trade of Crete reached its height in the sixteenth century. Although no detailed study of viticulture in Venetian Crete exists, contemporary sources make it clear that, buoyed by the immense profitability of wine exports, local growers devoted more and more land to the vine.[23] By the turn of the century, however, the wine-based export economy was giving way.

The reasons for this shift were several. Venice was increasingly uneasy with the avid devotion to viticulture on the island. Its objections, as we have seen, were primarily military in nature. Venice was concerned that the island would not be able to feed itself in the event of war with the Ottomans. The grain crisis was only made worse by the fact that less and less Ottoman wheat was available for export due to a ban on exports. In a desperate attempt to deal with this situation, the Venetians began forcibly uprooting vines in the 1570s and continued to do so in the seventeenth century.[24]

---

[20] Stergios Spanakēs, "1610 a 9 Genaro, relation de s. Dolfin Venier ritornato di duca di Candia," Krētika Chronika 4 (1950), 330.

[21] K. Konstantinidēs, "Ektheseis kai ypomnēmata apo tēn allēlografia tou gallikou prokseniou Krētēs" (Essays and notes from the French consulate in Crete), Krētika Chronika 8 (1954): 329.

[22] Stergios Spanakēs, "Relazione Francesco Moresini provveditore generale nel regno di Candia 1629," Mnēmeia tēs krētikēs istorias (Monuments of Cretan history), vol. 2 (Herakleion, 1950), 20.

[23] Thus Giacomo Foscarini, the reforming provveditor generale sent down to Crete just after the loss of Cyprus in the mid 1570s, when explaining the lack of wheat of the island, complained of "the planting of vines over great areas and in the best fields near the cities, because they get greater profit from wine due to its high price. A field that gives 10 mouzours of wheat can give 20 barrels of wine, which is sold at high prices because it is consumed on the island, in the west and in the east." Foscarini's report, which is in the San Marco library in Venice, has not been published but Spanakēs has consulted it and quotes from it at length in the notes to the relazione that he has published. For the preceding quotation see Spanakēs, "Relazione dell Sr. Benetto Moro," 159.

[24] This has already been discussed in chapter 2.

In addition, both the the onset of economic depression in Europe and the beginning of sweet-wine production in the western Mediterranean cut into the market for luxury goods, like sweet wine from Crete, from the eastern Mediterranean.[25]

It would be a mistake, however, to assume that the production of wine on Crete simply ended. The very fact that the Venetians continuously had to repeat the order to uproot vines and plant wheat suggests that its effectiveness was limited. Exasperated administrators certainly felt that they were making little or no progress. Viticulture continued even into the Ottoman period. The market for wine did become more local and regional, however, and thus almost invisible to the historian. This neglect has several causes. Local and regional trade is certainly harder to document, whereas there are abundant sources for trade with Europe. But historians of Ottoman commerce—and in this case Venetian as well—have also been guilty of a disproportionate preoccupation with exports to the west, to the neglect of the local economy, which, in the Ottoman case at least, was always much larger.[26] Their bias reflects contemporary views as well. The French consul in Chios, writing in 1759, said it was wrong to regard the caravan trade with disdain. A merchant, he continued, would have to carry a load of merchandise worth twenty times the original to equal profits that can be made on the caravan trade.[27] Thus it is precisely in the seventeeth century—when its commercial economy was becoming less international and more regional—that Crete's economic history becomes obscure.

The production and sale of wine did continue to be profitable, therefore, but in a different way. First, local consumption probably grew as the island became the recipient of significant military reinforcements. The report of 1589, referred to in chapter 2, states explicitly that "due to the large number of soldiers stationed on the island, the price of wine, wheat, and

[25] Tim Unwin, *Wine and the Vine: An Historical Geography of Viticulture and the Wine Trade* (London: Routledge, 1991): 186.

[26] Historians of Ottoman trade and commerce are beginning to take on this problem. In his pathbreaking study of Cairo and its commerce in the seventeenth and eighteenth centuries, Andre Raymond points out that Egypt's exports to Istanbul alone exceeded those destined for Europe: 178 million paras against 156 million paras in the years 1776–81. The trade with Istanbul, moreover, exhibited a remarkable stability, free of the violent fluctuations that characterized exports to Europe. André Raymond, *Artisans et commercants au Caire au XVIII siècle* (Damascus: Institut Français de Damas, 1973), 1:188. Suraiya Faroqhi succinctly sums up the bias of the scholarship: "The over-hasty inclination to proclaim the demise of Cairo as a center of international trade shows the persistence of a Eurocentric bias, which renders economic activities not responding to European needs or demands all but invisible." Suraiya Faroqhi, "Trade: Regional, Interregional and International," in *The Economic and Social History of the Ottoman Empire*, ed. Halil Inalcık with Donald Quataert (Cambridge: Cambridge University Press, 1994), 507.

[27] H. Pigne, "Eksoteriko kai dianisiotiko emborio stēn Chio tou 18th Aiōna" (International and interisland trade in 18th century Chios), *Ta Historika* 5, no. 8 (1988): 116.

all other provisions has doubled."[28] This development was bound to be viewed with disfavor by the Venetians. Whereas in earlier times the sale of Cretan wine in Venice and beyond had been very profitable for the Serenissima, now Venice found itself in the position of having to lay out considerable sums for the purchase of provisions for its soldiers stationed on the island. In the case of Crete, even the preparation for war—extended as it was over many decades—contributed to merchant profits.[29] Writers on early Ottoman Crete are quick to assume that the large numbers of soldiers on the island due to continuing tension in the eastern Mediterranean acted as a drag on the local economy.[30] In fact, the soldiers may well have stimulated commercial profits, just as they had in the Venetian period.

Second, regional markets for wine may well have held up even as exports to Europe declined.[31] Although we have no statistics, it is known that Cretan sweet wines were enjoyed in the Ottoman lands, as well as in the West. Foscarini noted that the wine of Crete was consumed "on the island, in the west, and in the east."[32]

The growing importance of regional markets for seventeenth-century Crete represents another reorientation in the economy at this time, equally as important as the move away from wine. The island's horizons had already shrunk once in the sixteenth century as the Dutch and the English rerouted the spice trade away from the Mediterranean.[33] Now, in the seventeenth century, they shrunk once again as northern ships began to avoid Cretan ports. Civran lamented their absence in his report: "The refusal of foreign ships to come to the kingdom, as they used to, brings a not inconsiderable damage both to the republic and to its citizens. With

[28] See note 86 in chapter 2.

[29] Mocenigo complained of how the newly rich displayed their new found wealth "nelli loro vestimenti superbi, et in quelli delle loro donne superbissimi; et nelle feste et nei conviti, et nei mortorij." Such wealth, he said, had not been seen before the war (over Cyprus in 1570)—that is, before the Venetians had started pouring soldiers into Crete. Spanakēs, "Relazione del Nobil Huomo Zuanne Mocenigo," 207.

[30] Baladie, for example, assumes that "The existence of a large mercenary army and of a sluggish and corrupt bureaucratic rule are the most obvious signs of the island's decline. The maintenance of the army whose mission it is, among other things, to hold onto conquered territory, exhausts the island's economic resources." Yolanda Triandafyllidou Baladie, *To emborio kai e oikonomia tēs Krētēs 1669–1795* (The commerce and economy of Crete, 1669–1795) (Herakleion: Municipality of Herakleion, 1988), 39.

[31] Tim Unwin acknowledges this possibility in his study of the history of wine: "The expansion of the Ottoman Empire in the eastern Mediterranean, which through the fourteenth and fifteenth centuries, gradually led to the Islamic conquest of mainland Greece . . . had the effect of restricting wine exports to Christian Europe from this region, but it is unclear whether this was the result of vineyard destruction or rather a reorientation in trade." Unwin, *Wine and the Vine,* 186. In the case of Venetian Crete, of course, the restriction of wine exports to Europe had nothing to do with Islam.

[32] See note 23.

[33] The spice trade and luxury trade from the East in general is completely absent from the reports of Venetians in Crete at this time.

the export of wine, muscat, and other products, the kingdom became wealthy and revenues increased considerably."[34]

The absence of European ships was not due solely to economic depression in Europe. The development of sweet wines in the western Mediterranean, underway already in the late sixteenth century, must have made the wines available further east less attractive. Piracy was also an important deterrent, maybe the most important, although it is impossible to be sure. The Venetians certainly gave more weight to the pirates than to anything else. Local shipping suffered from attacks as well, of course, but as the distances were shorter there would have been a greater incentive to continue trading.[35]

Notarial records from the seventeenth century indicate the considerable evolution in Crete's place in the Mediterranean.[36] No longer a way station in the long-distance trade from east to west, it was now part of a dense web of local exchange. Venice continued to be far and away the single most common port of destination, but Istanbul and the Egyptian ports received a good deal of Cretan traffic as well.[37] Merchants brought citrus juices to the Ottoman capital and came back with dried fish and caviar. John Struys, a Dutch mercenary who served in Crete in the 1650s, testified to the high reputation the island's fruit enjoyed in Istanbul and throughout the eastern Mediterranean:

> Here I have seen the wine-stocks grow thicker than anywhere else, which is a great argument of the excellent soil, with which this island is blessed, and besides that the vast bigness of the bunches, weighing mostly 8 or 10 pounds a piece,

[34] "Anco la renitenza de Vasselli forastieri nel capitar in Regno, com'erano soliti, apporta non picciolo pregiuditio alla Serenissima, et a sudditi stessi, perche coll'estrattione de vini, moscati, et altro, si rendeva oppolente, e danaroso il regno, et li Datij maggiormente profittavano." Spanakēs, "Relazione de Sr. Isepo Civran," 423.

[35] "These [pirate] boats surround Crete, and not one single little boat dares venture out from the islands. And with the frequency of journeys of the feluches that come with great speed (from the islands) the pirates don't make any exceptions." Apparently the frigates from Tinos, with official dispatches, were often attacked. Ibid., 448.

[36] What follows is based on Angelikē Panopoulou's pioneering work on seventeenth-century commerce. She has examined almost 400 notarial records for the period 1608–13 and 1634–40 (these were the guarantees that had to be given before a ship left). The war years and the years immediately preceeding the war are discussed in the seven books of the notary Michael Peri, covering the period 1635–61. Neither source is inclusive of all shipping in and out of the port. See Angelikē Panopoulou, "Opseis tēs nautiliakēs kinēsēs tou Chandaka to 17 aiōna" (Aspects of shipping in 17th Century Chandaka), *Krētika Estia*, 5, no. 2 (1980): 152–210, and her "Syntrofies kai nauloseis pliōn sto Chandaka 1635–1661" (Partnerships and chartering of boats in Chandaka, 1635–1661), in *Pepragmena tou ektou thiethnous krētologikou synedriou* (Proceedings of the sixth international Cretological symposium) (Chania: Philologikas Syllogos o Chrysostomos, 1991), 2:419–30.

[37] In the period 1608–13 109 ships were destined for Venice, 39 for Istanbul, and 16 for Alexandria. Between 1634 and 1640 66 ships set sail for Venice, 16 for Istanbul, and 21 for Rosetta. Another 16 were heading for the Archipelago. These four destinations accounted for 70 percent of the traffic.

The old harbor of Candia (Herakleion) in the opening years of the twentieth century. Credit: Princeton University Library

and those so delicate that after I had once tasted of those could not for some years after so much as taste the Spanish. And not only grapes, but also every other fruit the land affords is passing good and delicate, in so much that not only the Turkish Emperor but all the Princes and Potentates near this island have their fruits from hence for table use and banquets.[38]

Traffic was heavy with the nearby islands of the archipelago and grew during the war years to account for almost two-thirds of the ships that came into Candia. An interpreter for the Turkish language and a consul (console di Levantini) from the archipelago were in place early in the century in order to facilitate trading links with the Ottoman ports around the Aegean, where the Cretans picked up grain and wood. Distant traffic from northern Europe was much less: one out of five boats in the earlier period and one out of ten in the late 1630s.[39]

Finally, it was the seventeenth century that saw the beginnings of the trade in olive oil, the commodity that would come to replace wine as the coveted item of Cretan commerce in the eighteenth century.[40] It is important to emphasize the early seventeenth-century origins of the olive oil trade in Crete. Venetian Crete has been seen as the island of wine whereas

[38] John Struys, *The Voiages of John Struys* (London, 1684), 2:102.
[39] The percentages were actually 20 percent and 13 percent, based on Panopoulou's work.
[40] It was used in the manufacture of soap and textiles.

Ottoman Crete became the island of olive oil.[41] This is misleading on several counts. It ignores the transitional seventeenth century and, by so doing, implies that the shift in commercial orientation was the result of the change in political sovereignty. This assumption can then be used to suggest that familiar duo, Ottoman "backwardness" and its corollary, Venetian (i.e., western) capability and skill. In her study of the Cretan economy in the eighteenth century, Baladie suggests that olive, rather than vine, cultivation flourished under the Ottomans because the olive tree was more suited to a backward economy.[42] Nationalist historiography has preferred to see the advent of Ottoman rule as a dramatic (and catastrophic) rupture from the past, both in Crete and elsewhere in the Greek world. The dichotomy wine-oil nicely extends the idea of rupture into the commercial sphere.

In fact, it is abundantly clear that olive cultivation was gaining in popularity long before the Ottoman army set foot on the island. In 1589 Mocenigo wrote:

> The planting of olive trees increased after the [recently issued] prohibitions on viticulture, and is increasing still. I am afraid that if things continue as they are measures will have to be taken to discourage such cultivation, because otherwise olive tree cultivation will intrude on the growing of wheat, just as has happened with viticulture. Today olive trees are being planted not only in good fields, but even in the soccori, which are the best of all, particularly in the province of Sēteia."[43]

The Cretans were certainly responding to the rising demand on the part of the English, Dutch, and French for oil.[44] Demand was apparently strong enough that the authorities felt constrained to step in to ensure that there would be enough for local consumption.[45] From their base in Rethymnon during the war, the Ottomans also took steps to forbid the export of olive oil.

---

[41] This is the argument made by both Baladie and Masson. Baladie, *To emborio*, and Paul Masson, "Les échelles du Levant," in *Histoire du commerce français dans le Levant au XVII siècle* (Paris, 1896), 429–31.

[42] "The requirements for olive cultivation are different than those for the vine. The production of high-quality wine requires significant investment and expensive agricultural equipment . . . The olive does not require skilled labor or constant care. . . . Usually just women and children gather up the olives, while the men occupy themselves with more taxing or specialized tasks." Baladie, *To emborio*, 134. She also cites a lack of hands, due to population decline, for the labor-intensive work of vine cultivation as well as Ottoman "indifference" toward vines.

[43] Spanakēs, "Relazione del Nobil Huomo Zuanne Mocenigo," 185. *Soccori* was a term used to refer to fields that were located very close to the village.

[44] Carlo Cipolla, *Before the Industrial Revolution: European Society and Economy, 1000–1700*, 3rd ed. (London: Routledge, 1993), 51–52.

[45] Panopoulou, "Opseis tēs nautiliakēs kinēsēs tou Chandaka," 154.

The new importance of the trade in olive oil was underscored by the bitter complaints on the part of local families against Andrea Corner, the provveditore generale of Candia when the Ottomans attacked. They accused him of cornering the trade in olive oil, thereby cutting them out of this source of riches.[46]

Because the metaphors of rise and decline are so ubiquitous in the study of this part of the world, it seems necesary to address the question as to whether Venetian Crete—and particularly its capital city Candia—was in decline as a commercial center in the seventeenth century. This is difficult to say in the absence of comprehensive statistical information. Certainly the situation was lamentable in the eyes of the island's Venetian administrators. Civran's description in 1639 was a litany of woes, but it was given in the context of declining customs revenue.[47] These problems were in part about declining Venetian control over Cretan commerce, rather than a crisis in commerce itself. Even in its own colony Venice was suffering the same sorts of setbacks that were becoming common all over the eastern Mediterranean at this time.[48]

Piracy was, of course, a serious problem and sometimes had the effect of creating a commercial standstill. The most convincing evidence in this regard is Civran's statement that, because there had been so little trade, no one had bid for the customs revenue that year. On the other hand, it is also true that commercial relationships developed between "pirates" and merchants on Crete, just as they did on the smaller Aegean islands. Sagredo's report from 1604 discussed this illicit market in some detail. The English pirates, after driving all the "merchants and good men" from the seas, came to Crete and bought up all the wine with the money they had amassed from piracy. They were so wealthy that they didn't mind paying outrageously high prices. This hurt the "public interest" in two ways: first, it raised the cost of the wine that was sent on to Venice; second, people were persuaded to abandon wheat cultivation and resume viticulture. Apparently the pirates loaded wine at points all over the island so problems of transportation were eased. The market between these unnamed traders and the English pirates was developed enough that the Cretans had begun

[46] For more on the complaints against Corner, see chapter 2.

[47] Civran spoke of various problems: the shortage of boats and the loss of more boats to pirates, the fall of the "principali mercanti del Regno" and the reluctance of foreign ships to come to Crete. All of these factors had contributed to a disastrous fall in customs revenue. Spanakēs, "Relazione de Sr. Isepo Civran," 422–23.

[48] The literature on Venetian economic decline in the late sixteenth and the seventeenth centuries is vast. See Carlo Cipolla, "The Decline of Italy: The Case of a Fully Matured Economy," *Economic History Review*, 2d ser. 5 (1952–53): 178–87, and Dominique Sella, "Crisis and Transformation in Venetian Trade," in *Crisis and Change in the Venetian Economy in the Sixteenth and Seventeenth Centuries*, ed. Brian Pullan (London: Methuen, 1968), 127–45.

to throw small amounts of red table wine into the muscat bound for England "because the English like the wine to have color."[49]

Just as Venetian merchants no longer enjoyed a monopoly over the island's commerce, the lucrative trade in luxuries that had showered so much wealth on these merchants was also in eclipse. Spices, of course, no longer came through Crete, and wine exports to the west were way down. But local consumption was strong, and regional trade enjoyed a newfound prominence in the seventeenth century. This regional and local economy was more diverse than the wine-based monoculture of earlier times. Early in the seventeenth century oil, wine, cheese, salt, and honey were all listed as important exports.[50] It is highly likely that the profits from the long-distance luxury trade were more spectacular than those derived from regional commerce in the Aegean. Even so, an increased volume of trade could have compensated for the more mundane nature of regional trade.

Finally, the late sixteenth and the seventeenth centuries saw the rise of a new commercial class in Crete, which will be discussed at length in the following chapter. The combination of a new commercial class, a shift in geographical focus, and a more diversified commerical economy suggests that the seventeenth century saw a reorientation in the island's place in the Mediterranean. This is a more productive description than decline.

Early Ottoman Crete

With the surrender of Candia in 1669 the Ottomans finally established themselves as the undisputed masters of Crete. Yet the advent of Ottoman rule on the island did not significantly interrupt or alter the commercial changes already underway. In light of some of the more immoderate statements that have been made, it is important to point out that the sultan certainly did not deliver the deathblow to the island's commercial

[49] "dilletandosi coloro che sijno carichi di color." Stergios Spanakēs, "E ekthesē tou douka tēs Krētēs" (The report of the duke of Crete), *Krētika Chronika* 3 (1949):524–25. George Leon's comments on piracy in the seventeenth century are useful: "The seventeenth century was a period of anarchy in the Levant; Christian piracy shifted from the Mediterranean to the Archipelago. Pirates of all states, and especially the French, were active participants in the second half of the seventeenth century. It seems, however, that the damage done to Greek commerce and to the Mediterranean traffic in general has been exaggerated. . . . In the Archipelago, where the poverty of most of the Greek islands and certain of the coastal regions often provided a stimulus to Greek piracy, maritime banditry was active in direct proportion to the commercial activity of the region." George Leon, "The Greek Merchant Marine (1453–1850)," in *The Greek Merchant Marine*, ed. Stelios Papadopoulos, (Athens: National Bank of Greece, 1972), 19.

[50] "On this island there is plenty of oil, wine, cheese, salt and honey. The taxes on the extensive export of these products is the most important source of public revenue." Spanakēs, "Relatione dell Sr. Benetto Moro," 4.

life.[51] If the commercial history of the island, and of the capital city, is obscure during the early years of Ottoman rule, the reasons for this obscurity are little different than those which apply to the seventeenth century as a whole. Trade during this period was predominately local and regional, and no one product dominated the trade. This kind of commerce does not produce a wealth of documentation. The Ottoman period does suffer from the additional handicap that the island's rulers did not produce anything like the reports that the Venetians were in the habit of writing upon their return to Venice. The commercial history of Ottoman Crete, like the general history of the island at this time, must rely on much more fragmented sources like court records, consular reports, and the observations of the Venetians based on Souda.

There were changes, of course. The most dramatic one, which will be discussed in the next chapter, was in the composition of the commercial class in the city of Candia. In addition, the constant pressure of grain supplies was temporarily overcome and Crete actually exported grain for a period of time. Egyptian ports, already important in the Venetian period, became even more so and North Africa appears for the first time as a trading partner. Despite this, the continuities are more striking than the ruptures.

Exports

Both French consular reports and Ottoman documents indicate a diversified export economy in Crete in the first half century of Ottoman rule. In addition to the major exports of wine, raisins, olive oil, wheat, and cheese, other products like honey, linens, soap, and beeswax were also traded.

Wine, for instance, certainly continued to be produced and exported. This is not surprising given there was an established local and regional market for Cretan wine. A customs regulation issued less than two weeks after the surrender of Candia described wine as "a source of livelihood for the infidels" and assigned the higher, infidel tax rate on its export.[52] Between 1694 and 1722 the island exported an average of 50,000 mistat per year on French ships.[53] Clearly this is an enormous drop from the

---

[51] "The desertion of the cities, now inhabited mostly by Turks, destroyed urban life and hence any possibility of cultural advance. . . . The Cretan economy fell back on underdeveloped forms of agricultural and pastoral life. Trade, at least in the first fifty years of the occupation, was essentially nonexistent." Detorakēs, *Istoria tēs Krētēs*, 271–72.

[52] T.A.H. 3:104. The expression is "*keferlere rizk olmaıǧla.*"

[53] These figures are from the Marseille Chamber of Commerce. Baladie, *To Emborio*, 191. A mistat was used to measure both wine and olive oil in Crete and was common to both the Venetian and Ottoman periods. A mistat of olive oil was worth ten okkas in Crete, a mistat of wine between nine and twelve okkas, depending on the place. See T.A.H. 1:3. The standard Ottoman okka (kiyye) was 1.2828 kilograms. Suraiya Faroqhi, *Towns and*

50,000 tons of wine exported from Crete in 1512, a figure often cited by historians of the Venetian period.[54] The wine economy was at its height, however, in the early sixteenth century. Because wine exports were more limited in the seventeenth century, it may be that 50,000 mistat was not unrepresentative of the century as a whole. In the absence of any quantitative information, it is difficult to say.

The limited evidence available, all of it from travelers accounts', suggests that malvasia, the famous sweet wine, continued to be produced (no doubt along with other, more ordinary, wine as well). Jean Baptiste Tavernier wrote that "out of the island of Candy strangers export great store of wheat and sallet-oyl, all sorts of pulse, cheese, yellow wax, cottons, silks but more especially malmfey, wherein consists its chief trade."[55] In 1680 Bernard Randolph observed, "The wines are generally esteemed above all others" and added that the red muscadine was richer than its counterpart at Cadiz and much more pleasant. He then added, rather oddly, "Some are of the opinion that in the Warr [sic] the Muscadine grape was lost."[56] The French traveler Tournefort, in Crete in 1699, was not able to find any malmsey but the wine he received as a present from the monks of Arkadi Monastery impressed him: "the color of Alicant, without any lusciousness, rich, racy, strong bodied, deep colored, perfumed with a penetrating spirituousness." Later he added, "The wines are exquisite: red, white and claret . . . with that delicious balm which, in those who have once tasted the Candian wines, begets a contempt for all other wines." Richard Pococke visited Crete in 1739 and wrote that "The country around Candia produces great quantities of excellent wines."[57]

An Ottoman survey of tax farms in Crete at the end of the seventeenth century shows extensive territory given over to viticulture. In central and eastern Crete vineyards predominated, followed close behind by wheat.[58]

Townsmen of Ottoman Anatolia: Trade, Crafts and Food in an Urban Setting (Cambridge: Cambridge University Press, 1984), 211.

[54] Detorakēs, *Istoria tēs Krētēs*, 214.

[55] Jean Baptiste Tavernier, *Six Voyages through Turkey into Asia* (London, 1698), 118. Tavernier did not actually disembark at Candia. He was sailing from Alexandretta to Malta when the ship was becalmed off the coast of Crete for two days. His detailed discussion of the grape harvest, however, indicates that he was well informed.

[56] Bernard Randolph, *Travels in Crete* (London, 1700), 92. Rather oddly, because he did actually drink a muscadine wine while he was there. He wrote "the red muscadine they call here Leattico, tis a much richer wine than Tent at Cadize, and much more pleasant." During the Venetian period "vini logadi" referred to wine made from a variety of different grapes, whereas Leattico was identified as a wine made from just one grape variety. Spanakēs, "Relazione del Nobil Huomo Zuanne Mocenigo," 525.

[57] Richard Pococke, *A Description of the East* (London, 1739), 2:257, and M. Pitton de Tournefort, *A Voyage into the Levant* (Paris, 1717), 57, 95.

[58] T.A.H. 8:110. The tax farm survey of 1106/1694 covered ten subdistricts out of fifteen in the districts of Sēteia, Candia, and Rethymnon. Fifteen different crops were subject to the tithe. Grains—wheat, barley and oats—accounted for just 51 percent of the tithe collected that year, vines for 38 percent of the total. Vineyards (*bağ*) were the most valuable tax farm

Given that wine continued to be produced, and given that Candia continued to be the city most closely connected with wine-making, it is disappointing, though perhaps not surprising, that references to the wine trade are entirely absent from the records of the kadi court in Candia.[59] All sorts of other commodities appear with regularity in the court records, but never wine.

Of course, the trade did not operate outside the purview of the court. There must have been commercial disputes involving wine, after all. Certain peculiarities of the court documents suggest that cases involving wine were adjudicated, but that all the parties to the proceedings maintained a studious silence as to the exact nature of the goods under discussion.[60] The wine trade did continue, therefore, but in a period that is already obscure, it is almost invisible to the historian.

Not all the viticulture in early Ottoman Crete was devoted to wine-making. Raisins were also exported at this time. French trade in raisins was erratic but grew steadily throughout the eighteenth century. Between 1694 and 1704 French ships exported on average 46,219 okka of raisins per year, an average that rose to 65,374 okka between 1704 and 1718.[61]

---

in six out of eleven *nahiyeler* for which products were individually listed; wheat predominated in the other five. The other crops were flax, cotton, silk, oil, beans, onions, fruit trees, almonds, walnuts, carobs, and cucumbers. Linen, silk, and oil each accounted for 2 percent of the tithe, all the rest less than 1 percent. The tax farm survey does not include the province of Chania, which was heavily devoted to olive oil production. If we had a listing of all the tax farms of Crete, the figure for grain would certainly be even lower. In its diversity the eyalet of Candia resembled the kaza of Izmir, also a coastal region. Goffman has pointed out that grain cultivation typically devoured over 90 percent of peasant holdings in Balkan interior and in the central Anatolian plateau, but that it accounted for barely 40 percent of Izmir's production. Daniel Goffman, *Izmir and the Levantine World, 1550–1650* (Seattle: University of Washington Press, 1990), 20.

[59] See chapter 3 for the involvement of the city's janissaries in the domestic sale of wine.

[60] We know that the trade in wine was dominated by Christians. It is also true that, although Christians appear in only about one-third of the commercial cases brought before the kadi court between 1669 and 1720, they are an overwhelming majority in those cases where the goods in dispute are not named but are referred to as simply commodities, goods (*emti'a*), which must have been cases involving wine. For more on this, see my "The Court Records of Ottoman Crete" (paper presented at the Middle Eastern Studies Association annual conference, Washington D.C., December 1995). It is possible that the court saw itself as being guided by maslaha, that is, a responsible concern for the public interest. This was the position taken by the *ulema* in the sixteenth century on the controversial institution of cash vakıf. See Jon Mandaville, "Usurious Piety: The Cash-waqf Controversy in the Ottoman Empire," *International Journal of Middle East Studies* 10 (1979): 289–308. After all, the wine trade was undoubtedly a source of prosperity for the city, and merchants could not be expected to participate in it if contracts were unenforceable. Therefore, the court was only promoting the good of the city by admitting cases concerning wine in court, albeit discretely. Alternatively, the court could have ruled on the basis of hila or "ruse" in the sense of deciding to treat the whole thing as a contract, and contracts must be honored, no matter what the commodity being traded is. I thank Ken Cuno for the insight on hila.

[61] The volatile nature of the trade is clear from the commercial statistics. The French exported 16,852 okka in 1709 but only 8,800 okka in 1710. They bought no raisins at all in 1711 and 1712. Baladie, *To emborio*, 191.

The Ottoman elite on the island seems to have been involved in the raisin trade as well. Among the possessions of the former governor of Crete Ahmet Pasha, executed in 1684, were 3,250 okka of grapes (*üzüm*) on a ship in the harbor, ready to depart for the capital.[62]

In a striking departure from the Venetian period, Crete actually became a wheat exporter for a brief period in the late seventeenth and early eighteenth centuries. From the tax farm survey of 1106/1694, it is clear that wheat cultivation was widespread.[63] Wheat was the most important crop in the southeastern district of Ierapetra and in the central district of Lasithi, the site of the fertile upland plain of the same name. In the districts of Temenos and Malevizia, which formed Candia's hinterland, wheat was grown exclusively. French sources show that grain, mostly wheat but also some barley, was exported from Crete once in the 1680s and then quite regularly between 1690 and 1714. As with the trade in raisins, grain exports were extremely erratic.[64]

Thanks to the Ottoman system of requiring export permits for wheat, there is also a good deal of information on the wheat trade from local court records. The great majority of grain shipments went to Benghazi, Tripoli (Trablusgarb), and Darnah in northeast Africa in the years 1110–11/1698–1700.[65] Over the course of those three years, twenty-five shipments of grain left Crete and sixteen were destined for North Africa.[66] The most distinctive aspect of this grain trade with North Africa is the fact that it was all bunched into the space of two years. There are sporadic references to grain exports in the years following, but nothing like the burst at the very end of the seventeenth century.[67] This strongly suggests that the trade was a response to a temporary situation, most likely a scarcity or even a famine in North Africa. Two of the documents, in fact, make reference to a famine (in Darnah) and a shortage (in Tripoli).[68] This was

---

[62] T.A.H. 4:391. Such a large amount makes it highly unlikely that the grapes were intended for personal consumption In 1626–27 the Imperial Larder consumed 1,500 kantars—or roughly 66,000 okka—of raisins. In other words the shipment from Crete could have supplied 5 percent of the palace's annual consumption. Goffman, *Izmir*, 34.

[63] See note 58 for a description of this source.

[64] Baladie, *To emborio*, 174–75. On average, French ships carried away 3,454 mouzour of wheat per year. At its height in 1705, 13,295 mouzour of wheat was exported, but just four years later exports were a paltry 84 mouzour. A mouzour was used to measure grains and was equal to 12–15 okka, depending on the product. Georgiou Aikaterinide, "Laikos politismos" (Popular culture) in *Krētē: Istoria kai politismos* (Crete: History and civilization), ed. N. Panayiotakēs (Heraklion: Synthesmos Topikōn Enōseōn Demōn kai Koinotētōn Krētēs, 1988), 529.

[65] T.A.H. 7:5, 9:104–18.

[66] Because export permits were issued for all these shipments, it is unlikely that other shipments could have left without permission. Therefore, we can assume that this represents the trade for 1110 and 1111. Besides North Africa, grain shipments went to Kos, Chios, Egriboz (Negroponte), and Rhodes.

[67] In 1701, 1706, 1709, and three times in 1713 Crete exported grain again.

[68] T.A.H. 9:106, 108.

not, however, the first time that North Africa turned to Crete for grain: the English consul in Tripoli mentioned imports of grain from Crete as early as 1679.[69]

Imports

Venetian administrators paid very little attention to the island's import trade, as is reflected in the literature on the period. Thus it comes as something of a surprise to see that imports figure so prominently in the first Ottoman customs regulation (kanunnāme-i gümrük), issued in Candia less than two weeks after the city had surrendered.[70]

The customs regulation is clearly a piecemeal document and cannot be relied upon as a guide to the actual trade of Crete during the early Ottoman period. It passes over in silence most of the island's exports and even some of its imports. Olive oil, for instance, is not even mentioned, nor cheese or honey (although wine is included, as noted earlier). Coffee was an important import item but it, too, is missing from the customs regulation. Still, the focus on imports is a useful corrective to a commercial history that is preoccupied with exports. Such a preoccupation obscures the fact that local merchants could find the import trade extremely profitable. We shall see later on that several very wealthy merchants in Candia were primarily importers, rather than exporters, of goods.

The textile trade warrants a separate discussion, both because it is so prominent in the kanunnāme but also because some of the wealthiest merchants in early Ottoman Crete traded primarily in luxury textiles. Textiles claim pride of place in the kanunnāme; it opens with a list of thirteen different types of fabric, including luxury type weaves such as brocades and velvets.

It is highly likely that the textiles the Ottomans had in mind were imported from Venice, which specialized in the production of luxury fabrics. In 1127/1715 a ferman sent to Crete asked the customs office in Candia to send a list of the goods commonly imported from Venice to Crete, as part of the Sultan's effort to forbid imports from Venice during the war.[71] The customs official (gümrük emini) responded with a long list that put textiles at the very top. Twelve different types of textiles, most of them luxury-type fabrics, were listed.[72] The French consul in Candia in

[69] C. R. Pennell, ed., *Piracy and Diplomacy in Seventeenth Century North Africa: The Journal of Thomas Baker English Consul in Tripoli* (Rutherford, N.J.: Fairleigh Dickinson University Press, 1989), 38.

[70] T.A.H. 3:104. The date is 18 Cemaziyelevvel 1080/14 October 1669.

[71] T.A.H. 14:101.

[72] Such as brocades (*diba*), gold threaded textiles (*telli hatayi*), satins (*atlas*), watered silks (*hare*), velvets (*kadife*), and silk velvets (*kemha*). See T.A.H. 5:229; 7:70; 2:265, 386, for mention of these fabrics in the local court records.

1712 wrote that "French fabrics have not succeeded here, due to [the competition from] Venetian textiles."[73] Dutch and English fabrics were brought to the island as well by Armenians coming from Smyrna.[74]

Many of the other items in the custom official's list of 1715—all kinds of paper, glass, and iron products—were also traditional imports from Venice.[75] Fish (balık) and caviar (havyar), mentioned in the kanunnāme of 1080/ 1669, had been imported from Istanbul during the Venetian period—particularly during Lent—and this continued under the Ottomans.[76]

These older trades with Venice and with Istanbul seem to have continued along at a rather sedate pace in the early Ottoman period. One import market, however, was clearly booming and that was the relatively new business in coffee. Coffee, imported from Yemen, first made its appearance in the Ottoman lands toward the end of the sixteenth century. The center of the coffee trade was Cairo, which flourished throughout the seventeenth century and into the first half of the eighteenth, due to the lucrative trade in coffee.[77] Imports of Yemeni coffee into Crete, via Cairo, were significant, no doubt helped along by the island's proximity to Egypt. An early (1085/ 1674) list of urban tax farms in Candia included the tax farm of tahmis, that is the exclusive right to roast, grind, and sell all the coffee imported into the island.[78] Unfortunately, the tahmis was sold as part of the urban tax farm for Candia as a whole and thus we cannot know its specific value, but it was probably worth around 50,000 akçe.[79]

Official interest in the coffee trade in Crete was considerable. In 1699 the government inquired as to the amount of coffee presently in Candia so that it could levy an excise tax of five paras per okka.[80] The kadi reported

[73] Baladie, To emborio, 210. Detorakēs takes complaints from the French that their fabrics were not selling as evidence that the Cretan economy was at a standstill. Detorakēs, Istoria tēs Krētēs, 294.

[74] Konstantinidēs, "Ektheseis kai ypomnēmata," 353.

[75] Imports from the west were fabric, crystal, glass, paper, nails, silverware. From the east came spices, drugs, gum, caviar, and dried fish. Maltezou, "E Krētē," 139. The French, writing in 1717, noted that Venice furnishes "toutes les quincailles" (hardware) and "etoffes d'or et argent." Konstantinidēs, "Ektheseis kai ypomnēmata," 353. Some traditional Venetian industries like silk and glassmaking had recovered by the end of the seventeenth century. Sella, "Crisis and Transformation," 100.

[76] The other goods mentioned were furs, followed by beeswax (bal-i mum), butter (zeyt-i yağ), and some kind of lumber (kepenk). See Maltezou, "E Krētē," 139, for imports of caviar and dried fish, particularly during Lent. These were goods traditionally imported from the east.

[77] Raymond gives some figures. Toward the end of the seventeenth century a quintal of coffee could be bought in Alexandria for 28 or 29 piastres, and sold for 53 piastres in Livorno. Raymond, Artisans et commercants, 1:173.

[78] T.A.H. 5:132.

[79] In 1728 the urban tax farms of Candia were listed separately and the tahmis (a tax on coffee) sold for 50,000 akçe. T.A.H. 17:73. The total amount of all the urban tax farms was 576,000 akçe, little different from 1674 when the total was 537,000 akçe.

[80] This was an empirewide tax, not one for Crete in particular. Beginning in the seventeenth century the Ottomans increasingly derived revenue from excise taxes levied on the more

that there were 4,584 okka of coffee in the shops (*dukakin*) and storehouses (*mahzenler*) of Candia, as well as in the port.[81] In 1713 coffee was selling in Candia for forty-five paras per okka which means that the coffee reported to the Sultan in 1699 was worth over 9 million akçe.[82] By way of contrast, the three or four bales of French fabric sold yearly in Candia during the same period could not have amounted to more than 5,000 guruş or 20,000 akçe.[83]

By 1715, if not earlier, the excise tax on coffee throughout the empire was under the control of Istanbul elites. In that year a high-ranking military officer (sipahilar Agasi) bought the tax farm for the tax on all coffee imported into the empire, whether by sea or by land. The port of Candia was listed as one of those where merchants would be obliged to pay the tax and a copy of the ferman was sent to the kadi court.[84] The document betrays a considerable amount of anxiety lest this lucrative trade fail to be brought under Istanbul's control:

> neither the seyyids nor the kapikullari army nor the Egyptians and Syrian soldiers, the ships from Algiers, Tunis and Tripoli, in short, no soldiers, are to be exempt from paying this tax. Neither are the Muslim hacis [*huccac-i Muslimin*] or the notables and people of power to be exempt from paying this tax.

Trading Partners

During the long war for Crete the Venetians remarked bitterly more than once that France was secretly hoping for an Ottoman victory so that it could take over the island's trade. Whatever the validity of this sentiment, the fact is that, in commerce as in politics, the tie to Venice was slow to die and the tie to France slow to develop.

The enduring tie to Venice is one of the most remarkable aspects of commercial continuity in the early years of Ottoman rule in Crete. Despite the often antagonistic relationship between the Ottomans and the Venetians in this period, we have seen that Venetian goods were still in demand in Crete. Merchants from Venice also continued to trade with the island,

---

successful commercial goods. See Ariel Salzmann, "An Ancien Régime Revisited: 'Privatization' and Political Economy in the Eighteenth-Century Ottoman Empire," *Politics and Society* 21, no. 4 (December 1993): 399.

[81] T.A.H. 9:95. The document says "medine-i Kandiyede vaki' dukakin ve mahzenlerde ferman-i ali uzere bulunan kahvasi," as well as the coffee in the port "iskelesini sefine ile."

[82] The local price of coffee is derived from various contemporary court documents. The price of coffee was quite stable at this time. Between 1691 and 1700 the price of coffee in Cairo was 1.057 para per kantar; between 1711 and 1720 the price was 1.415 para per kantar (or 62.26 para per okka). Raymond, *Artisans et commercants*, 1:69.

[83] Baladie, *To emborio*, 215.

[84] T.A.H. 14:99.

although their base was now Chania rather than Candia. Bernard Randolph, in Crete in 1680, remarked that the products of the White Mountains (behind Chania), and particularly the cheeses, were snapped up by Venetian merchants and transported to France, Italy, and the Ionian islands.[85] Commercial cases involving Venice are almost entirely absent from the records of the kadi court but a deal that went awry in 1119/1707 reveals that the trade did exist.

A woman from the district of Pediada, east of the city, came to court because her son, Giannakēs, was sending her letters from Venice where he had been jailed. Apparently Giannakēs had gone with his two partners, both of them Cretans, to Venice with a load of olive oil, which they sold. A Venetian gave them 3,000 guruş which they were to use to buy linseed and cheese in Crete. As security for the money, however, the Venetian insisted on keeping Giannakēs as a sort of commercial hostage, in case the other two failed to send him the goods. When, in fact, the goods did not arrive, the Venetian had the unfortunate Giannakēs thrown into jail.[86]

Although French shipping was immediately important in the coastal trade, and will be discussed in the next chapter, trade between Crete and Marseilles developed quite slowly. In many ways this was simply a reflection of the dire commercial position of France in the Ottoman Empire as a whole. By the end of the seventeenth century France's Levantine trade had dropped from 30 million livres per year to 3 million livres (in 1661). The reasons for this were several and are well known. The triumph of French commerce in the eighteenth century—when France would become the empire's most important European trading partner—was based on the success of French textiles but this industry was still floundering at the end of the seventeenth century. Not until the 1720s could the French finally replace the English as the dominant supplier of cloth to the empire.[87] The

---

[85] Randolph, *Travels*, 86. These same Venetian merchants also bought up most of a certain drug that they called oldani. The drug, Randolph writes, "is a very great comforter of the head" when burned. Because of their concentration in Chania, Venetian merchants appear only infrequently in the court records of the capital city. See T.A.H. 4:329, 334. But for much of this early period they were obliged to trade under French protection, so they do show up in French archival sources. Baladie, who has examined these sources, says Venetian merchants appear very often (*To emborio,* 130).

[86] T.A.H. 11:153. And see T.A.H. 2:400 for a case of a Cretan Muslim shipping a large amount (7,000 mistat) of olive oil to Venice. The French exported, on average, about 92,000 mistat of olive oil a year. The Muslim shipper had his own agent in Venice.

[87] For the crisis of the French textile industry, see Traian Stoianovich, "Pour une model du commerce du Levant: Economie concurrentielle et economie de bazar 1500–1800," *International Association for South Eastern European Studies, Bulletin* 12, no. 2 (1974): 86. In 1692 Languedoc manufactured only 2,000 pieces of the type of cloth intended to directly compete with English exports to the Ottoman Empire. Between 1700 and 1705 the French managed to send about 10,300 pieces per year. The English were consistently sending between 20,000 and 25,000 pieces per year. The French did not surpass this number until the 1720s.

commercial and institutional reforms undertaken by Colbert in the second half of the seventeenth century had not yet borne fruit.[88]

Trade between France and Crete in the early Ottoman years reflected the general malaise. The inability to sell French textiles in Crete has already been mentioned. Between 1686 and 1697 only one boat left from Crete for Marseilles. Traffic became somewhat more lively after that but, even so, in the first two decades of the eighteenth century four or five years could go by without a departure for Marseilles.[89]

The turn toward Egypt, already present in the Venetian period, continued. In fact, it is highly likely that the Egyptian ports replaced Venice as the most common destination for ships leaving Crete.[90] The Cretans bought up Egyptian coffee, rice, and sugar, and in return it appears that Cretan exports found a ready market in Egypt. French archival sources show that, between 1698 and 1722, most of the raisins and wine loaded onto French ships were headed for Alexandria.[91] By the early 1690s property distributions drawn up by the religious court were no longer valued in akçe, but in the para of Egypt (para Misri) instead.[92] This suggests that in this early period commercial ties with Egypt were more important than with any other Mediterranean port.

From Raymond's study of Egyptian trade at this time it is clear that the Cretans used their proximity to Egypt not just to trade between the two places, but also to take charge of the substantial trade between Egypt and northern Ottoman ports.[93]

Under the Venetians, commercial ties to North Africa were weak. Michael Peri's records make no mention of North African ports and the Venetians seem to have viewed it as off limits. Given the vicious attacks by the Barbary pirates on Venetian shipping at this time, the absence of contact is not surprising. It must be admitted, however, that other western powers did manage to trade with North Africa even during the seventeenth century when corsairing was at its height. This suggests that, from the

---

[88] For the difficulties of the French in the seventeenth century, see ibid. and especially Masson, *Historie du commerce français dans le Levant au XVII siècle*, introd. Masson characterizes the seventeenth century as one crisis after another and one in which the French were continually threatened with the ruin of their commerce.

[89] Baladie, *To emborio*, 103.

[90] French shipping records for the caravan trade show that, between 1686 and 1718, more ships (152) left from Crete for the Egyptian ports than for any other destination. The next closest was Chios at 108. Ibid., 111.

[91] Ibid., 189. And consular reports frequently mention Egypt as a food supplier.

[92] T.A.H. 7:162. At the end of the eighteenth century the level of exchange between the two regions was still extremely high. Between the years 1776 and 1781 Cretan imports from Egypt were as much as half the level of Salonica's imports from Egypt. Crete sent almost half as many exports to Egypt as Izmir did. Raymond, *Artisans et commercants*, 1:201.

[93] "A Alexandrie egalement le commerce avec la Turquie était pour une bonne partie entre les mains de 1500 Turcs venant pour la plupart de Cos et de Candie." Raymond, *Artisans et commercants*, 1:201.

North African point of view, all westerners were not equal and that Venice and Venetian shipping were particular targets.

The advent of Ottoman rule in Crete allowed for the establishment of ties between North African ports and the island. French ships involved in the caravan trade in this early period went to Dernah (in today's Libya) more often than they went to Smyrna.[94] The wheat trade, discussed earlier, was one of the clearest manifestations of this new relationship although other products were exported as well.[95] North African merchants brought clarified butter (*sadeyağ*) to Crete in exchange for the island's goods.

Levels of Trade

As we shall see when we turn to a discussion of the olive oil trade, the international commercial economy began to expand around 1720. The question remains as to whether the period that preceded it—when regional trade accounted for almost all commercial activity—can be considered one of economic depression. One way to try and answer this question would be to look at the amount of shipping in and out of the island during these years. On the basis of French archival sources, Baladie has supported the idea of commercial depression by emphasizing how little was exported during this time.

French shipping records are certainly an invaluable quantitative source. But it is a mistake to assume that all shipping was French and thus that statistics from Marseilles represent the entirety of commercial activity at this time. Such an approach certainly underestimates the commercial sector, as a few examples from Ottoman archives can show.

In 1110/1699 a sea merchant (*reis tuccari*) named Georgi petitioned the court in Candia for permission to export 4,000 mouzour of wheat (*hinta*) to North Africa on his own (non-French) boat.[96] The amount is instructive. The largest annual export of wheat in this early period was 30,000 mouzour (1699), and it was often far less.[97]

[94] Twenty-nine times between 1686 and 1718 as opposed to twenty-six for Smyrna. Shipments to all three North African destinations (Dernah, Tripoli, and Tunisia) surpassed Smyrna by far. Baladie, *To emborio,* 111.

[95] See T.A.H. 9:105: Mustafa Agha from Tripoli in North Africa asked for permission to export honey (*asel*) as well as wheat. A traveler's comment from the early nineteenth century suggests that trade with North Africa endured, long after Crete ceased to be an exporter of wheat. In this case the commodity was slaves. "A ship from Tripoli arrived in the port, with nearly fifty Negro slaves on board, who were soon landed, and sold singly to Turkish inhabitants as house servants. . . . This ship soon sailed again for Tunis. Many Turkish merchants, who had waited for an opportunity, went with it." F. W. Sieber, *Travels in the Island of Crete in the Year 1817* (London, 1823), 38.

[96] T.A.H. 9:107. With the term *reis tuccari,* the court probably wants to emphasize that this is a merchant who owns his own boat.

[97] Baladie, *To emborio,* 170.

Local shipping was also significant in the cheese trade. In 1110/1698 one Mehmet Reis received permission to load 250 kantars of cheese and the same amount of olive oil onto his boat (*sefine*) and to take it to Izmir.[98] This shipment of cheese was equivalent to 11,000 okka at a time when annual French purchases of cheese were estimated by the consul at 50,000 okka.

The absence of statistics on local shipping—which was clearly important—is compounded by the problem of contraband trade. In 1723 the French consul said he had heard of boats leaving the island with as much as 2,000 mistat of contraband oil on board. Cheese, wax, and silk were all smuggled as well.[99]

If it is not possible to establish the size of the commercial economy at this time, the limited quantitative evidence available to us does allow us to sketch out relative trends in the regional economy with more confidence. The number of French ships engaged in the coastal trade rose modestly, and not always steadily, between 1686 (the first year statistics are available) and 1717. After a two-year plunge, coastal shipping rose sharply and continued at a higher level than before until the mid-1750s.[100]

Figures for the urban tax farm of Candia do not contradict this picture of modest gains in trade, followed by a sharp upswing around 1720.[101] After hovering around 550,000 akçe for most of the period, the contract was rented for 10,000 guruş (1 million akçe) in 1132/1720.[102] By this time, as well, the tax farm had been converted into a life-term contract (*malikāne*), a sign that it was viewed as a particularly lucrative source of income.[103]

The reports of the French consuls (and the vice-consul in Candia) started off gloomily but quickly improved. In 1686 the consul in Chania commented, "Quant au commerce de ce royaume c'est fort peu de chose ne

---

[98] T.A.H. 10:117.

[99] Konstantinidēs, "Ektheseis kai ypomnēmata," 363, and Baladie, *To emborio*, 195.

[100] See Baladie's chart, *To emborio*, 110. From Baladie's figures we can see that between 1686 and 1710 an average of twenty ships a year left Candia; between 1711 and 1718 it was twenty-seven. For Chania twenty ships left a year in the period between 1686 and 1710 while in the subsequent period it was fifteen a year. Twenty-one ships per year entered Candia's port between 1686 and 1710 and twenty-seven for the years 1711 to 1718.

[101] Although that does not necessarily mean that the level of trade explains the amount of the tax farm. See Murat Çizakça's article, "Taxfarming and Financial Decentralization in the Ottoman Economy, 1520–1697," *Journal of European Economic History* 22, no. 2 (1993): 219–50, where he shows that the price of tax farm contracts did not automatically reflect changes in the level of trade.

[102] The eight tax farm contracts can be found in the court records: T.A.H. 3:250; 4:295, 442, 449, 458; 5:251–52; 13:99; 15:332.

[103] See Ariel Salzmann, "Centripetal Decentralization: Life-Term Taxfarming in the Eighteenth Century Ottoman Empire," in *Political Economies of the Ottoman, Safavid and Mughal Empires*, vol. 1, ed. Tosun Aracanli, Ashraf Ghani, and David Luden (forthcoming), for a discussion of the significance of *malikāne*.

consistant qu'en huile et en blés . . ." and "enfin le commerce de cette ile est le moins considerable du Levant et le plus incertain."[104]

By 1701 the report from Chania was openly enthusiastic: "Candie est une des îles la plus abondante en huiles, blés, cires, soies et fromages qu'il y aient en la mer Mediterranée."[105] In 1723 the vice-consul in Candia wrote that the caravan trade was so profitable that after just two years in the Levant sea captains could buy a load of oil to bring back to France or Italy.[106]

As noted elsewhere, piracy continued throughout this period, and no doubt operated as a brake on commerce. But nothing suggests that it was any worse than before the war, and in this sense, too, the commercial conditions of the early Ottoman years are little different from those which held before the war.

Finally it is true that, during the first half century of Ottoman rule, Crete was an exporter of grain. Following Braudel's argument, we may ask then if this means Crete was poor. In his discussion of Mediterranean islands in the sixteenth century, Braudel points out that it was "the poorer and more backward islands, which had fewer inhabitants and above all were not exploited by crops grown for export," that could sometimes afford the luxury of exporting wheat.[107]

But whether this description of Crete is accurate in the period 1669–1715 is debatable. Certainly Tournefort, in Crete in 1699, made the connection between abundance in grain and population loss.[108] On the other hand, there is at least some evidence that grain exports did, on occasion, compete with consumption on the island. In 1110/1699 the bakers of Candia complained that the grain merchants were refusing to sell grain to them at the agreed upon price, and in 1112/1700 they reported that they could not make bread since no grain was to be had.[109] In other words, grain exports during this time do not necessarily indicate a lack of local demand. Wheat prices were high in Europe at this time.[110] What is clear is that, as the trade in olive oil began to pick up in the second decade of the eighteenth century, the Cretans were quick to abandon grain cultivation and resume their more traditional role as a consumer, rather than a producer, of grain.

---

[104] Konstantinidēs, "Ektheseis kai ypomnēmata," 325–26.

[105] Ibid., 343.

[106] Ibid., 355.

[107] Braudel, *The Mediterranean*, 1:152.

[108] The island, he wrote, "produces more grain than the inhabitants can consume." Tournefort, *A Voyage*, 69.

[109] T.A.H. 9:118, 12:73.

[110] Yolanda Triandafyllidon Baladie, "Les conditions du commerce en Crete pendant les premiers deannies de la domination ottomane," in *Pepragmena tou Dartou Diethnous*

In light of the considerable disruptions of this period—piracy, two more wars with Venice, and the presence of the hains—it may seem curious that there was any surplus to trade. But the evidence does suggest that the fertility of the island compensated, at least partially, for the difficulties of the time. The French commented, "la terre qui est très fertile, ne refuse rien au laboureur diligent."[111] A ferman sent to the pasha of Crete in 1084/1674 said:

> Due to the scarcity in Crete in the year 1081, it had been ordered that none of the island's products be sold outside. But because yields after that have been satisfactory and produce has gone unsold, nobody has been showing any inclination toward agriculture. I have been informed that if this order stays in effect for this year the situation will get even worse and will inflict a great injustice on the inhabitants of the island generally. Therefore I order that no one prevent the islanders from selling their produce to the merchants that come to the harbors of the islands in their boats.[112]

Toward the Island of Oil

The first Ottoman statement on the olive oil trade in Crete came a decade after the Turks had arrived on the island and showed provisionist concerns similar to those of the Venetians. The serdar, or head military officer, through an order sent to the governor and janissary agha of Rethymnon, forbade the loading of wheat and olive oil onto ships arriving from "other islands."[113] Like the Venetians before them, the Ottomans sought to put limits on the commerical economy in order to ensure supplies for their troops. Even so, it is clear that trade in olive oil continued throughout the war years.

While the battle for Crete was still ongoing, a Greek named Makrygiannēs from the Aegean island of Skopelos followed his brother to Crete and settled in Rethymnon for trade. Subsequent to this he set off for Izmir with a load of olive oil, but during the voyage he was set upon by the Venetians, who seized the goods and took him hostage. Thrown into their galleys, he died in the course of a battle.[114] Just a few months after the serdar issued his partial ban on the trade in olive oil, a Muslim trader from

---

Krētologikou Synedriou (Proceedings of the Fourth International Cretological Symposium) (Athens: 1981), 3:301.
[111] Konstantinidēs, "Ektheseis kai ypomnēmata," 353.
[112] T.A.H. 5:131.
[113] T.A.H. 1:148.
[114] T.A.H. 1:126.

the island of Tenedos died in Rethymnon. His property distribution listed over thirty people who owed him money for olive oil.[115]

References to the olive oil trade continue to appear in the court records of Candia after the final conquest of the island, although in the immediate aftermath of the war supplies must have been extremely limited, due to the great number of trees that had been chopped down during the war. In 1106/1694 a Cretan merchant named Haci Musli beşe b. Ahmet loaded a substantial amount of raisins, olive oil, and honey onto a French ship and sailed for Alexandria.[116] In 1117/1706 Haci Ahmet b. Mehmet of Candia loaded 7,000 mistat of olive oil onto a French ship going to Venice.[117] Just one year later three Greeks took a load of olive oil to Venice as well.[118]

Even so, olive oil appears in the court records as a commodity like any other in the early years of Ottoman rule in Candia.[119] Neither the local elite nor the Sultan in Istanbul took a particular interest in it. French reports from the period show an interest in the oil market, but not to the exclusion of other goods. Writing in 1686, the French consul in Chania commented "Quant au commerce de ce royaume c'est fort peu de chose ne consistant qu'en huile et en blés."[120] By 1701 the French were more enthusiastic about the island's potential but, still, olive oil received no special attention: "Candie est une des îles la plus abondante en huiles, blés, cires, soies et fromages qu'il y aient en la mer Méditerranée."[121] Randolph, in Chania in 1680, said "the French have a great trade for oyl, wools, wax, cheese and several other commodities."[122]

All this began to change early in the eighteenth century. Between the years 1700 and 1721 the French exported an average of 92,000 mistat of olive oil per year, or slightly double the amount of wine they exported.[123] Just four years later, that number had jumped to 200,000 mistat.[124] Shipping to Marseilles had previously been sporadic, but beginning in 1717 somewhere between twenty and forty ships a year began regularly to load

[115] T.A.H. 1:146.

[116] T.A.H. 8:30. He paid a freight of 1,500 esedi guruş round trip. French archival sources show that, between 1725 and 1764, the average round trip freight between Crete and Alexandria was 749 esedi guruş.

[117] T.A.H. 2:400.

[118] T.A.H. 11:153.

[119] Admittedly it would certainly appear more in the court records of Chania, which was the center of the olive oil trade. These records, however, have not survived.

[120] Konstantinidēs, "Ektheseis kai ypomnēmata," 325.

[121] Ibid., 343.

[122] Randolph, Travels, 90.

[123] Baladie, To emborio, 138, 191.

[124] According to the estimate of De Monhenault, French consul in Chania. Konstantinidēs, "Ektheseis kai ypomnēmata," 362.

olive oil.[125] About the same time, Ottoman interest in the trade began to pick up. In 1130/1717 a ferman was sent to Crete imposing a tax of three akçe or 22 percent on every okka of olive oil exported, to be paid by the exporter. The reasons for this tax were stated explicitly:

> Because of the bounteous production of olive oil in the provinces and villages of Crete, Ottoman and foreign merchants purchase it in great quantity. Despite their being able to buy olive oil all over the island, when they load it at Candia, Souda, Chania, Rethymnon, and the other islands they pay only a small customs tax, just as is done with other products, and nothing more for the public treasury. While these merchants make a great profit, the income of Crete—according to the latest survey—does not cover her expenses. . . . If a tax for the public treasury is levied on the great amount of olive oil exported from the harbors of Crete, there will be a great benefit to public treasury. . . . It is understood that because this tax will not burden the indigenous population, it will not be a source of unhappiness for them while at the same time the public treasury will benefit.[126]

The similarity to Venetian arguments for a tax on wine a century and a half previous is striking. In both cases the wealth of the merchants was contrasted to the poverty of the state, a poverty directly linked to the cost of defending the island. Whereas during the war the Ottomans had been concerned to limit the olive oil trade, by 1718 they were coming to rely on the profits generated by one highly lucrative commodity, just as the Venetians had before them.

When Mocenigo urged a tax on wine in 1589, however, the Venetians had a century of difficulty ahead in Crete. Their desire for the profits of the wine trade conflicted with the need to keep the island adequately provisioned in case of war.

The Ottomans were in a fundamentally different position in 1718. After three hundred years and six major wars, the Venetians had finally been driven from the eastern Mediterranean. In a peace treaty signed that year, bringing the war of 1715–18 to a close, the Venetians had given up all their remaining possessions in the East, including the two small islands off the northern coast of Crete that they had managed to hold onto since 1669.[127] The Russian naval threat in the Mediterranean was still over half a century away. The French were a major presence, of course, but they were not yet a military threat. Indeed, as I argued earlier, they made it easier for the Ottomans to hold onto Crete than it would have been

---

[125] Baladie, *To emborio,* 103.

[126] T.A.H. 15:80. The customs tax referred to would be that laid down in the customs regulation (kanunnāme-i gümrük).

[127] The third island, Grambousa, was lost during the course of the long war with the Venetians 1684–99, when the Venetian contingent surrendered to the Ottomans in return for safe passage to Istanbul.

otherwise. There was a price to be paid, of course, for this support, and once the Venetians were out of the way the French were more willing to press their claims. When the Ottomans attempted to raise the export tax to six akçe in 1720—a 100 percent rise from the 1718 rate—the French consul fought back and managed to knock it down to four akçe.[128]

Despite tensions with the French, the Ottomans had just weathered a difficult phase in Crete and now they could look forward to a relatively quiet period in the eastern Mediterranean. This serenity allowed them to encourage the development of a lucrative export economy on the island, just as the Venetians had before them, but this one was based on olive oil, not wine.

Evidence for the new concentration on olive oil is not hard to come by. French consular reports were now full of discussions about the trade, to the exclusion of all else. In 1716 the French consul, Delane, wrote to the minister of the navy, the duc d'Orléans, begging him to speak to the French ambassador in Istanbul with a view to getting the ban on the export of oil rescinded. He warned that if the ban wasn't lifted, most of the French merchants in Crete will leave since there is nothing else to trade in: "il faudra que la plupart de nos négociants fassent retraite si la permission de sortir les huiles ne nous est continuée, ni ayant dans tout ce royaume que très peu de soie, cires et laines qui n'occuperaient pas un seul petit marchand."[129] He finished his plea by saying that, if this affair were not resolved satisfactorily, "cette échelle est absolument ruinée."[130] Even if we allow for a certain amount of special pleading on Delane's part, it is clear that interest in olive oil was growing rapidly. French exports of olive oil increased by 50 percent between 1720 and 1741.[131]

On the Ottoman side the development of an indigenous soap industry increased the competition for access to the yearly crop. Soap factories made their first appearance in Candia and Chania in the 1720s, and their numbers multiplied during the course of the eighteenth century.[132] In 1742 the French consul observed that competition for the oil was much greater than it had been in the past.[133] Writing at midcentury, a subsequent consul

---

[128] Although not until 1724. See T.A.H. 15:79, 306, as well as Baladie, *To Emborio*, 56, for the Ottoman attempt and the French response.

[129] Konstantinidēs, "Ektheseis kai ypomnēmata," 350.

[130] Ten years later the next French consul in Chania expressed identical sentiments. Olive oil, he said, was "la seule richesse du royaume" and without it "le pays serait absolument ruiné et le Grand Seigneur aurait de la peine à en retirer de quoi fournir aux frais qu'il est obligé d'y faire pour l'entretien des garrisons des places. . . . On doit donc regarder l'huile comme la base et l'unique object du commerce du royaume." Ibid., 362.

[131] Baladie, *To emborio*, 174.

[132] See Baladie's article "L'industrie du savon en Crete au XVIII siècle: Aspects economiques et sociaux," *Etudes Balkaniques* 4 (1975): 75–87. Ottoman surveys show that there were six soap factories in Candia in 1723, twelve at midcentury, fifteen in 1783, and eighteen in 1787. French sources indicated that there were fifty soap factories in Chania in 1772.

[133] Baladie, *To emborio*, 140–41.

complained that the Ottoman soap industry used 50 percent of the olive oil crop in a good year and almost all when the harvest was bad.[134]

The growth in oil exports and the proliferation of soap-making factories were not the only signs of the island's new orientation. Crete ceased to be a wheat exporter right around the time that elites began to pay attention to the olive oil trade. In 1715 the city of Foca in Anatolia sent 10,000 kilograms of wheat to Candia to supplement the city's supplies.[135] In 1722 alone the Greek mainland sent more than twenty-two shipments of wheat.[136]

In the early years of Ottoman rule on Crete, when war was a constant possibility, the sultan was determined to protect the island's grain supply, just as the Venetians had been before him. He had the pasha of Candia strangled for selling wheat "aux chrétiens" while the war between the empire and the Holy League was raging.[137] But with the final departure of the Venetians from the eastern Mediterranean in 1718, he was willing to have the island import its grain supply, if need be, in order to be able to concentrate on more lucrative commodities.

Metropolitan elites were determined to benefit from Cretan olive oil, just as Venetian officials, in centuries gone by, had reaped the rewards of Cretan viticulture. In 1738 the tax farm for Cretan olive oil (resm-i revgan-i zeyt mukataasi) was sold to Ragip Mehmet, a member of the grand vezir's household.[138] In the mid-1740s the same tax farm, together with the tax farm on Cretan soap, was awarded to the governor of Egypt, Mehmet Pasha.[139] The sultan even went so far as to try and reserve Cretan olive oil exclusively for the capital city. In 1776 he sent a ferman to the island that forbade the export of any olive oil that did not have as its destination the city of Istanbul.[140] Given the importance of foreign shipping in the empire it is unlikely that he was able to enforce the ferman, but the similarity to Venetian policy in the Levant—whereby Venice tried to force its colonies to trade exclusively with Venice—is striking.

[134] Ibid., 141. The French had to worry about local merchants, as well as the demands of Istanbul elites. Writing in 1748 Magy worried: "Les marchands grecs et juifs de cette ville ont chargé depuis peu trois bâtiments ragusois et un de ce pays, d'huile pour la porter à Trieste. Si ce commerce continuait il porteroit un grand préjudice à celui que nous faisons dans cette échelle." Ibid., 284.

[135] T.A.H. 14:113.

[136] Baladie, To emborio, 291.

[137] Konstantinidēs, "Ektheseis kai ypomnēmata," 330. The note is undated but was attached to note number one, sent in 1686.

[138] T.A.H. 18:78.

[139] In the years 1158/1160 (February 1745 to December 1748) the tax farm for Cretan soap and olive oil (resm-i miri sabun ve resm-i revgan-i zeyt mukataasi) was awarded to the vali of Egypt, Mehmet Pasha. Yavuz Cezar, Osmanli maliyesinde bunalim ve değişim dönemi: XVIII.yy'dan Tanzimat'a mali tarih (The period of crisis and change in Ottoman finance: A financial history from the eighteenth century to the Tanzimat) (Istanbul: Alan Yayıncılık, 1986), 44.

[140] Baladie, To emborio, 144–45.

The turn away from grain cultivation can explain the divergent remarks of Tournefort and Pococke on the hinterland surrounding the capital city. Tournefort, writing in 1699, said there were fruitful plains all around Candia "enriched with all sorts of grain."[141] Forty years later, Pococke said that the country around Candia "produces great quantities of excellent wines."[142]

It is clear what happened in the ensuing forty years. Landowners in the vicinity of Candia took advantage of peace, as well as the willingness (and ability) of the Ottomans to supply the island with grain, to return to the viticulture that had been predominant there in the sixteenth century. Wine, of course, was now very much secondary to olive oil in the commercial economy. Nevertheless, the return to viticulture in the province of Candia, the boom in olive oil, and the turn away from grain cultivation all point in the same direction: a move away from the regional and diversified commerce of the seventeenth and early eighteenth centuries, and back toward the earlier pattern of a highly lucrative, export-oriented commercial agriculture based on the intensive cultivation of one crop.[143] This reversion brought back some of the old problems as well, despite the relative proximity of grain. On one occasion in 1745 the authorities seized all the boats in the harbor—both local and foreign—and sent them off to find grain in other parts of the archipelago. Toward the end of the century Baron de Tott observed that Crete was habitually short of grain.[144]

Chania and Candia

The growth of the olive oil trade led to a rise in the international stature of Chania and an increasing divergence from the port of Candia. Whereas in the early decades of Ottoman rule the two cities had seen roughly equal amounts of the caravan trade (Candia had slightly more), now Chania became the city of international exchange and Candia the center of regional trade.[145] In a letter of 1725, the French consul in Chania, De Monhenault,

---

[141] Tournefort, *A Voyage*, 44. This observation is supported by the Ottoman tax farm survey of 1694 cited earlier.

[142] Pococke, *A Description*, 257.

[143] Masson observes that French commerce in Crete was unlike that with any other *échelle*, in that it was dominated almost entirely by one product, olive oil, which Marseilles and Toulon used in their soapmaking industries. Masson, *Histoire du commerce français dans le Levant au XVII siècle*, 430.

[144] Baron de Tott, *Memoires sur les Turcs et les Tartares* (Amsterdam, 1784), 2:221. In 1745 the local authorities seized all the boats in the harbor—both local and foreign—and sent them off to find grain in other parts of the archipelago, just as the Venetians had before them. Baladie, *To emborio*, 144–45.

[145] Between 1686 and 1720 an average of twenty-six French boats per year engaged in the caravan trade left the port of Candia, while twenty-four departed from Chania. Baladie, *To emborio*, 111–16.

estimated that the French loaded 200,000 mistat of olive oil per year, 150,000 of it in Chania alone.[146]

This division of labor was not unlike that between Rosetta and Damiette on the Egyptian coast. Rosetta was the port of international exchange where the Europeans went, whereas Damiette was the center of the trade with Syria, and its merchant community was largely Syrian Catholic.[147]

Predictably, the interest of foreign merchants in olive oil after 1715 led them to denigrate Candia's importance as a commercial city, but in fact the city now became the most important center of caravan trade on the island. Coastal traffic out of the city actually increased in the first half of the eighteenth century. This may well have been the result, at least partially, of the return to viticulture in the city's hinterland. At any rate, the port's trade continued to be characterized by a diversity of commodities, unlike Chania.

Writing in 1723, the vice-consul in Candia reported "ce port est d'un fort grand abord de bâtiments français qu'on appelle caravaneurs, c'est à dire naviguant d'un port à l'autre de Turquie, chargé de différentes marchandises pour compte des sujets du Grand Seigneur."[148] He then went on provide a long list of the goods that passed through the port.[149] A report of 1725 said the port of Candia had hardly "trois ou quatre bâtiments français par an pour y charger pour Chrétienté; mails il y va beaucoup de caravaneurs."[150]

The disdain for Candia is probably not explained by commerce alone. With its heavily Muslim population and relative lack of foreigners (Tournefort noted that there were "no more than three or four French families"), it was a more threatening place than Chania. Panayiōtēs Nikousios's strongly anti-Latin stand—to be discussed in chapter 6—may also have added to the feeling of discomfort for the French at least.[151]

In any event, Candia remained the political center of the island—as it had been under the Venetians—but under the Ottomans Chania came to aquire an importance that it had not enjoyed in previous centuries.

[146] Konstantinidēs, "Ektheseis kai ypomnēmata," 362.

[147] Thomas Philipp, *The Syrians in Egypt, 1725–1975* (Stuttgart: Seiner-Verlag-Wiesbaden, 1985), 24.

[148] Konstantinidēs, "Ektheseis kai ypomnēmata," 355.

[149] Soap, honey, and cheese went to Istanbul, Chios, Alexandria, and Smyrna. Oil was also sent to Istanbul, while Alexandria bought up Cretan raisins, wine, linen, and licorice. Large amounts of raisins were sent to Salonica and Tunis. Textiles, iron goods, rice, coffee, flax, linen, sugar, legumes, salted fish, hides, and wood were all imported. Konstantinidēs, "Ektheseis kai ypomnēmata," 354–55.

[150] Ibid., 365.

[151] Thomas Philipp alerts us to the possibility of an economic motive behind "anti-European" sentiment: "One European travel account of the time claimed that the Syrian Christians in Damiette deliberately spread rumors about the hostility of the local population against Europeans in order to prevent the latter from settling there and to maintain their own monopoly over trade in the city." Philipp, *The Syrians in Egypt*, 24.

Five

Merchants of Candia

Nay, which is yet more wonderful, Why
Should the Apostates that command these
ships (who were whilst Christians, admired for
their Valour and Conduct) turn presently
inconsiderable, as if with their Faith they
became Bankrupts of their Natural talents too!
  Earl of Castlemaine[1]

Candia and Venetian Decline

The dramatic reversals suffered by Venetian trade, navigation, and shipbuilding in the late sixteenth and especially the seventeenth centuries are
well known to historians. French, Dutch, and English newcomers managed
to wrest the Levantine trade away from the Venetian merchants who had
thrived for centuries in their role as middlemen between East and West.
The new arrivals in the eastern Mediterranean showed themselves to be
adept not just at trading but at shipbuilding and seafaring as well. Between
1550 and 1590 the cost of constructing a ship at Venice quadrupled and
the strength of the merchant marine fell by half.[2] Meanwhile, the Dutch
enjoyed lower insurance rates because of their reputation as superior naviga-
tors.[3] Increasingly, leading Venetian families turned their back on the sea

---

[1] Earl of Castlemaine, *An Account of the Present War between Venetians and Turks with
the State of Candie (in a Letter to the King from Venice)* (London: Printed by J.M. for
H. Herringman, at the Anchor on the Lower Walk of the New Exchange, 1666), the opening
"Epistle Dedicatory."

[2] See Frederic Lane, *Venice: A Maritime Republic* (Baltimore: Johns Hopkins University
Press, 1973), 385, for information on the costs of shipbuilding at Venice. Dominique Sella,
"Crisis and Transformation in Venetian Trade," in *Crisis and Change in the Venetian Economy
in the Sixteenth and Seventeenth Centuries*, ed. Brian Pullan (London: Methuen, 1968), 92,
discusses the strength of the merchant marine in later centuries.

[3] Lane, *Venice*, 419. Venice acknowledged the superiority of the Dutch and others in 1683
when it established a school for the training of masters and mates.

and began to invest in agriculture and industry on the mainland. Although Venice continued to be a busy center of regional trade, as well as a major consumer of imported goods itself, the merchants who handled this trade were a new class of people. Many of them were recently naturalized immigrants, and a gap between the ruling class and the trading class developed.[4]

Little attention has been given, however, to the repercussions of these developments for Venice's principal colony. In the preceding chapter I suggested how the commerce of Crete moved out from under Venice's shadow in the seventeenth century. In this chapter we continue the story and show how a local group of merchants, independent of Venice, emerged at this time to take advantage of the island's increasingly separate course.

The Rise of Local Merchants

From earliest times it was Venetian policy to exclude non-Venetians from the lofty summits of international trade, a restriction that naturally applied to the Greeks of Crete as well. Thus a Cretan merchant named Costa Michel managed to ship a cargo of pepper to Venice early in the fourteenth century, but when he reached the city the pepper was seized because his name did not appear on a list of Venetian citizens.[5] Venice also insisted that all goods originating in its possessions in the Ionian and Aegean seas— in places like Crete, Nauplion, Corfou, and Dalmatia—be transported directly to Venice, with no deviations allowed.[6] Gradually, however, Venice began to loosen various aspects of these restrictions. The reasons for this are not entirely clear, but the changes began in the fifteenth century, when the Ottomans were rapidly expanding into the Mediterranean, and possibly there was a desire to appease the local Orthodox population. Thus, for instance, the Senate took various measures in 1434 and 1455 to lessen the dues levied on goods transported between the Venetian-held towns

[4] Ibid., 418. Thus in a speech to the Senate in 1784 the Venetian noble Andrea Tron called on his fellow nobles to return to maritime commerce as their ancestors had done. But "he disparaged the spurt of Venetian shipping and trade during the war of the American revolution because the profits did not go to solid, established Venetian families but to foreigners or new men, agents of foreigners. Jews had become important shipowners and also manufacturers. Andrea Tron helped put through new restrictions on Jews." This gap may also explain the ill-advised measure taken by the Senate in 1662 to lower the customs tax on imports while continuing to tax reexports as heavily as ever. The measure was repealed twenty years later.

[5] F. Thiriet, "La vie des hommes de les rapports des collectivités," in *La romanie venitienne au Moyen Age* (Paris: De Boccard, 1959), 280.

[6] Venice had a similar policy for the Adriatic, which was expressed in the phrase "ogni merce che entra nell'Adriatico o esce dall'Adriatico, deve toccar Venezia." Chr. Panayiōtopoulos, "Ellēnes nautikoi kai ploioktētes apo ta palaiotera oikonomika vivlia tēs Ellēnikēs Adelfotētas Venetias 1536–1576)" (Greek sailors and shipowners according to the oldest account books of the Greek Society of Venice, 1536–1576), *Thēsaurismata* 11 (1974): 287.

of Coron and Modon in the southwestern Peloponnese and the Byzantine city of Mistra.[7]

No doubt as a result of this gradual easing, Cretan names appear in the archival documents with increasing frequency as the centuries go by. By the sixteenth century merchants from Crete were no longer unusual, even on the longer routes. In 1514 Emmanual Skordilēs sailed from Candia to the Negroponte, and Marko Kallergēs left for southern Italy from Candia in 1532.[8] Georgēs Noufris of Candia sailed all the way from Venice to Flanders in 1539.[9] As early as 1551 one Evdokimos Chortatsēs was teaching in Candia, instructing the locals in the Italian language and commercial documents.[10]

The merchants' position in society has been little studied but it appears to have been fairly modest.[11] Those engaged in trade were not the large landowning class, but were rather from the new class of city-dwellers produced by urban expansion in the sixteenth century. In addition to trade many would have found positions in local industry and administration. Some even owned land.[12] Merchants occupied a middle ground between impoverished urban dwellers (the *popolo*) and the landed elite (whether noble or not), which continued to monopolize political power.

The Greeks were not yet in a position to challenge seriously the western European powers for the control of international trade, individual examples notwithstanding. Such an expansion in their role would not come about

---

[7] Thiriet, "Les premiers effets de l'expansion ottomane," chap. 2, in *La romanie venitienne*, 420.

[8] Maltezou provides the names of other Greek traders of the sixteenth century: Nikolu Ververe, Manole Papadopoulu, and Nikolo Pyromalle. Chr. Maltezou, "E Krētē stē diarkeia tēs periodou tēs venetokratias" (Crete during the period of Venetian rule), in *Krētē: Istoria kai politismos* (Crete: History and civilization), ed. N. Panayiotakēs (Herakelion: Synthesmos Topikōn Enōseōn Dēmōn kai Koinotētōn Krētēs, 1988), 141. All three men were members of the Greek Society of Venice and all three were shipowners. Panayiōtopoulos, "Ellēnes nautikoi kai ploioktētes," 321, 323.

[9] Panayiōtopoulos, "Ellēnes nautikoi kai ploioktētes," 334.

[10] Maltezou, "E Krētē," 141.

[11] Thus Maltezou and Detorakēs differ in their characterization of the emerging merchant class. Maltezou identifies the merchants with the cittadini (the urban privileged class) while Detorakēs argues that both cittadini and nobilitas cretensis (the Cretan nobility) practiced trade. Maltezou, "E Krētē," 114, and Theocharis Detorakēs, *Istoria tēs Krētēs* (History of Crete) (Athens, 1986), 210. As Papadia-Lala points out, both descriptions are misleading because they confuse a strictly legal status (cittadini and nobilitas cretensis) with a group that is better defined in economic terms. There were nobles (both Venetian and Cretan) engaged in commerce, for instance, but they were invariably those nobles who had lost their fiefs and were living in reduced circumstances (just as ordinary, but wealthy, subjects had been able to buy fiefs without, however, being able to obtain a title of nobility). Anastasia Papadia-Lala, " 'Cittadini' kai katoikoi poleōn: Koinōnike diastrōmatosē sta venetokratoumena Chania (mesa 16–17 ai.)" ('Cittadini' and the urban Population: Social stratification in Venetian Chania [from the middle of the 16th to the middle of the 17th century], in *Praktika tou Diethnous Symposiou Istorias Neoellēnikē Polē (Proceedings of the International Symposium on the History of the Modern Greek City)* (Athens, 1985), 61.

[12] Papadia-Lala, " 'Cittadini' kai katoikoi poleōn," 62.

until the second half of the eighteenth century. They could, however, take advantage of Venice's declining ability to mandate that all trade from its colonies (in the seventeenth century, Crete and the Ionian islands) be shipped directly to Venice for redistribution from there. Whereas its grip on the commerce of the Adriatic was not definitively shattered until 1719 when the Hapsburg emperor was able to establish the free port of Trieste, Venice lost control of points further east much earlier.[13] Already in the early seventeenth century, as we have seen in the previous chapter, the Cretans set sail for ports in the eastern Mediterranean almost as often as they set out for Venice. The reports of the provveditori and archival evidence make it clear that local merchants were directing this local and regional trade. Mocenigo wrote in 1589,

> The cities, and especially Candia and Chania, produce many good sailors. It is said, as a proverb, that when a villager is born in Crete, a galley slave is born and when a child is born in the city, a sailor is born. The Cretans sail with their boats in times of peace to Syria, to Alexandria, to Constantinople, to the archipelago and to other places in Turkey in every sort of boat and skiff; they are skillful and daring men.[14]

The daring of the local sailors is clear from an account left to us by Tournefort, who went from Crete to the Cycladic islands at the end of the seventeenth century. He preferred to wait for a French boat because the local boats, not being above fifteen feet long, were easily overset "with a sudden gust of the north wind."[15]

Notarial documents from the port of Candia in the seventeenth century provide evidence of extensive Greek involvement in commercial and maritime affairs.[16] All shipments leaving the port had to have a guarantor who would vouch that the ship was not carrying slaves or olive oil above the amount permitted for export. Many of these guarantors, who were at the same time investors in the shipment, were Cretan merchants.[17] Although in most cases the origin of the captain (or, possibly, owner-captain) was

---

[13] Lane, *Venice*, 417.

[14] "Questi navigando in tempo di pace nella Soria, in Allessandria, in Constli, in Arcipelago, et in altri luoghi della Turchia con ogni sorte di vasseli, et di barche, si fanno molto risicati, et valent' huomini." Stergios Spanakēs, "Relazione del Nobil Huomo Zuanne Mocenigo ritornato provveditore generale del regno di Candia presentata nell'eccellentissimo consillio 17 Aprile 1589," *Mnēmeia tēs krētikēs istorias* (Monuments of Cretan history) (Herakleion, 1940), 23.

[15] M. Pitton de Tournefort, *A Voyage into the Levant* (Paris, 1717), 152.

[16] See note 33 in chapter 5 for a description of Panopoulou's work on seventeenth-century commerce.

[17] Angelikē Panopoulou, "Opseis tēs nautiliakēs kinēsēs tou Chandaka to 17 aiōna" (Aspects of shipping in 17th century Chandaka), *Krētika Estia* 5 no. 2 (1980): 157.

not given, in those cases where it was he was usually a Greek.[18] Extensive local involvement in maritime commerce continued through the war years and may even have grown as the Ottoman army cut the city off from its hinterland.[19]

The case of George Mormore is a good example of a Cretan merchant who became wealthy pursuing the diversified regional trade that was so prominent in the seventeenth century, even under wartime conditions.[20] His commercial papers from the 1650s and 1660s show that he traded in olive oil, coffee, wheat, and cheese. He was also a moneylender and was himself indebted to a Jew named Menechem Dal Madego.[21] At least as far back as 1644 the Venetian administration had extracted loans from the island's merchants in order to pay for the militia, and in 1663 Mormore loaned the state the princely sum of 28,116 reals.[22] (The construction of the Moresini fountain in Candia in the 1620s, probably the major public work undertaken in the seventeenth century, had cost 13,000 reals in its entirety.)[23] Just two years later Mormore handed over another 13,281 reals.[24]

By the seventeenth century Cretan merchants had clearly gone beyond the shores of their native island and spread throughout the eastern

[18] Panopoulou, "Opseis," 163.

[19] "In addition to the merchants and shipowners, a large number of the people of Candia, from all levels of society (citizens, priests, artisans) had accumulated capital for which maritime trade was the only outlet. These people usually invested in the cargo or loaned money to merchants." Angelikē Panopoulou, "Syntrofies kai naulōseis pliōn sto Chandaka 1635–1661" (Partnerships and chartering of boats in Chandaka, 1635–1661), in *Pepragmena tou Ektou Diethnous Krētologikou Synedriou* (Proceedings of the Sixth International Cretological symposium) (Chania: Philologikos Syllogos O Chrysostomos, 1991), 2:426.

[20] We know about George Mormore because his sister, Theonymphe Mormore, brought the papers of her deceased brother with her to Venice in 1667. George died in 1666. S. A. Antoniadēs, "E Kinētē Periousia tou Geōrgiou Mormore metaferetai ap tēn Krētē stē Venetia 1667" (The property of George Mormore is brought from Crete to Venice), *Pratika Akadēmia Athenōn* 40 (1965): 258–67.

[21] He accepted pawns as collateral for loans, which implies that he lent money to the poorer strata of Candia. But high-ranking Venetian officers (in Crete) borrowed from him as well.

[22] Ibid., 262. The Spanish real was by this point the most common coin in Crete, as it was throughout the Mediterranean in the seventeenth century. Şevket Pamuk, "Money in the Ottoman Empire, 1326–1914" in *An Economic and Social History of the Ottoman Empire*, ed. Halil Inalcık with Donald Quataert (Cambridge: Cambridge University Press, 1994), 965.

[23] Stergios Spanakēs, "Relazione Francesco Moresini provveditore generale nel regno di Candia 1629," *Mnēmeia tes krētikēs istorias* (Monuments of Cretan history), (Herakleion, 1950), 28.

[24] S. A. Antoniadēs, "Oikonomikē katastasē tōn poleōn tēs Krētēs 1645–1669" (The economic situation of Crete's cities, 1645–1669), *Thēsaurismata* 4 (1967): 40. The loan was earmarked for the city's militia. Writing in 1666, Palmer said that a common soldier received 3 or 4 reals a month. In 1645 when the city of Chania was under attack George's father, Emmanual, loaned the authorities 3,000 ducats. It is a sign of Venice's deteriorating position that, unlike in 1645, the receipt for the loan in 1665 bore the disclaimer "the creditor will not be able to collect compensation on the basis of this receipt, which is nothing more than a simple certification of the amount of 13,280 reals."

Mediterranean. There were already enough Greek sailors and captains in Venice in the middle of the sixteenth century, for instance, for the Greek community there to decide to levy a tax on every Greek boat that anchored in the city's port. The tax was intended to help pay for the construction of the Church of Saint George of the Greeks, which was the center of the community in Venice.[25] Between 1536 and 1576 roughly twenty Greek boats a year arrived in Venice, and Cretans were more numerous than any other group.[26]

The Cretan commercial presence in the Ottoman lands before the island became a part of the empire has received much less attention from historians. Still, scattered evidence suggests that long before the final surrender to Köprülü's army, merchants, both Muslim and Christian, moved easily between Crete and the rest of the eastern Mediterranean, which was by now entirely in Ottoman hands. This was a natural consequence of the gradual uncoupling of Crete from the commercial fortunes of Venice.

In the seventeenth century Cretans were just as likely to be sailing to Izmir or Alexandria as they were to Venice. Similarly, Muslim seamen were not a rarity on the island. In the late 1620s Moresini had to handle the delicate situation of two Ottoman galleys, one belonging to the bey of Negroponte, which sailed into the harbor of Candia with white flags hoisted. The crews, mostly Russian slaves, had mutinied and then sailed to Crete seeking refuge. The Venetians were anxious to avoid any incident with the Sultan and hastily arranged for the return of the two boats (but not the slaves) to the Ottomans. A rendevous was set at the Aegean island of Milos. Venetian galleys would accompany the Ottoman galleys part of the way, and, for reasons that are not entirely clear, Moresini decided to man these galleys with Turks. He readily found these Turkish sailors (*marinari*) among the small boats (*vasselli et saiche*) that were in the harbors of Chania and Candia.[27]

One of the Venetians put in charge of this affair was Captain Piero Zucho of Rethymnon, who was described as "interprete della lingua turca." The existence of such a position on the island is another indication of a growing Muslim commercial presence. No doubt part of Zucho's job was easing the way of those Turks who came with their vasselli and saiche to

[25] Panayiōtopoulos, "Ellēnes nautikoi kai ploioktētes," 288. The Council of Ten granted permission for the erection of the Church of Saint George of the Greeks in 1514 and the foundation was laid in 1539. Seven years went by and the construction was slowing due to lack of funds. So the decision was made (1546) to levy a tax on every Greek boat that anchored in Venice.

[26] Ibid., 302. From the records of the Adelfotita, Panayiotopoulous has culled the names of 405 sailors, merchants, and shipowners. The city of origin is known in 112 cases and of those the most (16) are from Candia followed close behind by Corfou. The port of departure is known in 42 cases. Of these Candia appears the most frequently by far—29 departures as compared with no more than 4 from anywhere else.

[27] Spanakēs, "Relazione Francesco Moresini," 90.

do business in Candia and Chania.[28] Archival evidence gives specific examples of Muslims traders in Crete during this period.[29]

Therefore when Ottoman court records tell us of the death of Abd ur-Rahman, a Muslim merchant from Tenedos, in Rethymnon (which the Ottomans now held) in 1069/1659, we cannot conclude that Muslim businessmen arrived with the Ottoman armies.[30] Commercial ties between Crete and the surrounding Ottoman world predated the Ottoman conquest of the island. The court records also show that relations between Muslim and Christian businessmen could be quite close, even during wartime. Again in 1069/1659 a certain Poulēmenos, formerly of Athens now settled in Chania, came to the Muslim court to register his partnership with an imperial janissary named Ali beşe. Ali gave him 80,000 akçe (presumably to trade with, although the document does not specify), and they agreed that the accounts would run from March to March, profits would be split on an equal basis, and Ali could withdraw his money at any time.[31] It is likely that Muslim and Christian merchants moved in common circles to a certain extent during the Venetian period as well. Turkish merchants like "Ghidun turco de Faches" were able to find guarantors in Venetian Candia, without which they would not have been allowed to depart from the city's port.[32]

Shipping and Shipbuilding

Venice's declining ability to monopolize Cretan trade was one reason why a local merchant class was able to develop in Crete in the sixteenth and seventeenth centuries. Another important factor was the ability of the islanders to build their own boats.

The shipping crisis that gripped Venice at the end of the sixteenth century certainly had its local counterpart in Crete. The state arsenal at Candia, used to repair and maintain the war ships stationed in Crete for the island's defense and to make equipment such as oars for the new galleys that were sent down from the metropole, was in constant difficulty during the last century of Venetian rule.[33] There were never enough galleys in the arsenal, and the workers, if they could be had at all, were unsatisfactory.

---

[28] On 17 May 1629 Manoli Aramandani was chosen in Candia as the "dragomano publico" and "interprete della lingua Turca." His salary was five ducats a month. Panopoulou, "Opseis," 172.

[29] In 1611 "Ghidun turco de Faches" was in Candia with his "saica." Ibid., 186.

[30] T.A.H. 1:146.

[31] T.A.H. 1:154.

[32] His guarantor was Nicolo Cacni q. Luca.

[33] Angelikē Panopoulou, "Oi technites naupēgeiōn tou Chandaka kai tōn Chaniōn kata to 16 kai 17 aiōna" (The shipyard workers of Chandaka and Chania in the sixteenth and

Writing in 1589, Mocenigo informed the Senate that few boats were being built in Candia's arsenal. The great expense involved, the general economic crisis, and the meager profits all contributed to the problem.[34] The shipyard workers, seeing that there was little work available, then went elsewhere, principally to Istanbul. In 1602 Moro reported that he had instructed two galleys to be built in Chania but that they remained unfinished at the time of his departure due to Venice's failure to send the necessary wood.[35] Venice, of course, was in no position to send timber to Crete. By the end of the sixteenth century severe timber shortages were forcing Venice to buy expensive wood on the international market even for its own needs.[36] In 1639 Civran remarked that Venice, which used to send new galleys out to Crete, had not sent any in almost two decades.[37]

Venice made a concerted effort to raise salaries and thus bring back skilled workers to the arsenal in the seventeenth century, an effort that paid off in terms of increased numbers.[38] In 1608 Agostino Sagredo reported with satisfaction that he had manged to bring back those who had been scattered "not only in the kingdom but also many of those who had been abroad."[39] Even so, quality continued to be a problem. Francesco Moresini fired fourteen workers in Candia in 1629, some because they were actually housebuilders rather than shipbuilders, others because they were "così inutili."[40] He added that there were just as many useless workers, if not more, in Chania and that they had received their jobs through patronage.[41]

Clearly the Venetians had many reasons for dissatisfaction in Crete. But, as with trade itself, the situation looked quite different from the local point of view. It was difficult to retain skilled workers in Candia precisely because they had so many opportunities elsewhere in the eastern Mediterranean. Mocenigo mentions Istanbul, where workers were well paid and money was plentiful.[42] And Venice had become so dependent on Greek sailors

seventeenth centuries), *Krētikē Estia* 4, no. 3 (1989–90): 173. State arsenals outside Venice were at Corfou, Zakynthos, Candia (Chandaka), and Chania.

[34] "rispetto che le gran spese, et le carestie di questi tempi, et li traffichi pochi, et di poco guadagno, che si fanno, causano che al presente si fabricano pochissimi vasseli." Spanakēs, "Relazione del Nobil Huomo Zuanne Mocenigo," 171.

[35] Stergios Spanakēs, "Relatione dell Sr. Benetto Moro ritornato di proveditor general del regno di Candia, letta in pregadi a 25 giugno 1602," *Mnēmeia tēs krētikēs istorias* (Monuments of Cretan history), vol. 4 (Herakleion, 1958), 12.

[36] Lane, *Venice*, 384–85.

[37] Stergios Spanakēs, "Relazione de Sr. Isepo Civran tornato di Prov. r Gen.l di Candia 1639," *Krētika Chronika* 21 (1969): 383.

[38] Panopoulou, "Oi Technites," 176.

[39] "non solo nel regno ma molti anco fuori d'esso in paesi esterni." Ibid., 182.

[40] Spanakēs, "Relazione Francesco Moresini," 60. Moresini says there were 130 but this is such a high number that it almost certainly includes assistants and students. Panopoulou, "Oi technites," 182.

[41] Spanakēs, "Relazione Francesco Moresini," 60–61.

[42] In his words "le arti vagliono bene, et il danaro corre largamente." Spanakēs, "Relazione del Nobil Huomo Zuanne Mocenigo," 171.

that in the ill-fated Navigation Laws of 1602, which sought to penalize western shipping and favor Venetian navigation by requiring that the crews of ships of Venetian registry had to be two-thirds Venetian, an exception was made for the Greeks who, for the purposes of this law, could be counted as Venetians.[43]

Even within Crete, sailors, caulkers, carpenters, and oar-makers had other options besides the city of Candia. When Sagredo reported in 1608 that he had been able to bring back those who had been scattered *within the kingdom*, he was no doubt referring to the mountainous area of southwestern Crete known as Sfakia. The inhabitants of these mountains, which border the sea on the southern side of the island, were skilled seamen and boatbuilders who worked periodically in the arsenal at Chania.[44]

The crisis of shipbuilding in the state arsenal at Candia does not mean that there was an overall crisis in the construction of boats. In the very same report in which he informed the Senate that few boats were being built in Candia's arsenal, Mocenigo also wrote the following of the urban populations in both Candia and Chania: "Among the population of the cities there are a number of master workers who are used to occupy themselves with the construction of galleons and other ships. And if, in fact, their numbers are small today relative to what would we need in time of war, I must point out that it is possible to find a way to increase their numbers."[45] No doubt the Cretans as well with their modest boats accounted for the "navigatione continua e frequentissima" along the northern coast of the island noted by Moresini in 1629, and for the vital procurement of wood from the archipelago cited in 1630.[46]

In other words, just as commerce continued in the seventeenth century but is less visible to us because it was local and regional, so shipbuilding continued into the seventeenth century as well. It moved out of the state

[43] Lane, *Venice*, 415, and A. Tenenti, *Naufrages, corsaires, et assurances maritimes à Venise 1592–1609* (Paris: S.E.V.P.E.N., 1959), 21.

[44] See a petition to the provveditore of Chania in 1594 where the Sfakianoi introduced themselves as "servitori di San Marco, et Marangoni, calafati, et Maestri che fanno il legname, et pegole (retsina), e quali sono stati sempre pronti nelli servitii delli Arsenali der Sermo. Principle nostro." Stergios Spanakēs, "Relatione di Me Filippo Pasqualigo ritornato di cap.o di Candia et prov.r della Canea 1594," *Mnēmeia tēs krētikēs istorias* (Monuments of Cretan history), vol. 3 (Herakleion, 1953), 165. The reports of 1589, 1602, 1630, and 1639 all refer to the seafaring and boatbuilding skills of the Sfakianoi as well.

[45] "delli medisimi popoli delle Città si cava qualche numbero di maestranza, la quale si va sostentando con le fabriche dei galeoni, et altri vasseli, et se ben è hora poca in verita, rispetto al bisogno che se ne ha ad havere in tempo di guerra; si può però facilmente trovar modo di accrescherla, e di mantenerla, come mi obbligo di raccordare." Spanakēs, "Relazione del Nobil Huomo Zuanne Mocenigo," 23.

[46] "As far as the procurement of wood is concerned, the situation would be very bad if it weren't for the little boats [*legne*] that go to the archipelago and bring it back, because there isn't enough wood in Crete for the needs of Candia." Stergios Spanakēs, "Relazione Pietro Giustiniano Capitan Generale de Resmo 1630." *Mnēmeia tēs krētikēs istorias* (Monuments of Cretan history), vol. 5 (Herakleion, 1969), 20, 227.

The Monastery of the Holy Trinity of Tzangarolōn, northeast of Chania. During the Ottoman period it had its own shipyard. Credit: Princeton University Library

shipyards, however, and into the more elusive world of small, private shipyards such as those in Sfakia or even smaller one-man operations. We know that in the Ottoman period, for instance, the monastery of the Holy Trinity of Tzangarolōn on the peninsula that juts out just northeast of Chania had its own shipyard (*tersane*) and used its boats to bring supplies more easily from Chania. Other monasteries might well have had shipyards, too.[47]

In order to build boats, of course, one must have wood, which explains the centrality of Sfakia in the history of Cretan seafaring. Without the wood supplied by the prodigious forests of Sfakia there would have been little boatbuilding, and the ability of the Cretans to strike out on their own, independent of Venice, would have been more limited. The Venetian reports make many references to the forests of Sfakia and to shipbuilding in that part of the island. The Sfakianoi, Mocenigo wrote, "extract resin and cut wood, because there is a lot of wood there [where they live]."[48] In 1630 Giustiniano described the "many mountains of Sfakia with boundless forests of cypress, oak (*roueri*), and other trees." The Sfakianoi, he contin-

[47] See Elizabeth Zachariadou, "Monks and Sailors under the Ottoman Sultans" (paper presented at the conference on *The Ottomans and the Sea* at the Skilliter Centre for Ottoman Studies, Newnham College, Cambridge University, 29–30 March 1996), for examples of monastic boatyards in the Aegean.

[48] "cavano pegola, et tagliano legnami, essendovi in quel contorno boschi assai." Spanakēs, "Relazione del Nobil Huomo Zuanne Mocenigo," 8. Moro referred to the Sfakianoi as "tagliaboschi." Spanakēs, "Relatione dell Sr. Benetto Moro," 75.

ued, bring this wood to the city where it is used to build boats and galleys, as well as houses.[49]

Early in the seventeenth century, however, the local wood industry—and, by extension, local shipbuilding—appears to have suffered a severe, if temporary, setback. According to Civran, writing in 1639, there had been a terrible fire almost thirty years earlier: "From the wood of those forests, all of it cypress and hornbeam (*carpini*), the inhabitants used to build great ships with great skill. But in 1612 there was a huge fire which lasted more than a year without them being able to put it out. As a result of that fire the forests were almost completely destroyed and now little wood can be gotten from there."[50]

Given this explicit reference to a fire in 1612, it is odd that Giustiniano, writing in 1630, refers to the "boundless forests" of Sfakia. Most probably he was simply including outdated information in his report to the Senate, perhaps as part of a conventional description of the island.[51] Later on in the report he shows himself to be very much aware of a shortage of wood on the island, a shortage that might have been partially the result of a fire in Sfakia. The situation on Crete, he wrote, would be very dire if it weren't for the little boats (*legne*) that bring wood from the archipelago. When they failed to bring wood, the bakeries in Candia were not even able to bake bread.[52]

Still, even Civran, who provides the information for the fire in Sfakia in 1612, refers to the "many forests" (*molti boschi*) on the island.[53] In the end it is difficult to be sure of the state of the forests in Sfakia during the last decades of Venetian rule. Even if there was a fire, however, the setback was only temporary because the shipbuilding tradition in Sfakia is very much in evidence in the early Ottoman period, as we shall discuss shortly.

Whatever the origin of the boats in use in Crete, it is clear that, just as local and regional trade grew in importance during the course of the seventeenth century, so too did the reliance on smaller vessels to carry

[49] "Vi sono anco nelle parti della Sfacchia molti Monti co(n) boscagli di Ancipressi, Roueri et altri arbori in infinito, di dove si conducono nelle Città, tauole, traui, et legnami per far Galee, et Vasselli, coprir case et altri negotij." Spanakēs, "Relazione Pietro Giustiniano," 22. Civran, writing in 1639, also referred to shipments of wood from Sfakia to the cities. Spanakēs, "Relazione de Sr. Isepo Civran," 402.

[50] "De legnami di quei boschi, che sono tutti Cipressi e Carpini, altre volte si fabricavano Vasselli di gran portata, che riuscivano a perfettione, ma essendo del 1612 seguito un grand'incendio, che durò un anno, et più, senza potersi smorzare; restano i medesimi boschi, quasi disfatti, con gran perdita, e danno, ne si può più cavar legnami di consideratione." Spanakēs, "Relazione de Sr. Isepo Civran," 402. Hornbeam is a tree very close to the beech tree.

[51] His discussion of the workers in the state arsenals (Spanakēs, "Relazione Pietro Giustiniano," 247) reproduces Mocenigo's 1589 report word for word.

[52] Ibid., 227.

[53] Spanakēs, "Relazione de Sr. Isepo Civran," 387.

that trade.[54] Moro's discussion of the type of boat known as the marciliana makes clear the cost-cutting advantages of using smaller boats.[55] Because of the marciliana, he complained, galleons were no longer being built on the island:

> Ever since the introduction of the marciliane, they [the galleons] have been completely abandoned, to such an extent that during my entire time there only one [galleon] was built, and that with great difficulty. It is not sufficient to offer subsidies in order to get them to build galleys because they know that the merchants will not give up the freight advantage that they gain by loading their goods onto marciliane. The galleys are more expensive because they require more crew, whereas the marciliane are cheaper because they sail with fewer sailors.[56]

The marciliana was developed in Venice as an attempt by the private sector, faced with Dutch and English competition, to lower operating costs.[57] Its use in Crete as well serves to underscore the fact that, in both Crete and Venice, private initiative stepped in to fill at least some of the gaps left by the retreat of the state from commerce, navigation, and shipbuilding.[58] Another similarity was the frustration felt by Venice both at home and in its principal colony at commercial trends that appeared to threaten the military concerns that Venice held paramount. In the previous chapter we have already seen how the Cretan insistence on viticulture and then olive cultivation was opposed by the Venetians, who wanted to ensure an adequate supply of grain in case of war. These conflicts extended into the arena of shipping and navigation as well. The marciliana is a good example.

The Venetian government was opposed to the use of marciliane (in 1602 it forbade them to go beyond the island of Zakynthos in the Ionian Sea) because their use detracted from Venice's military preparedness. Venice preferred that big caracks be used in long voyages because the caracks could double as naval auxiliaries in time of war. It also wanted to ensure that Venetian (or Greek) sailors knew how to rig lateen sails (the marciliana used square sails) because the war galleys were lateen-rigged. Venetian complaints about the marciliana in Crete were the same:

> In addition it is clear that the shipowners have been attracted by the small expense involved in the building of these boats and in equipping them with crews. As a result they have almost completely stopped building larger ships.

---

[54] Panopoulou notes that in the second period for which she has contracts (1634–40) smaller, lighter boats predominated. Panopoulou, "Opseis," 159.

[55] The marciliana was in use in Venice as well. See Lane, *Venice*, 385–86.

[56] Spanakēs, "Relatione dell Sr. Benetto Moro," 148.

[57] Lane, *Venice*, 385. My discussion of the marciliana in Venice closely follows Lane's account.

[58] At the level of international trade, of course, it was the Dutch and the English who came to replace Venice.

But your Excellency knows that it is these large ships and the galleys that are needed in time of war, to ferry supplies and soldiers and to stand up to other galleys.[59]

In Crete, of course, the Venetians faced the very real possibility of an actual war, whereas the vantage point from Venice was quite different. Despite this, merchants in Crete showed themselves just as willing to disregard Venetian strategic concerns as their counterparts in the metropolitan city itself.

A Model for the Sixteenth and Seventeenth Centuries

The ability to build their own boats certainly helped Cretan merchants, sailors, and captains to strike out on their own, independent of Venice. This was not the only way, however, to participate in the world of maritime commerce. Cretans could and did sail for others as well. Probably a minority, in fact, owned the vessels they served on or loaded their cargo onto. According to Panayiōtopoulos, most of the Greek sailors and captains in Venice in the middle of the sixteenth century were serving on Venetian boats. One Greek sailor of Venice was working for an Ottoman Turkish merchant.[60]

This is a point worth emphasizing. Historians of Greek seafaring during the centuries of Ottoman rule have preferred to concentrate their energies on the eighteenth century, when an entirely Greek merchant marine was formed in the Aegean islands, particularly on the island of Hydra. Discussions of the place of Greek maritime skill in the Ottoman Empire before the eighteenth century have emphasized servile labor and the military requirements of the Ottoman state.[61]

Such an emphasis on the commercial activity of the Greeks when it was a relatively self-contained and ethnically homogeneous undertaking has served well the requirements of nationalist historiography, but it has tended to obscure the characteristics of an earlier age. The example of Crete in the sixteenth and seventeenth centuries suggests another model. In 1590 a Venetian official complained that workers in the arsenal in Candia had abandoned the shipyard and gone off to become ship captains (*patroni*).[62]

---

[59] Spanakēs, "Relatione dell Sr. Benetto Moro," 149.

[60] The names of the boats show that most were Venetian. It was the custom of the time for boats to be named after their owners and most of the names are Venetian. Panayiōtopoulos, "Ellēnes nautikoi kai ploioktētes," 302.

[61] Vassilis Sfyroeras's excellent study is typical of this genre in that it is organized around the place of the Greeks in the Sultan's navy. Vassilis Sfyroeras, *Ta hellenika plerōmata tou tourkikou stolou* (The Greek Crews of the Turkish fleet) (Athens, 1968).

[62] Panopoulou, "Opseis," 180.

Both Venice and Istanbul relied in part on Greek labor to maintain their navies and their merchant marines, and, as this comment shows, the Greeks were able to use this service in the shipyards as a stepping-stone in their own maritime careers. In contemplating their choices, they did not limit themselves to Greek-owned enterprises but rather moved with ease into the multinational world that characterized maritime commerce in the seventeenth century eastern Mediterranean. This was a world in flux. Venice no longer ruled the seas and the domination of France had yet to be established. This transitional age was one of opportunity for the Cretans, as it was for the Greek islanders in general.[63]

The Ottoman Period

The earl of Castlemaine was no doubt flushed with Christian pride when he wrote to the king of England how, when Christian sailors converted to Islam, they not only changed their faith but also, wonderfully, lost their ability to navigate. Something of the same attitude has led to the assumption of an abrupt change in commercial life and culture in Candia after 1669. Some writers have even spoken of the death of commerce: "The Cretan economy reverted to primitive forms of agricultural and pastoral life, while trade, at least during the first fifty years of the occupation, came to a halt. . . . The flourishing shipping of an earlier age was forgotten."[64]

As we have already seen in the previous chapter, commercial life did continue in early Ottoman Candia and in many ways showed important continuities with the late Venetian period. Moreover, some of the changes that became manifest at this time, such as the orientation toward Egypt, had taken root earlier in the century. Even with regard to the merchants themselves, certain aspects of the recent past endured. In one respect, however, there was a dramatic change and that was in the identity of the merchant community in Candia. Most of the city's merchants were now Muslim rather than Christian, and this fact more than any other, I believe, has led historians of Crete, in harmony with Castlemaine, to write as if the commercial world of Muslim Candia could have nothing to do with the Candia of an earlier, Christian age.

[63] Such a model holds for the Cycladic islands as well. Slot writes "Dès le milieu du XVIIe siècle la navigation autochtone cycladienne fait l'objet d'une expansion marquée, particulièrement à Mykonos. . . . On trouve incidentellement des marins cycladiens à peu près partout. Ils proviennent non seulement de ces îles à navigation importante, mais également d'autres îles. Ainsi nous trouvons en 1600 un Naxien fait prisonnier par un corsaire néerlandais à bord d'un vaisseau vénitien en route pour le Brésil." B. J. Slot, *Archipelagus Turbatus: Les Cyclades entre colonisation latine et occupation ottomane c. 1500–1718* (Istanbul: Nederlands Historisch-Archaeologisch Instituut te Istanbul, 1982), 1:20.
[64] Theocharis Detorakēs, *Istoria tēs Krētēs* (History of Crete) (Athens, 1986), 271, 296.

A Merchant World Both Old and New

The predominantly Muslim identity of the city's merchants is not surprising given the fact that the population was now overwhelmingly Muslim.[65] More to the point is the fact that the majority of the city's merchants were of local origin. The Ottoman conquest of the city did not result in the wholesale displacement of indigenous merchants.

The local roots of Candia's merchants are not difficult to establish. First, the court records were in the habit of carefully distinguishing between natives and nonresidents. The neighborhood of residence in Candia was always given for a native, while the place of origin (typically a province or a city) was supplied in the case of a visitor. Because of this, we can be sure that, except for the case of the wheat trade with North Africa, native merchants were far more numerous than any other group.[66]

Second, individuals with some affiliation to the janissary corps clearly dominated commerce in Candia, as they dominated so many other areas of urban life.[67] As we know from an earlier chapter, many of the city's soldiers were local converts to Islam. It follows, then, that many of these soldier-merchants were Cretans. In some cases we are lucky enough to have a confirmation of this theory. One of the richest merchants in Candia at this time was one Bezirgān Haci Hüseyin beşe, who was an ordinary soldier (yoldaş) from the ninety-ninth corps (cema'at) of the imperial janissaries.[68] The absence of a patronymic in his property distribution already suggests a convert origin. This suspicion is confirmed in the section listing credits extended where we learn that his Christian brother in Nicosia owed him fifty-three paras at the time of his death.[69]

Haci Hüseyin beşe was an ordinary soldier, a yoldaş, and most of the janissaries involved in trade in Candia were also at the humble rank of beşe.[70] This too suggests a locally based merchant class, since it was the

[65] The following section on merchants is based on a comprehensive review of all commercial documents found in the court records for the period 1669–1720. I have counted both records of commercial cases brought before the court and terekes, or property distributions of merchants, as commercial documents. One hundred seventy documents were found for this period. Over 80 percent of the documents involved Muslims (although not necessarily Muslims exclusively).

[66] Sixty-eight percent of the merchants named in the court documents were from Crete (excluding those involved in the wheat trade). A resident of Candia was typically identified by the words "medine-i Candia sakinlerinden."

[67] They are present in 40 percent of all court documents concerning commerce.

[68] The Ottoman military garrison in Egypt was divided into seven corps, called ojaqat or jama'at. Ahmad Damurdashi, al-Damurdashi's Chronicle of Egypt, 1688–1755, trans. and annotated by Daniel Crecelius and Abd al-Wahhab Bakr (Leiden: E. J. Brill, 1991), 17.

[69] T.A.H. 7:70. "Nikosalu zimmi karandaşında."

[70] For one of many examples, see T.A.H. 8:16 where six janissaries, all at the low rank of beşe, are identified as being from the tujjar taifesi (the group of the merchants).

average soldier, not the officer of high rank, who was most likely to be from Crete. This characteristic also suggests a certain continuity with the Venetian period, in that the city's merchants occupied a middle ground in the urban hierarchy. They were, presumably, better off than those who had no military affiliation but their status could not compare with the wealthy military officers (many of them from Istanbul) who farmed the island's agricultural wealth.

Although Muslims were now the dominant group, trade in Candia was not an exclusively Muslim concern. In fact, despite their small number, Christians in the city were highly visible in commercial life.[71] Christian merchants were somewhat more likely to be non-Cretans and many were identified in court as temporary residents (*misafiran sakin*).[72] The importance of Candia to Christian merchants from other parts of the empire is suggested by the fact that, less than a year after the conquest, a ferman directed that the yave cizye, a head tax levied on nonresident minorities, be collected in Candia. The yave cizye was traditionally imposed in important centers of commerce, such as Aleppo, where merchants would stay for extended periods, and, in fact, the ferman specified that the tax was to be collected "from infidels who came from outside Crete for business."[73]

Even for those Christians who were residents of the city, a place of origin was nevertheless given, indicating that they were recent immigrants. These immigrants tended to come from the cities and towns around the Aegean, places like Salonica, Monemvasia, Athens, and the islands. Through Papa Apostolos, of the island of Skopelos, we learn something of the affairs of Moschos, from Larissa on the mainland, who settled in Rethymnon for purposes of trade, and his brother, Makrygiannēs. During a sojourn in Skopelos, Makrygiannēs had married Papa Apostolos's daughter and the couple had had a son. Makrygiannēs then went down to Rethymnon where he picked up a cargo of olive oil and headed off to Izmir to sell it. On the way, however, he was caught by Venetian ships patrolling the Aegean and forced to serve as a galley slave. In the course of a subsequent battle, he died. Before his departure from Rethymnon he had entrusted his brother, Moschos, with 700 esedi guruş, the focus of Papa Apostolos's interest. He wanted a share of the money for his daughter and his grandson. According to the court document, the existence of this family came as a surprise to Moschos, not least because while in Rethymnon his brother Makrygiannēs had married a woman named Eleni with whom he had a son.[74]

---

[71] Christians appear in 36 percent of all documents relating to commerce.
[72] About one-third.
[73] T.A.H. 3:103. "Girit hududu sükkānindan gayri āhir diyardan gelüb kar ve kesb uzere kefere."
[74] T.A.H. 1:71.

Another inheritance dispute, this one from 1108/1697, involved two Greek brothers who had emigrated to Crete from Monemvasia (probably upon the fall of that city to the Venetians in 1690, although the document does not say).[75] One of the brothers, Nikola veled-i Georgaki, had recently died of the plague on Chios while bringing back dried fish from Istanbul. The public treasury then declared that there were no heirs and took over the property. One month later his brother, Yianno veled-i Todoro, showed up in Candia to demand his brother's goods, and from his testimony we learn of the brothers' emigration to Crete from Monemvasia. In order to prove his relationship to his brother, Yianno was able to call on the testimony of three Christians and three Muslims, all of them émigrés from Monemvasia as well.

Christian immigration into Candia at this time is one indication that, although the city was now predominately Muslim, it was in no way cut off from larger Aegean world that had been so important to the island in the Venetian period. Numerous other documents also show a close relationship between Candia's merchants and traders in other ports in the eastern Mediterrranean.

At the time of his death in 1083/1673, for instance, a janissary soldier named Ali Ahmet beşe b. Mehmet owned 50 percent of the gear on board a frigate (*firkata*) moored in the harbor of Candia.[76] The gear was a jumble of pistols, cannons, kitchen utensils, and sailing equipment. One of the other two owners was a sea captain from Chios, Sakizli Mustafa Kapudan, while the third was a high-ranking officer, a pasha. The deceased's wife sold her husband's share for 600 esedi guruş to an agha from Üsküp (in Macedonia).

Mehmet beşe b. Davud of Candia had a trading partnership (*şirket*) with a merchant from the island of Kos by the name of Haci Mustafa b. Süleyman. They did business together in Egypt.[77] Hussein beşe, a janissary and a cloth merchant, was supplied with cloth by a Christian in Chios.[78] Two Muslim merchants from Rhodes emigrated to Crete sometime before 1103/1691 and subsequently occupied themselves in the coffee trade with Egypt, where they had a third partner (*şerik*) who was also a Muslim.[79]

In addition to these rather straightforward links, a case of piracy and a contract of guarantorship (*kefala*) show the complex lines of communication and obligation that could be sustained over a large area, even during wartime. In 1099/1687 Ahmet b. haci Ali, a North African merchant sailing from Alexandria, was taken hostage by Portuguese corsairs

---

[75] T.A.H. 10:12, 13.
[76] T.A.H. 4:138.
[77] T.A.H. 4:183.
[78] T.A.H. 7:70.
[79] T.A.H. 7:86.

("Portugal kefere korsanlarina asir olup").[80] When they reached the Aegean island of Aegina near the Greek mainland, he was ransomed by Asmati veled-i Georgi. This Asmati showed up in Candia fourteen months later, to collect the ransom fee from a merchant of Candia named Mehmet b. Abdullah.

Merchants from many parts of the Aegean came together to court in 1106/1695 to register an act of guarantorship. Two Muslim merchants from Chania, a Greek from Monemvasia, and three other Greeks from Chios all offered themselves as guarantors for Mihal veled-i Manol and his partner Manoli.[81] The partners were originally from Monemvasia (perhaps they fled when the Venetians took the city in 1690) but were now resident in Chios. The guarantors swore that the two (referred to as "Egyptian merchants" [*Misr Bezirganlar*]) would not go to enemy territory or to Chios when they departed from Candia. Given that the Venetians were occupying Chios at the time the court document was issued, it is clear that the Ottoman authorities were concerned lest the two gentlemen from Chios be tempted to take their goods to that island or otherwise engage in some sort of intrigue.

It is striking that, even as war with the Venetians raged in the Aegean, Christians were admitted by the court as guarantors of good conduct. One of the explanations may be the strength of established custom; guarantors were an established part of commercial life in Venetian Candia and the bond of guarantorship had crossed religious lines then as well.[82]

A Diversified Commerce

The diversified commerce that someone like George Mormore had pursued with such success in the 1650s and 1660s continued to be characteristic of Candia's merchants in the early Ottoman period. Numerous property distributions (*tereke/terekāt*) survive in the records of the local court, thanks to which we can construct a fairly detailed picture of the commercial world of some of Candia's most successful merchants at this time.[83]

[80] T.A.H. 5:192. A similar case occurred a few years later. A Jewish merchant of Candia named Samul veled-i Danil came to court demanding the remainder of the ransom fee (which had been 1,250 esedi guruş) for freeing four Muslims from Nauplion where they had been held by the Venetians during the war.

[81] T.A.H. 8:36.

[82] See also T.A.H. 9:107: Georgi, a merchant sea captain (*reis tuccari*) required a guarantor in order to secure permission to export wheat to North Africa. He turned to a Muslim sea captain, Benefşeli Çolak Hassan reis.

[83] The problem with this source is the fact that most property distributions never came to court and the wealthy are overrepresented. While this source cannot provide a picture of all economic classes in the city, it does give us a profile of the city's wealthiest merchants. For the strengths and weaknesses of the mukhallafat as a source, see Bruce Masters, *The Origins*

On 27 Cemeziyüyelevvel 1103/15 February 1692, the kadi court in Candia drew up the property distribution of bezirgān Haci Hüseyin beşe, the merchant from the ninety-ninth corps of the imperial janissaries who was discussed earlier in the context of his Christian brother in Nicosia.[84] Hussein beşe's assets were worth 706,348 akçe. This amount, plus the fact that he owned a Russian slave, indicates that he was a wealthy man.[85] He was almost certainly a fabric merchant, since several items of cloth in his tereke were far more expensive than any of his other possessions. He had 179 zira (somewhere between 100 and 150 yards) of fine English wool (*Elvan Londra çukasi*) worth 51,201 akçe.[86] He also had significant amounts (over 100 zira each) of *kemha*, a silk fabric embroidered with gold and silver threads used for kaftans; another type of silk fabric called *hatai*, possibly used as underclothing; and *atlas*, a plain silk.[87]

Although he only had eight okka of coffee in his possession (worth 1,312 akçe), the record of his debts shows that he owed one Ahmed beşe 23,800 akçe for coffee, so it seems likely that he traded in coffee as well. Finally, three merchants owed him 32,000 akçe for silver goods (*sim eşya*) he had sent to Egypt with them.

Most of Hussein beşe's customers were the Muslim military elite of the city.[88] At the time of his death he had extended credit to them in the

---

of Western Economic Dominance in the Middle East: Mercantilism and the Islamic Economy in Aleppo, 1600–1750 (New York: New York University Press, 1988), 165.

[84] T.A.H. 7:70.

[85] This was equivalent to 176,587 para. For changing guruş into akçe or para, or vice versa, I rely on exchange rates given by the judge either in the property distribution itself or in one drawn up as near as possible to the date of the document under consideration (exchange rates, while common, are not given in every instance). Hussein beşe's assets were certainly substantial, especially in the context of a small city like Candia, but whether this made him wealthy is more difficult to say. In Cairo the average estate of a merchant involved in the coffee or spice trade (the group that Raymond calls the "grands commerçants") between 1679 and 1700 was 299,344 para. The para was the basic silver coin and unit of account in Egypt. For merchants in less lucrative sectors the figure was 46,734 para. André Raymond, *Artisans et commerçants au Caire au XVIII siècle* (Damascus: Institut Français de Damas, 1973), 1:290. Raymond's account, however, does not make clear whether this is the value owed before or after monies owed are taken into account. Although Hussein beşe owed (and was owed) a substantial amount, he was also heavily in debt. At the time of his death, his debts amounted to 80 percent of his assets, a much higher percentage than what Masters has noted for Aleppo, where the highest figure was 21 percent. Masters, *The Origins of Western Economic Dominance*, 166. Clearly Hussein beşe was highly dependent on credit for the functioning of his business.

[86] In the seventeenth century English and French wool enjoyed a reputation as the finest wool available. A zira, an "arm's length," was a measurement for cloth running anywhere from 21 to 29.5 inches, depending on the place. Reşat Ekrem Koçu, *Türk giyim süslenme sözlüğü* (The dictionary of Turkish dress) (Istanbul: Sümerbank Kültür Yayinlari, 1969), 82.

[87] See Koçu, *Türk Giyim*, the entries under *atlas*, *kemha*, and *hatai*.

[88] This credit relationship between the city's merchants and the military elite may well have predated the Ottoman period. Among the private papers of the Greek merchant George Mormore who was active in the 1650s and 1660s were records of many loans extended to the Venetian elite of the city. Antoniadēs, "E Kinētē Periousia tou Geōrgiou Mormore," 264.

amount of roughly 252,000 akçe, over a third of his assets. Significantly his only Christian customer was the powerful secretary to the Porte, whose status and wealth would allow him to pursue the same luxury consumption that his Muslim counterparts enjoyed.

If Hussein beşe extended credit generously, he was also the beneficiary of liberal credit arrangements. His debts amounted to 558,904 akçe or 80 percent of his assets. One of the larger debts, 38,400 akçe, was to an Armenian merchant, and he owed 22,840 akçe to a Greek of Chios for fabric (*kumaş*). As mentioned earlier, he also owed a substantial amount for coffee.

By considering Hussein's customers and suppliers together, a picture of his place in Candia's commerce emerges. He was a merchant who supplied the city's elite with luxury items like coffee and fine textiles. He himself did not travel to Egypt, Chios, or Izmir (the center of the trade in English cloth) to purchase these goods but was instead supplied by Greeks and Armenians who came from the Aegean and Muslims who came from Egypt to Candia with these goods. He was, in other words, a middleman but not of the sort most often discussed in Ottoman historiography. He was not a minority merchant mediating between a westerner and the Muslim elite, but rather a Muslim who connected the traveling merchants of the eastern Mediterranean to Candia's wealthy officer class. Outstanding debts to two brokers (*dallals*) suggest that he sold imported goods in the marketplace as well, in addition to his direct relationship with the city's aghas and pashas.

If the debts discussed so far are relatively easy to explain, a series of much more substantial liabilities is more difficult to understand and points to another side of Hussein's activities. He owed 50,000 akçe to Nuama Efendi, the former scribe of the janissaries (*katib-i yeniçeriyan-i sabik*), another 80,000 akçe to Ali Agha, the chief lieutenant of the local janissaries (*kethuda-yi yeniçeriyan-i yerli*), and 25,200 akçe to the current scribe of the local janissaries (*katib-i yeniçeriyan-i yerli*). Because there is no obvious reason why these officers would lend him money so extensively, one must conclude that these amounts represent debt for goods received. Considering the high rank of those involved, the goods in question must have been agricultural produce given to Hussein to market, possibly to the traveling merchants who came to the port. This explanation makes sense, although it must be admitted that no agricultural products of any significant amount appear in his property distribution. Perhaps he simply happened to have none in his possession at the time of his death.

Hussein's success, as well as the sophistication of his business methods, is further indicated by two extensive, additional sections in his property distribution that do not appear in the records of other merchants of Candia. These final two parts are described by the scribe as "the price of goods owed, payment for which has not yet been received, found in the notebook of the deceased," and "akçe owed to the deceased through certificates, not yet received."[89] Hussein beşe was clearly literate and relied on written records and specialized documents to keep track of his many business dealings. The court was willing to admit these documents in the official tallying of his estate, a fact that suggests that it was not unaware of the requirements of commerce.[90] It is difficult to know why these debtors, recorded in his notebook (*defter*) or holding certificates (*temessükkat*), were recorded separately from the debtors that appear in the initial listing of Hussein's assets. The implication is that the first were purely oral agreements. At any rate, his close connection to the military elite remained the same. The vast majority of his debtors were janissaries and many of those were aghas. One of the largest credits outstanding at the time of his death was to a janissary officer on the island of Mytilene.[91]

Hussein beşe's business records sugggest that he moved comfortably in Christian, Muslim, and Jewish society. Here we must speculate, but it does not seem unreasonable to suggest the following: converts to Islam who were also able to construct some sort of an affiliation with the janissary corps could enjoy several advantages in their commercial life. On the one hand, they gained high-ranking military officers as clients and benefactors. We learn from this document that, even though Hussein beşe was only a lowly yoldaş, he was able to designate an agha as his debt collector after his death. For a man who extended credit as liberally as Hussein beşe did, the ability to rely on a janissary officer to make sure his debtors paid must have been vitally important.[92] On the other hand, his ties to his (former) coreligionists in the Christian community may have helped him in maintaining business relationships throughout the Aegean world.

The merchant (*Bezirgān*) Mustafa Yazici, who died six years after Hussein beşe in the winter of 1100/1698, was similar in many ways.[93] He was an imperial janissary and the absence of a patronym suggests that he, too, was a convert. Like Hussein beşe he was certainly literate because he extended credit through temessükkat and kept track of loans in a defter. Unfortunately, the scribe did not record individual debtors so we know

---

[89] "müteveffa-yi mezbûrun defterinde bulunub zimemde olan eşta pahalaridir ki el-haletül hazihi tahsil olmayub zikr-i āti üzere beyan olunur" and "müteveffa-yi mezbûrun temessükkat-ile zimemde olan akçeleridir ki el-haletül hazihi tahsil olmayub zikr-i āti üzere beyan olunur."

[90] Despite the emphasis in Islamic law on oral testimony, the Ottoman courts seem generally to have admitted the use of written documents in settling claims. R. C. Jennings, *Christians and Muslims in Ottoman Cyprus and the Mediterranean World* (New York: New York University Press, 1993), 87, 92.

[91] "humbaraci Hassan Aga, Aga Midullu."

[92] In the property distributions of Candia a debt collector was often designated, although it was by no means always a janisssary officer. Hussein beşe paid the Khasseki Agha 40,000 akçe for performing this service: "balada tahrir olunan zimemler tahsili içün Haseki Aga'ya tarik-i ücret ve ma'harac mubaşir."

[93] T.A.H. 5:229.

much less about his customers than we would like.[94] His assets were slightly less than Mustafa Yazici's—about half a million akçe—but his debts were not as large.[95] He had a home in the most exclusive neighborhood in Candia, the one around Köprülü's mosque. One-third of his wealth was held in the various coins of the time—the Dutch silver coin known as esedi guruş, Venetian ducats, Egyptian paras, and şerifi altun, an Ottoman gold coin. Like Hussein beşe he was a coffee and textile importer who must have had close ties to the Egyptian economy.[96]

The exclusively urban orientation of these two soldier-merchants emerges more clearly when compared with the profile of a merchant and tax farmer who died in the autumn of 1712.[97] Esir Haci Ahmet's assets (the name suggests that he had been taken hostage at some point in his life) were roughly equal to those of Hussein beşe but, unlike him, he had ties to the Cretan countryside. He was owed 11,840 para for olive oil, wheat, barley, and flax for some villages that he held as a tax farm (*iltizamin-da*). He also lent money in the countryside and at the time of this death Christian villagers owed him some 22,200 para. Probably he sold the agricultural surplus to others to market, since he was owed a large amount for wheat, barley, and flax that he had sold from his storehouse (*der anbar*).[98] His largest debt (25,600 para) was to a Jew named Musa, no doubt one of the merchants he dealt with.

Haci Ahmet was not just a tax farmer, however. The records reveal that he imported goods from Egypt, including rice, flax, and sugarcane and was owed 14,162 paras for unspecified goods he had sold from Egypt. He owed rent on a shop in Candia, so he was involved in the retail trade as well. Finally, the scribe noted that his debts were recorded in a defter, which suggests that he, too, was literate.

Haci Ahmet lacks a title, which makes him difficult to place within Candiot society. Nevertheless, it is clear that he was not, as were the other two, an ordinary soldier. The yoldaş and beşe of Candia might, on occasion, accumulate substantial fortunes through the kind of regional trade that we have been discussing, but they were shut out of the agricultural economy—whether through tax farming or landownership—where the real profits lay. Like their counterparts in the late Venetian period, they tended not to be landowners or tax farmers themselves but occupied themselves instead with the more mundane needs of a medium-sized city within a dense network of regional trade.

---

[94] The scribe just recorded the total amount owed, 845 guruş.
[95] Five-hundred guruş or approximately 66,000 akçe.
[96] He had modest amounts (between 30 and 40 yards) of many different types of cloth and over 200 okka of coffee worth 200 guruş. He also had 53 pieces of leather.
[97] T.A.H. 2:324.
[98] The amount owed was equal to 25 percent of his total assets.

There is, of course, much more information on the island's elites. The French consular agents, for one, occupied themselves with little else but negotiations with this or that pasha over wheat and, later, olive oil. The documents generated by the fall of Yiannas Skordili, a Greek official of the highest rank (see chapter 6), in 1695 illustrate the very different contours of elite investment.

After Skordili fled the island, the governor of Candia went ahead with the sale of the former official's property, the proceeds of which were to be stored with the defterdar. The defterdar, the governor, and the kadi each sent a representative to Skordili's village of Monastiraki in Amari district (south of Rethymnon) in order to take an inventory of his estate.[99] Skordili's heavy investment in the agricultural economy of Crete is immediately apparent from this inventory. In addition to his house in the village, he had an olive press, a vineyard, 220 sheep, various livestock including 8 oxen, 103 mouzour of wheat, fields for grazing, new iron tools, and various household goods. Several months prior to this sale, Ottoman officials had found 5,000 French gold pieces—efrenji altun—buried on his property. These were turned over to the defterdar who was instructed to pay the janissaries with them.

Shipping

In her study of the Cretan economy during the first one hundred years of Ottoman rule, Yolanda Baladie argues for an almost seamless transition from Venetian shipping to French shipping once the Ottomans came into possession of the island.

> During the period of Venetian naval supremacy in the Mediterranean, her ships monopolized transportation. For the Cretans to have competed with her would have been pointless. Immediately after the Ottoman conquest, the French replaced the Venetians in this sector. They took over not only long-distance shipping, but also shipping within the empire itself.[100]

This analysis, while perhaps not inaccurate in the long run, ignores the transitional era of 1570 to 1720. By the seventeenth century the Venetians most certainly did not enjoy naval supremacy in the Mediterranean and the Cretans were, in fact, able to compete with her very effectively. As we have seen in chapter 4, indigenous shipping continued after the Ottoman conquest as well.

[99] T.A.H. 8:58.
[100] Yolanda Triandafyllidou Baladie, *To emborio kai e oikonomia tēs Krētēs 1669–1795* (The commerce and economy of Crete, 1669–1795) (Herakleion: Municipality of Herakleion, 1988), 61.

The tradition of urban shipbuilding does seem to have died out, probably because the Ottomans chose not to revive the state shipyards at Candia and Chania.[101] Sfakia, however, continued to produce boats. Because of the preoccupation with nationalist concerns, the role of the Sfakiot ship-owners in the uprisings of 1770 that swept the Greek world has received the lion's share of the attention. The leader of the revolt in Crete was a Sfakiot shipowner and merchant named John Vlachos, popularly known as Daskaloyiannēs.[102] Less well known is the fact that, prior to 1770, the Sfakiots continued to build ships for the merchants of Candia, just as they had in the Venetian period. In 1761 the French consul in Chania wrote, "The Turks here order their boats from Sfakia. They have quite a number of them and they give them over to Greek captains [to sail].[103]

The Sfakiots, then, may well have built some of the forty-eight boats listed in an important Ottoman document from the year 1164/1751.[104] In that year the Sultan ordered that a list be drawn up of the commercial fleet of the city of Candia. The boats, which were almost entirely Muslim-owned, compared very favorably both in size and number with other fleets that are known to us from the eastern Mediterranean at this time, "The example of Herakleion," writes one scholar, "is the second that we know of, after Missolonghi, of a thriving merchant marine at such an early date." The impetus behind the fleet's creation was directly linked to the city's important role in regional trade; it was used to sell Cretan soap around the eastern Mediterranean.[105] The largest boat in the fleet weighed in at 169 tons, well within the capacity of the Sfakiot shipyards at this time.[106]

It is difficult to know how soon after the conquest this relationship between Sfakia and Candia was reestablished. A spy letter dated 1686 implies that Sfakia was already supplying Candia with wood (in this case

[101] Aik. Bekiaroglu-Eksadaktylou, *Othomanika naupēgeia ston paradosiako ellēniko choro* (Ottoman shipyards in the Greek world) (Athens: ETBA, 1994), 120. In the court records from the first fifty years there is only one reference to boatbuilding in the city of Candia itself. In 1674 Candia's harbormaster (*liman reisi*) complained to the court that a boat in the harbor of Chania, currently in the possession of one Receb beşe b. Mehmet, was actually his boat. He had rented it to one Yiannis of Chania, who had sailed off and never been heard from again. Despite the addition of a deck (*güverte*), which had been added by the thief as a disguise, the harbormaster recognized the boat. Three residents of Candia testified that it was, indeed, the harbormaster's boat. They recognized it from the stern (*kiç*) since *it had been built in this city* (emphasis added): "medine-yi mezbure limanindan bina olunmağla, kiçinden biliriz." T.A.H. 5:148.

[102] These uprisings are known as the Orloff uprisings because of the critical role played by Theodoros Orloff, Catherine the Great's emissary to the Morea in 1769. For more on the Orloff uprisings, see the conclusion.

[103] Quoted in V. Kremmydas, "Katagrafē tōn emborikōn pliōn tou Irakleiou to 1751" (A list of the commercial boats of Herakleion in 1751), *Mnēmon* 7 (1978): 16.

[104] This document from the Ottoman archives in Candia is discussed by V. Kremmydas in his article. Ibid., 12–17.

[105] Ibid., 16–17.

[106] Ibid., 15.

for military purposes) but on an occasional basis only.[107] Certainly there is little mention of Sfakiot seafaring and shipping in the early years of Ottoman rule. Pococke mentioned Sfakiot seafaring in his trip to the island in 1739. He said they carried on a "a great coasting trade around the island in small boats, by carrying wood, corn and other merchandises."[108] His description suggests that by the middle of the eighteenth century shipping was recovering, but that shipbuilders could not yet handle the large boats that appear in the document of 1751. The explanation for limited shipping in the early Ottoman period must be ecological: if the fire of 1612 was as severe as Civran says it was, the forests would have taken many decades to recover.

The relative quietude of Cretan shipbuilding in the first half century of Ottoman rule does not mean that the island's merchants were completely dependent on French shipping. The anecdotal nature of the information on Ottoman shipping contained in the court records makes it impossible to assess the relative weight of Ottoman versus French shipping.[109] Andre Raymond's work on Egypt, however, suggests that Ottoman ships may well have been a common sight in the island's ports.

In the seventeenth and eighteenth centuries, he writes, about half of the trade between Egypt and the rest of the empire was carried on local ships ("navires turcs et grecs"). In trade with southern Anatolia Ottoman shipping actually predominated.[110] As we know, Crete enjoyed very close ties with Egypt at this time, to the point where it was Cretan merchants in Alexandria who controlled the trade with the rest of the empire.[111] It is plausible that, at least as far as trade with Egypt was concerned, many of the ships leaving Crete for Alexandria were native.

Cretans had access to some of these ships through their ties to merchants and shipowners in other parts of the empire. In 1081/1670, for instance, a Christian sailor named Anton veled-i Asarmat became involved in a dispute with Recep reis b. Abdullah, a sea captain from the Imperial Dockyards in Istanbul (*tersane-i Amire reislerinden*). Anton, Recep, and

---

[107] Archivio di Stato, Venice, Senato, Provveditori da Terra e da mar, Lettere del. Provv. straordinario a Suda, Busta 889. "No. 55 Sig. Andrea Milioti de di primo(?) Feb. 1686 S.V. Candia. Di gia e statto proposto restelare L'Arzere di queste Fosse, ma per mancanze di Legname non l'hanno adempito, hora con l'occasione, che di sfachioti litigarano con Loro Aga *sono pregati condure a Matala m/10 Travi* [emphasis added], che gli sarebbe datto di pagamento doi milla misure di formento quindici (15) per misura, et Licenza da quel Luoco per Sfachia, dove che prima e stato proibita L'estrattione con repesti che questo formento si portase in socorso dell'Armata . . . gia hano dato da 60 misure, che tanto capiva(?) una loro barcheta con promissione del resto, ordinandoli La portatura con premura(haste)."

[108] Richard Pococke, *A Description of the East* (London, 1739), 2:241.

[109] Whereas fairly comprehensive documents exist for the Venetian period (albeit for certain years only), the only systematic shipping records for the Ottoman period, the customs registers, have not survived.

[110] Raymond, *Artisans et commercants*, 1:168.

[111] See note 91 in chapter 4.

the sailor's guild (*gemici taifesi*) all owned shares (*pay*) in a caique and the dispute was over how much Recep's share should be, now that the voyage was over. Both agreed that Recep had given Anton the boat one year previous and that the latter had sailed to Rhodes. The system of joint ownership, then, allowed Anton access to a boat that he might not have had otherwise, and the sea captain from Istanbul, who was probably wealthier than the Cretan sailor, made a return on his capital (the boat).[112]

Two Muslim merchants from Chania loaded goods worth 510 esedi guruş onto Mihal veled-i Manol's frigate in Istanbul in 1084/1673, for passage to Crete.[113]

The harbormaster of Candia co-owned a fregatta with one el-haci b. el-haci Ali who was temporarily resident (*misafiran sakin*) in Candia in 1096/1685. After settling the balance sheet, they dissolved their partnership, and the harbormaster remained the sole owner of the boat.[114]

Finally, the defterdar of Crete used a boat from Rhodes owned by two Muslims—and captained by a Greek—to ship wood from Rhodes to Crete in 1083/1672, while the pasha of Candia hired one Christodoulou reis from Mytilene to take war matériel from Candia to Rethymnon on his boat in 1105/1694.[115]

The consideration of this evidence as a whole suggests the following model. French shipping did not take over in Crete where Venetian shipping left off at the end of the sixteenth century. Rather, local shipowners and shipbuilders were vigorous participants in the chaotic seventeenth century when piracy was rife and no one sea power, Ottoman or western, was dominant. The long years of the war, combined with the tremendous successes of French shipping toward the end of the seventeenth century, certainly dealt a blow to Cretan shipping and seafaring but not a fatal blow. French domination of the coastal trade of the Ottoman Empire (as opposed to the international trade between Marseilles and Levantine ports) was remarkably short-lived. The period of expansion came to an end in 1717, after which time local merchant marines again entered a period of growth.[116] In Crete shipowners were able to draw on a durable local

---

[112] It is not clear why the preference would have been joint ownership of the boat rather than a simple profit-sailing arrangement. But the document is not absolutely clear; it is possible that shares in the boat actually meant shares in the profits of the boat. T.A.H. 2:139.

[113] T.A.H. 5:30.

[114] T.A.H. 4:427. The document is ambiguous as to whether it was the boat itself that was owned in common or the profits from a commercial venture.

[115] T.A.H. 3:92, 8:70.

[116] In the debate over the causes of the decline in French domination of the Ottoman coastal or cabotage trade, some scholars ascribe it to local competition, others to French disinterest in the cabotage trade, relative to the possibilities of international shipping. See Traian Stoianovich, "L'espace maritime segmentaire de l'empire ottoman," in *Material Culture and Mentalities: Land and Sea*, vol. 4 of *Between East and West: The Balkan and Mediterranean Worlds*. (New Rochelle, N.Y.: Aristide D. Caratzas, 1995), 55, and George

tradition that united the shipbuilders of Sfakia with the merchants of Candia. As in so many other areas of commercial life in Ottoman Crete, the merchant fleet registered in the kadi court in 1751 represented not a break but rather a resumption, in modified form, of a pattern dating back to the beginning of the seventeenth century.

Commercial Practice

Did the transition from Venetian to Ottoman rule mean a devolution in the sophistication of the merchant community? This might seem like a pointless question if one assumes that legal niceties like insurance and, indeed, contracts in general went out the window with extensive military (i.e., janissary) involvement in commerce. Baladie, for instance, dispenses with the question of commercial culture in one sentence: "The janissaries threw themselves into trade and became rich by taking advantage of the judicial immunity that privileged members of the military enjoyed in the Ottoman Empire."[117]

This argument has several problems. First, it fails to distinguish between political elites and the ordinary merchant.[118] Among the elites there was of course constant conflict over access to the supply of lucrative goods, conflict that was not settled at the level of the courts. This was a game played by everyone: pashas, tax farmers, and foreign merchants as well as janissaries. From the French consuls in Crete we learn that the pashas had first claim on the wheat harvest, and French merchants moved quickly to buy it up, lest it fall into the hands of the janissaries.[119] This situation is little different than that of the 1640s when local families complained that the Venetian provveditore generale Andrea Corner was controlling the olive oil market.

Second, it is true that there is ample evidence of coercive behavior on the part of the various urban militia.[120] The institution of himaye, whereby

Leon, "The Greek Merchant Marine," in *The Greek Merchant Marine, 1453–1850*, ed. Stelios Papadopoulos (Athens: National Bank of Greece, 1972), 29.

[117] Baladie, *To emborio*, 39.

[118] In his study of the janissary corps, and urban culture in general, in the seventeenth century, Cemal Kafadar notes the "serious rift" between the officers and the rank and file of the corps. As a result, "The economic exploits of an ordinary Yeniçeri must have been hardly comparable to the ventures of Bektaş Aga, a financier and wholesaler." Cemal Kafadar, "Yeniçeri-Esnaf Relations: Solidarity and Conflict" (Master's thesis, McGill University, 1981), 97.

[119] K. Konstantinidēs, "Ektheseis kai ypomnēmata apo tēn allēlografia tou gallikou proxseniou Krētēs" (Essays and notes from the French consulate in Crete), *Krētika Chronika* 8 (1954): 338.

[120] A letter of complaint written from late-seventeenth-century Cairo informed the sultan that "the market supervisor does not dare test the bakers' bread because they are under [the janissaries'] protection. . . . They raise the prices of fruits and vegetables. The mint is inside

a merchant would join a military unit (*ocak*) in exchange for protection, was widespread in Cairo at this time (including some of the wealthiest merchants) and has been cited as an example of military coercion in the marketplace. Even so, a more populist view of the himaye relationship has been put forward by Andre Raymond, who argues that the protection granted to merchants by the ocaks was largely defensive and directed against the oppression of the pasha and his agents. It was "une sorte d'assurance preventive contre les violences et les exactions de la caste dominante aux depens des sujets."[121]

The relationship of the janissaries to the market, then, was a complex one and is still too little understood to argue that it was unequivocally one of privilege. In Candia one of the strongest arguments against the privileged position of the ordinary beşe merchant is the fact that he often appears in the court records where he seems to be treated much the same as any other merchant.[122] Like other merchants, he had to find ways to finance commercial endeavors, collect debt, and perform the myriad of other tasks inherent in the pursuit of commerce.

A systematic comparison of commercial practice in Crete in the late Venetian and early Ottoman period is rendered difficult by the sparsity of information on the Ottoman side. In the earlier period, notaries in the Venetian city generated a wide variety of documents that were the result of centuries of Latin maritime development.[123] Freight agreements, records of sea loans, acts establishing partnerships, certificates of insurance, lading documents, and records of boat sales were regularly issued by the industrious notaries of Candia. Next to this the Ottoman city provided only the kadi court, whose involvement in commerce was hardly systematic.[124]

The problem can be approached more profitably by using the Ottoman materials as a supplement, and instead comparing commercial practice in

---

their barracks and they mint whatever weight of coin they please." Damurdashi, *al-Damurdashi's Chronicle*, 137–42. Kafadar, too, notes that rank-and-file members of the corps and officers "were both given to disruption of the market system through zorbalık," a term derived from Persian meaning coercion. Kafadar, "Yeniçeri-Esnaf Relations," 97.

[121] Raymond, *Artisans et commercants*, 2:703.

[122] See, for instance, T.A.H. 5:15 where a janissary sold some leather to a Greek named Cholaf Lampo. After trying without success to collect the money from Lampo, he turned to Lampo's partner, Yianni veled-i Karanu. Yianni acknowledged that such a sale had taken place but said that his partnership with Lampo did not include guarantorship ("şirket kefalati mutazammina olmamağin"). This was sufficient for the court, which told the janissary to drop the suit. The situation was similar in Cyprus. "Janissaries, although members of the military elite, frequently used the court of Lefkosa, where in most matters they were subject to the same procedures as any other users of the court." Jennings, *Christians and Muslims in Ottoman Cyprus*, 112.

[123] These notarial records (*atti*) for Crete can be found in the Archivio di Stato, Venice.

[124] No doubt the Ottomans also maintained customs registers for the port because such documents have survived for other cities. It currently appears that no such records have survived for Candia in this period.

late Venetian Crete to the custom followed on other, much better known, islands such as Hydra. This comparison suggests that, even before the arrival of the Ottomans, merchants in Candia belonged to the world of the Ottoman-dominated eastern Mediterranean, rather than to that of northern Italy. This was so despite the long and intimate relationship—unique in the Greek world—between Italy and Crete. The advent of Ottoman rule, then, did not mean that the more sophisticated business techniques that characterized Italy were replaced by the relatively backward methods that typified the eastern Mediterranean.

For example, Venice had long ago left behind the egalitarian and nonspecialized organization of commerce that was typical of Europe in the early medieval period and was one of the first to move beyond profit sailing—where all on board shared in the profits of a successful voyage—to wage sailing, where sailors received a fixed wage.[125] The professionalization of commerce was underway as early as the fourteenth century when the declining use of the commenda went hand in hand with the decline in the role of the part-time investor. As the role of the occasional investor diminished, a clearer line developed between merchant and nonmerchant.[126]

Crete did not follow in the path of its overlord but retained more archaic forms of business organization. Records of the Greek community in Venice in the mid-sixteenth century show that often the Greek crews (and most commonly the ships had come from Crete) were not salaried but rather "participated in the losses and profits of the voyage."[127] In Crete itself the contracts recorded in the files of Michael Peri, a notary in Candia whose records span almost thirty years in the middle of the seventeenth century, show that a ship's crew was often among the investors in commercial ventures. These ventures were typically characterized by a large number of small investors and credit was also provided by a broad cross section of ordinary society, rather than a specialized group of financiers.[128]

---

[125] See R. Jackson, "From Profit-Sailing to Wage-Sailing: Mediterranean Owner-Captains and Their Crews during the Medieval Commercial Revolution," *Journal of European Economic History* 18, no. 3 (Winter 1989): 605–28.

[126] "With the routinization of commerce and the concomitant decline of the commenda, commerce became more professional. The role of the occasional investor diminished and the division between merchant and nonmerchant became more clearcut." B. Kedar *Merchants in Crisis: Genoese and Venetian Men of Affairs and the Fourteenth Century Depression* (New Haven: Yale University Press, 1976), 58.

[127] Panayiōtopoulos, "Ellēnes nautikoi kai ploioktētes," 289. In the typical profit-sailing arrangement in the medieval West, according to Jackson, 50 percent of the total profits went to the owner, 50 percent to the crew. In the tax levied on each Greek ship coming to Venice, in order to pay for the erection of the Church of Saint George, the sailors were collectively liable for half the tax while the shipowner was responsible for the other half. This divvying up of the tax suggests that the profit-sailing arrangement was also half and half, like the traditional contract in the medieval West.

[128] For example, the abbot and the deacon of the Monastery of Saint Catherine's in Candia, along with a woman named Sofia Cornaropoulo, were all investors in the ship *Saint John*

Both of these practices were typical of the eastern Mediterranean. On the Aegean island of Hydra, for instance, whose nautical traditions were characteristic of the Greek maritime world, profit sailing was the norm well into the nineteenth century when the traveler Henry Holland observed, "Every Hydriot sailor is therefore more or less a merchant."[129] Even Dalmatian sailors, right across the Adriatic from their salaried counterparts in Venice, operated on the shares system.[130] In other words, long after it had been abandoned in the western Mediterranean, the relatively backward practice of profit sailing continued to be the norm further east.[131] Somewhat further afield, a description of the organization of commerce in Aleppo in the seventeenth century could easily be applied to late Venetian Crete:

> The buying and selling of merchandise was an almost ubiquitous endeavor for the city's citizenry. It might seem, therefore, that a listing of those elements of the urban population that comprised the merchant "class" would be useless, for it appears that almost all Aleppines who had any excess capital were at one time or another engaged directly in trade or in credit relationships involving commerce.[132]

---

the Baptist, which traveled regularly between Candia and Volos on the Greek mainland, bringing wheat and legumes to Crete. Panopoulou, "Syntrofies kai navloseis," 422. Panayiōtopoulos cites three instances where a sea captain was also a priest. Panayiōtopoulos, "Ellēnes nautikoi kai ploioktētes," 300.

[129] Holland noted: "It is the system of the Hydriotes . . . that every person on board their ships, even to the cabin boy, has a share in the speculations, either in lieu of wages, for which the proportion is duly regulated, or by the investment of the savings which any one may have made. *Every Hydriot sailor is therefore more or less a merchant* [emphasis added] and is furnished with strongest motive to habitual industry, in the opportunity thereby of advancing his fortune in life." Henry Holland, *Travels in the Ionian Isles, Albania, Thessaly, Macedonia during the years 1812 and 1813* (London, 1819), 2:204. Every sailor a merchant, of course, was precisely what characterized commercial venture in the western Mediterranean before the commercial revolution of the early fourteenth century. The leading role played by Hydra in establishing maritime custom is evident in the response given by the islanders of Poros to the new Greek government in 1829, when asked to provide information on local custom, law, and practice. "As for maritime contracts and judgements," they responded, "all these are customarily executed according to the custom of Hydra." Sp. Vryonis, "Local Institutions in the Greek Islands and Elements of Byzantine Continuity during Ottoman Rule," *Annuaire de L'Université de Sofia: Centre de Recherches Slavo-Byzantines "Ivan Dujčev"* 83, no. 3 (1989): 96.

[130] Lane, *Venice*, 387.

[131] I say backward because the shift to wage sailing came about as a result of an expanding economy, which allowed the owner-captain to assume more risk. Profit-sailing, where the owner does not have to pay anything in advance has been "the common form of engagement in maritime activities that fail to command adequate capital." Jackson, "From Profit-Sailing to Wage-Sailing," 609. Jackson notes that profit sailing persisted in small-scale trade in Italy up through the nineteenth century. For more information on commercial organization in the eastern Mediterranean on the eve of the revolution see Tr. Konstantinidou, *Karavia, kapetanoi kai Syndrofonautoi 1800–1830* (Boats, captains and sailors, 1800–1830) (Athens, 1954), 72–76.

[132] Masters, *The Origins of Western Economic Dominance*, 48.

Two cases from the court records of Candia provide a rare glimpse of lay involvement, as it were, in trade in the early Ottoman period. In 1120/1708 three Christians—a woman named Fotoka bint Drakou, Korkia Tsirile veled-i Nikola, and Lonou veled-i Nikola from the eastern province of Sēteia—sold their caique to a bishop for 100 guruş. It is likely that the boat was involved in trade between Crete and the island of Kos, since the witnesses in the case were from that island. The case ended up in court only because the woman involved complained that Lonou had failed to give her her share of the proceeds from the sale.[133]

In a slightly earlier case, also involving a woman, Fatima—represented by her husband in court—testified that she gave twenty esedi guruş in a mudarebe contract to one haci Hussein.[134] The mudarebe, of course, is none other than the Muslim equivalent of the European commenda, the standard contract for commercial venture in the medieval Mediterranean. Long after it had died out in the western Mediterranean, it continued to be used further east.[135] It seems likely that the many small debts that appear in merchants' property distributions in Candia reflect a society where a large cross-section of the population was in the habit of investing small amounts in commercial ventures, but in the absence of more information it is impossible to say for certain. What the above two cases suggest, however, is that in a situation where commerce was pursued quite informally, and by the population at large, women were able to pursue commercial endeavors, even in an Islamic context.

Although it is clear that Crete belonged to the commercial world of the eastern Mediterranean, some aspects of the commercial revolution of the Middle Ages—whose epicenter was the Italian maritime cities—did make it to Venice's colony.[136] Insurance contracts were in regular use in seventeenth-century Candia. We know this because they are preserved in the notarial records. In this case the departure of the Venetians probably meant a reversion to older techniques for insuring against risk. The commenda, for instance, carried with it an implicit insurance function since the traveling partner (i.e., the one who invested his labor rather than his capital) was not liable for any losses incurred. The sea loan—in use in the Aegean throughout the Ottoman period and with roots in the Byzantine era—also had this feature since it was collectible only as long as the ship returned safely to port.[137]

---

[133] T.A.H. 11:224.

[134] T.A.H. 8:128.

[135] Masters, *The Origins of Western Economic Dominance*, 50.

[136] See Lane, *Venice*, chaps. 10–12. The medieval commercial revolution brought momentous changes in many areas, from nautical technique to business organization and the recruitment of labor.

[137] For the use of insurance in Venice, see Tenenti, *Naufrages, corsaires et Assurance maritimes à Venise 1592–1609*. For its use in Crete, see Panopoulou's work.

The example of insurance does suggest the one radical change in commercial practice that Ottoman rule effected, namely the abrupt transition from a written, bureaucratic culture to a semi-oral one. In Venetian Candia a professional class of notaries stood ready to draw up the necessary documents any time a ship left the port, but the involvement of the Ottoman kadi in trade was sporadic and dependent upon specific circumstances, which are not always clear to us today.[138] Under the Ottomans, commercial practice in Candia no doubt came closer to the situation that prevailed in the smaller Greek islands. In 1833, in response to the inquiries of the newly constituted Greek government, the residents of Spetses described the very informal methods used to amass capital for a maritime venture:

> Each captain desiring to amass capital [*sermayia*] sent out his secretary or he went out alone, and the sum total of money which he received he would record in his ledger. To some he gave receipts, to others he did not [give receipts]. After the completion of his trip he turned the interest over to his secretary with a notice, who then [in turn] distributed it to each one wherever he might find him, either in his house, or in the market place, or in some shop, or on the road. Whoever of these asked [also] for the capital, they first notified the captain and if the captain did not find him himself, he turned it over to his wife in good faith without demanding a quittance or receipt (even if he had given one) and thus their relation was dissolved.[139]

Although this is probably an accurate description of how many commercial transactions were handled in Candia as well, Ottoman Crete diverged from the Aegean islands in important ways. Most important for our discussion, the Ottomans did establish an Islamic legal system in Crete, something they did not bother to do in the smaller islands with their minimal Muslim population. Candia was more like Aleppo, or Nicosia in Cyprus, in this respect than it was like Hydra or Psara. This difference raises an intriguing question: did the presence of Islamic lawcourts impinge in any way on the customary law that was so pronounced in the area of commercial practice?[140] Was there such a thing as an "Islamic" zone of commerce in the eastern Mediterranean? The answer, I believe, is no. All the available evidence suggests that, both before and after the Ottoman conquest, local merchants pursued trade in a manner consistent with commercial practice throughout the eastern Mediterranean. This is, in fact, precisely what one would expect,

---

[138] "It would appear that the vast majority of day-to-day transactions were the products of verbal agreements, and if they did not later engender litigation over the terms of the contract, they were unrecorded by the courts. As a result, the court records have preserved a very selective sampling of commercial transactions." Masters, *The Origins of Western Economic Dominance*, 61.

[139] Vryonis, "Local Institutions in the Greek Islands," 105.

[140] In his writings Vryonis shows the origins in customary law of commercial practice in the Greek world.

given that Islamic law—and particularly the Hanafi school to which the Ottomans belonged—has traditionally conceded a large role to custom in the conduct of commercial life.[141]

When state interests were involved, the court could and did involve itself in commercial life in a much more systematic manner. We know a good deal about the wheat trade in Crete, for instance, because the kadi regularly issued permits for the export of grain. The case of Georgi, a merchant sea captain (*reis tuccari*) who approached the court in 1110/ 1699 is a typical illustration of the court's role. He asked for permission to export 4,000 mouzour of wheat (*hinta*) to Tripoli in North Africa. Permission was granted contingent upon the fulfillment of certain conditions. He had to provide a guarantor, to bring back a document (*hüccet*) from the kadi of Tripoli (presumably showing that the grain had been delivered) as well as an unspecified amount of clarified butter (*revgan-i sade*).[142] In their desire to regulate the trade in certain key commodities, and to provision the island adequately, the Ottomans shared the concerns of their Venetian predecessors. Venetian involvement was simply more systematic and routine; no ship could leave Venetian Candia without a guarantor who swore to a notary that no slaves or other prohibited goods were on board, nor olive oil above the permitted amount.

Finally, a small but significant linguistic shift at the end of the sixteenth century is perhaps a good way to end this discussion of commercial practice in Crete. At this time the notaries began to use the Turkish word for capital, *sermaye*, in the documents that they routinely prepared before a ship's departure. This change foreshadowed the island's future, and it suggests that long before the Venetians left, the Ottomans had already arrived.

[141] A. Udovitch, "Islamic Law and the Social Context of Exchange in the Medieval Middle East," *History and Anthropology* 1 (1985): 457. Especially in the Hanafi school, and particularly in the sphere of economic life, the resort to custom as a guide to proper economic conduct is prominent indeed. Udovitch points out that when custom is in collision with the requirements of legal reasoning (for instance, the problem of one man ordering a pair of shoes from another since one cannot contract for something that does not exist), the lawyers are often quite candid about saying "This is the custom and we are going to let it stand."

[142] T.A.H. 9:107. In almost 40 percent of the shipments of wheat to North African cities, the merchant had either brought clarified butter to Crete or had promised to bring butter back with him on the return trip. In numerous other export permission requests, the goods that the merchant had brought to Candia were mentioned. This suggests that merchants were expected to help in the provisioning of the island, in exchange for permission to export.

Six

The Slow Death of
the Ancien Regime

The Captain-General Morosini having in the
meantime imbarked his Forces, sailed to Suda
to provide and fortify that place, Spina Longa
and Carbusa, poor rocks and Appendages to
the greater Ilse of Candia with all necessary
supplies of Victuals and Ammunition which
only serve for a prospect into Candia, and to
keep alive the Title of the Venetian Republic
to that Kingdom.
  Sir Paul Rycaut[1]

An Uncertain Sovereignty

As Rycaut's remarks suggest, the Venetians were not at all reconciled to
the loss of Crete in 1669. They used the opportunity provided by the War
of the Holy League (1684–99) to try and retake Chania in 1692. It was
only with the loss of all its remaining territories in the eastern Mediterranean (except for the small island of Cerigo) during the last Ottoman-
Venetian war of 1715–18 that Venice's ambitions in Crete were finally
extinguished. Until that time Venetian challenges to Ottoman sovereignty
on the island, of which the brief siege of Chania was only the most visible
sign, remained a serious concern to the Ottoman Empire.

By no means did Venice rely on military force alone. Unlike the French,
the Venetians knew the island and the islanders well and they used that

---

[1] Paul Rycaut, *A History of the Ottoman Empire from the Year 1623 to the Year 1677*
(London: 1680), 278–79.

knowledge to create an impressive network of spies, some of whom were in the highest reaches of the local government. Venice was also helped, oddly enough, by the fact that the only indigenous institution to survive the transition from Venetian to Ottoman rule was the Greek Orthodox Church. Despite centuries of Latin-Orthodox enmity, it seems that the Venetians were able to take advantage of the desire in Crete to maintain local control over religious life. This determination led certain members of the clergy to go so far as to declare the Orthodox Church of Crete independent of the patriarch in 1715.

Rejoining the Orthodox World

Of all the peculiarities of this late Ottoman conquest perhaps none was more striking than the fact the Crete was rejoining the Orthodox world after almost half a millennium under Latin rule. The transition was not an easy one.

Venetian policy toward the Orthodox Church on Crete had effectively prevented the development of an indigenous church elite. In addition to depriving the church of much of its property (the same policy was followed vis-à-vis private landowners), Venice abolished the Orthodox bishoprics and replaced them with Latin ones.[2] Throughout the period of Venetian rule no Orthodox bishop was allowed on the island and Benetto Moro forcefully restated this policy in 1602 when he wrote that this was a "prohibitione certo prudentissima," which had been observed "in tutti li tempi."[3] The lack of Orthodox bishops made ordination very difficult

---

[2] Chr. Maltezou, "E Krētē stē diarkeia tēs periodou tēs venetokratias" (Crete during the period of Venetian rule) in *Krētē: Istoria kai politismos* (Crete: History and civilization), ed. N. Panayiotakēs (Herakleion: Synthesmos Topikōn Enōseōn Demōn Kai Koinotētōn Krētes, 1988), 131. Among western states Venice was not alone in following this type of policy toward the Orthodox bishops. It had been established as early as the First Crusade when the Crusaders found themselves confronted with the problem of the eastern churches in the Holy Land. See J. Prawer, "Social Classes in the Crusader States: The 'Minorities,' " in *The Impact of the Crusades on the Near East*, ed. Norman Zacour and Harry Hazard, vol. 5 of *A History of the Crusades*, ed. Kenneth Setton (Madison: University of Wisconsin Press, 1985), 59–116.

[3] Stergios Spanakēs, "Relatione dell Sr. Benetto Moro ritornato di proveditor general del regno di Candia, letta in pregadi a 25 giugno 1602," *Mnēmeia tēs krētikēs istorias* (Monuments of Cretan history), vol. 4 (Herakleion, 1958), 93. Moro's paranoia concerning the Orthodox Church is evident from his discussion of the bishops: "These bishops must be completely excluded from the Kingdom and never accepted . . . because the Greeks have a tremendous respect for their priests as well as for their bishops. When they see a religious person of some authority they immediately accept him, invite him into their homes and trust him completely. One can presume that these people (the bishops), who are ill-disposed toward the Roman Church and the Latin Rite, secretly sow the seeds of dissension between Greeks and Latins when they hear confession."

(unless the candidate was willing to accept ordination from a Latin bishop) and resulted, among other things, in a certain amount of irregularity. Mocenigo reported, with great horror, that there were priests presiding over the mass who were not even ordained.[4]

This uncompromising attitude persisted even as Venice sought other ways to placate the Orthodox population. Venice did allow for Orthodox churches, and by the seventeenth century there were over 100 such churches in Candia.[5] Moro noted with satisfaction that Orthodox and Latins frequented each others' churches, which had not been the case in the past. Latin attendance at Greek churches was particularly beneficial because, by showing support for Orthodoxy, the Latins could win the trust of the Greeks, and he urged state officials to attend Orthodox churches as often as possible.[6] Officials also worked hard to prevent what they saw as provocative behavior on the part of the Catholic Church. The Latin clergy, Moro wrote, must not be allowed to use their pulpits to speak against the Greek faith.[7] At one point Venice even considered providing a stipend for Orthodox priests in the villages, as a way of ensuring Orthodox fidelity to the flag of Saint Mark.[8] More than anything else, Venice was determined to avoid the consequences of religious conflict. "The two faiths, the Greek and the Latin," wrote Isepo Civran in 1639, "must remain united in love and peace. They must be equal and refrain from dissension.

[4] The Cretans, as Mocenigo noted, had to go elsewhere if they wished to be ordained by an Orthodox bishop, as no Orthodox bishops were allowed on the island. It was Venice's preference that they go to the Ionian islands, also under Venetian control, where Orthodox bishops were permitted, and secure their ordination there. According to Mocenigo, however, many preferred to go to "Asia and other forbidden places" (Asia, et in altri luoghi prohibiti), that is places under Ottoman control, and receive ordination there. He claimed that the reason for this was to avoid the stricter standards applied for ordination in the Ionian islands. It also happened on occasion that an Orthodox bishop would arrive undetected on the island and ordain hundreds of candidates in great secrecy. It is not clear whether Mocenigo is referring to these cases when he speaks of unordained priests, or if there was, in fact, an additional group of priests and monks who had not been ordained by any authority. Stergios Spanakēs, "Relazione del Nobil Huomo Zuanne Mocenigo ritornato provveditore generale del regno di Candia presentata nell'eccellentissimo consillio 17 Aprile 1589," *Mnēmeia tēs krētikēs istorias* (Monuments of Cretan history), vol. 1 (Herakleion, 1940), 15–16.

[5] Although there were only twenty Latin churches, they tended to be much more opulent. St. Alexiou, "To kastro tēs Krētēs kai ē zoē tou ston 16th kai 17th aiōna" (The fortess of Crete and its life in the 16th and 17th centuries), *Krētika Chronika* 19 (1965): 170. The church historian Nicholas Tomadakēs gives the figures of 113 Orthodox and 17 Latin churches. Nicholas V. Tomadakēs, "Syndomon diagramma tēs istorias tēs ekklēsias krētēs epi Tourkokratias" (A short sketch of the history of the church of Crete during Turkish rule), *Deltio tēs Istorikēs kai Ethnologikēs Hetaireias tēs Hellados* 14 (1960): 19.

[6] "et gli latini, per acquistarsi gli animi de'greci, si mostrano divoti, et frequentano le Chiese greche" and "il far il medesimo captivandosi glia nimi de'Greci in quel modo più che in ogni altra maniera." Spanakēs, "Relatione dell Sr. Benetto Moro," 87, 89.

[7] "Non si conviene ne anco tollerar che li Predicatori latini parlino nelli pulpiti cose contrarie al rito greco." Ibid., 103.

[8] Stergios Spanakēs, "Relazione de Sr. Isepo Civran tornato di Prov r Gen.l di Candia 1639," *Krētika Chronika* 21 (1969): 449.

There is nothing that can damage the public interest more, and create unrest, than the question of respect for religion."[9]

Orthodox monasteries were also permitted and, for reasons that are still unexplored, the island's monasteries experienced a period of economic and intellectual revival beginning in the middle of the sixteenth century.[10] Crete began to produce so many capable abbots that Saint Catherine's at Mount Sinai in Egypt was effectively run by the Cretans in the sixteenth and seventeenth centuries.[11]

Despite Venice's attempts to do so, the Cretans were in no way cut off from the larger Orthodox world. They were active participants in the vicious world of church politics in Istanbul, and they filled some of the highest positions in the church hierarchy. The future patriarch of Alexandria, Meletios Pigas, was a pupil at a school in Candia run by the Sinai monks, as was Kyrillos Loukaris, a Cretan who became one of the most famous patriarchs of Istanbul in Orthodox history.[12]

At the level of the ordinary believer, ironically enough, the absence of bishops on the island actually encouraged contacts between the Orthodox in Crete and their coreligionists in the Ottoman Empire. Foscarini, the reforming provveditore of the 1570s, worried about the fact that so many Cretans went to the patriarch in Istanbul to ask forgiveness for their sins. He feared that they would then be persuaded to agitate against Venetian rule in Crete and he briefly considered reinstating the church hierarchy in

[9] Ibid. The specific circumstances of the seventeenth century even created a measure of common ground between Venice and the Orthodox Church, as both stood in opposition to the missionary thrust of the Counter-Reformation. See Gunner Hering, *Oikomeniko Patriarcheio kai evropaikē politikē 1620–1638* (The Ecumenical Patriarchate and European politics, 1620–1638) (Athens: National Bank of Greece, 1992).

[10] In a general way, monastic life in Crete must have benefited from the gradual softening of Venetian attitudes toward the Orthodox Church in Crete, as the Ottoman threat to the island grew. More specifically, one historian of the Byzantine monuments on the island has suggested that, beginning in the sixteenth century, the Venetians encouraged the founding of new monasteries, or the strengthening of existing ones, in remote areas where the monasteries could play a role in the defense of the island. Such would seem to have been the case, for instance, with the monastery of Akrotiriani, named Toplu ("with cannons") by the Ottomans. Situated on the northern coast of the remote province of Sēteia, an area that was a prime target for piracy, it ressembles a fortress and evidence suggests that the wall surrounding the monastery was built with funds supplied by Venice. Nikos Psilakēs, *Monasteries and Byzantine Memories of Crete* (Herakleion: Karmanor, 1994), 27, and *Ta monasteria tēs Krētēs* (The monasteries of Crete) (Athens: Bank of Crete, 1986), 178.

[11] N. Panayiotakēs, "E paideia kata tēn Venetokratia" (Education during the period of Venetian rule) in *Krētē: Istoria kai politismos* (Crete: History and civilization), ed. N. Panayiotakēs (Herakleion: Synthesmos Topikōn Enōseōn Demōn Kai Koinotetōn Kretes, 1988), 186.

[12] Patriarchal letters from the period of Parthenios the First (1639–44) demonstrate the patriarch's courtship of the Cretans in order to win their support for his stewardship of the church. The Cretans were so disenchanted with his predecessor (Kyrillos the Second) that they had refused to recognize him as patriarch. I. K. Chasiotēs, "To oikomeniko patriarcheio kai e Krētē meta to thanato tou Kyrillou A' tou Loukareos" (The ecumenical Patriarchate and Crete after the death of Kyrillos Loukareos the first), *Thēsaurismata* 6–7 (1969–70): 201–36.

Crete so the Orthodox wouldn't have to go to Istanbul. As it was, he confined himself to forbidding the rectors from exiling Cretans to places outside the island.[13]

The Ottomans were swift to bestow their favor on the Orthodox Church in Crete, even as the capital city's many churches became mosques, and showed themselves willing to overturn Venetian policies of long standing. Long before the fall of Candia they had installed Neofytos Patelaros, a native of Chania and monk from the monastery of Arkadi, as archbishop of Crete with seven Orthodox bishops under him.[14] The patriarch in Istanbul must have been gladdened, too, by the deep involvement of Panayiōtēs Nikousios in the surrender and subsequent resettlement of Candia. Nikousios was mentioned only briefly in previous chapters. Here a proper introduction is required in order to understand what he represented, both for Crete and for the larger Orthodox world.

Panayiōtēs Nikousios was born in Istanbul and educated, as was traditional for the Greek elite, in Italy, where he acquired Italian, French, and German in addition to the eastern languages he already possessed. Returning to his native city in 1649, he was appointed as diplomatic negotiator, or dragoman, for an embassy to the Austrians. He performed this task so well that the grand vezir Mehmet Köprülü (father of Fazil Ahmet) named him grand dragoman to the Imperial Court (Divon-ı Hümayun), a first. It was Nikousios, then, who began the tradition of Greek domination of this important office in the Ottoman bureaucracy, a tradition that would continue uninterrupted until 1821, the year of the Greek revolution.[15]

---

[13] Sp. Theotokēs, "Iakovos Foscarini kai e Krētē tou 1570" (Iakovos Foscarini and Crete in 1570), *Epeteris tēs Hetaireias Kretikōn Spoudōn* 1 (1938): 186–206. Foscarini was resident in Crete from 1570 to 1573.

[14] The Venetian senator Andrea Valiero's history of the war of Crete relates that Patelaros approached Hussein Pasha, the military governor of Crete, in 1653 with the idea of establishing an archbishopric in Crete in order to "conciliarsi l'affetto de'popoli, et introdurre abborrimento al nome venetiano." Apparently Hussein Pasha found this to be a good suggestion: "These propositions having been absorbed by Hussein Pasha, he wrote to Constantinople where the advice was well received. The patriarch was commanded to institute an archibishop metropolitan in the Kingdom of Candia, under which would be ordained another seven bishops, and that the aforementioned Patelaro be elevated to the first office." Andrea Valiero, *Historia della guerra di Candia di Andrea Valiero* (Venice, 1679), 311–12, quoted in Nicholas V. Tomadakēs, *Istoria tēs ekklēsias Krētēs epi Tourkokratias 1645–1898* (The history of the Cretan church during the period of Turkish rule, 1645–1898 (Athens: Iordanou Myrtide, 1974), 71–72. The new archbishop was a relative of the then patriarch Athanasios III. Theocharis Detorakēs, "E ekklēsia tēs Krētēs kata tēn Tourkokratia 1645–1898" (The church of Crete during the period of Turkish Rule, 1645–1898), in Panayiotakēs, *Krētē: Istoria kai politismos*, 439. It is not clear how many bishoprics were in existence in the early years of Ottoman rule. Valiero says seven, but the Cretan historian Detorakēs refers to a manuscript of 1659 which listed twelve bishoprics. Detorakēs, "Ekklēsia," 439.

[15] *Megalē Ellēnike Engyklopaideia*, vol. 11, (Athens: Eleutheroudakē 1962–), s.v. "Nikousios."

In addition to his pioneering career in the service of the sultan, Nikousios was also famous as a zealous defender of Orthodoxy. Rycaut referred to him as "a person of Parts and Learning." Monsignor Urbano Cerri, who as secretary to the Propaganda Fide wrote a report for Pope Innocent XI (1676–89) on *The State of the Roman-Catholick Religion throughout the World*, saw fit to mention Nikousios.

> Tis very strange that so many Greeks, educated in the Greek College at Rome, should not contribute in the least to bring the Schismaticks into the Bosom of Holy Mother Church. On the contrary, many turn Schismaticks again, and become more violent Enemies to the Catholics, after they have learned our Sciences, and are acquainted with our Imperfections. To give an Instance of it; Paionotto, a Schismatical Bishop (and heretofore the Grand Vizier's Interpreter,) who was educated in our Greek College, has proved the greatest Persecutor of the Catholicks, and contrived false Writings to deprive them of the Holy Sepulchre.[16]

The chevalier d'Arvieux, French consul in Aleppo toward the end of the seventeenth century and inveterate traveler in the Levant, complained about Nikousios in 1672 in a report to the king: "Sur cet article Votre Majesté doit être avertie que . . . Le Grand Vizir favorise en toutes choses Panaioty son premier Drogman, et celui-ci soûtient les Grecs ses Compatriotes de toutes des forces."[17] Nikousios was as willing to take on the Armenians as he was the Catholics. Together with Patriarch Paissios (twice patriarch in the 1650s), he prevented the Armenians in the Holy Land from taking over the Basilica of Bethlehem.[18]

Nikousios, the fervent defender of Orthodox Christianity, was a close associate of Köprülü's, the grand vezir who was known for his piety.[19] It was Panayiōtēs Nikousios, together with Ankebut Ahmet Agha (destined to become the first governor of Candia), who received the Venetian

---

[16] Paul Rycaut, *A History of the Ottoman Empire from the Year 1623 to the Year 1677* (London, 1680), 279–80, and Sir Richard Steele, *An Account of the State of the Roman-Catholick Religion throughout the World, Written for the Use of Pope Innocent XI by Monsieur Cerri, Secretary of the Congregation de propagande Fide*, 2nd ed. (London, 1716), 51.

[17] Laurant d'Arvieux, *Memoires du Chevalier d'Arvieux, contenant ses voyages à Constantinople, dans l'Asie, la Syrie, la Palestine, l'Egypte et la Barbarie*, comp. J. B. Labat (Paris, 1735), 5:12.

[18] Ch. Wardi "The Question of the Holy Places in Ottoman Times," in *Studies on Palestine during the Ottoman Period*, ed. Moshe Ma'oz (Jerusalem: Magnes Press, 1975), 389–90.

[19] Unusally for a grand vezir, Köprülü had initially trained for a career in the religious bureaucracy. He had already reached the elevated rank of professor when his father persuaded him to accept a vezirate. Madeline Zilfi, *The Politics of Piety: The Ottoman Ulema in the Postclassical Age, 1600–1800*, (Minneapolis: Bibliotheca Islamica, 1988), 85. See also my chapter 1 for his ties to the kadizadeli movement of religious reform. The encyclopedia entry on Nikousios claims that Köprülü "loved him as a brother and respected him as a father" and hoped that Nikousios would convert to Islam.

delegation that rowed over to the Ottoman camp to surrender the city. Nikousios was included among the pashas and aghas who represented the Ottoman side during the peace negotiations.[20] Pavlos Kladopoulos, priest and author of a poem (mid-eighteenth century) on the history of the metropolitan Church of Saint Minas, linked the two together in the opening lines of his composition: "Köprülü was the vezir at the time when, under a violent storm, Crete changed masters. He dragged an interpreter with him from Constantinople Panayiōtēs the wise, as you all know."[21] Nikousios also bought the Church of Saint Matthew in Candia, which became the nucleus of the Orthodox community in the early years of Ottoman rule.[22]

Saint Matthew's and a church for the Armenian community—also bought by a wealthy outsider—were the only churches in Candia at this time. Rycaut remarked on the fact that no church of the Latin denomination was established: "But the Turks were not more pious towards their Moschs than the Christians were careless and cold towards their Churches, for the Venetians inserted not one Article in favor of a Christian Church or a Religious House, which would have been granted as soon as demanded."[23] Rycaut's remark is intriguing, as it suggests that it was Venice's failure to ask rather than Köprülü's unwillingness to give, that explains the absence of a Latin church in the capital city. Given a lack of any other evidence, one can only speculate as to why this might have been so, but it is possible that Nikousios's hostility toward Catholicism might have had something to do with it. Instead, the Latins very quickly established a presence in Chania. The Capuchins, who previous to the war had maintained a small presence in Candia, now relocated to Chania. The European preference for Chania has been seen as a natural, given that the city was the center of Crete's olive oil trade. But in 1669 the olive oil trade was

---

[20] Silahdar Fındıklılı Mehmet Agha, *Silahdar Tarihi* (Istanbul: Devlet Matbaasi 1928), 517–19.

[21] Greek historians have long been aware of this poem and its author. A first edition of the poem was published as early as 1912 in a local Cretan journal. Research has revealed that Pavlos Kladopoulos was born in 1682 and became a priest at the age of twenty-seven. He was ordained by his uncle, who was the bishop of Knossos, and went on to become a presbyter at the metropolitan Church of Saint Minas. An edited edition of this poem is given in Tomadakēs, *Istoria tēs Ekklēsias Krētēs*, 77–99. The poem is entitled simply *Peri tou Naou tou Agiou Mēna Chandaka* (Concerning the Church of Saint Minas in Chandaka). As the title suggests, its subject is the circumstances surrounding the founding of the metropolitan church in Candia. *Peri tou Naou*, 77–78, lines 9–12.

[22] *Peri tou Naou*, 79, lines 23–31. The Church of Saint Matthew is still standing and is still a dependency (*metochio*) of Saint Catherine's in Sinai. It is currently undergoing reconstruction.

[23] Rycaut, *A History of the Ottoman Empire*, 279. He continued: "only a Greek who was Interpreter to the Grand Vezir called Panaiotti a Person of parts and Learning, at the expense of 2500 Dollars and an Armenian Merchant called Apro Chelebi at the charge of a thousand four hundred purchased two Churches for their respective nations."

The Church of Saint Matthew today, hidden away in the southwest corner of the city. It is still a dependency of Saint Catherine's in Sinai and is currently undergoing reconstruction. Credit: Photograph by author

still little developed, and the concentration of Catholics in Chania might have had more to do with Nikousios's claims on Candia than with matters connected to the olive oil trade.

Given that Nikousios came to Crete as a firm believer in the prerogatives of the Orthodox Patriarch, it is ironic that his actions in Candia seemed to have ushered in a troubled period in the relationship between the Orthodox Christians of Crete and the mother church in Istanbul.

The problem began with the Church of Saint Matthew, which Nikousios had bought. According to Kladopoulos, he intended to turn it over to the new metropolitan, Neofytos Patelaros, but the two had a quarrel.

> [Patelaros] fell into scandals with Panayiotakē, quareling about things that I cannot write down on this piece of paper. And see what damage the poor metropolitan suffered as a result of these scandals; Panayiotēs ran straight away to the Sinai Monks who were here in Candia those schemers and he gave Saint Matthew to them, and Patelaros was shut out.[24]

[24] *Peri tou Naou*, 79, lines 37–44. A patriarchal encyclical also records that Nikousios gave the church, as well as another in the district of Rizokastro, to the Sinai monks. Tomadakēs, *Istoria tēs ekklēsias krētēs*, 308.

The Monastery of Saint Catherine on Mount Sinai had traditionally had a large presence on Crete, including a church (not the same church that Nikousios bought) and a famous school in the city of Candia itself.[25] Probably Nikousios bestowed Saint Matthew on the monks as the only institutional alternative to the metropolitan.

Unfortunately, the sources from the period are silent as to the reasons behind the quarrel between Nikousios and Patelaros. Whatever the reasons, it resulted in a long and extraordinary estrangement between successive metropolitans and the Sinai monks.

The first round of the battle centered around Metropolitan Neofytos's unsuccessful attempts to obtain his own church in the city. In 1083/1672 he bought a bathhouse near Chania gate, probably with the intention of turning it into a church since it was so large.[26] A year and a half later, however, he was in court again, this time to sell the bathhouse to two Muslims, Hassan beşe and Haydar beşe. Although he was unable to convert the building into a church, it is not certain that the Sinai monks were behind his failure.[27]

The monks did, however, foil the attempt of the new metropolitan—Athanasios Kallipolitēs—to obtain a church some years later. In 1104/1692 a ferman arrived from Istanbul in response to a complaint lodged by one Mahmut, the administrator of a vakıf in Candia. Mahmut had informed the Sultan that a certain priest (the name was not given) was trying to convert a building that had previously served as a janissary barracks into a church. The sultan forbade him from so doing, claiming that it would be a violation of Islamic law to allow a church to be erected in a space which was next to a vakıf (Mahmut's) and which had previously housed Muslims.[28]

Although the Sinai monks are understandably not mentioned in the ferman, the poem makes clear the central role that they played in preventing Athanasios from getting his church.

[25] The Church of Saint Catherine's was turned into the Kethuda Bey mosque. When Crete fell to the Venetians early in the thirteenth century the archbishop of Sinai traveled all the way to Venice to ask for the preservation of the monastery's holdings on the island, as well as the continuation of its traditional rights and privileges. The request was granted. See E. G. Pantelakēs, "To Sinai kai ē Krētē" (Sinai and Crete), *Epetēris Hetaireia Krētikōn Spoudōn* 1 (1938): 165–85.

[26] T.A.H. 3:178.

[27] T.A.H. 5:67. In his comments on the Ottoman document, Stavrinidēs is certain that they were. He writes, "The metropolitan Neofytos would have been planning to convert the building and to use it as a church for the Christians of Candia. The intrigues and machinations of the powerful Sinai monks, however, would oblige him to sell the building." Nicholaos Stavrinidēs, *Metafraseis tourkikōn istorikōn engrafōn* (Translations of Turkish historical documents), vol. 2 (Herakleion: Municipality of Herakleion, 1986), 163. Kladopoulou, while making much of the fact that the metropolitan did not have his own church, does not mention the events of 1672–73.

[28] T.A.H. 7:134. The poem (lines 95–99) makes it clear that earlier fermans, solicited by the metropolitan, had granted permission for the church to be built.

There was a cunning abbot brought here to the cursed church of Sinai. His name was Daniel and see what this cunning dog managed to do. There was an alim named Timinzi [?] who would agree to undertake any difficult job. He went to him and gave him a lot of money and sent him to the city to do the trick. He gave him letters to take and weighed him down with akçe, and nobody here discovered this [plot]. He sent him to Yiannas Skordili in the city because both were dogs. And he [the abbot] told him not to be slow, but to do this quickly and willingly. He told Skordili to spend what he had to but to make sure that the church which had been built would be destroyed.[29]

Three years later, the Sinai monks and the metropolitan Athanasios were in court again, quarreling about jurisdiction over the local flock.[30] A number of monks from Saint Matthew brought the metropolitan to court, complaining that he was interfering in the work of the Sinai monks by attempting to catechize the Christians, to read them the Gospels, to care for their sick and newborns, and to bury the dead. The metropolitan, they argued, should restrict himself to collecting the fees that were due him. In response Athanasios said that, as metropolitan, he had the right not only to collect certain taxes but also to concern himself with all the affairs of the Christian community, including the specific areas referred to by the Sinai monks. The court effectively sided with the Sinai monks by conceding to them their traditional privilege, given the absence of any explicit directive to withdraw that privilege. It examined the berat or patent of privileges that the metropolitan had brought with him and noted that, beyond granting him the right to collect certain fees, nothing was said about allowing him to interfere in the affairs of the Sinai monks. The Christians, the court concluded, were free to consult with any priest they wished and the court warned the metropolitan not to interfere in the affairs of the monastery.[31]

Kladopoulos's poem conveys the extraordinary situation that ensued as a result of these battles, as the Metropolitan of Crete found himself without a church to celebrate the mass in.

To be the archbishop of Crete, to rule Crete, and to lack a church to chant the mass in. Instead to wander about in the villages looking for a place to hold a service, and lamenting in vain. To watch another feeding off his flock, and to

---

[29] *Peri tou Naou*, 81, lines 103–18. A patriarchal encyclical of 1777 mentions the same incident and the role of the Sinai monks. Tomadakēs, *Istoria tēs Ekklēsias Krētēs*, 312.

[30] T.A.H. 8:54.

[31] A ferman issued just eleven days earlier stated in a general way that the metropolitan could not interfere in the affairs of the Sinai monks. No doubt because of this ferman the monks decided to go to court to press their case against the metropolitan. T.A.H. 10:20. Concerning the rights of the church, no document has yet been found establishing the rights of the church at the time of the conquest. In the 1930s the newspaper *Vima* in Rethymnon published several documents from the Rethymnon archives. These documents were subsequently destroyed during World War II. One, dating from 1719, was from the metropolitan Fotios to the governor of Crete. He wrote that he was due "by custom" one Ottoman lira

not have anything to eat himself. He was archbishop in name only while the Sinai monks took all the income.

Writing almost a century later, Patriarch Sofronios II referred to the "scandals" and "dissension" that had bedeviled relations between the metropolitan and the Sinai monks at this time.[32]

The conflict soared to new heights in 1715, during the middle of the last Ottoman-Venetian war, when a remarkable ferman arrived from Istanbul in response, it said, to complaints lodged by the reaya in Crete.[33] From this day forward, the sultan wrote, the metropolitan must be a native of the island who would be chosen not by the patriarch but rather by the reaya and the local notables (*kocabaşilar*) of the island. The current metropolitan, Kōnstantine, was deprived of his duties, and a bishop from Kisamos, in the extreme west of the island, became metropolitan in his stead.[34] In order to select a new metropolitan an "open" berat would be issued, which would be given to a worthy cleric in Crete. Together with the reaya and the local notables, the cleric would then fill in the name of the chosen person, who would, in this way, become the new metropolitan of Crete. Presumably the 10,000 akçe that had traditionally been paid to the patriarch upon the acension of a new metropolitan would no longer be required, although the ferman does not say this. On several occasions, however, the ferman does state in no uncertain terms that the patriarch is not to intervene.[35]

The ferman ushered in a decade of turbulence in the relationship between the Ecumenical Patriarchate and the Christians of Crete, as the patriarch responded to this challenge to his authority. In the words of the poet, Crete had "apostasized."[36] Within three years, the patriarch managed to get Kōnstantine reinstated and one of Kōnstantine's chief attackers, a

---

from each priest and twelve para "gerous" (unadulterated) from each subject. Tomadakēs, "Syndomon diagramma," 7.

[32] *Peri tou Naou*, 79, lines 49–56. Tomadakēs, *Istoria tēs ekklēsias Krētēs*, 314. Stavrinidēs refers to a "tumultuous period in the history of the Church of Crete." Nicholaos Stavrinidēs, *Metafraseis tourkikōn historikōn engrafōn* (Translations of Turkish historical documents), vol. 3 (Herakleion: Municipality of Herakleion, 1987), 402.

[33] See T.A.H. 2:253 for the ferman declaring the church of Crete to be autocephalos.

[34] Kōnstantine's fall was foreshadowed by a number of complaints sent about him to Istanbul. Some months earlier the patriarch had complained to the Sultan about two reaya in Crete who were "full of hatred" toward Kōnstantine. T.A.H. 2:248. The two reaya must have been Moschakēs and Bonakēs, Greek notables who occupied influential positions in the Ottoman administration. They are discussed later on in this chapter.

[35] For example, line three of the document reads "patriklarin tarafindan madakhala olunmayub" (There is to be no interference on the part of the patriarchs).

[36] *Peri tou Naou*, 83, line 199. The poem also informs us (line 200) that Gerasimos, a bishop from the district of Kisamos, in the extreme west of the island, became the new metropolitan. See also Nicholaos Stavrinidēs, *Metafraseis tourkikōn istorikōn engrafōn* (Translations of Turkish historial documents), vol. 4 (Herakleion: Municipality of Herakleion, 1984), 13.

Greek official named Moschakēs, was put to death.[37] A certain level of uncertainty persisted, however. Although Moschakēs had been gotten rid of, his associate, Bonakēs, managed to take over Moschakēs' former position for several years.[38] In 1135/1722 Kōnstantine was exiled again. The bishop of Rethymnon, a man named Daniel, became the new metropolitan.[39]

This rapid turnover of officeholders, of course, was entirely routine in the seventeenth- and eighteenth-century Ottoman Empire and extended all the way up to the office of the patriarch and even the grand vezir himself. But Kladopoulos writes that Daniel was thinking of again trying to take the church of Crete out of the control of the patriarch, and this indeed may have been the reason behind his dismissal in 1137/1725.[40]

And he [Daniel] managed well in Crete. But then he began thinking about apostasizing and separating from the Ecumenical throne, but he lost his chance because he was tricked. He began to put his plan into action, his plan to apostasize. I am going to declare Crete autocephalos, he said to himself. So he sent letters to his friends in the city to do as he said and not let the plans go awry; but these letters fell into the lap of the patriarch and immediately a synod was convened.[41]

This time the patriarch responded by appointing a man who was both a Cretan and an insider at the patriarchal court in Istanbul, as metropolitan of Crete.[42] Although the attempt, led by the Sinai monks, to deny him his own church would persist for another decade, it was under Gerasimos that the question of the independence of the Cretan church was finally put to rest and the island placed firmly under the control of the patriarch. At some point during his tenure an agreement was reached with the Sinai monks to share the income deriving from the Christians of the city.[43] Gerasimos served until 1756 and in 1735, sixty-six years after the Ottoman

[37] T.A.H. 15:78 for Moschakēs' execution and T.A.H. 6:303 for the reinstatement of Kōnstantine. Register number 6 is deteriorated and is no longer available to researchers. I have used Stavrinidēs' translation. Stavrinidēs, *Metafraseis*, 32.

[38] T.A.H. 15:91. And see T.A.H. 15:341 for Mehmet Agha's (Bonakēs) exile to Rhodes.

[39] T.A.H. 16:94. I have consulted Stavrinidēs' translation of this document. Stavrinidēs, *Metafraseis*, 124.

[40] T.A.H. 2:203.

[41] *Peri tou Naou*, 84, lines 217–28.

[42] Kladopoulos provides a full biography. After rising in the hierarchy at the Patriarchate he went to serve as the bishop of Monemvasia (newly recovered from the Venetians). He gave up that position to become the metropolitan of Crete. *Peri tou Naou*, 84–85, lines 237–57.

[43] As the only church in Candia, the Church of Saint Matthew had been the recipient of all revenues accruing to the Bishopric of Candia. Tomadakēs, *Istoria tēs ekklēsias Krētēs*, 308. Fermans from 1756 and 1823 laying out the revenue rights of the metropolitan in Crete specified that none of this applied if the metropolitan had not been ordained in Istanbul. Tomadakēs, "Syndomon diagramma," 9.

This view of the Candia (Herakleion) in the early twentieth century bears testimony to Crete's complex religious history. In the foreground is the Catholic Church of the Madonna, converted into a mosque by the Ottomans upon their conquest of the island. In the background rises the new metropolitan church which, in the last quarter of the nineteenth century, replaced the much more modest Saint Mina as the main church of the Orthodox community. Its size and central location were indicative of the rising strength of Greek nationalism on the island. Credit: Princeton University Library

conquest of Candia, a metropolitan church was established in the capital city. "Where there had been darkness, now there was light!" our poet wrote rapturously.[44]

The Defense of the Ancien Regime

These are the quarrels that have been preserved in contemporary documents and no doubt there were others, of lesser magnitude, of which we remain ignorant. The question remains as to their meaning.

Despite the obscurity of this period of Cretan history, several Greek historians have touched upon the dissension in the Cretan church at this time. Yet all of them are remarkably cryptic and show an unwillingness to

[44] *Peri tou Naou*, 92, lines 525–28. Stavrinidēs has translated the ferman giving official, permanent status to Saint Minas as the metropolitan church in 1742. Stavrinidēs, *Metafraseis*, 4:270.

Saint Minas, the original metropolitan church of the Orthodox community under the Ottomans, established in 1735. Its construction signaled the end of Cretan aspirations for an autocephalous church on the island. Credit: Photograph by author

explore the issue. Argine Frangoulē, a Greek of Egypt and amateur historian, writes only "a huge fight broke out between the metropolitan of Crete and the Sinai monks" without saying what the fight was about.[45] The church historian Tomadakēs, despite having published a number of church documents that directly bear on the issue, including the long poem by Kladopoulos, did not refer to it in his introduction to the sources.[46] Both Detorakēs, who has written a general history of Crete, and Stavrinidēs,

[45] Argine Frangoule, *E Sinaia Scholē tēs Ag. Aikaterines sto Chandaka* (The School of Saint Catherine's in Chandaka) (Athens, 1981), 60.
[46] Although he might have intended to discuss it in the second volume he planned on the history of the church in Crete, his death prevented him from completing the work.

the leading authority on the early Ottoman period in Crete, prefer to see the matter in purely economic terms. Detorakes notes that the Sinai monks blocked the construction of a metropolitan church for sixty-six years (1669–1735). This was done "largely for economic reasons."[47] Stavrinidēs' language implies that he thinks the monks were up to more than mere moneygrubbing. He speaks rather mysteriously about the "machinations" of the "powerful Sinai monks" and "a tumultous period in the history of the Church of Crete."[48]

Certainly local resentment of the economic demands of the church hierarchy must have played a part in the events in Crete. But while the cupidity of the church was everywhere resented, the struggles in Crete were unique in the Greek-speaking Orthodox world.[49] A single-minded focus on economic issues risks missing the larger aspect of the drama, which was about the place of Crete in the Orthodox world now that the Venetians had departed. The failure of Greek historians to raise this issue, I believe, is due not to ignorance but rather to a reluctance to entertain the possibility that resistance to the metropolitans and the patriarch was about more than money.[50]

The events of 1669–1735 resulted from the intersection of two factors: the attempt to maintain local control over religious life on the island and the willingness of the Venetians to support that struggle because, in their view, it kept alive their chances of someday regaining Crete.

The battle waged by the Sinai monks against successive metropolitans was an attempt to defend privileges acquired during the period of Venetian rule. Just as the ancien regime was slow to die in other spheres, patterns of religious life established over the course of half a millennium (or even longer since the Sinai monks were in Crete even before the Venetians) were not immediately extinguished with the arrival of the Ottomans.

Christian Orthodoxy existed in Venetian Crete in a peculiarly truncated form. While monasteries survived and, in the later centuries, even flourished, the church hierarchy—bishops and metropolitans—was entirely absent. In other words, during the Venetian period the Orthodox monasteries had assumed the leadership of the Orthodox community, and one can

---

[47] Detorakēs does discuss the turbulent decade 1715–25 in some detail and refers to the formation of pro- and antipatriarchal factions. Although he goes so far as to write of the "hatred" between these two groups, he does not discuss the reasons for it. Detorakēs, "E ekklēsia tēs Krētēs," 443.

[48] See Stavrinidēs' comments on the Ottoman texts in *Metafraseis*, 163, 3:402–04.

[49] They bear some resemblence to events in Levant, as we shall see.

[50] Michael Ursinus, basing himself on a document from 1675, notes that in Crete "there is evidence which suggests that Christians, on occasion, resented and openly opposed, the fiscal regime imposed on them by their bishops, *rather than the payments as such*." (emphasis added). Michael Ursinus, "Petitions from Orthodox Church Officials to the Imperial Diwan, 1675," *Byzantine and Modern Greek Studies* 18 (1994): 244.

imagine that such a position was not easily surrendered, especially when one adds into the picture the traditional enmity between monks and bishops that was such an enduring feature of Byzantine life.

The struggle for control over the Christian community in Candia is evident in the court case discussed above when, in 1106/1695, the monks of Saint Matthew's complained that the metropolitan was interfering in the work of the Sinai monks. It is significant that, in their complaint, the monks did not object to the metropolitan collecting the fees that were due him. What they did object to were his attempts to minister to the community. It is true that the monks enjoyed a monopoly on certain incomes directly attached to the city of Candia, but it isn't hard to imagine that, in addition to the financial encroachments, they were unwilling to surrender to the patriarch and his representatives the authority that they had enjoyed under the Venetians.[51] This unwillingness to cede any authority to the bishop must also explain the attempt to prevent a metropolitan church from being built in Candia. It is not known whether the individual Christian had a preference for the leadership of the Sinai monks or the metropolitan—there seems to have been a split—but it seems likely that the monks could exploit the resentment over Istanbul's demands to their own benefit.[52]

Up to a point, the patriarch was willing to accommodate the monks' desire for autonomy. The church and its holdings in Crete were assigned the coveted status of stavropeigeiko. A patriarchal encyclical of 1769 informs us that:

> it [Saint Matthews] was attached [by Nikousios] to the blessed Monastery of the Holy Mountain of Sinai and it was awarded patriarchal stavropeigeiko status through patriarchal encyclicals, to wit that it is a stavropeigeiko holding [meto-chio] of Mount Sinai. As such no one is allowed to interfere with it for any reason except the Ecumenical Throne [the patriarch].[53]

This status had roots in the Byzantine period where it was the subject of a great deal of controversy. A stavropeigeiko monastery placed itself under the direct authority of the patriarch and by so doing denied the local bishop any rights of interference at all. Monasteries saw this as an advantageous arrangement because, in practice if not in law, this often gave them greater freedom of action. The patriarch, unlike the local bishop, was far away. The patriarch benefited both in a material sense—he was entitled to a

---

[51] A patriarchal encyclical of 1769 lays out the financial privileges that Saint Matthew's enjoyed as the only Christian institution in Candia. Tomadakēs, *Istoria tēs ekklēsias Krētēs*, 308.

[52] Stavrinidēs discusses the poor state of relations between the Cretans and the patriarch due to the former's unwillingness or inability to pay their church taxes. Stavrinidēs, *Metafraseis*, 3:403.

[53] Tomadakēs, *Istoria tēs ekklēsias Krētēs*, 308.

certain amount of revenue from the monastery—and in the sense of being able to extend his authority into the provinces, at least theoretically.[54]

Bishops, quite naturally, were adamantly opposed to this practice and their criticisms multiplied toward the end of the eleventh century when the practice of declaring a monastery stavropeigeiko became increasingly common.[55] They resented what they saw as patriarchal usurpation of episcopal rights over monasteries.

The events that transpired between 1715 and 1725 must have convinced the patriarch that the Sinai monks at Saint Matthew's had to be reined in, lest the Christian community in Crete slip out of his grasp altogether. The high profile of the new metropolitan of Crete—Gerasimos—must have been due, in part, to the patriarch's decision to back him against the Sinai monks. Not only did Gerasimos manage finally to build a proper metropolitan church in Candia but also to modify Saint Matthew's stavropeigeiko status. Again, a later patriarchal encyclical of 1777 gives us the history of these events. The encyclical, anxious to project an image of Christian unity, emphasizes how Gerasimos obtained the consent of the Sinai monks before proceeding with the erection of Saint Minas (as the metropolitan church came to be called) and how the whole Christian community was united in this effort to build a metropolitan church. It was agreed that the new church would not affect the stavropeigeiko status of Saint Matthew's and its holdings. Nevertheless, once the church was complete, differences arose. The encyclical refers to "a war of words" conducted against the bishop (i.e., Gerasimos). As a result of this damaging dissension in the Christian community, an agreement was reached to cede jurisdiction over half of Saint Matthew's income to the metropolitan of Crete. Thus, in the words of the encyclical, "scandal and dissension" were finally brought to an end in Candia.[56]

Although the encyclical presents the final arrangement as an agreement between the monks of Sinai and the metropolitan of Crete, it in fact represented a victory of episcopal over monastic authority in Crete. This victory was evident even in spatial terms: any visitor to the Cretan capital today can see that Saint Mina's occupies a much more central place in the city than does Saint Matthew's, which is off in the southwestern corner of the city (both churches, however, are well out of the northwestern corner where the Ottoman elite, as the Venetians before them, located all their major public buildings). The patriarch was persuaded to support

[54] But not always in fact. In the chaotic conditions following 1204 stavropeigeiko monasteries may have been nomially subordinate to the patriarch, but they were effectively under lay control. This was, in fact, the motivation for declaring them stavropeigeiko in the first place. Michael Angold, *Church and Society in Byzantium under the Comneni, 1081–1261* (Cambridge: Cambridge University Press, 1995), 339–45.

[55] Ibid., 56.

[56] Tomadakēs, *Istoria tēs ekklēsias Krētēs*, 310–14.

episcopal authority precisely because bringing the island back into the bosom of the Orthodox Church had proved to be more difficult than anticipated. With Gerasimos's ascendancy, the church of Crete was now firmly within Istanbul's orbit.

Autonomy and Ottoman Christian Communities

In order to appreciate the significance of the division of labor between the Metropolitan and the Sinai monks—whereby he collected the monies owed to him and they administered to the needs of the community—it will be helpful to look at a similar arrangement in a very different context, which is Syria in the early eighteenth century.

Thomas Philipp's research into the genesis of the Greek Catholic communities in Damascus and Aleppo reveals the following chain of events.[57] After the death of the reigning Greek Orthodox patriarch of Antioch in 1724, the Orthodox community in Damascus took the dramatic step of electing and installing their own candidate, Cyrillus VI, who was "an avowed Catholic," as patriarch of Antioch. At the same time a Greek from Cyprus named Sylvester, who was the choice of the patriarch in Istanbul, was accepted as the new patriarch by the Orthodox community in Aleppo.[58] The reigning pasha in Damascus, Uthman Pasha, supported Cyrillus and it was he who officially confirmed the results of the community's election. But when Uthman was subsequently recalled, Cyrillus found himself without a local protector (Catholicism not being an officially recognized millet, or religious community) and was forced to flee to Mount Lebanon. Sylvester, the choice of the central authorities in Istanbul, became patriarch.

Very shortly, however, he managed to alienate the community in Aleppo through his anti-Catholic zeal. He forcefully searched a French church during a service to see if any Aleppine Christians were participating, and he extorted considerable sums from the community by arbitrarily accusing individuals of being Catholic and confiscating their property. Faced with the wrath of his own community, Sylvester fled. The Aleppines were now apparently fed up with Istanbul as well. The community sent a delegation to Istanbul, demanding the detachment of Aleppo from the Antioch Patriarchate and the appointment of a bishop chosen by the community itself. This demand, apparently, was accepted in Istanbul, and the Aleppines chose Maximus, a native of the city. Interestingly, Maximus took a completely different attitude toward the Catholic proclivities of his flock. He

---

[57] For a fuller discussion, see Philipp, *The Syrians in Egypt, 1725–1975* (Stuttgart: Steiner-Verlag-Wiesbaden, 1985), 1–54.

[58] Philipp surmises this was less out of a sense of loyalty to the patriarch in Istanbul than out of a desire to compete with Damascus over control of the patriarchal. Ibid., 19.

allowed them to attend whatever church they chose and complained only when lack of attendance in his own Orthodox churches threatened to reduce his revenue. Local notables moved quickly to guarantee his income, and tranquillity returned. A European doctor in Aleppo in the mid-eighteenth century observed that "the Greek bishop leads a solitary life. Formally recognized and paid for by the community the people do not attend his church but go to the Marnoites or attend services at home. The clergy is all Greek-speaking."[59] Thus, "the Greek Orthodox community in Aleppo could now be described as having turned completely toward Catholicism."[60]

Philipp has argued, convincingly I believe, that these struggles represented the attempt of an increasingly wealthy and educated Christian community to wrest control of its communal life away from Istanbul and he points out that it was the issue of local control to which the patriarch in Istanbul reacted most vociferously.[61] Many of Cyrillus's predecessors had been of Arab origin but none before him had been elected by the local Christians. The turn toward Catholicism, an option provided for them by French missionaries who came to the eastern Mediterranean in the seventeenth century, was also primarily "a symbolic expression of their demand for local communal autonomy congruent with their recently achieved social and economic status."[62] Local Christians seemed quite uninterested in matters of dogma.[63]

The similarities with the Cretan case are several. First, in both Damascus and then Aleppo there was an attempt to select important church officials through local election, rather than through directives coming from Istanbul. Second, there was a preference for indigenous leaders (Cyrillus and Maximus were both Arabs). Finally, the compromise that was arrived at in Aleppo was not unlike the arrangement in Candia: the bishop (in the case of Aleppo) or the metropolitan (in the case of Candia) received his due, and in return the community was free to worship where it chose.

These similarities strongly suggest that, as in Syria, the Sinai monks and those within the Greek community who installed Gerasimos as metropolitan in 1715 (and possibly Daniel in 1722) were also fighting for local

[59] Ibid.
[60] Ibid., 15.
[61] "Local autonomy was the key issue in the genesis of the Greek Catholic community." Ibid., 19.
[62] Ibid.
[63] Thus when Jirjis Mishaqa desired to marry a Catholic woman in the 1750s and "his prospective in-laws demanded that he convert to Catholicism, he first asked what Catholics were. He was taken to the San Salvatore monastery to observe the practice of the religion. After a few days he came to the conclusion that the prayers were the same, the liturgical language was Greek and the garb of the monks was similar to that of the Greek Orthodox monks. 'The Catholics are Greek Orthodox; why did you change your name when your denomination is the same as mine?' " Ibid., 17.

control over the Orthodox community and Orthodox life. The larger context, however, was completely different, and the fortunes of the two communities were heading in opposite directions.

In Syria, the movement for autonomy represented the future. Local Christians were moving out of the shadow of the patriarch and in due time would go so far as to move to the coastal cities of Syria and Lebanon where local strongmen could protect them from harassment by Orthodox authorities. The Catholics and all other Uniate communities were recognized as millets by the Ottoman government in the 1830s.[64] The Cretans, on the other hand, were moving back into the realm of the patriarch of Istanbul after having been outside it for 500 years. The events of the late seventeenth and early eighteenth centuries in Crete represented the slow death of local control over religious life rather than its birth. This was very much part of the larger process, which I have argued elsewhere in this book, whereby Crete became more tightly integrated into the Ottoman Empire in the course of the eighteenth century. The formation of the Greek Catholic community in Damascus and Aleppo, in contrast, came at a time when the Syrian lands were developing a considerable amount of autonomy vis-à-vis Istanbul.[65]

Another difference between the two places is that the metropolitans in Crete, unlike Maximus in Aleppo, from the very beginning were not willing to surrender stewardship of the community to the Sinai monks or to tolerate locally chosen officials. What led to the different outcome in the two cases is uncertain, but it is worth pointing out that the experience of Aleppo was not typical for the eighteenth century. In that century the patriarch in Istanbul actually managed to extend his control over archbishoprics that had previously enjoyed some measure of independence, both in the Balkans and the Middle East.[66] The jurisdictional unity that he managed to create by the second half of the century (and which endured into the nineteenth century) was then taken by many historians as the model of the Orthodox Church throughout the Ottoman period, and Greek nationalist historians were only too happy to support this view of the patriarch as the head of all the Orthodox peoples. In fact Konortas's work has shown that the Orthodox world before 1750 was much more divided. The experience of Crete, then, should be seen as an early example of the success of the patriarch in reexerting his authority over recalcitrant communities. Crete's uniqueness lies in the fact that most of the areas that

[64] Ibid., 23.
[65] Ibid., 7.
[66] It was in the second half of the eighteenth century, for instance, that the Ecumenical Patriarchate succeeded in absorbing the formerly independent Archbishoprics of Achris and Ipekion (in today's Macedonia and Serbia respectively). Paris Konortas, "From Ta'ife to Millet: Ottoman Terms for the Ottoman Greek Orthodox Community," in *Ottoman Greeks in the Age of Nationalism,* ed. D. Gondicas and Ch. Issawi (Princeton: Darwin Press, 1999), 171.

enjoyed a measure of independence between the fifteenth and eighteenth centuries were ethnically mixed or even entirely non-Greek. The Cretan desire for autonomy was due not to ethnic factors but rather to the difficulty of reestablishing formal ties with Istanbul after 500 years under Latin rule.

Finally, Catholicism was not a factor in the events in Candia between 1669 and 1735. French missionaries were conspicuous by their absence in Crete, which does not figure in the missionary literature of the time.[67] According to Philipp, however, Catholicism was not initially an issue in Syria either, at least not in the sense of a dogmatic challenge to Orthodoxy (later on, of course, Middle Eastern Catholics would develop an elaborate and very specific separate identity). What the French missionaries and their churches represented was instead a chance for local control of religious life. This was not unlike what the Sinai monks represented in Candia.

The Role of the Venetians

I had mentioned earlier that the struggles within the Orthodox community reflected not only the attempt to maintain local control over religious life on the island, but also the willingness of the Venetians to support that struggle. Now it is time to examine the Venetian role in these events. We must backtrack a little in order to do this.

In the incident from 1692 when Kallipolitēs was prevented from building his church, Yiannas Skordili was introduced without explaining who he was. Similarly, I mentioned, very briefly, two Greek officials, Moschakēs and Bonakēs, who were involved in the events of 1715 and beyond. What these three men had in common was that at one point they had each served as the secretary to the divan (kapu yazicisi), the highest office open to a Christian on the island. This was a new position created by the Ottomans, and it carried considerable responsibility and power, as well as risk.[68] The secretary, who had to be a native of the country as well as someone fluent in both Turkish and Greek, was charged with assisting the defterdar in the collection of taxes, with recruiting labor when necessary,

---

[67] The Jesuits, the Capuchins, and the Franciscans were the most prominent missionary orders in the eastern Mediterranean in the seventeenth and eighteenth centuries. Crete figures very little, if at all, in the various accounts of their missions, which centered much more on the smaller islands of the Aegean.

[68] These secretaries were initially chosen by the provincial leaders, the castel kethudas, that is, by local Christians of some prominence. Later on, no doubt because of the unreliability of the early secretaries, the official was appointed by the pasha or the kadi of Candia. The berat would then come from Istanbul confirming him. For more on this office, see Nicholaos Stavrinidēs, "O thesmos ton grammatikōn tēs Portēs stēn Krētē" (The institution of the secretary of the Porte in Crete), in *Pepragmena tou D Diethnous Krētologikou Synedriou* (Proceedings of the Fourth International Cretological Symposium) (Athens: 1975), 3:397–401.

and generally with acting as an intermediary between the local community and the Ottoman administration.[69] The wealth of Yiannas Skordili's estate at the time of his fall is a testimony to the possibilities for enrichment open to these secretaries.[70]

Kladopoulos's poem makes clear the central role played by Moschakēs and Bonakēs in the rupture with the patriarch in 1715.

> There was a notable here, whose name was Moschakēs, and another, who became a Turk, who was called Bonakēs. And the metropolitan got ensnared by these two. They managed to get him exiled, and he left Crete. And Moschakēs fixed it so that Crete apostasized. Gerasimos from Kisamos was installed as archbishop, without permission from the patriarch, that's how they wanted it. But in a few years divine judgment was rendered, and Kōnstantine found justice. Moschakēs was strangled.[71]

Moschakēs' violent death was not at all unusual for these early secretaries to the divan. Andreas Mēliōtēs, the first secretary to the divan who served the Ottomans for many decades, was hung from a tree in his native village of Margarites. Although the exact date of his death is not known, the years 1688 or 1692 are the most likely.[72]

At the time of the Ottoman invasion of Rethymnon in 1646, Mēliōtēs was among the prominent cittadini of that city.[73] Rather than flee like many of his compatriots, he initially chose to stay and was able to hold onto his considerable property, both urban and rural. Subsequent to this, however, and for reasons that are unknown, he fled to Venetian-held Candia sometime before 1653 and the property was duly sold. By 1653

---

[69] Richard Pococke, who visited the island in the late 1730s, has provided us with a valuable description of Christian involvement in the tax collection system. "The caia, or prime minister of the Pasha, gives an account of all duties to be levied, to the Christian secretary of the Pasha, who sends it to the castel caia, or high constable, and he goes round to the capitaneo of each village who levie the sume laid on the village from every house." Richard Pococke, *A Description of the East* (London: 1739), 2:266.

[70] See the discussion of Yiannas Skordili's wealth in chapter 5.

[71] *Peri tou Naou*, 83, lines 195–205.

[72] Local tradition designated a particular olive tree as "the olive tree of Miliotis," that is, the tree from which he was hung. Stavrinides, "O Thesmos tōn Grammatikōn," 398. Stavrinides writes that he was most likely arrested and executed in the wake of the hysterical atmosphere produced by the Venetian seige of Chania in 1692. For an account of Mēliōtēs' career, see Nicholaos Stavrinides, "Andreas Mēliōtēs, prōtos grammatikos tēs Portēs en Krētē" (Andreas Mēliōtēs, the first secretary to the Porte in Crete), *Krētika Chronika* 2 (1948): 555. Correspondence from the Venetian archives suggests 1688 as the more likely date.

[73] Under the Venetians, the cittadini were urban residents possessed of certain legal privileges. Anastasia Papadia-Lala, " 'Cittadini' kai katoikoi poleōn: Koinōnikē diastrōmatosē sta venetokratoumena Chania (mesa 16–17 ai.)" ("Cittadini" and the urban population: Social stratification in Venetian Chania [from the middle of the 16th to the middle of the 17th century], in *Praktika tou Diethnous Symposiou Istorias Neoellēnikē Polē* (Proceedings of the International Symposium on the History of the Modern Greek City) (Athens, 1985), 59–66.

he was back in Rethymnon, having agreed to submit to the Ottomans.[74] It is a sign of his considerable talents that, despite this rather checkered background, he was able to regain most of his property and then go on to obtain the tax farm on sheep and goats for the entire province. Although the Ottoman documentary record is nonexistent for the 1660s, Mēliōtēs must have gone from success to success because he appeared as one of the negotiators on the Ottoman side for the surrender of Candia in 1669. At some point prior to this he must have been appointed as the first occupant of this newly created office, secretary to the divan, because he was already going by that title in the early 1670s when we encounter him in Candia, buying and selling real estate in elite neighborhoods.

Mēliōtēs appears again in the archival records in 1685, still in possession of the title of secretary to the divan, although some time previous he had temporarily relinquished it to his nephew Loukas. Sometime between then and the mid-1690s—the most likely date is 1688—he was executed by the Ottomans, charged with spying for the Venetians, who were once again at war with the empire and actively trying to regain Crete.

Yiannas Skordili, whom Stavrinidēs calls "the great demon of Crete," was from a prominent family. It was another Skordili, Stefanos, who negotiated the surrender of Candia on the Venetian side. When his patron, Findik haci Mehmet Pasha, the pasha of Candia, fell from grace in the summer of 1694, Yiannas fled to Chios and thence to Istanbul where he was eventually killed, although when and under what conditions are not known.[75]

The story of Moschakēs, and his successor Bonakēs, is a particularly convoluted one. Moschakēs, who was executed in 1718 for his role in declaring the church autocephalous, had been in trouble at least twice before.[76] A ferman was registered in court in 1126/1714 calling for his dismissal, arrest, and imprisonment.[77] According to the ferman, Moschakēs had been relieved of his duties before and a fetva had been issued calling for his execution. He had managed to escape this fate, however, by converting to Islam and fleeing to Istanbul. Six or seven years later, he was once again the secretary to the divan in Crete. Once back in Crete, he may have presented himself as a Christian, since the document refers to

---

[74] Most of the refugees in Candia did not find a very welcome reception. Many were put to work in the shipyards where they died of ill treatment. This may have played a role in Mēliōtēs' decision not to remain in the capital city. Stavrinidēs, "Andreas Mēliōtēs," 550.

[75] The order for the pasha's execution is preserved in the archives. T.A.H. 8:113. See also Stavrinidēs, "O thesmos tōn grammatikōn," 399. These events are also included in the poem. *Peri tou Naou*, 83, lines 179–80.

[76] T.A.H. 15:78. The document calling for his execution does not, of course, mention his role in declaring the church of Crete autocephalous. It is a purely formulaic document which charges him with routine abuses such as exploitation of the reaya.

[77] T.A.H. 2:246.

him as an apostate (*mürted*).[78] The support of the pasha's chief lieutanant, a man named Ali Kahya who was "of the same heart and the same feelings" with Moschakēs, was critical in allowing him to regain his position. He then resumed his extortionist policies, according to the ferman, and thus had to be removed. According to a later document, his former ally Bonakēs was behind his execution.

Moschakēs was duly executed but Bonakēs survived. As the poem relates, he converted to Islam (and was given the name Mehmet) and became the new secretary to the divan.[79] As Mehmet Agha he was removed from office in 1132/1720 and exiled to the island of Rhodes.[80]

In the document relieving Mehmet Agha of his office, one charge stands out from the routine description of abuses. At some point he had apparently been thrown into prison for spying on the sultan's army.[81] In the earlier proceedings against Moschakēs, too, he had been accused of spying for the Venetians.[82] Are these simply trumped-up charges, manufactured for the purpose of disposing of someone whose luck had changed? In fact, the Ottomans had good reason to suspect the loyalty of the Greek secretaries to the divan.

The Venetian Spy Ring

Rycaut remarked that the three Venetian-held islands off the northern coast served as "a prospect into Candia," and archival records reveal that Venice did run an extensive spy operation from its offshore base. Judging from the relative weight of the documentation, the island of Souda was the center of this effort. This makes sense since it was the most strategically placed of the three islands and the one where Venice concentrated its resources. Souda overlooks the entrance to Souda Bay, just five miles east of Chania, and it remains a major naval base today.

The Venetians maintained a provveditore straordinario on Souda who forwarded correspondence on to Venice. The correspondence remains there today, in the state archives, where it is filed in the series Provveditore

---

[78] And the document of 1718, T.A.H. 15:78, repeats the same charge. After hiding for a while, he became a *mürted* (apostate) and took up the position of secretary to the Porte again. Stavrinidēs gives a similar version of events, namely that when Moschakēs went to Istanbul to get his berat he accepted Islam, but when he came back he presented himself as a Christian. Stavrinidēs, "O thesmos tōn grammatikōn," 400.

[79] In the words of the poem, Bonakēs "etourkepse" or turned Turk—that is, converted to Islam. *Peri tou Naou*, 83, line 196. See also T.A.H. 15:91. T.A.H. 15:341 refers to Mehmet Agha as a new convert to Islam.

[80] T.A.H. 15:341.

[81] "ordu-i humayn-a [   ] casusluk tuhmet-ile." Despite this, he had managed to escape through the help of someone influential. T.A.H. 15:78.

[82] T.A.H. 15:78.

From the small island of Souda, located in the middle of Chania bay, the Venetians communicated with their network of spies. Credit: Princeton University Library

da Terra e da Mar.[83] The provveditore sent along both his own reports, which consisted mostly of oft-repeated requests for supplies, and spy letters, which he tucked into the pages of the general correspondence. It is not clear how spy letters got from Candia (and Chania) to the provveditore on Souda, but Randolph remarked "there is a good correspondence betwixt the Inquisitore of Suda, and the Bafha [sic], who often send letters to one another." Most likely illicit communications were included in this general stream.

This correspondence reveals that the Venetians were able to penetrate the Ottoman government on Crete at the highest levels. In numerous letters directed to the Venetian provveditore on Souda, spies relate the lengthy conversations they held with the pashas of Candia and Chania, and their retainers.[84]

[83] Correspondence from the smaller islands of Gramvoussa (off the extreme northwest corner of Crete) and Spinalonga (off the eastern coast) as well as from Cerigo (halfway between Crete and the Peloponnese) is also filed in the same series.

[84] For example a spy letter of 28 September 1687 relates how the pasha of Candia gathered with "suoi familgiari" (among them the Venetian spy writing the letter) to solicit their views on the progress of the war. A year later (a letter dated 21 Gener 1688) a Venetian spy found himself at the home of the pasha's chief lieutenant (the kahya) where he was able to converse freely about the war with the commander of the garrison at Milopotamo (a renegade) because of the close bonds of friendship (*streta amicicia*) which united them. Archivio di Stato, Venice, Senato, Provveditori da Terra e da mar, Lettere del. Provv. straordinario a Suda, Busta 889.

Andreas Mēliōtēs, the long-serving secretary to the divan, married to a Venetian woman, and the most powerful Christian on the island, was a Venetian spy. We know this because several of his letters has survived in the archives and references to him are numerous. A letter from "Sig. Andrea Milioti" dated February 1686 informed the Venetians that the Ottomans were considerering some repairs to the fortifications but were having difficulty finding the wood necessary to carry them out.[85] Mēliōtēs was in the employ of the Venetians for quite a while, possibly from the time of the war, because a letter from the provveditore on Souda dated 1677 refers to him at length. The provveditore makes it clear that Mēliōtēs was central to the Venetian operation in Candia. Mēliōtēs, he wrote, is the principal spy in the kingdom (as the Venetians continued to refer to Crete), and for this reason the provveditore has delegated him to carry out the "most accurate investigations" possible to find out the reasons for the recent arrival of a number of soldiers in Crete.[86]

In a letter dated 3 July 1688, the spy's name is given only in code, but it is highly likely that the author was Mēliōtēs. We know that the year 1688 is a likely date for his execution, and this letter was written from prison where, as he put it quite poignantly, his life was "hanging by a thread."[87] In the letter he notes that both he and his nephew stood accused of informing the Venetians as to the whereabouts of the Ottoman armada, as a result of which a number of galleys were captured. This nephew in question must certainly be Loukas, who was a close associate of his uncle's and even held the position of secretary to the divan for a brief period in the 1680s. The letter is a plaintive request to the Venetian authorities for money so that he can bribe himself out of an otherwise certain death sentence. "I am imprisoned in the house of Mussa Bey [the governor of Rethymnon]," Mēliōtēs writes, "where I can't even stretch out as I would like. My life is hanging by a thread. I received the letters from Your Grace and was starting to reply when they imprisoned me. Now everything is up in the air." Mēliōtēs informed the Venetians that he had been able to lay his hands on 2,400 dinars, but that it still was not enough. "They want the money right away and thus I bring the request to Your Grace

---

[85] "Di già e statto proposto restelare L'Arzere di queste Fosse, ma per mancanze di Legname non l'hanno adempito, hora con l'occasione, che di sfachioti litigarano con Loro Aga sono pregati condure a Matala m/10 Travi (beams/girders)." Ibid. Then, as now, the main road running to the south coast from the capital city ended at Matala.

[86] "Contribuisco L'intiero di mie applicationi per ripportar dalli Confidenti in Regno tutti [   ] raugagli, che fossero degni di notitia, et appunto Andrea Miliotti, principale di essi" Archivio di Stato, Venice, Senato, Provveditori da Terra e da mar, Lettere del. Provv. straordinario a Suda, Busta 886.

[87] "La vita pende al fillo della morte infalibille." Lettere del. Provv. straordinario a Suda, Busta 889.

to see to sending the rest because if you do not help me I will die in prison."[88]

Yiannas Skordili, who served as secretary to the divan after Mēliōtēs, is identified in a Venetian document as someone who provided information to Venice on the military strength of the Ottomans in Crete.[89] A letter from a spy (his name is in code) a few years earlier, written in the large and prosperous village of Margarites, acknowledges having received from "Sig. Scordili" a letter, numbered 48 and dated 14 April, from Venice.[90] Furthermore, it is possible that both Mēliōtēs and Skordili wrote many of the letters that were sent to the provveditore straordinario on Souda. In most cases the name is given only in code, making it difficult to identify the author.[91]

Neither Moschakēs nor Bonakēs has appeared in the correspondence I have examined. But in light of the charges against them, and the history of earlier secretaries to the divan, the likelihood of their working with the Venetians as well must be considered very high.

The Sinai monks clearly worked together with people like Skordili and Moschakēs on a number of occasions. Both shared an interest in preserving some sort of church organization independent of Istanbul. Does that mean that the Sinai monks had ties to the Venetians as well? It is worth noting that Tomadakēs's explicitly charged at least some of the clergy in Crete with spying for the Venetians. The miserable peasantry, he writes, were stirred up by the "priest-spies of the Venetians."[92]

[88] "Prigione in Casa di Mussa Bey, a Retimo il miserabille, non posso estendermi come volgio; La vita pende al fillo della morte infalibille; Ho ricevuto Le lettere di Vostra Ser(ma), et nel cominciare a scrivere m'imprigionai, et resterono le cose sospese . . . li volgiono subbito e porto l'istanze a Ser(ma) per veder a che resto, perche quando non mi socori morirà prigione." Ibid.

[89] "Nota dell'Armo della Citta di Candia spedito à [   ] Confidenti della medisima sono L'anno decorso del 1695 come pure L'Armo dell'stessa spedito da Giannachi Skordili L'anno 1694 al Precedemente Nostro [   ] Imperial Contarina." A list of the soldiers in Candia follows, and then another list, which is Skordili's original report: "Copia dell'Armo spedito al [   ] Prec. Contarina sono li 24 Marzo 1694 di Giannachi Skordili." Archivo di Stato, Venice, Senato, Provveditori de Terra e da mar, Lettere del. Provv. straordinario a Suda, Busta 890.

[90] "Del sig. [the name is in code], dal Sig. Scordili ricevo una di V.S. di X:48 di 14 April nella quale mi aviso Lo ricevuta de miei numeri dal X. 7." Lettere del. Provv. straordinario a Suda, Busta 889. Clearly a considerable amount of effort was put into keeping track of correspondence.

[91] In one case someone, probably the recipient of the letter, wrote "confidente Milioti" above the code. Ibid., a letter of 28 Luglio (no year is given but considering the surrounding documents it was probably 1686).

[92] "papades-praktores tōn enetōn." Tomadakēs, *Istoria tēs ekklēsias Krētēs*, 28. Tomadakēs also mentions that some members of the Orthodox hierarchy were able to gain access to the resources of the Latins by pretending to be in favor of submission to the pope, and he includes the Sinai monks among those who followed such a policy. The Orthodox had "to face the propaganda of the papists but at the same time they managed to exploit the resources of the Latin Church by falsely presenting themselves as being in favor of Uniate churches."

The Venetian correspondence does not specifically mention the monks of Sinai. At least one abbot, however, was in regular correspondence with the Venetians and a spy letter written shortly after Mēliōtēs' fall strongly implies that other abbots were linked to Venice as well.

A "Padre" and "Abbate" in Chania wrote a letter to Venice in 1687 and he numbered it "102," suggesting that he was keeping a regular correspondence. In it he told them of the location of soldiers within the city, as well as the fruitless search of a "Passa di Barbaria" for a ship to take him to Constantinople.[93]

A spy letter written in the wake of Mēliōtēs' execution gave the following account of the response to his fall from grace: "he [Mēliōtēs] was hung from a tree . . . as a result of which the abbots of Arcadi and Arsami, as well as Chiaretti, withdrew and threw themselves into the sea in order to board a French ship, which transferred them to Milos and from there they passed to the feet of the captain of the Armada."[94] Francesco Chiaretti was one of the more prolific Venetian spies—many letters from him survive in the archives—and Arcadi Monastery was (and continues to be) the most prominent monastery on the island.

To sum up, the indigenous Greek elite in this period was to be found either in the Ottoman divan—where it exercised a monopoly over the position of secretary—or in the upper echelons of the monastic establishment. These two groups had ties to each other and both had ties to the Venetians.

Apostasy and Sovereignty

The full significance of these contacts with Venice cannot be understood without considering the possibility that they extended to the island's Muslim officials as well. The evidence for this is limited (at this point) but very suggestive.

In the ferman of 1130/1718 calling for Moschakēs' execution, the pasha's chief lieutanant, Ali Kahya, was charged with having helped

Ibid., 34. By itself, however, this does not mean that the Sinai monks and others were actually involved in spying for the Venetians. In the Cyclades, too, it was very common to proclaim Uniate sentiment in order to obtain the support of the Latins against, say, the attacks of western (Catholic) pirates. No espionage was involved in this dynamic.

[93] "Dell. Pad.e Abbate Hieroteo Mormori de di 17 Marzo S.N.Canea No.102." The year is not given but it appears after a letter written at the end of December 1686, so the letter was probably written in March 1687. Lettere del. Provv. straordinario a Suda, Busta 889.

[94] "atacatto ad'un Arborenella via di Parema, causa di che si ritiro pure l'Abbate d'Arcadi e l'Abbate d'Arsami e Chiaretti, che getandosi a nuotto per esser imbarcatto sopra un Vascello Francese, come laude S.V.M. segui con trasferirsi a Millo e di la passar a piedi di S.S. Capi [   ] all'Armata;" The date of the letter is 14 October 1688. Ibid.

Moschakēs regain his position as secretary.[95] Ali Kahya, the ferman said, was "of the same heart and the same feelings" with Moschakēs. It is difficult to know what is meant exactly by this cryptic remark. At the very least it certainly means that Ali Kahya, one of the most powerful men on the island, backed Moschakēs in his political ambitions. It could also mean that Ali Kahya belonged to the same faction as Moschakēs, a faction that was in contact with Venice.

A spy letter, dating probably to 1687, is much more revealing as to the equivocal position of some high-ranking Ottoman officials.[96] In it, the spy relates a long and leisurely conversation that he had over dinner with the agha of the imperial janissary corps in Candia. The relationship appeared to be a close one.

> I had the opportunity not only to be in his company many times but even to find myself at dinner with him as a friend. Having shown myself to be seeking his favor with presents and other services, I was able to talk with him at length and to discover all that was possible [to discover]. He told me about the various Turkish campaigns in Hungary in great detail, having been himself at the fighting. In particular he told me that there was no way the Turks could further resist the imperial forces.[97]

Apparently the spy felt this to be an admission of some despair, because he then suggested to the officer that he come over to the Venetian side.

> Then I said to him, speaking familiarly, if indeed all is lost, why don't you look to provide for your own, rather than be lost with them?

The agha seemed to grasp immediately what was being suggested to him.

> He responded, "It is of no use to me, since my son is serving in the army. If it proves possible to become the turnacibasi, that is the chief military officer, of this place [Crete], then at that time we will see what can be worked out from these dogs." And he said this acting as a Christian, since he knew that his mother, as a Christian, had secretly had him baptized when he was born. [It was] as if he wanted to say that, having this office, he would be able to find a way to correspond with the Christians while enjoying high office at the same time. Then if he wanted he could leave Turkey.

[95] T.A.H. 15:78 Pococke's description of the tax collection system (see note 69) makes clear the close relationship that existed between the pasha's lieutenant (kahya) and the Christian secretary to the divan.

[96] It is in a series of documents that cover the years 1685–88, and in the letter reference is made to the acension of the new sultan. This must be Süleyman II, who came to the throne in 1687. Lettere del. Provv. straordinario a Suda, Busta 889. The author of the letter is unknown since the name is given in code.

[97] In part: "ho incontratto appertura non solamente di attocarmi secco più volte, ma titrovarmi a cena con lui, come Amico, che mi mostra havendolo ollbigatto con Regaliet altri serviciii in maniera, che ho havutto modo di discorer lungamente con lui."

The spy was skeptical of the agha's claim that he couldn't leave because he would be forced to abandon his son in the army. He said the agha "well knew" that he could have his son with him if he chose to flee and was in fact angling for some offer of a position with the Venetians. Apparently the agha was expecting a visit from yet another spy (whose name is written in code), with the implication being that this, too, was connected with the issue of a suitable offer from the Venetians.[98]

This remarkable letter suggests that some Ottoman officials on Crete, as well as local Christians, also kept the door open to Venetian overtures, both through Venice's spies and perhaps even directly. The agha told the spy that "Caramusa" in Rethymnon (the pasha of the city) was corresponding with Souda.[99] Most likely these officials did not have a definite plan in mind but simply wanted to make sure that, if Venetian rule returned to the island, they would be well placed to survive. Others, perhaps like the agha of the spy's letter, may have been looking to flee if Ottoman military fortunes took a turn for the worse.

Ambiguity in religious identity is a persistent undercurrent in the stories of high-ranking officials—both Christian and Muslim—in Crete at this time. Moschakēs was rumored to have converted to Islam while in Istanbul and then to have returned to Christianity when he resumed his post in Crete. His associate Bonakēs did actually convert and held the post of secretary to the Porte as a Muslim. Similarly, the Venetian spy who has left us an account of his dinner with the janissary agha of Candia spoke of the agha "acting like a Christian" and of his secret baptism. This suggests that a certain fluidity in religious identity at the level of the ordinary subject—already discussed in chapter 3—was replicated at the highest levels of society.

At the level of elite politics this oscillation between Christianity and Islam was a reflection, I believe, of the uncertain nature of Ottoman sovereignty on the island. Social marginality in these circumstances—the sense on society's part that an individual belonged truly to neither the Christian nor the Muslim camp—may actually have worked to increase an individual's options in terms of political choices, although, of course, it was not without its dangers.

In claiming an extended period (until 1715) of uncertain Ottoman sovereignty on Crete, I am arguing against the distinction that is usually drawn between the history of the larger Greek islands (Crete and Cyprus) and the small islands of the Aegean. In the case of the latter, historians have rightly emphasized the extremely limited Muslim presence on the islands themselves and the persistence there of Western (Latin) power long

---

[98] "e lo ben consciuto che potesse haver il suo figliolo con lui fugirebbe certo da Cristiani, ma desidera haver merito prima con loro."

[99] "ho informacione che tiene correspondenza alla Suda, et altre cose similli."

after the conquests of Hayreddin Barbarossa in 1538 formally brought the Aegean under Ottoman control. Up through the beginning of the eighteenth century, the Aegean was very much a contested zone, and this central fact of political life meant that individuals who stood astride two (or more) communities were likely to prosper.

Consider, for example, the career of Vasilis Logothetis, who in the first half of the seventeenth century was one of the richest merchants in the Cycladic islands. He was also the consul of France, England, and Venice. During the early years of the war, when sea battles between the Ottomans and the Venetians raged throughout the Aegean, he kept his title as Venetian consul and spied for Venice, but was at the same time considered a friend by the Ottomans. He was very effective at ransoming Muslims taken prisoner by the Venetians and was used in special missions by the Ottoman admiral of the navy.[100] Logothetis also effectively straddled the Orthodox-Latin divide. Although a Greek Orthodox, he gave a church on the island of Milos to the Jesuits and provided for the upkeep of a Franciscan cleric.[101] In his stance toward the two churches, Logothetis represented "the traditional Cycladic attitude of laissez-faire."[102]

More striking is the story of the early seventeenth-century Ottoman Kapudan Pasha Sinan Pasha Cicala. Sinan Pasha, a convert to Islam, was originally from Naples. His father was a famous Christian corsair and his brother—a Catholic named Carlo Cicala—was briefly the bey of Naxos, an office he secured through Sinan Pasha's efforts. Another brother, Vincenzo, was a Jesuit. Sinan Pasha's mother was born Muslim but, after being captured in a raid by the Pasha's father, had converted to Christianity.[103] Through his brother Vincenzo—who was an agent of the Spanish court—Sinan established contact with the Vatican, which hoped to persuade him to surrender Naxos to the Christian powers. Although nothing eventually came of these contacts, the very fact that they existed at all suggests Sinan Pasha's receptiveness to Western plots. In the words of B. J. Slot, "Sinan ne prit guère l'attitude indignée qu'on attendrait d'un loyal ministre de l'empire ottoman."[104]

The in-between status of the Aegean world has been much remarked, but a different sort of model has been posited for Crete. The presence of Ottoman officialdom and Ottoman institutions on the island, the fact of a large Muslim community, and the prominent role of the janissaries has led historians to posit an abrupt and wrenching reorientation, from capital

[100] B. J. Slot, *Archipelagus Turbatus: Les Cyclades entre colonisation latine et occupation ottomane c. 1500–1718* (Istanbul: Nederlands Historisch-Archaeologisch Instituut te Istanbul, 1982), 162–92.
[101] Ibid., 153.
[102] Ibid., 161.
[103] Ibid., 103, 122.
[104] Ibid., 122.

of the Venetian overseas empire to loyal outpost of the Ottoman state. This, in fact, was not the case. Despite a strong (relative to the Aegean) Ottoman presence, the island's elite during the first half-century of Ottoman rule was strongly marked by the multiple identities so common in the Aegean. Crete, in other words, shows that Muslims, too, were active participants in a world that extended beyond the Aegean to include the eastern Mediterranean as a whole. In this world personal ties and religious conversion blurred the lines among the Latin, Orthodox, and Muslim communities.

This world was on its last legs in early Ottoman Crete. In the wake of the last Ottoman-Venetian war (1714–18) and the final Venetian withdrawal from the eastern Mediterranean, France emerged, at last, as the unrivaled Latin power in the eastern Mediterranean. But the French presence in the eighteenth century was of a totally different order than that of the old Latin powers—principally Genoa and Venice—who had dominated the area since the Fourth Crusade.[105] French merchants and diplomats held themselves apart from local society, and this is evident in the sources. The French consular reports and the Venetian correspondence from Souda are a study in contrasts. The French reports, overwhelmingly concerned with commerce, present an anonymous society composed of well-defined groups: Jews, Turks, and Greeks. They foreshadow the era of nationalism. The Venetians and their spies write of individuals whose history they know—this pasha who is a good soldier, that agha whose mother is a Christian, and this renegade soldier who is from Sfakia. The tone of the Venetian sources is a natural outgrowth of the long and complex intermingling of Latins, Orthodox, and Muslims in the early modern Mediterranean. Sinan Pasha Cicala was from Naples; he could not have been from Marseilles. Under French influence, the boundaries between East and West in the eighteenth century Mediterranean began to acquire a solidity that they had previously lacked.

---

[105] It was even different from the French presence in the seventeenth century. See Slot, *Archipelagus Turbatus*, 236–38, for Louis XIV's largely successful efforts at the end of the century to "clean up" the French colony in the Aegean and break the ties between it and the local population.

Conclusion

IN THE SPRING OF 1770 a Cretan notable and shipowner from Sfakia named John Vlachos, known to history as Daskaloyiannēs, led a band of 2,000 well-armed men out of the mountains and down into the plains of western Crete.[1] After a week of preparation with messianic overtones, spent in eating, drinking, and dancing, they fanned out into small bands and began to kill the Muslims in the area, in an unsuccessful effort to convince their fellow Cretans to join them in throwing off Ottoman rule.[2] This revolt was part of a wider event, known in Greek historiography as the "Orloff uprisings," which shook the eastern Mediterranean in 1770. The uprisings occurred as part of the Russo-Turkish War (1768–74) when Catherine the Great's naval commander Gregory Orlov sailed boldy into the Aegean (by way of the English Channel) and sacked the Ottoman fleet anchored at Chios and Çeşme. Encouraged by Russian agents, many local Greek leaders on the islands and the mainland attacked Ottoman forces in the hopes of exchanging Ottoman for Russian rule.[3] Daskaloyiannēs himself, on the strength of Russian promises, had sailed to Trieste the previous fall and bought a large number of weapons with his own money. But the Russian attack in the Aegean was eventually turned back—with the help of local Greeks who did not support the insurrection and a large number of Albanian troops—and the unfortunate rebels suffered severe reprisals.

In Crete the uprising was swiftly put down. The Russian fleet never appeared in the port of Chania, as promised, and the Ottomans moved decisively against the rebels. Sfakiot villages were burned, and the Sfakiots themselves retreated higher and higher up into the mountains. Toward the end of 1770 Daskaloyiannēs decided to give himself up, and the rebellion came to an end.[4] Among the terms of surrender was one that forbade the Sfakiots from having any contact with Christian ships that

---

[1] My account of the uprising of 1770, as well as Daskaloyiannēs' career prior to 1770, is based on the description given in V. Psilakēs, *Istoria tēs Krētēs* (History of Crete) (Athens: Arkadi, 1970), 3:63–106.

[2] Daskaloyiannēs and his band of men, accompanied by twenty priests, came out of the mountains on Easter Sunday, 1770, a day traditionally seen as the one when the nation would be delivered. The week spent eating, drinking, and dancing was the Octave of Easter, also known as "Bright Week," a period that was considered an extension of the Easter celebrations.

[3] For a brief discussion of the war of 1768–74, and Orlov's naval expedition, see P. Sugar, "The Change of Fortune," in *Southeastern Europe under Ottoman Rule, 1354–1804* (Seattle: University of Washington Press, 1993), chap. 9.

[4] Despite promises of amnesty, Daskaloyiannēs was put to death by the pasha of Candia in 1771.

might sail into their harbors other than the obligation to arrest the ship's crew and send them on to Candia.[5] Already the Ottomans had hit hard at Sfakiot seafaring by destroying its merchant marine in the opening months of the rebellion.[6]

The events of 1770 marked a turning point both in Crete and in the larger world of the eastern Mediterranean. The attack on the Sfakiot nautical tradition is notable because it signaled a profound shift in the relationship between Candia and the seafarers of Sfakia. Although the mountains had always been viewed as a wild area that was difficult to rule, for two centuries city and mountain had been linked by the boats and the wood that the Sfakiots supplied to Candia's merchants. By attacking the merchant marine—and attempting to prevent contact between Sfakia and the Christian powers—the Ottomans signaled that the world of Sfakia now stood in opposition to the world of Candia and its merchants.

Daskaloyiannēs' career itself belonged to a new Mediterranean constellation that was emerging, and would continue to emerge, even after the disastrous events of 1770. Prior to the uprising, the rebel leader had been a successful merchant with four large boats to his name. What distinguished him both from the merchants of an earlier age and the merchants of Candia was his connection to Russia. Daskaloyiannēs spoke Italian but he also spoke Russian, and he traveled often to the Black Sea where Russia was expanding, slowly but steadily, at the expense of the Ottoman Empire. Lacking an indigenous mercantile population sufficient to exploit the fertile Black Sea area, Catherine the Great was happy to welcome the Ottoman Greeks, her coreligionists, who flocked to southern Russia, especially after the conclusion of the war in 1774.[7]

This expanding Greek disapora in the Black Sea area was closely linked to Russia, who harbored political ambitions of her own vis-à-vis the Ottomans. The naval battle at Chios and Çeşme signaled the return of Great Power struggle to the eastern Mediterranean after a long hiatus. Napoleon's famous expedition to Egypt in 1798 is the more conventional watershed—among other things it ushered in a period of intense Anglo-French competition in the eastern Mediterranean—but the French were never as important to the political aspirations of the Greeks as the Russians.[8]

[5] For the other terms of the surrender, see Theocharis Detorakēs, *Istoria tēs Krētēs* (History of Crete) (Athens, 1986), 310–11.

[6] Yolanda Baladie Triandafylidou, *To emborio kai E oikonomia tēs Krētēs 1669–1795* (Trade and economy in Crete, 1669–1795) (Herakleion: Municipality of Herakleion, 1988), 278. The attack on the Sfakiot merchant marine is mentioned in a letter of the French consul in Chania, June 22, 1770.

[7] For a concise history of the Greeks in southern Russia, see Patricia Herlihy, "Greek Merchants in Odessa in the Nineteenth Century," *Harvard Ukrainian Studies* 3–4 (1979–80): 399–420.

[8] This is not to say that many Greeks, and especially those in the diaspora, were not inspired by the vision of the French Revolution, and Napoleon's subsequent proclamations in favor

Russia was eager to use the Greeks to further its goals and, as the case of Daskaloyiannēs illustrates so well, some Greeks were willing to link their fate to Russia's. Its encouragement of the Greeks was part of the classic pattern of the Eastern Question whereby a Great Power extended "protection" to a selected minority in the Ottoman Empire in the hopes of extending its own influence. This aspect of the long Ottoman-Russian struggle distinguished it from the earlier, and equally durable, Ottoman-Venetian rivalry in the eastern Mediterranean. In that conflict the Greeks were essentially invisible, whereas Russian sponsorship was one of the factors that allowed the Greeks, eventually, to wrest control of the Aegean, and even the eastern Mediterranean, away from the Ottomans and to turn it into Greek national space.

Daskaloyiannēs' uprising was part of that long-term process, although its vision was not a national one but rather one in which Christian Orthodox Russia would replace the Ottoman Turks in Constantinople and the East in general. A section from the long *Song of Daskaloyiannēs*, a poem describing the events of 1770, indicates the new society envisioned by Daskaloyiannēs, one that had no place for the mixed cities of Crete's northern shore.

> Every Sunday and every Easter Sunday he
> would don his hat and go to the priest
> and say: "I will bring Moscow here and Sfakia
> will help her throw out the Turks. Then
> together we will set out for the Red Apple.
> And whoever wants to stay in Crete, had
> better pray to the Cross and become a Christian."[9]

Daskaloyiannēs' exclusivist vision, of course, was the one that finally triumphed in Crete and throughout the Greek world. It was in the rural areas that the fight against the Ottomans was launched and finally won, and thus to the peasant's traditional enmity toward urban life was added the powerful tonic of a national vision that exalted the authentic countryside over the corrupt Ottoman city. Therefore, it is fair to say that, even though the Ottomans brutally crushed the Sfakiots in 1770, the city of Candia, and the older Mediterranean world of which it was a part, were buried in the events of that year. The result has been to render Ottoman Candia invisible to this day.

Different scholarly traditions have presented us with distinct narratives of the early modern Mediterranean. Next to Braudel's pan-Mediterranean

---

of Greek liberty. But Russia's involvement in Greek affairs, for better or worse, was of much longer standing and much more direct. Culturally, too, many more Greeks could relate to the idea of an avenging Orthodox tsar than they could to the republican and secular vision of the French Revolution.

[9] Psilakēs, *Istoria tēs Krētēs*, 75.

world of olive trees, shipwrecks, and banditry, Ottoman historians have given us the Mediterranean of the sultan's navy and, after the sixteenth century, the eastern Mediterranean as the preserve of new western powers, intruders from the north. Greek historiography has provided the local reflection of this tradition by studying, first, Greek service in the sultan's navy and then the rise of Greek shipping and commerce in the latter half of the eighteenth century in the context of cooperation and competition with the western powers. This book has argued that there was another Mediterranean world and suggested the ways in which it was distinctive. For those who would persist in seeing it as a battleground between hostile civilizations, the central irony must certainly be this: that the survival of this society depended precisely on its ability to exclude the world beyond the sea. When that was no longer possible, the end was only a matter of time.

Bibliography

ARCHIVAL SOURCES

Ankara

The cadastral surveys of the Ottoman Empire, by and large, are stored in Ankara at the Tapu ve Kadastro Genel Müdürlüğü.
   Register no. 4 (eastern Crete)

Crete

The most extensive Ottoman documentation for the history of Ottoman Crete is located in Crete itself. I have used the records of the Islamic court (*mahkeme*) in Candia—today's Herakleion—which are housed in the Vikelaia Municipal Library in Herakleion under the heading Turkish Archives of Herakleion (henceforth T.A.H.). There are 162 volumes covering two and one-half centuries of Ottoman rule in Crete. The following volumes were consulted for this study: 1–5, 7–11, 13–15, and 20. These volumes cover the years 1080–1132/1669–1720. (Volumes 6 and 12 are in a deteriorated condition and are no longer available to researchers.)

Istanbul

The central records of the Ottoman administration are housed in the Başbakanlık Arşivi (Prime Ministry's Archive). I consulted the following three series.

Baş Muhasebe Mukata'a Defterleri series
   Register nos. 10138–62

Maliyeden Müdevver.
   Register no. 634
   Register no. 658
   Register no. 745
   Register no. 2636

Tapu Tahrir Defterleri series
   No.801.
   No.825
   No.980

Venice

The majority of the documentation on Crete in the vast Venetian Archivio di Stato (State Archives) concerns the period before 1669 when Crete was a Venetian possession. For the post-1669 period, however, reports gathered by the Venetian provveditore on Souda are an extremely valuable source.

Senato. Provveditore da Terra e da mar. Lettere del. Provv. straordinario a Suda
   Busta 886
   Busta 888

Busta 889
Busta 890
Busta 891bis

TRAVEL ACCOUNTS

Castlemaine, Earl of. *An Account of the Present War between Venetians and Turks with the State of Candie (in a Letter to the King from Venice)*. London: Printed by J.M. for H. Herringman, at the Anchor on the Lower Walk of the New Exchange, 1666.

Dandini, Girolamo. "A voyage to Mount Libanus; wherein is an account of the customs and manners of the Turks. Also, a description of Candia, Nicosia, Tripoli, Alexandretta, etc. Written originally in Italian by the Rev. Father Jerome Dandini." In *A General Collection of the Best and Most Interesting Voyages and Travels*. Vol. 10. London, 1811.

d'Arvieux, Laurant. *Memoires du Chevalier d'Arvieux, contenant ses voyages à Constantinople, dans l'Asie, la Syrie, la Palestine, l'Egypte et la Barbarie*. Comp. J. B. Labat. 5 vols. Paris, 1735.

Evliya Çelebi. *Seyahatnamesi* (Travelogue). Vol. 8. Istanbul: Devlet Matbassi, 1928.

Holland, Henry. *Travels in the Ionian Islands, Albania, Thessaly, Macedonia during the years 1812 and 1813*. 2 vols. London, 1819.

Pashley, Robert. *Travels in Crete*. 2 vols. 1837. Reprint, Athens: Dion N. Karavias, 1989.

Pococke, Richard. *A Description of the East*. Vol. 2. London, 1739.

Praktikidou, Zachariou. *Chōrografia tes Krētēs* (Description of the places of Crete). 1900. Reprint, Herakleion: Technical Board of Greece, 1983.

Randolph, Bernard. *Travels in Crete*. London, 1700.

Rycaut, Paul. *A History of the Ottoman Empire from the Year 1623 to the Year 1677*. London, 1680.

―――. *The Present State of the Ottoman Empire*. London, 1669.

Sieber, F. W. *Travels in the Island of Crete in the Year 1817*. London, 1823.

Struys, John. *The Voiages of John Struys*. London, 1684.

Tavernier, Jean Baptiste. *Six Voyages through Turkey into Asia*. London, 1678.

Tott, Baron de. *Memoires sur les Turcs et les Tartares*.
Vol. 2. Amsterdam, 1784.

Tournefort, M. Pitton de. *A Voyage into the Levant*. Paris, 1717.

SECONDARY SOURCES

Abou-El-Haj, Rifa'at Ali. *Formation of the Modern State: The Ottoman Empire, Sixteenth to Eighteenth Centuries*. Albany: State University of New York Press, 1991.

―――. "The Ottoman Kanun as an Instrument of Domination." Paper presented at CIEPO, International Committee of Pre-Ottoman and Ottoman Studies, Seventh Symposium, Pecs, 7–11 September, 1986.

————. *The 1703 Rebellion and the Structure of Ottoman Politics.* Leiden: E. J. Brill, 1984.

Aikaterinide, Georgiou. "Laikos politismos" (Popular culture). In *Krētē: Istoria kai politismos* (Crete: History and civilization), edited by N. Panayiotakēs, 521–50. Herakleion: Synthesmos Topikōn Enōseōn Demōn kai Koinotetōn Kretes, 1988.

Alexiou, St. "To Kastro tēs Krētes kai ē zoē tou ston 16th kai 17th aiona" (The fortress of Crete and its life in the 16th and 17th centuries). *Krētika Chronika* 19 (1965): 146–78.

Allbaugh, L. *Crete: Case Study of an Underdeveloped Area.* Princeton: Princeton University Press, 1953.

Anderson, R. C. *Naval Wars in the Levant.* Princeton: Princeton University Press, 1952.

Angold, Michael. *Church and Society in Byzantium under the Comneni, 1081–1261.* Cambridge: Cambridge University Press, 1995.

Ankori, Zvi. "From Zudecha to Yahudi Mahellesi: The Jewish Quarter of Candia in the Seventeenth Century." In *Salo Wittmayer Baron Jubilee Volume*, edited by Saul Lieberman, 1:63–127. Jerusalem: American Academy for Jewish Research, 1974.

Antoniadēs, S. A. "E kinētē periousia tou Geōrgiou Mormore metaferetai ap tēn Krētē stē Venetia 1667" (The property of George Mormore is brought from Crete to Venice). *Praktika Akadēmia Athenōn* 40 (1965): 258–267.

————. "Oikonomikē katastasē ton poleōn tēs Krētēs 1645–1669" (The economic condition of Crete's cities, 1645–1669). *Thēsaurismata* 4 (1967): 38–52.

Baladie, Yolanda Triandafyllidou. *To emborio kai e oikonomia tēs Krētēs 1669–1795* (The commerce and economy of Crete, 1669–1795). Herakleion: Municipality of Herakleion, 1988.

————. "Les conditions du commerce en Crete pendant les premiers deannies de la domination ottomane." In *Pepragmena tou D Diethnous Krētologikou Synedriou* (Proceedings of the Fourth International Cretological Symposium), 3:297–304. Athens, 1981.

————. "L'industrie du savon en Crete au XVIII siècle: Aspects economiques et sociaux." *Etudes Balkaniques* 4 (1975): 75–87.

Barkan, O. L. *Osmanli Imparatorluğunda ziraat ekonominin hukuki esaslari* (The legal basis of the agricultural economy in the Ottoman Empire). Istanbul: Burhaneddin Matbaasi, 1945.

Bekiaroglu-Eksadaktylou, Aik. *Othomanika naupēgeia ston paradosiako ellēniko choro* (Ottoman shipyards in the Greek world). Athens: ETBA, 1994.

Bernard, Jack. *Italy: An Historical Survey.* Newton Abbot: David and Charles, 1971.

Bernardy, Amy. *Venezia e Il Turco nella seconda metà del secolo XVII.* Florence: G. Civelli, 1902.

Bierman, I. "The Ottomanization of Crete." In *The Ottoman City and Its Parts,* edited by Irene A. Bierman, Rifa'at A. Abou-el-Haj, and Donald Preziosi, 53–75. New Rochelle, N.Y.: Aristide D. Caratzas, 1991.

Bracewell, Catherine Wendy. *The Uskoks of Senj: Piracy, Banditry and Holy War in the Sixteenth Century Adriatic.* Ithaca: Cornell University Press, 1992.

Braudel, Fernand. *The Mediterranean and the Mediterranean World in the Age of Philip II*. 2 vols. New York: Harper and Row, 1973.

Brummett, Palmira. *Ottoman Seapower and Levantine Diplomacy in the Age of Discovery* Albany: State University of New York Press, 1994.

Cameron, P. *Blue Guide to Crete*. 4th ed. London: Ernest Benn, 1986.

Cezar, Yavuz. *Osmanli maliyesinde bunalim ve değişim dönemi: XVIII.yy'dan Tanzimat'a mali tarih* (The period of crisis and change in Ottoman finance: A financial history from the eighteenth century to the Tanzimat). Istanbul: Alan Yayıncılık, 1986.

Chasiotēs, I. K. "To oikomeniko patriarcheio kai E Krētē meta to thanato tou Kyrillou A' tou Loukareos" (The ecumenical Patriarchate and Crete after the death of Kyrillos Loukareos the First). *Thēsaurismata* 6–7 (1969–70): 201–36.

Cipolla, Carlo. *Before the Industrial Revolution: European Society and Economy, 1000–1700*. 3d ed. London: Routledge, 1993.

———. "The Decline of Italy: The Case of a Fully Matured Economy." *Economic History Review*, 2d ser. 5 (1952–53): 178–87.

Çizakça, Murat. "Taxfarming and Financial Decentralization in the Ottoman Economy, 1520–1697." *Journal of European Economic History* 22, no. 2 (1993): 219–50.

Cuno, Kenneth. *The Pasha's Peasants: Land, Society and Economy in Lower Egypt, 1740–1858*. Cambridge: Cambridge University Press, 1992.

Damurdashi, Ahmad. *al-Damurdashi's Chronicle of Egypt, 1688–1755*. Translated and annotated by Daniel Crecelius and 'Abd al-Wahhab Bakr. Leiden: E. J. Brill, 1991.

Darling, Linda. *Revenue-Raising and Legitimacy: Tax Collection and Finance Administration in the Ottoman Empire, 1550–1660*. Leiden: E. J. Brill, 1996.

Detorakēs, Theocharis. "E ekklēsia tēs Krētēs kata tēn Tourkokratia 1645–1898" (The church of Crete during the period of Turkish rule, 1645–1898). In *Krētē: Istoria kai politismos* (Crete: History and civilization), edited by N. Panayiotakēs, 437–58. Herakleion: Synthesmos Topilcōn Enōseōn Demōn kai Koinotetōn Kretes, 1988.

———. *Istorias tēs Krētēs* (History of Crete). Athens, 1986.

———. "E Tourkokrateia stēn Krētē" (The Turkish period in Crete). In *Krētē: Istoria and politismus* (Crete: History and civilization), ed. N. Panayiotakēs, 333–436. Herakleion: Synthesmos Topikōn Enōseōn Demōn kai Koinotetōn Kretes, 1988.

Donia, Robert, and John Fine. *Bosnia and Hercegovina: A Tradition Betrayed*. London: C. Hurst, 1994.

Encyclopaedia of Islam. New ed. Leiden: E. J. Brill, 1960– .

Faroqhi, Suraiya. "Finances." In *An Economic and Social History of the Ottoman Empire*, edited by Halil Inalcık with Donald Quataert, 531–44. Cambridge: Cambridge University Press, 1994.

———. "Making a Living: Economic Crisis and Partial Recovery." In *An Economic and Social History of the Ottoman Empire*, edited by Halil Inalcık with Donald Quataert, 433–73. Cambridge: Cambridge University Press, 1994.

———. "On Population." In *An Economic and Social History of the Ottoman Empire*, edited by Halil Inalcık with Donald Quataert. Cambridge: Cambridge University Press, 1994.

———. "The Ruling Elite between Politics and the Economy." In *An Economic and Social History of the Ottoman Empire*, edited by Halil Inalcık with Donald Quataert, 545–75. Cambridge: Cambridge University Press, 1994.

———. "Social Life in Cities." In *An Economic and Social History of the Ottoman Empire*, edited by Halil Inalcık with Donald Quataert, 576–608. Cambridge: Cambridge University Press, 1994.

———. "Trade: Regional, Interregional and International." In *An Economic and Social History of the Ottoman Empire*, edited by Halil Inalcık with Donald Quataert, 474–530. Cambridge: Cambridge University Press, 1994.

———. *Towns and Townsmen of Ottoman Anatolia: Trade, Crafts and Food in an Urban Setting*. Cambridge: Cambridge University Press, 1984.

Frangoule, Argine. *E Sinaia Scholē tēs Ag. Aikaterinēs sto Chandaka* (The School of Saint Catherine's in Chandaka). Athens: 1981.

Goffman, Daniel. *Izmir and the Levantine World, 1550–1650*. Seattle: University of Washington Press, 1990.

Gradeva, Rossitsa. "War and Peace along the Danube: Vidin at the End of the Seventeenth Century." Paper presented at the conference on *The Ottomans and the Sea* at the Skilliter Centre for Ottoman Studies, Newnham College, Cambridge University, 29–30 March 1996.

Greene, Molly. "The Court Records of Ottoman Crete." Paper presented at the Middle Eastern Studies Association Annual Conference, Washington D.C., December 1995.

———. "An Islamic Experiment? Ottoman Land Policy on Crete." *Mediterranean Historical Review* 11, no. 1 (June 1996): 60–78.

Hammer, J. von. *Histoire de l'Empire ottoman*. Vols. 10 and 11. Paris, 1838.

Hathaway, Jane. "The Military Household in Ottoman Egypt." *International Journal of Middle East Studies* 27, no. 1 (February 1995): 39–52.

———. *The Politics of Households in Ottoman Egypt: The Rise of the Qazdaglis*. Cambridge: Cambridge University Press, 1997.

———. "Problems of Periodization in Ottoman History: The Fifteenth through the Eighteenth Centuries." *Turkish Studies Association Bulletin* 20, no. 2 (Fall 1996): 25–31.

Hering, Gunner. *Oikomeniko Patriarcheio kai evropaike politike 1620–1638* (The Ecumenical Patriarchate and European politics, 1620–1638). Athens: National Bank of Greece, 1992.

Herlihy, Patricia, "Greek Merchants in Odessa in the Nineteenth Century." *Harvard Ukrainian Studies* 3–4 (1979–80): 399–420.

Hess, Andrew. *The Forgotten Frontier: A History of the Sixteenth Century Ibero-African Frontier*. Chicago: University of Chicago Press, 1978.

Inalcık, Halil. "The *çift-hane* System: The Organization of Ottoman Rural Society." In *An Economic and Social History of the Ottoman Empire*, edited by Halil Inalcık with Donald Quataert, 143–54. Cambridge: Cambridge University Press, 1994.

Inalcık, Halil. "Introduction: Empire and and Population." In *An Economic and Social History of the Ottoman Empire*, edited by Halil Inalcık with Donald Quataert, 11–43. Cambridge: Cambridge University Press, 1994.

———. "Islamization of Ottoman Laws on Land and Land Tax." In *Festgabe an Josef Matuz*, edited by Christa Fragner and Klaus Schwarz, 101–19. Berlin: Klaus Schwarz Verlag, 1992.

———. "Military and Fiscal Transformation in the Ottoman Empire, 1600–1700." *Archivum Ottomanicum* 6 (1980): 283–337.

———. "The Policy of Mehmed II towards the Greek Population of Istanbul and the Byzantine Buildings of the City." *Dumbarton Oaks Papers* 23–25 (1969–70): 231–49.

———. "Sources of Revenue." In *An Economic and Social History of the Ottoman Empire*, edited by Halil Inalcık with Donald Quataert, 55–76. Cambridge: Cambridge University Press, 1994.

———. "State, Land and Peasant." In *An Economic and Social History of the Ottoman Empire*, edited by Halil Inalcık with Donald Quataert, 103–78. Cambridge: Cambridge University Press, 1994.

———. "State-owned Lands (*miri*)." In *An Economic and Social History of the Ottoman Empire*, edited by Halil Inalcık with Donald Quataert, 103–19. Cambridge: Cambridge University Press, 1994.

———. "Suleiman the Lawgiver and Ottoman Law." *Archivum Ottomanicum* 1 (1969): 105–38.

Jackson, R. "From Profit-Sailing to Wage-Sailing: Mediterranean Owner-Captains and Their Crews during the Medieval Commercial Revolution." *Journal of European Economic History* 18, no. 3 (Winter 1989): 605–28.

Jelavich, Charles, and Barbara Jelavich. *The Establishment of the Balkan National States, 1804–1920*. Seattle: University of Washington Press, 1977.

Jennings, R. C. *Christians and Muslims in Ottoman Cyprus and the Mediterranean World*. New York: New York University Press, 1993.

Kafadar, Cemal. "Yeniçeri-Esnaf Relations: Solidarity and Conflict." Master's thesis, McGill University, 1981.

Karathanasēs, Ath. "Anekdotē allēlografia tou Fr. Morosini kai allōn Venetōn me Krētikous sta chronia tou polemou (1659–1660)" (Unpublished correspondence of Fr. Morosini and other Venetians with Cretans during the years of the war [1659–1660]). *Krētika Chronika* 25 (1973): 21–124.

Katib, Çelebi. *The Balance of Truth*. Trans. G. L. Lewis. London: George Allen and Unwin, 1957.

Kedar, B. *Merchants in Crisis: Genoese and Venetian Men of Affairs and the Fourteenth Century Depression*. New Haven: Yale University Press, 1976.

Koçu, Reşat Ekrem. *Türk giyim süslenme sözlüğü* (The dictionary of Turkish dress). Istanbul: Sümerbank Kültür Yayinlari, 1969.

Konortas, Paris. "From Ta'ife to Millet: Ottoman Terms for the Ottoman Greek Orthodox Community." In *Ottoman Greeks in the Age of Nationalism*, edited by D. Gondicas and Ch. Issawi, 169–80. Princeton: Darwin Press, 1999.

Konstantinidēs, K. "Ektheseis kai ypomnēmata apo tēn allēlografia tou gallikou prokseniou krētēs" (Essays and notes from the French consulate in Crete). *Krētika Chronika* 8 (1954): 323–65.

Konstantinidou, Tr. *Karavia, kapetanoi kai Syndrofonautoi 1800–1830* (Boats, captains and sailors, 1800–1830). Athens, 1954.

Kremmydas, V. "Katagrafē tōn emborikōn pliōn tou Irakleiou to 1751" (A list of the commercial boats of Irakleion in 1751). *Mnēmon* 7 (1978): 12–17.

Kunt, Metin. *The Sultan's Servants: The Transformation of Ottoman Provincial Government, 1550–1650*. New York: Columbia University Press, 1983.

———. "The Waqf as an Instrument of Public Policy: Notes on the Köprülü Family Endowments." In *Studies in Ottoman History in Honour of Professor V. L. Ménage*, edited by Colin Heywood and Colin Imber, 189–98. Istanbul: Isis Press, 1994.

Lambros, Sp. "Enthymiseon, etoi chronikōn semeiomatōn" (Enthymeseon, or notes in the margins of chronicles). *Neos Ellēnomnēmōn* 7, nos. 2–3 (1910): 8–313.

Lane, Frederic. *Venice: A Maritime Republic*. Baltimore: Johns Hopkins University Press, 1973.

Leon, George. "The Greek Merchant Marine (1453–1850)." In *The Greek Merchant Marine*, edited by Stelios Papadopoulos, 13–52. Athens: National Bank of Greece, 1972.

Lowry, Heath. "The Island of Limnos: A Case Study on the Continuity of Byzantine Forms under Ottoman Rule." In *Continuity and Change in Late Byzantine and Early Ottoman Society*, edited by Anthony Bryer and Heath Lowry, 235–59. Washington D.C.: Dumbarton Oaks, 1986.

Maltezou, Chr. "E Krētē stē diarkeia tēs periodou tēs venetokratias" (Crete during the period of Venetian rule). In *Krētē: Istoria kai politismos* (Crete: History and civilization), edited by N. Panayiotakēs, 105–62. Herakleion: Synthesmos Topikōn Enōseōn Demōn kai Koinotetōn Kretes, 1988.

Mandaville, Jon. "Usurious Piety: The Cash-waqf Controversy in the Ottoman Empire." *International Journal of Middle East Studies* 10 (1979): 289–308.

Manna, Adel. "The Rebellion of Naqib Ul-Ashraf in Jerusalem, 1703–1705," p. 10 (unpublished manuscript). A Hebrew language version of this paper was published in *Cathedra* 53 (1989): 49–74.

Manousakas, M. I. "E para Trivan apografē tēs Krētēs (1644) kai o dithen katalogos tōn krētikōn oikōn Kerkyras" (The 1644 census of Crete [found in] Trivan and the supposed list of Cretan families in Corfu). *Krētika Chronika* 3 (1949): 35–44.

———. "Symvolē eis tēn istorian tēs krētikēs oikogeneias Chortatse" (A contribution to the history of the Chortatse family from Crete). *Epetēris Hetaireias Vyzantinōn Spoudōn* 26 (1956): 231–301.

Masson, Paul. *Histoire du commerce français dans le Levant au XVII siècle*. Paris, 1896.

Masters, Bruce. *The Origins of Western Economic Dominance in the Middle East: Mercantilism and the Islamic Economy in Aleppo, 1600–1750*. New York: New York University Press, 1988.

McGowan, Bruce. *Economic Life in Ottoman Europe*. Cambridge: Cambridge University Press, 1981.

———. "The Elites and Their Retinues." In *An Economic and Social History of the Ottoman Empire*, edited by Halil Inalcık with Donald Quataert, 658–79. Cambridge: Cambridge University Press, 1994.

McGowan, Bruce. "Merchants and Craftsmen." In *An Economic and Social History of the Ottoman Empire*, edited by Halil Inalcık with Donald Quataert, 695–709. Cambridge: Cambridge University Press, 1994.

McKee, Sally. "Greek Women in Latin Households of Fourteenth-Century Venetian Crete." *Journal of Medieval History* 19 (1993): 229–49.

————. "Uncommon Dominion: The Latins and Greeks of Fourteenth Century Venetian Crete." Ph.D. dissertation, University of Toronto, 1993.

Mertzios, M. "Dyo katalogoi tōn en Kerkyra kai Zakyntho krētōn prosfygōn kata ta etē 1682 kai 1683" (Two lists of Cretan refugees in Corfu and Zakynthos in the years 1682 and 1683). *Krētika Chronika* 5 (1981): 7–31.

Moschopoulos, G. N. "Metoikēsē Kretōn stēn Kefalonia stē diarkeia tou krētikou polemou (1645–1669) kai ystera apo tēn alosē tou Chandaka" (The emigration of Cretans to Kefalonia during the course of the Cretan war and after the fall of Chandaka). In *Pepragmena tou D Diethnous Krētologikou Synedriou* (Proceedings of the Fourth International Cretological Symposium), 2: 27–291. Athens, 1981.

Murphey, Rhodes. "The Ottoman Resurgence in the Seventeenth Century Mediterranean: The Gamble and Its Results." *Mediterranean Historical Review* 8, no. 2 (December 1993): 186–200.

Nani, Battista. *Historia Veneta di Nani*. 2 vols. Venice, 1687.

Pamuk, Şevket. "Money in the Ottoman Empire, 1326–1914." In *An Economic and Social History of the Ottoman Empire*, edited by Halil Inalcık with Donald Quataert, 947–80. Cambridge: Cambridge University Press, 1994.

Panayiotakēs, N. "E paideia kata tēn Venetokratia" (Education during the period of Venetian rule). In *Krētē: Istoria kai politismos* (Crete: History and civilization), edited by N. Panayiotakēs, 163–96. Herakleion: Synthesmos Topikōn Enōseōn Demōn kai Koinotetōn Kretes, 1988.

Panayiōtopoulos, Chr. "Ellēnes nautikoi kai ploioktētes apo ta palaiotera oikonomika vivlia tēs Ellēnikēs Adelfotētas Venetias 1536–1576 (Greek sailors and shipowners according to the oldest account books of the Greek society of Venice, 1536–1576). *Thēsaurismata* 11 (1974): 284–352.

Panopoulou, Angelikē. "Opseis tēs nautiliakēs kinēsēs tou Chandaka to 17 aiōna" (Aspects of shipping in 17th century chandaka). *Krētikē Estia* 5, no. 2 (1980): 152–210.

————. "Syntrofies kai naulōseis pliōn sto Chandaka 1635–1661" (Partnership and chartering of boats in Chandaka, 1635–1661). *Pepragmena tou Ektou Diethnous Krētologikou Synedriou* (Proceedings of the Sixth Cretological Symposium), 2: 419–30. Chania: Philologikas Syllogos O Chrysostomos, 1991.

————. "Oi technites naupēgeiōn tou Chandaka kai tōn Chaniōn kata to 16 kai 17 aiōna" (The shipyard workers of Chandaka and Chania in the sixteenth and seventeenth centuries). *Krētikē Estia* 4, no. 3 (1989–90): 173–94.

Pantelakēs, E. G. "To Sinai kai ē Krētē" (Sinai and Crete). *Epetēris Hetaireia Krētikōn Spoudōn* 1 (1938): 165–185.

Papadia-Lala, Anastasia. " 'Cittadini' kai katoikoi poleōn" Koinōnikē diastrōmatosē sta venetokratoumena Chania (mesa 16–17 ai)" ('Cittadini' and the urban population: Social stratification in Venetian Chania [from the middle of the 16th to the middle of the 17th century], in *Praktika tou Diethnous Symposiou Istorias*

Neoellēnikē Polē (Proceedings of the International Symposium on the History of the Modern Greek City), 59–66. Athens, 1985.

———. *To Monte di Pietà tou Chandaka, 1613–mesa 17 aiona: Symvolē stēn koinōnikē kai eikonomikē istoria tēs venetokratoumenēs Krētēs* (The Monte di Pietà of Kandiye, 1613–mid-17th century: A contribution to the social and economic history of Venetian Crete). Athens, 1987.

Papadopoulos, Stelios, ed. *The Greek Merchant Marine (1453–1850)*. Athens: National Bank of Greece, 1972.

Pennell, C. R., ed. *Piracy and Diplomacy in Seventeenth Century North Africa: The Journal of Thomas Baker English Consul in Tripoli*. Rutherford, N.J.: Fairleigh Dickinson University Press, 1989.

Philipp, Thomas. *The Syrians in Egypt, 1725–1975*. Stuttgart: Seiner-Verlag-Wiesbaden, 1985.

Pierce, Leslie. *The Imperial Harem: Women and Sovereignty in the Ottoman Empire*. Oxford: Oxford University Press, 1993.

Pigne, H. "Eksoteriko kai dianisiotiko emborio stēn Chios tou 18th aiōna" (International and inter-island trade in 18th Century Chios). *Ta Historika* 5, no. 8 (1988): 115–22.

Prawer, J. "Social Classes in the Crusader States: The 'Minorities.' " In *The Impact of the Crusades on the Near East*, edited by Norman Zacour and Harry Hazard. Vol. 5 of *A History of the Crusades*, edited by Kenneth Setton, 59–116. Madison: University of Wisconsin, 1985.

Psilakēs, Nikos. *Ta Monasteria tēs Krētēs* (The monasteries of Crete). Athens: Bank of Crete, 1986.

———. *Monasteries and Byzantine Memories of Crete*. Irakleion: Karmanor, 1994.

Psilakēs, Vasileiou. *Istoria tēs Krētēs* (History of Crete). 3 vols. Chania, 1909. Reprint, Athens: Arkadi, 1970.

Rafeq, Abd ul-Karim. "The Local Forces in Syria in the Seventeenth and Eighteenth Centuries." In *War, Technology and Society in the Middle East*, edited by V. J. Parry and M. E. Yapp, 277–307. London: Oxford University Press, 1975.

Raymond, André. *Artisans et commercants au Caire au XVIII siècle*. 2 vols. Damascus: Institut Français, 1973.

———. "Soldiers in Trade: The case of Ottoman Cairo." *British Journal of Middle Eastern Studies* 18, no. 1 (1991): 16–37.

Salzmann, Ariel. "An Ancién Régime Revisited: 'Privatization' and Political Economy in the Eighteenth-Century Ottoman Empire." *Politics and Society* 21, no. 4 (December 1993): 393–423.

———. "Centripetal Decentralization: Life-Term Taxfarming in the Eighteenth Century Ottoman Empire." In *Political Economies of the Ottoman, Safavid and Mughal Empires*. Vol. 1. Edited by Tosun Aracanli, Ashraf Ghani, and David Ludden. Forthcoming.

Sarpi, Paolo. *The Opinion of Padre Paolo of the Order of the Servites, consultor of State, given to the Lords the Inquisitors of State. In what manner the Republick of Venice ought to govern themselves both at home and abroad to have perpetual dominion. Deliver'd by publick order in the year 1615*. Translated by William Aglionby. London: R. Bentley, 1689.

Sella, Dominique. "Crisis and Transformation in Venetian Trade." In *Crisis and*

Change in the Venetian Economy in the Sixteenth and Seventeenth Centuries, edited by Brian Pullan, 127–45. London: Methuen, 1968.

Setton, K. M. *Venice, Austria and the Turks in the Seventeenth Century*. Philadelphia: American Philosophical Society, 1991.

Seymour, Anthony. "Caveat Lector: Some Notes on the Population Figures of the Jewish Communities of the Ionian Islands: II." *Bulletin of Judeo-Greek Studies* 15 (Winter 1994): 33–40.

Sfyroeras, Vassilis. *Ta hellēnika plerōmata tou tourkikou stolou* (The Greek crews of the Turkish fleet). Athens, 1968.

Silahdar Fındıklılı Mehmet Aga. *Silahdar Tarihi*. Istanbul: Devlet Matbaasi, 1928.

Slot, B. J. *Archipelagus Turbatus: Les Cyclades entre colonisation latine et occupation ottomane c. 1500–1718*. Istanbul: Nederlands Historisch-Archaeologisch Instituut te Istanbul, 1982.

Spanakēs, Stergios. "E ekthesē tou douka tēs Krētēs (The report of the duke of Crete). *Krētika Chronika* 3 (1949): 519–33.

———. *Poleis kai choria tēs Krētēs sto perasma tōn aionōn* (Cities and villages of Crete throughout the ages). Herakleion: G. Detorakes, 1991.

———. "Relatione del. prov(r) genal dell'armi in Candia E. Antonio Priuli 1667, 30 Marzo." *Mnēmeia tēs krētikēs istorias* (Monuments of Cretan history). Vol. 6. Herakleion, 1969.

———. "Relatione dell Sr. Benetto Moro ritornato di proveditor general del regno di Candia, letta in pregadi a 25 giugno 1602." *Mnēmeia tēs krētikēs istorias* (Monuments of Cretan History). Vol. 4. Herakleion, 1960.

———. "Relatione di Me Filippo Pasqualigo ritornato di cap. o di Candia et prov.r della Canea 1594." *Mnēmeia tēs krētikēs istorias* (Monuments of Cretan history). Vol. 3. Herakleion, 1953.

———. "Relazione de Sr. Isepo Civran tornato di Prov. r Gen.l di Candia 1639." *Krētika Chronika* 21 (1969): 365–458.

———. "Relazione del Nobil Huomo Zuanne Mocenigo ritornato provveditore generale del regno di Candia presentata nell' eccellentissimo consillio 17 Aprile 1589." *Mnēmeia tēs krētikēs istorias* (Monuments of Cretan history). Vol. 1. Herakleion, 1940.

———. "Relazione Francesco Morosini provveditore generale nel regno di Candia 1629." *Mnēmeia tēs krētikēs istorias* (Monuments of Cretan history). Vol. 2. Herakleion, 1950.

———. "Relazione Pietro Giustiniano capitan generale de resmo 1630." *Mnēmeia tēs krētikēs istorias* (Monuments of Cretan history). Vol. 5. Herakleion, 1969.

———. "1610 a 9 Genaro, Relatione de s. Dolfin Venier ritornato di duca di Candia." *Krētika Chronika* 4 (1950): 313–52.

Stavrakē, Nikolaou. *Statistikē tou plēthysmou tēs Krētēs* (A statistical survey of the population of Crete). Athens: N. Karavia, 1890.

Stavrinidēs, Nicholaos. "Andreas Mēliōtēs, protōs grammatikos tēs Portēs en Krētē" (Andreas Miliotis, the first secretary to the Porte in Crete). *Krētika Chronika* 2 (1948): 546–68.

———. *Metafraseis tourkikōn istorikōn engrafōn* (Translations of Turkish historical documents). 5 vols. Herakleion: Municipality of Herakleion, 1984–87.

———. *E teleutaia periodos tēs poliorkias tou M. Kastrou* (The final stage of the siege of Candia). Herakleion, 1979.

———. "O thesmos tōn grammatikōn tēs Portēs stēn Krētē" (The institution of the secretary of the Porte in Crete). In *Pepragmena tou D Diethnous Krētologikou Synedriou* (Proceedings of the Fourth International Cretological Symposium), 3:397–401. Athens, 1981.

Steele, Sir Richard. *An Account of the State of the Roman-Catholick Religion Throughout the World, Written for the Use of Pope Innocent XI by Monsieur Cerri, Secretary of the Congregation de propagande Fide.* 2nd ed. London, 1716.

Stoianovich, Traian. "L'espace maritime segmentaire de l'Empire Ottoman." In *Material Culture and Mentalities: Land and Sea.* Vol. 4 of *Between East and West: The Balkan and Mediterranean Worlds,* 49–62. New Rochelle, N.Y.: Aristide D. Caratzas, 1995.

———. "Model and Mirror of the Premodern Balkan City." In *Economies and Societies: Traders, Towns and Households.* Vol. 2 of *Between East and West: The Balkan and Mediterranean Worlds,* 79–119. New Rochelle, N.Y.: Aristide D. Caratzas, 1992.

———. "Pour une model du commerce du Levant: Economie concurrentielle et economie de bazar 1500–1800." *International Association for South Eastern European Studies, Bulletin* 12, no. 2 (1974): 61–120.

Sugar, Peter. *Southeastern Europe under Ottoman Rule, 1354–1804.* Edited by Peter Sugar and Donald Treadgold. Seattle: University of Washington Press, 1993.

Tenenti, A. *Naufrages, corsaires et assurance maritimes à Venise 1592–1609.* Paris: S.E.V.P.E.N., 1959.

———. *Piracy and the Decline of Venice, 1580–1615.* Berkeley: University of California Press, 1967.

Theotokēs, Sp. "Iakovos Foscarini kai E Krētē tou 1570" (Iakovos Foscarini and Crete in 1570). *Epetēris tēs Hetaireias Kretikōn Spoudōn* 1 (1938): 186–206.

Thiriet, F. *La romanie venitienne au Moyen Age.* Paris: De Boccard, 1959.

Todorov, Nikolai. *The Balkan City, 1400–1900.* Seattle: University of Washington Press, 1983.

Tomadakēs, Nicholas V. "E Iera Monē Agias Triados tōn Tzangarolōn en Akrotirio Melecha Krētēs" (The Blessed Monastery of the Holy Trinity on Cape Melecha in Crete). *Hetaireia Byzantinōn Spoudōn* 9 (1932): 289–350.

———. *Istoria tēs ekklēsias Krētēs epi Tourkokratias 1645–1898* (The history of the Cretan church during the period of Turkish rule, 1645–1898). Athens: Iordanou Myrtide, 1974.

———. "Syndomon diagramma tēs istorias tēs ekklēsias Krētēs epi Tourkokratias" (A short sketch of the history of the church of Crete during Turkish rule). *Deltio tēs Istorikēs kai Ethnologikēs Etaireias tēs Ellados* 14 (1960): 3–32.

Udovitch, A. "Islamic law and the social context of exchange in the Medieval Middle East." *History and Anthropology* 1 (1985): 445–64.

Unwin, Tim. *Wine and the Vine: An Historical Geography of Viticulture and the Wine Trade.* London: Routledge, 1991.

Ursinus, Michael. "Petitions from Orthodox Church officials to the imperial diwan, 1675." *Byzantine and Modern Greek Studies* 18 (1994): 236–47.

Uzunçarşílí, Ismail Hakki. *Osmanli devleti teşkilātindan: kapukulu ocaklarí* (The institutions of the Ottoman state: The military corps). 2 vols. Anakara: Türk Tarihi Kurumu Basimevi, 1943.

Vatin, Nicholas. *L'Ordre de Saint-Jean-de-Jérusalem, l'Empire ottoman et la Méditerranée orientale entre les deux sièges de Rhodes 1480–1522.* Vol. 7 of *Collection Turcica.* Paris: N.R.S., 1994.

Veinstein, G. "On the Çiftlik Debate." In *Landholding and Commerical Agriculture in the Middle East,* edited by C. Keyder and F. Tabak, 35–56. Albany: State University of New York Press, 1991.

Vryonis, Spyros. "Local Institutions in the Greek Islands and Elements of Byzantine Continuity during Ottoman Rule." *Annuaire de L'Université de Sofia: Centre de Recherches Slavo-Byzantines "Ivan Dujčev."* 83, no. 3 (1989): 85–144.

Wardi, Ch. "The Question of the Holy Places in Ottoman Times." In *Studies on Palestine during the Ottoman Period,* edited by Moshe Ma'oz, 385–93. Jerusalem: Magnes Press, 1975.

Yiannopoulou, I. *E dioikētikē organosis tēs stereas Ellados kata tēn Tourkokratian 1393–1821* (The administrative organization of mainland Greece during the period of Turkish rule, 1393–1821). Athens: Athens University, 1971.

Zachariadou, Elizabeth. "Monks and Sailors under the Ottoman Sultans." Paper presented at the conference on *The Ottomans and the Sea* at the Skilliter Centre for Ottoman Studies, Newnham College, Cambridge University, 29–30 March 1996.

Zilfi, Madeline. *The Politics of Piety: the Ottoman Ulema in the Postclassical Age, 1600–1800.* Minneapolis: Bibliotheca Islamica, 1988.

Zois, L. Ch. "Krētes prosfyges tou 1667" (Cretan refugees from 1667). *Krētika Chronika* 9 (1956): 346–52.

Index